MW00906401

"One of the first acts of dictators when they come into power is to destroy and ban books. In this important book, Patrick Boyer reminds us that to protect democracy, we have to protect the written word and the free access to it; in other words, we have to recognize and celebrate the role of public libraries in making books accessible to the public."

MARINA NEMAT, *author of* Prisoner of Tehran *and inaugural recipient of the European Parliament's "Human Dignity Award" on December 15, 2007*

"A fundamental pillar of a well-functioning, free and open democracy is an informed citizenry. For citizens to effectively participate in a democracy, form opinions freely and protect their rights and interests, they need access to information. Public libraries are crucial in providing such access regardless of income, age, education, race, politics or religion. Boyer colorfully and masterfully illuminates the gift libraries are to us as citizens and to democracies around the world."

DR. PAMELA RYAN, *Managing Director, Issues Deliberation Australia (international public policy think tank)*

"If an informed public is the foundation of a democracy, then libraries and a free press are like twin cornerstones. In *Local Library, Global Passport*, Patrick Boyer reminds us just how essential libraries and an unfettered press are to the functioning of democratic society."

DIANA M. DANIELS, *General Counsel, The Washington Post Company (1988–2007) and past president, Inter American Press Association*

"From my perspective as an historian with responsibility for a library, Patrick Boyer's book appeals on many levels. As he so eloquently sets out in the context of Bracebridge, libraries are far more than bricks and mortar that house books. Libraries are fundamentally linked to their communities, whether it is Bracebridge or Parliament Hill. These communities provide the support not just for the bricks, mortar and books, periodicals and newspapers that fill the shelves, but increasingly computers, databases and online versions of all these things as well. In turn, libraries have a responsibility not only to be repositories of knowledge but also to make this knowledge available to their community. This is the vocation of a librarian—to serve as the conduit of knowledge to those who seek it—in the service of their community."

WILLIAM R. YOUNG, *Parliamentary Librarian of Canada, Ottawa*

A CENTURY OLD. Standing prominently atop Queen's Hill on the main street, the Carnegie library in Bracebridge has been a passport for residents and visitors to explore the world since 1908. *Joe Ursano*

Opening page Since 1935 Andrew Carnegie has figuratively watched over his library in Bracebridge from this oil painting. The young women now connecting to the world through the Internet, where he formerly saw patrons reading books, represent one of most revolutionary changes in the past century of the library's evolution. *Jan Pitman*

Cover/dust jacket The Bracebridge Carnegie library, viewed from the east, following the 1985 restoration and expansion that honoured the architecture of the original 1908 building. *Chamberlain Architect Services*

LOCAL LIBRARY
GLOBAL PASSPORT

The Evolution of a Carnegie Library

J. PATRICK BOYER

Blue Butterfly Books
THINK FREE, BE FREE

Blue Butterfly Book Publishing Inc.
2583 Lakeshore Boulevard West, Toronto, Ontario, Canada M8V 1G3
Tel. 416-255-3930   Fax 416-252-8291
www.bluebutterflybooks.ca

TRADE DISTRIBUTION (CANADA)

White Knight Book Distribution
Warehouse/fulfilment by Georgetown Terminal Warehouse
34 Armstrong Avenue, Georgetown, Ontario L7G 4R9
Tel. 1-800-485-5556   Fax 1-800-485-6665

TRADE DISTRIBUTION (U.S.A.)

Hushion House Publishing Inc.
Warehouse/fulfilment by APG Books
7344 Cockrill Bond Boulevard, Nashville, Tennessee 37209
Tel. 1-800-275-2606   Fax 1-800-510-3650

ON-LINE PURCHASE (WORLD WIDE)
www.bluebutterflybooks.ca

LIBRARY AND ARCHIVES CANADA CATALOGUING IN PUBLICATION

Boyer, J. Patrick
Local library, global passport : the evolution of a Carnegie library /
J. Patrick Boyer

Includes bibliographical references and index.
ISBN 978-0-9784982-2-1 (bound). – ISBN 978-0-9781600-8-1 (pbk.)

1. Bracebridge Public Library – History.
2. Carnegie libraries – Ontario – Bracebridge – History.
3. Public libraries – Ontario – Bracebridge – History. I. Title.

Z736.B64B69 2008   027.4713'16   C2008-900573-2

Design and typesetting by Fox Meadow Creations
Text is set in Fournier. Front cover titling is Fell Great Primer, digitally
reproduced by Igino Marini (www.iginomarini.com).
Printed in Canada on acid-free paper by Transcontinental-Gagné

This book is dedicated to Italian essayist Natalia Ginzburg
who wrote that we should teach our children

not the little virtues but the great ones.

Not thrift but generosity and an indifference to money;

not caution but courage and a contempt for danger;

not shrewdness but frankness and a love of truth;

not tact but love for one's neighbour and self-denial;

not a desire for success but a desire to be and to know.

Contents

A Portal to the World *by Vartan Gregorian*   x

Foreword *by Adrienne Clarkson*   xiii

Preface   xvii

ONE   Passport to a Larger World   1

TWO   Books in the Bush   18

THREE   Early Library Beginnings   32

FOUR   Saga of the Mechanics' Institute Library   49

FIVE   Democratizing the Bracebridge Library   63

SIX   The Patron Saint of Libraries   76

SEVEN   Seeking a Carnegie Library   91

EIGHT   Building a Carnegie Library   123

NINE   A Library through Times of War and Depression   141

TEN   Everything Old is New Again   193

ELEVEN   Librarian Dynamics, Dynamic Librarians   257

TWELVE   Shhh! Children in the Library   285

THIRTEEN   The Library and the Schools   304

FOURTEEN   Prisoners of the Library   315

FIFTEEN   Always the Book, Never the Book   325

SIXTEEN   A Library of the Future   334

Credits   344

Sources   347

Notes   351

Index   354

A Portal to the World

by Dr. Vartan Gregorian
President, Carnegie Corporation of New York

L ibraries have always occupied a central role in our culture. They contain the heritage of humanity, the record of its triumphs and failures,
the record of its intellectual, scientific and artistic achievements. They are
the diaries of the human race. They contain humanity's collective memory. They are not repositories of human endeavor alone. They are instruments of civilization. They provide tools for learning, understanding and
progress. They are a source of information, a source of knowledge, a
source of wisdom, hence they are a source of action. They are a labo-
ratory of human endeavor. They are a window to the future. They are
a source of hope. They are a source of self-renewal. They are the symbol of our community with the rest of humanity. They represent the link
between the solitary individual and the wider world which is our community.

The library is the university of universities, for it contains the source
and the unity of knowledge. It constitutes a commonwealth of learning.
It is the portal that one passes through in order to find the wider world.

But it is not only the doors of the biggest or most expansive libraries
in great urban centers that provide such portals—any library, no matter
how small, offers the same opportunity to enter new worlds. In towns
and cities across the globe, somewhere today, someone is about to step
into a library and have a life-changing experience, because they are going
to enter the world of books. As author Rita Mae Brown succinctly put it,
"When I got my library card, that is when my life began." U.S. Supreme
Court Justice Clarence Thomas also found a place to think and dream
and plan in a library—a Carnegie library, in fact, no doubt similar to

PORTAL TO THE WORLD. Picking up the theme of this book's title, Vartan Gregorian writes that the local library "is the portal that one passes through in order to find the wider world." The nobility of this idea is enhanced by a dignified entranceway, as successive generations climbing these steps into the Bracebridge Carnegie Library have experienced over the past century.

the Bracebridge library that Patrick Boyer so vividly brings to life in the pages of *Local Library, Global Passport*.

Not long ago, Justice Thomas came up to me at a conference on the judiciary and handed me his business card; on the back, he had written: "The Carnegie library in Savannah, Georgia, was my sanctuary. It was the library that served blacks, since we were not allowed to go to the Savannah Public Library. It continues to have a very special place in my heart."

Certainly, times change. Technology has become a predominant force affecting almost every part of our daily doings. It has also speeded up our expectations, linked us to nations and peoples far and wide, and opened the floodgates of information that bombards us twenty-four hours a day, seven days a week—more information than any one person can possibly sort through, much less analyze and process into substantive knowledge. But one thing technology cannot do is replace libraries and books. Books are still cultural icons in our society. They are still among the first gifts that people give to beloved children, that friends and lovers exchange with one another. You can dedicate a book to someone you love but we haven't reached the point yet where we dedicate floppy disks!

There are 3,222 public libraries in Canada; 116 of them were created by Andrew Carnegie, with grants totaling more than $2.5 million dollars, in a time—the early years of the twentieth century—when that amount was a vast fortune to be spent on almost anything, let alone on building libraries to serve "the common man," and women, of course, along with children. But Andrew Carnegie understood that books and libraries were exactly what people needed in order to learn, to enrich their education, to expand their dreams and aspirations and, ultimately, help them succeed at whatever they chose to do in life.

I only wish that Andrew Carnegie were around today to see what his legacy has provided to countless people down through the generations, and how his gift of libraries continues to be of incalculable value to those who cherish them.

In telling the story of the Bracebridge library, Patrick Boyer is actually sharing many stories: he brings us the evolution of Andrew Carnegie's idea that education is the foundation of civilization, that philanthropy is an investment in the future, and that libraries are one of the strongest building blocks of democracy. As president of Carnegie Corporation of New York, founded by Andrew Carnegie in 1911 to promote the advancement and diffusion of knowledge and education, and as the former president of The New York Public Library, I welcome this volume into the brotherhood of books and of learning that we are all privileged to share.

Vartan Gregorian

New York City
January 29, 2008

Foreword

by The Right Honourable Adrienne Clarkson

I am delighted to introduce this fine and engaging book by Patrick Boyer about the importance of libraries in general and the Carnegie library in Bracebridge in particular.

Personally, I have to say that I would not be the person I became if I had not had the access to Andrew Carnegie's enormous gift to North America with his Carnegie Libraries. He supported 2,500 communities throughout the English-speaking world to build libraries. Regina, for instance, was given $50,000 in 1907, which was an enormous amount of money then. They knew what they were about because their library crest read (and I think it still does), *Qui Legit Regit* —"The one who reads, rules."

The library was central to my life as a child going to public school in Ottawa because, happily for me, the library was half-way between my school and my home. I quickly learned to understand that great Hebrew saying: "Hold the book in your hand and you are a pilgrim at the gate to the new city."

I learned very early that the book could open us as human beings to the emotions, worlds, everything that we could not possibly live in all our lives combined.

The education I got in the public library in Ottawa added to my education in a completely unstructured way. I think public libraries did that for a lot of people.

The broad social benefits issuing from libraries were never more obvious than during the great depression. My dear friend Doris Anderson, who in her lifetime gave opportunities and insights to so many through her leadership in publishing and causes for equality, told me that the social need for libraries was particularly real on the Prairies when she was growing up. It was very important for men who could not get jobs, but who had some education, to be able to go to the public library and read books. Many unemployed people, refusing to succumb to despair, turned to their local libraries. They found in them the path to education, or a source of pleasure in a very bleak time. That's what books can do, and that's what they will always do. They help us to understand, to think in large terms, to gain some hope and prepare ourselves for what can come next.

When I was Governor-General I was able to visit a large number of libraries all across this country and see how they have changed and evolved with the needs of the neighbourhoods in which they find themselves. There is a remarkable one in Vancouver's downtown Eastside. It's in old Chinatown and it has an urban Aboriginal community. It deals with serious poverty, drugs and homelessness. Its nearest neighbours are soup kitchens and church halls where food and clothing are distributed. But, in the midst of this, the Carnegie Centre is a place of tremendous hope. It is like a giant living room for this whole neighbourhood, with newspapers and magazines in different languages, drop-in areas and workshop rooms where you can come to write poetry, do crafts, or simply chat. It has a cafeteria with healthy food at very good prices. It epitomizes community: and gives the real mission of a library.

Our great writer, Robertson Davies, said: "Culture is simply the way in which people live ... One of our difficulties in Canada is that too many of us insist in thinking of culture as a kind of lacy frill that is attached to the edge of the garment of life, whereas to be worth anything, it must be the whole fabric of life."

The word "public" is critical in dealing with libraries. It means that libraries are for everybody. It does not mean that everybody will get the same thing out of them. An egalitarian society means that everybody gets an equal start, a field of opportunity that is level. But, it certainly doesn't mean that everyone ends up homogenized.

George Locke, the Chief Librarian in the Toronto system eighty years ago, wrote "the pride of a library is not the mere possession of books but rather the explanation of the significance of those treasures and the development of interest and pleasure among those who may have the taste, but not the material means of satisfying it." It is our society that gives to everybody the material means to find out what is in books.

It's significant that when George Locke became the Chief Librarian, in addition to the French and German volumes at the library already held, he began to stock the Toronto libraries with books in Russian, Yiddish, Italian and Lithuanian specifically to meet the needs of arriving immigrants in the period immediately following the First World War. Our libraries must meet the needs of many diverse populations.

All those who work for the good of public libraries know that we will need careful navigation to get them to a safer harbour. Andrew Carnegie understood that in his day. We in our turn have to do it because the future of our country is at stake in good libraries, because we have our role to play in helping new Canadians become totally comfortable and totally at home with everything that our culture stands for.

I have started the Institute for Canadian Citizenship, which is to help new Canadians (who have already lived in the country or they wouldn't be citizens) become part of what we who have been here a long time know as Canada. With 250,000 new Canadian citizens every year, we must be sure that the public libraries will be able to serve them and answer new needs. We will discover different things because our new citizens come with a strong sense of family and community bonding, even if they come from countries in anarchy, lacking true democracy. Remember they are not just taking from us; we are learning from them. Like the relationship between an author and a reader, it's a two-way street.

Public libraries around the world, and Carnegie libraries especially, were at the root and heart of thousands of communities, in towns like Bracebridge and cities like Regina, Ottawa and Vancouver. The local library, wherever we live, is our passport to a larger and better world. It is up to all of us to help them remain that way.

Adrienne Clarkson

Toronto
January 25, 2008

SYMBOLIC ENTRANCEWAY. The grand portico framing the entrance to the original Bracebridge Carnegie library building was a strong visual reminder for patrons of the importance of the gift within—a passport to the world through books. Following extensive renovations and expansion to the library in 1985, the main entrance was moved to a level, more accessible location at the side of the building. The portico nonetheless remains a prominent street-side feature that leaves no doubt this is a public building of high purpose. *Joe Ursano*

Preface

W hether our relationship with a library is fundamental or fleeting, whether it is with the community library or a school library, our home library or any of the other places books are gathered and organized for use, the hold such centres have on our lives is tighter than we may even realize.

Libraries as institutions are self-invested with historic responsibility as collectors and conveyors of our culture in all its literary forms, but our personal encounter with their holdings of books and written records is highly personal and essentially private. This blending of a library's importance as a repository of knowledge and our almost intimate links to its contents create a unique relationship that is easier to know than to explain. Once our natural curiosity is awakened, a powerful magnetism begins drawing us to books and the Internet and into libraries and across the threshold of the human imagination.

While this phenomenon—part institutional, part individual—may be hard to "explain," this book seeks to honour the reality of that bond by showing how it takes shape. We see how a library does not exist apart from its community but is an expression of it, with the Bracebridge Public Library both reflecting and forming the book-centred culture of its community from first settlement in the 1860s into the present moment. We discover a number of the ways a library binds us together, directly and indirectly, collectively and individually.

Andrew Carnegie a century ago paid for the construction of the Bracebridge Public Library and nearly three thousand others in many places around the world, an unprecedented act of cultural craftsmanship on a global scale. The architects designing these "Carnegie Libraries" implemented many ideas that were new and even revolutionary at the time. Their purpose, on instructions from Carnegie, was to inspire people by the possibilities of public buildings and to ease their free access to this communal resource of the world's learning and literature. The freedom to read, which is the larger gift given by Andrew Carnegie through his library buildings, can lift an individual's horizons as she or he discovers new territory and further realms of thought, whether such reading is for self-education or entertainment, or, quite often, the two combined. Our joy in good reading cannot be bound by the classification system a well-ordered library itself needs to keep track of its extensive holdings.

The greatest gift of freedom to read and the availability of books on any topic, supported systematically and on a grand scale by Andrew Carnegie, was revolutionary in the long history of control over information and paternalistic attitudes about the general population. Even if we do not use the library much ourselves, other citizens do. They enjoy unrestricted access to information on any topic of interest or inquiry. Because self-reliant and self-educating citizens are the lifeblood of a resilient society and a self-governing democratic state, the library holds an additional special virtue as one of our pre-eminent democratic institutions.

In the century since they first appeared, Andrew Carnegie's libraries have seen many changes. A number have been demolished, several abandoned and quite a few transformed for other purposes, but a majority still carry on, usually with additions to the original facilities. The Bracebridge Public Library underwent expansions twice in the past century and is preparing for the next enlargement commensurate with its vibrant role in a growing town. More than the physical size and attributes of the library buildings themselves, however, the last hundred years have seen dramatic changes in the nature and uses of the local library. The fine oil painting of Andrew Carnegie hanging prominently in the Bracebridge Public Library since 1935 allows "the Patron Saint of Libraries" to look today over a scene of computer terminals where those who once sat with a book now surf the planet's information resources. Their access to the body of knowledge is not provided by a well-trained reference librarian guiding them to the printed resources under the library's roof, but by a search engine that offers them a million or more sources for information on a topic, in seconds.

This history of one town's Carnegie library, commemorating its centennial by celebrating the ways a local library provides us with a passport to the larger world, traces the particular components of a more universal story—the indispensable cultural role of local libraries and their evolution as centres of dynamic stability over a century of transformative change.

J. Patrick Boyer

Bracebridge, Ontario
March 4, 2008

PORTALS TO THE UNIVERSE. In the quiet order of the main library hall of Bracebridge's original 1908 Carnegie library, now the upper level of much expanded precincts, young women follow their interests into the limitless information society of planet earth. *Jan Pitman*

ONE

Passport to a Larger World

A passport, property of the government but issued uniquely to each individual, helps us cross borders and enter new lands. Likewise the library, asset of the community but open to each individual, is an institutionalized kind of passport. Although our booklet-type passport enables us to encounter new territory for experiencing adventures and gaining insights, the local library is usually more convenient, and certainly far cheaper, than travel overseas. Here the foreign also becomes familiar. Here access is free. Here the climate is welcoming year round; there is no "off-season" for adventures of the mind.

A library is coveted by people in controlled societies precisely because of this freedom it offers, just as those whose governments control travel abroad prize an unrestricted passport. Both are pathways to freedom, precious to safeguard if one is fortunate enough to have them.

Possession of a government-issued passport is a proof of citizenship, but ownership of a library card admits its bearer to the precincts of what Andrew Carnegie called "the free republic of the library." We may bring back souvenirs and trophies from travels abroad, but the citizen of a library can take works off-site for further private study—on a dock, in a bath, at a desk—wherever he or she can seize the opportunity and enjoyment of reading books.

Not everyone is fortunate enough to be admitted to this free republic. Some people lack passports.

Across northern Ontario isolated First Nations communities were denied this freedom by the absence of books in the opening years of the twenty-first century. Ontario Lieutenant-Governor James Bartleman,

I

motivated by his own experience as an Aboriginal youth discovering books in his local library, acted to change that. He persuaded Canadian book publishers to donate volumes, citizens to give money, and the Aboriginal air service to fly the boxes of books into Canada's remote lakeside reserves. Families began building up precious home libraries. Some youngsters helping unpack the boxes from the small aircraft were so keen they even opened the books and started reading while still unloading. Lieutenant-Governor Bartleman's initiative was so impressive that Ontario Premier Dalton McGuinty took the unprecedented step of asking him to address the Ontario Legislative Assembly about it.

Bartleman grew up in the Muskoka village of *Obajewanung* or Port Carling in central Muskoka. By following the example of his father, the boy became an avid reader. Interest in reading led him into an ever-widening circle of new worlds. First he encountered adventure-filled domains across the colourful pages of comic books retrieved from the village dump close to where his family lived in a tent or purchased at Whiting's Drugstore and Ice Cream Parlour with his meagre earnings from selling newspapers and fish. Next he became fully absorbed by the immediacy of world dramas and human passions splayed over the news columns of the *Toronto Daily Star*, often reading the entire newspaper before delivering copies to his impatient customers. Then, following his iconoclastic father to the Port Carling library one day, the boy discovered the most amazing world of all. The librarian welcomed him. He could borrow books for free. Each book along the seemingly endless shelves offered him free travel to a new universe. In the Port Carling Public Library Jimmy Bartleman discovered a whole new world, a route of escape from the prison of poverty and racism of his time and place, just as impoverished Andrew Carnegie as a boy discovered the library's passport to a larger world.

"Exposed to the real thing," wrote Bartleman in his memoir *Raisin Wine*,[1] "the boy never returned to comic books." From then on, as he recounted in part when talking about the power of books to an audience at Bracebridge Public Library in November 2006, his worldwide adventures in the highest levels of Canadian diplomatic service and international relations have physically carried Jim Bartleman to all corners of the earth, but even when he had grown up to represent his country abroad and was able to travel with ease on a Canadian diplomatic passport, he always kept his other passport close as well, quietly slipping into the realm of adventure between the covers of a handy book. Now offering this same open passage to other First Nations children, James Bartleman has given expression to the same instinct that a century ago drove

OUT OF MUSKOKA. His Honour Ontario Lieutenant-Governor James Bartleman, at Bracebridge Public Library on November 1, 2006, shares his boyhood stories about discovering a larger world through books in the nearby library of Port Carling, Muskoka, where he grew up. Many attentive listeners included his brother Robert Bartleman, who lives in Bracebridge, and their mother, Maureen Benson Simcoe (seated, foreground), of Port Carling.

James Bartleman has written four memoirs with stark honesty and vivid creativity about his experience as an aboriginal Canadian, his courage in public service, and how his life is intensely interwoven with literature. As an impoverished "half-breed" struggling to grow up in Port Carling, the local library became his global passport, as signified in the title of his first memoir in 2002, *Out of Muskoka*.

To encourage aboriginal young people to expand their horizons and enrich their lives through books, he initiated the Lieutenant-Governor's Book Program in 2004, collecting over 1.2 million used books to stock school libraries in First Nations communities, particularly in Northern Ontario. In 2005, to further promote literacy and bridge-building, His Honour initiated a program to pair Native and non-Native schools in Ontario and Nunavut, and set up summer camps for literacy development in five northern First Nations communities. *Mark Clairmont, MuskokaTODAY*

Andrew Carnegie to ensure that everyone could be equal citizens in the free republic of the library.

Another example of how people are denied such citizenship was the exclusion of Blacks from libraries in the United States, especially in the South, where segregationist policies kept half the population of certain states effectively barred from the education and enjoyment offered by the free public libraries of their communities for long twilight years of racial oppression. Richard Wright first became interested in books as a 17-year-old factory worker when he came across a newspaper editorial denouncing a book by H.L. Mencken. "Having already formed an acute appraisal of the oppression found in the South," recounts Matthew Battle in his "unquiet history" of the library throughout time, Wright "determined that if a Southern paper disliked what Mencken had written, he must have something worthwhile to say." However, the library was closed to Blacks and Wright knew "that the developmental scheme librarians promoted in the nineteenth century had no room for him."[2] Despite dangers that included death by lynching, Wright persuaded a man to lend him his library card so he could go where he was prohibited. He went into the library with the titles of two Mencken books written on a slip of paper, meekly saying he was "on an errand" to fetch some books for the white man whose card he showed. When he read *Prejudices* it unlocked for the teenager the power of books, "the sheer force of expression itself." In time, Richard Wright would himself write his wrenching autobiography *Black Boy*. "Wright used a borrowed library card," said Battle, "like a passport to cross into that world of self-discovery."[3]

If this passport is denied to some by the physical absence of books, as with Aboriginal children in remote communities, or by the taunting presence of books in the community that are kept where some are denied access to them, as in the case of those held behind the barrier of racism, still others may be denied the freedom of reading because their own society imposes restrictions in the name of religious ideology. Marina Nemat, who discovered far away places in the companionship of books growing up as an only child in Iran, found this world closing down in darkness around her as the Iranian revolution prohibited the freedom she had previously known. As Marina describes with intelligent sensitivity in *Prisoner of Tehran*, or as we find portrayed by Azar Nafisi in *Reading Lolita in Tehran*, in Deitrich Bonhoeffer's *Letters and Papers from Prison*, Martin Luther King Jr.'s *Letter from the Birmingham City Jail*, Jacob Timmerman's *Prisoner without a Name, Cell without a Number*, Aleksander Solzenitsyn's *The Gulag Archipelago*, or any of the other searing testimonials by those struggling to survive the loss of their freedom, its priceless power can really only be grasped in the bleak and tawdry twilight of its disappearance.

As Marina Nemat herself emphasized, when writing to me about *Local Library, Global Passport* and the importance of books in society, "One of the first acts of dictators when they come into power is to destroy and ban books." From her harrowing experience in her own country of Iran, she passionately reminds us that "to protect democracy, we have to protect the written word and the free access to it; in other words, we have to recognize and celebrate the role of public libraries in making books accessible to the public." Her own witness to this cause inspires others. Knowing well how societies close down under ideological oppression, Europe's parliamentarians, many of them too familiar with this form of state imprisonment under fascism and communism, named Marina Nemat as the inaugural recipient of the European Parliament's "Human Dignity Award" on December 15, 2007.

Other barriers may keep people from making this journey. Those who are not literate would have little incentive to make the trip, being trapped as they are in a cyclical problem of not reading because they can't and not being able to read because they don't. Wendy Nicholson, librarian at Bracebridge and Muskoka Lakes Secondary School, buys graphic novels in her quest to just get kids interested in reading, and tells me her concern is with literacy. "If they stay in the library and keep reading, that's a good step." This struggle in a small Ontario town is indicative of a larger condition in contemporary society and a growing pattern wherever libraries are multimedia centres and books are marginalized. The library's evolution, however, has always reflected the society in which it is. The information society, virtual reality, and the communications revolutions imprint the library precisely because it is part of and essential to them all. The matter of freedom to read, however, is something else. The early examples set in the development of a person's life awaken or close down the natural curiosities, and so long as curiosity and interest stay alive, a person will sooner or later find books, like Jimmy Bartleman did in Port Carling. It is only when you travel that you realize what a passport is.

People may simply be shy about going into a public building with which they are unfamiliar because the door into the library had somehow never been on their route before in life. One of my cousins in Bracebridge had a paralyzing fear of flying and so never travelled. Since she nervously made her first tentative trip abroad four years ago, however, it is now hard to keep her off an airplane. A library's meeting rooms opened to the community, such as those conveniently in the centre of town at the Huntsville Public Library north of Bracebridge, have revealed a similar phenomenon. Some members of groups or organizations meeting in the library who never had a particular connection to books, reading or the personal research and learning that is possible in a library, make a joyous discovery later in life. Simply by being on the premises for other reasons, but in passing experience the pleasant setting of a contemporary library and its rich offerings, a number of individuals with these community groups, including many seniors, have become enthusiastic first-time members of the local library.

If the library extends into the community through its patrons who freely come and go, it also reaches beyond its physical locale through its mobile library service, extension programs to schools, volunteer-operated "books-on-wheels" links between shut-ins and the library, satellite operations in seniors' residences or branches (which for Bracebridge includes a branch at a local prison), and inter-library loans for works not otherwise available locally. Just as a booklet-style passport on its own is not always enough, the citizen of the free library finds these extension services and supplemental programs transform the potential of experiencing the new and encountering the foreign into a reality.

However one uses the library, though, the experience is always personal. This journey of the mind is custom-made by individual interests and private tastes working within the large tableau of available resources from our global culture, our literary inheritance, and our information technologies. Just as a thousand people may use their government passports to visit another country, a thousand people may show their library card and access the rich resources of the local library. Yet in either case no two people will ever have an identical experience. We may share foreign travel or the local library with countless others, but our experience of them both is invariably unique.

A library performs its grand role of upholding tradition and preserving our cultural inheritance by bridging the past to the future in the present, which it does by maintaining what might best be called, oddly, its dynamic stability.

Libraries change over time. Shifts take place in the philosophy behind their architectural design. Evolution of technology affects the coding and classification of books. Changing social values and new branches of learning affect acquisitions policies. Like any institution, the library evolves by

EXAMINING THE TRAVEL DOCUMENTS. In the adult section of Bracebridge Public Library, Heather McFadyen browses the books to select the next
place she will let one take her. *Jan Pitman*

adapting to its changing context, more even than surface appearances and
terminology might suggest. Although it may be stable, a good library is
dynamic, not static.

This paradoxical quality of dynamic stability helps libraries retain their
core role as custodians of culture and purveyors of literature, even while
they evolve as centres of learning and users of new technologies. As a
result, good libraries transition through time as centres for civilized order
in a world constantly re-inventing itself.

A significant feature of the library, perhaps one of the important though
seldom mentioned reasons for its dynamism or vitality, is the way it
enhances the privacy of the individual, especially important in an age
when our personal privacy is so eroded.

This is another paradox of the public library. This public institution is open to anyone who strolls in, a place of public exposure in many ways, but it is also a place that respects individuality and enshrines the privacy of each person. You can obtain virtually any book, either from the stacks or through inter-library loan, then take it to the privacy of your home.

Those reading and studying in the library perhaps lack space or privacy at their own home. Joe Ursano, a retired school teacher and currently a dedicated member of the Bracebridge Library Board, first came to the local library as a boy because his family's small home in the early days following their arrival from Italy in the 1950s was without private space for him to do his schoolwork. "My parents were only able to go as far as Grade 3 in Italy and were not able to help me with homework. I also did not have a study desk at home. I liked the surroundings because they were warm, quiet and I usually had an entire large table where I could spread out my work," he recalled decades later.

Some people are in the library because they are using reference works that cannot be borrowed. Once launched into their work, they are left alone to do it. "I make sure a person has found the right source materials," explained reference librarian Nancy Wilson of the Bracebridge Public Library, "but then leave that individual in their own private world."

This culture of private space in a public place is respected not just by the librarian but by fellow users as well. There may be sideways glances of curiosity or flirtatious attraction, yet each person's universe remains guarded by an invisible protective barrier of courtesy and respect for individual privacy.

Respect for privacy supports the larger celebration of each person's individuality. The successful workings of a good library is a collective project held together by shared respect for books and the quest of human inquiry in an atmosphere of co-operation. Despite these essential elements of a collective and communal nature, however, they are deployed in the greater service of individualism.

For each individual traveller, the local library is thus an endless supply of books, a cornucopia of information. It is a place of quietude made vital by intensely focused individuals in front of computer or microfiche screens or pouring over documents and spread-out books who have all but disappeared into the expanding realms of their research on the pros and cons of pasteurizing milk or the structural attributes of seventeenth-century sailing ships.

Yet if we also think about the library in a larger way, we see it differently as a community institution. In this context it is a specific structure and organization with staff and money and plans to fulfill its public mandate of making books and information freely available to all. It is a physical building that needs to be maintained, and occasionally expanded when the collection once more exceeds available shelf space, and when a leaky roof can jeopardize the holdings. This organization and structure is as vital to an individual's experience of a library excursion as the aircraft on which a global traveller embarks on international trips.

If we step back even further to see the local library in its largest context, we discover how it actually embodies the entire culture of our society. As both gatekeeper and purveyor of "culture" the library is itself a vehicle for beliefs, values, actions and memories that influence the way we see and think about the world around us—its architecture, its sports and other religions, its economic activity and political behaviours, its clothing designs and sexual practices—and how we in turn envisage our place in that diverse world. Opening ourselves to literature and learning through novels and non-fiction, periodicals and research scans, we enter a larger world by discovering the relationships that connect all human experience. The library, in this sense, has a role in structuring our very idea of who we are. As we think, so we become.

Not everybody, it is true, uses their local library. People who do not connect directly to library life in its many forms and attributes still benefit from its impacts as the rippling out effect of activities and thoughts of library patrons touch the lives of others. The very presence of the library institution itself influences and shapes the common community which both its patrons and non-users cohabit.

This point is important in an age of measurement, our era of polling and percentages, of "value for money" audits. Culture by its very nature is not something we can quantify nor that we should diminish by even trying. When Bracebridge opened the doors of its new Carnegie public library in 1908 to the 2,500 citizens in the town and the 2,500 residents in the surrounding hinterland of farms and villages, only some 800 were regular users of the facility—a minority. By the 1950s, with a town population of 3,000 and a like number again in the surrounding environs as well as a growing "summer" population of cottagers and vacationers who took some advantage of the Bracebridge Public Library, the number of members holding library cards had risen to 1,200—still a minority. Today, amidst a population setting of about 18,000, the town library has

A SPACE OF THEIR OWN. Bracebridge library has a designated section for Young Adult readers. Teens need a space apart from the children's library but more specific to them than the Robert J. Boyer Reading Room for all ages. The next expansion of the library will no doubt provide even more accommodation for young adults, but in the meantime Jonathan Cho and Ashley Pierre find it a quiet, clean and safe place to launch themselves into wherever their books take them. *Jan Pitman*

some 6,200 active members. Nationally, these ratios are consistent with the pattern in other Canadian communities, and correspond generally to the numbers of residents and library users in most municipalities in the United States as well. Nowhere do all the people, or even a majority, use their community's library.

While the statistics on library patrons may indicate the formal attachment people have to the library, they cannot accurately measure who really uses a library nor indicate its centrality to the community as a whole. Circulation statistics, another index of measurement, perhaps looked at by granting bodies or municipal councillors at budget-time, are only marginally helpful in evaluating the library as a vital community institution. Nor does the number of borrowings from the library's collection, though a specific number, tell us whether a couple of different people may have read the book while it was checked out, or whether books borrowed were actually read at all. Another limitation of circulation statistics, at least for measuring the influence of the library, is that they do not capture how much is read by how many patrons while at the library premises.

Numbers can provide guidance, but they just don't help much in the larger qualitative scheme of things, especially when it comes to the role of those who are "the mind, taste and voice" of the community.

In this larger cultural view, it is clear that the local library is an important democratic institution, right up there with the public school.

This attribute is not quantifiable either, but it is of immense importance in training up young people to be self-reliant, freestanding, rights-bearing citizens. The library, like a good school, can be a perfect match for a youngster's natural curiosity. Later in life, the library continues its relevance as a democratic institution by providing inquisitive citizens with different channels of information, enabling them to independently think through to alternate positions from those being advanced by the powers-that-be or the conventional wisdom of the day.

A library thus not only provides intellectual yeast for its community, but also enables the local citizenry to be independent, the ultimate bulwark of "a free and democratic society" grounded in the Canadian Charter of Rights and Freedoms. Not everyone may go to the library for such consciously high-minded purposes, but that does not matter. Just to have the freedom to select from a wide range of novels and non-fiction works or to enjoy reading the current newspapers and recent periodicals is itself an integral part of this larger pattern of self-referencing behaviour by independent-minded people.

Freedom of expression, as John Ralston Saul pointed out when president of PEN Canada, the organization that supports and seeks the release of writers imprisoned by repressive regimes, does not exist in a vacuum. It also requires, he said, "that people are free to read and discuss what is being written." Without an audience of readers, why would most authors even bother to write? The library's wide availability of diverse and essentially uncensored materials makes a citizen's freedom of choice real, which in turn encourages creation of more books and articles.

Once again, the numbers do not matter. Statistics cannot calibrate the importance to society as a whole of those who are acculturated to see their freedom of choice as a right. That is why the same Charter, in also guaranteeing to individuals "freedom of information," does not attempt to measure what that means other than to stipulate that such freedom can only be limited by laws of general application consistent with a free and democratic society—such as statues assuring privacy of one's medical records and income tax returns.

That is also why, on the other hand, rulers who seek to control their country's population clamp restrictions on information, control messages in the news media, censor certain books and sometimes even publicly burn them. Nazis burned books in Germany in the 1930s because like all totalitarians they understood how the power of ideas and independent access to knowledge empower a freestanding citizenry, which is not something one wants if the intent is to subvert democracy. To make sure these bonfires of learning would, as Joseph Goebbels put it, enable "the soul of the German people again to express itself," the uniformed Nazi vandals' trashing of literature prominently took place in public.

This brutish method of addressing ideas one does not share neither began nor ended in Nazi Germany. Cicero's treatise *On the Nature of the Gods* was burned by pagans. The followers of Luther and then Calvin burned books expressing the Catholic world-view. Alberto Manguel adds to this genealogy of missing books whose shadows alone occupy empty shelf space in libraries of our time: "the works of the 'bourgeois' writers proscribed by Stalin, the publications of the 'Communist scribblers' exiled by Senator McCarthy, the books destroyed by the Taliban, by Fidel Castro, by the government of North Korea, by the officials of Canada Customs."[4]

Devastating threats to libraries also come in less dramatic forms too, and can be even more insidious for being less obvious—death not in a single burn but by a thousand little cuts: discarding books because of overcrowding, water damage caused by failure to maintain facilities, governments cutting budgets and avoiding accountability, a shifting of the library into the role of an amusement centre, and so much more. This is all seen here in one town's embattled quest, from the 1870s through to the present and projecting into the future, to provide citizens of Bracebridge as well as visitors to the town with their freedom through books.

The library is a passport to a larger world because it is a source of information about not just our own culture but potentially all cultures. The people of a particular community behave a certain way because they are acclimatized to the particular cultural practices and beliefs in which they live. For any community, be it a local village or an entire country, institutions are indispensable for passing on cultural values from one generation to the next. Among the institutions central to this role are book publishers and news media, courts and legislatures, the civil service and the military, families and religious organizations, and of course schools and libraries.

Yet even though they are important in making us who we are, and for embracing and transmitting our culture, institutions like schools and libraries are themselves the product of forces that make them vary significantly from one place to another, from one culture to another, from one era to the next. Consequently, the structure of our cultural life is itself of vast importance in taking stock of just who we are. In looking at the evolution of one North American town's public library over more than a century, we discover how this evolving structure not only expresses the dynamic culture of our North American continent, but also shapes it. This is another dimension of the "dynamic stability" alluded to earlier. Such symbiotic relationship between structure and culture is nowhere displayed better than in our most democratic of institutions, the public library.

In 1938, Bracebridge librarian Patricia Johnson wrote a weekly newspaper column, "Library Corner," and in it reviewed a new book in the library's collection by Alice Tisdale Hobart, entitled *Yang and Yin*. "The title of the book is an Eastern phrase meaning, in its general sense, the two forces that create life—'yang' the active element and 'yin' the passive. All life must keep the harmony between these two elements, the creative and the receptive," Johnson wrote. She spoke of the "deep imperative need to keep the balance" running through all life. Few institutions address that imperative the way a library can.

Whether a library is in a throbbing metropolis or a sleepy village, its centrality to the community consists of a two-way exchange. This yin-yang balance flows between, on one hand, the library premises and its contents, and on the other, those who make use of the facilities and services. The following chapters trace how this balancing act works in the specific ups and downs and ins and outs over time of one particular community and its library. What they portray is a relationship of mutual dependence.

However, the structural nature of a library to our society entails much more than balance and mutual dependence. Libraries were born out of communities whose citizens already had books, appreciated them, and wanted a larger and better-organized relationship with the world of published information. In the case of Bracebridge, for example, a gradual development of book-related services over several decades first provided the stepping-stones toward the innovative Carnegie-style library in 1908.

A COMPELLING DRAW. Student Alex Mason of Gravenhurst, who says he finds the Bracebridge Public Library even better than his school library, joins a lengthening parade of students attracted to this same space over the years. At this corner carrel his focus at the moment is the endless world of Wikipedia information on the computer screen. *Jan Pitman*

The first Bracebridge library followed the form and philosophy of subscription libraries inaugurated in the United States by Benjamin Franklin in 1779 and in Britain by skilled tradesmen and engineers whose collections of books were available to members only. Both were a co-operative structure for those wanting access to a larger number of books than they could afford individually. The British version of this was advanced by Mechanics' Institutes which perfected the model for their time and place.

To modern ears the name "mechanic" does not at first conjure up an association with books or libraries perhaps. In the nineteenth century, however, with increasing application of science to create new industrial processes, educated tradesmen began appearing on the scene in much greater numbers. These individuals were knowledgeable in mechanical engineering. They were skilled workers interested in science. They saw the connection between things and sought integration of knowledge, understanding that the fragmentation of learning through specialization would be limiting if not re-integrated into a larger awareness through what today is sometimes called a "holistic" approach. These educated men, whose applied intelligence provided the brains to go with the brawn in the pragmatic task of building up a new society in the province, enthu-

14

siastically formed a Mechanics' Institute to further these educational, literary and social interests.

The Mechanics' Institutes would establish a library in the community where they were constituted by interested locals, and invariably added other services such as reading rooms and special lectures to round out their mission of uplifting and engaging skilled working people through education. Many Canadian communities established Mechanics' Institute libraries and by 1851 the Legislature enacted a statute to broadly encompass their operation, so that the structure was a clearly developed model for creating a local library by 1874 when adopted in Bracebridge. Although this structure was the common one, it reflected a deeper cultural attribute of its age: it was a private institution. The more revolutionary idea of open public libraries had not yet taken form in a workable structure.

Several decades after formation of the Mechanics' Institute Library in Bracebridge, however, a different model was emerging: the Free Library. "Free libraries" were structured to be open to all members of the commu-

SAME STAGE, NEW PLAY. Over a hundred years, time-lapse photography of this section along the south wall of the library would chronicle many re-enactments of the same basic plot, with different actors, new scripts, changed furniture and contemporary methods. Today, people at computer terminals busily occupy the area in the centre, and locked cases along the right wall secure the Muskoka Collection archive. In the 1970s, as shown here, a librarian sat at her desk and young people worked at a library table. In the 1950s, there was a potted palm to the right, a square stairwell to the left where the patch of carpet is visible, and at the same large table in the same place you see in this picture, the author sat making notes in what was then the reference section about the development of computer technology. Back in the 1930s . . .

nity without fee or charge, and as such qualified to receive government grants. This structure, too, became part of the Bracebridge experience at the turn of the last century.

Both of these models can now be seen, in retrospect, to have been transitional phases leading to yet another structure of the community library in the early 1900s when Bracebridge joined the swelling ranks of towns and cities with Carnegie-constructed public libraries. During the intense quarter-century when the Bracebridge library was in transition from the Mechanics' Institute Library to the Free Library and then to the Carnegie library, each model had a definite structure that significantly influenced the way it operated, and was even capable of operating, in the community.

In *Free Books for All*, a study of the public library movement in Ontario, University of Guelph librarian and historian Lorne Bruce recaptures the "Dream for Ontario" that empowered leaders from 1850 to 1930 to believe that public libraries had important roles to fulfill. In telling the story of a movement that used the power of local governments to deliver rate-supported library services for all citizens, which he felt "typified the efforts of Victorians and Edwardians to improve Canadian society and enrich its culture," Bruce observed that men and women supporting the library movement saw libraries as only part of a larger picture, "one of a number of reforms and working concerns in which they were engaged." He suggested it was because of their work in this larger arena that "the majority did not write extensively about their library experiences" with the result that this part of their story slipped from view and became harder to document as time passed by.

Yet Bruce found rewarding results from his laborious gathering of source materials scattered across the province to document the large story of an important public movement. "It is my hope," he concluded, "that this book will stimulate readers to turn to the history of Ontario's libraries for themselves, thus deepening our understanding of the processes that have shaped modern public libraries in Canada." He urged advancing from the general to the specific, a "turn to the history of Ontario's libraries" to deepen "our understanding of the processes that have shaped modern public libraries in Canada." *Local Library, Global Passport* is a reply to that invitation. Telling the story of library services in the Canadian town of Bracebridge fulfills, in one specific instance, his scholar's wisdom in recommending that we can better understand the general picture by seeing its particular details.

The passport quality of the library and its contents applies regardless of the size of one's community. By focusing on a small town's library in Bracebridge, we see just how a collection of books and the expansion of knowledge they provide for citizens become pivotal to the culture and vitality of the library's host community. At the same time, this microcosmic view of a universal phenomenon also reveals how the struggle to establish and maintain a local library is tortuous and often uncertain, more than could ever be known if one only looked at the large general picture of provincial library associations or national library movements.

Before a library can even be built, there must be books and people who want to read them, a condition that does not, however, develop uniformly: more than half a century after Bracebridge had its library, larger towns in the province still had none. How a community's "book culture" develops, as an essential prelude to emergence of a library, is thus a good starting point for unravelling the mystery of why every library, although doing essentially the same thing and composed of primarily the same elements, is nevertheless unique.

TWO

Books in the Bush

For at least five millennia, from the first-known human activity at the present site of Bracebridge until the past couple hundred years or less, Aboriginals got by without books. This illuminating counterpoint to our written tradition reminds us of alternative possibilities, not only historically but in contemporary contexts as well. It also provides a "base line" for our case study of how a book-centred culture eventually emerged in this same Muskoka setting.

The Ojibwa peoples were happily free from worries about fines for late books or getting behind in their reading. For centuries their words conveyed meaning in central Muskoka without ever being written down. One of the largest of the Algonquian-speaking tribes in Canada, the Ojibwa were this district's original summer tourists, moving regularly up and down the Muskoka River system along their major canoe route between the Ottawa River valley and Georgian Bay, visiting their hunting grounds, trap lines, fishing areas and summer encampments.

Knowledge of these destinations and the safest routes to reach them, the skills in gathering and hunting food, all the wisdom and ways of generations, were continuously passed down from parent to child, and exchanged between one and all, through the spoken word alone. They knew where to find the large woodland clearing above the falls because their father had told them of it, not because they had read about it in an old text. The Ojibwa lived within an oral tradition. People could survive and prosper without books. They created a fundamentally different society from ours based on attentive listening, close observation, respect for elders, narrative and legend, acquisition of skills rather than "head learning," reliance on instinct and intuition, memory and personal experience.

Just as the Ojibwa existed without books, other older parts of the world existed before the advent of books and their history in intrinsically part of the story of how books, one of our oldest technologies, were created and developed. This was not the case for Bracebridge. Here habitation only commenced 400 years after Johannes Gutenberg in Germany had invented moveable type, revolutionizing printing in a way that remained essentially unchanged into the 20th century, made mass printing of books possible and available to all who wanted them, and ensured that when Bracebridge was settled in the 1860s it would be by people to whom books were as essential as bread, who brought them with them into the bush and who were soon printing them in their new community. Before that could happen, however, the area had to be mapped and settled.

Maps, indispensable documents for knowing and navigating our places on the planet, crucial providers of information at turning points in history both large and small, are another format used by a society that records its information on paper and other media.

Cartography is handmaiden to literacy and literature. Getting the right image is often instrumental to our fate and fortune as humans. How accurate people's maps are at the time they make decisions and take actions based on them can be linked directly to their success or failure. Maps of Muskoka thus played a crucial role in determining how the District developed, with direct consequences both for when the area was opened for settlement and what kind of people it was who came here with their books.

One of the first map to show the three lakes of Muskoka to the east of Georgian Bay appeared in 1751, identified by the British military engineers who prepared it as "The Lakes of the Hurons." Here began a long saga of official misunderstanding and, like all misunderstandings by those in positions of power, it would have significant consequences and create much hardship. This lesson played out in the human interaction with settlement and development of Muskoka, heartbreaking tales in many cases, poor families sent into the swarming blackflies to hack a farm out of forest when all they found beneath the roots were boulders for women and children to pile up like gravemarkers for an agricultural experiment commissioned by distant officials who did not have the image of the land right.

The military cartographers of 1751, as Lyman B. Jackes notes in *Indian Legends of Muskoka and the North Country*, "did not come up into Canada with their surveying instruments and tape measures. They got most of their information concerning what is now Ontario from Indians who had crossed Lake Ontario and who were familiar with the waterways and lakes of the regions to the north of Lake Ontario."[1]

With the exception of a brief survey done in 1812, in conjunction with the war of that period, nothing else was done until 1826 when, to better test the accessibility of this unknown region, Lieutenant Henry Briscoe of the Royal Engineers travelled north from Toronto into Muskoka. His extensive records of this voyage into and out of Muskoka mark a notable first in producing a written record in the District, but these accounts were lodged with the Public Records Office in London, England.[2] Mysterious Muskoka's connection with the printed word still remained marginal, to say the least.

Three years later, travelling in the opposite direction, Alexander Sherriff arrived on the scene and wrote the first descriptive words about Muskoka to take published form. In 1831, Sherriff's account of this expedition was published in *Transactions of the Literary and Historical Society of Quebec*. At least this was not as far away as London, but as D.H.C. Mason wryly observes in his book *Muskoka: The First Islanders*, "Thus buried, it contributed little to the knowledge of the country."[3] A civilization based on writing had so far extended only the tiniest of tentacles toward Muskoka.

In 1835, two lieutenants from the Royal Engineers were sent to create a new map of the area. The men probably had a spectacular trip, perhaps were even rendered speechless by Muskoka, but their lakeland excursion served little value to others. Their descriptions are brief and apparently no mapping was done.

If there was one person in the world, however, who could map and make excellent written records, it was David Thompson. A man of superior intelligence and resilient physical stamina to match his robust sense of adventure, Thompson was emerging as one of the greatest cartographers. The man mapped the northern half of the North American continent, from Muskoka to the mountain peaks of the Rockies in British Columbia. Dispatched into the *terra incognita* of Muskoka in 1837 by an impatient provincial government with instructions to make a quick survey of the three lakes, in August that year he and his survey team from the North West Company portaged around the falls at the future site of Bracebridge. He took his measurements and made maps of this district around the Muskoka River, or *Musk-ka-ko-skow-see-pie* in the language of the Ojibwa, meaning "Swamp Ground River" from the topography of its entrance to the lake. In rapid order, Thompson accomplished his work to perfection, recording for the first time a scientific picture of the Muskoka landscape and the first map with any pretence to accuracy.

The problem with written records such as maps and books, however, is that they can be misplaced, lost or even maliciously hidden, which was never a problem for the Ojibwa. In David Thompson's case, his records of the 1837 Muskoka survey were salted away deep and long forgotten in the records of government offices. This sabotage was intentional. Jealous colleagues were happy to see his efforts buried and superiors with vested financial interests in land ownership and transportation corridors sought to control information about accessible routes through certain areas of the province they preferred remain *terra incognita*. So it was not surprising for both these reasons that the stellar results of Thompson's map-making in Muskoka "disappeared." As Robert J. Boyer notes in *Early Exploration and Surveying of Muskoka*, the books and charts David Thompson created in Muskoka in the 1830s were conveniently "lost" for years. "His fine map of the lakes," adds Colonel Douglas H.C. Mason in *Muskoka: The First Islanders*, "lay apparently unknown in some government office while such maps as were available to the public were largely guess-work, some showing three lakes, some two and some one."

Nothing more happened until 1853 when geologist Alexander Murray crossed Lake Muskoka and roughly mapped the north and east shores. By 1860, when settlers began creeping into the silent forests and traversing the pristine waterways of isolated Muskoka, the public knowledge of the District was minimal and mostly confined to Lake Muskoka. Only Thompson had visited Lake Joseph and his map was unknown. Had his maps and written documents about this district been available for public and governmental use, they would have given Muskoka a very different history of development. Thompson's detailed information about the lakes and bays of Muskoka, many of which he named, could have guided distant government planners contemplating the prospects for opening up the territory.

As a result, the district remained an isolated interior part of the province for decades, where the Ojibwa peoples continued to contentedly live as they had for unrecorded centuries.

In fact the delay in colonization of Muskoka had a double impact, affecting both the timing of settlement and those who came, with significant implications in turn for the nature of the society that would eventually emerge, with their books, in this heavily forested region.

The province of Upper Canada itself was being settled much later than surrounding regions of North America, and within the province Muskoka District itself would not opened for settlement until southern parts of the province had already become well established. Only eight brief years before Confederation did the very first settler even make it to the falls on the north branch of the Muskoka River. This relatively late start meant those who arrived in Bracebridge included many educated people for whom life without books was unthinkable. Before settlement began in Muskoka, there were plenty of hopeful souls departing for British North America in general and Upper Canada in particular. Their efforts to settle in the bush included more than hacking farms out of forests. Given a fresh start in the New World these same individuals who had been considered the dregs of Britain displayed "sterling qualities of character" that made them, said McDougall, "the muscle and sinew of the new civilization." Although many immigrants to Upper Canada possessed the mutually reinforcing qualities of being poor and illiterate, a smaller number of educated and literate immigrants at the same time became for the province "its mind, its taste, and its voice."[4]

In this territory a small but influential number of those taking up new lives were accordingly seeking, not to re-create the existing world order, but rather to extend the one they already knew. This extension ran into the wilderness on the twin rails of literacy and books. In 1834, the province's first town, Kingston, had formed a Mechanics' Institute Library, the most advanced form of community library at that time, when "a numerous and most highly respectable body of mechanics, interspersed with some few of the town's inhabitants" took the initiative to create a library in their community.[5] This was already three years after a Mechanics' Institute Library had been formed in York, later to be renamed Toronto. The book had thus arrived on the shores of one of the province's southern Great Lakes, but not yet in Muskoka.

By 1859 yet another man paddled up the Muskoka River, coming into a large dark bay to face a rocky horseshoe-shaped canyon ahead. A slanted rocky opening in the centre channelled the splashing and swirling white waters of a thundering falls. John Beal could go no further so pulled his canoe ashore to his left on the northern bank below the falls and clambered up the rocks, hiking and hacking his way northward to the first suitably flat piece of elevated land where he built a shanty and became recorded, two years before even a colonization road reached the falls, as the first European to settle at the site of the future town of Bracebridge. This impossible jumble of steep hills and rocky outcroppings was no place to site a settlement, but Beal was not thinking in those terms. He just wanted quiet isolation and had found it.

At last the saga of books in the bush that launched the Bracebridge book culture was about to begin.

By the summer of 1860 the Muskoka Road that government contractors were pushing through the wilderness had penetrated as far as the south branch of the Muskoka River, which had yet to be bridged, at a site three miles south of John Beal's one-member settlement. The roadmakers cleared their way to Beal's place in 1861, arriving in a surrealistic scene at his small clearing in the bush to lay a road right past his doorstep. The patient John Beal looked up from reading his Bible, the first book in the bush, bemused that the world he had sought to escape in the deep wilderness of Muskoka was beating a path to his door. It must be a sign.

That the Bible was among the first books a settler would bring into the bush is not surprising. It was called "the Good Book" for a number of reasons. It served as an all-in-one lifetime reading companion, a compendium of sensual poetry and horror stories, magic encounters and deadly dramas, morality plays and mystical revelations. If travelling by canoe or packing lightly for an overland trek, the Good Book was in fact a great book. It provided a whole library between two covers.

And it was easily transportable. Today the entire Bible has been compressed digitally so that it is as small as the head of a pin, but even in the 1700s and 1800s when theologians sought to clarify the unknowable by debating how many angels might dance on the head of a pin, skilled printers already displayed the more practical miracles of the graphic arts by crafting highly portable Bibles. Set in microscopic type by hand, these miniature Bibles were readable only with a magnifying glass. Although such miniature editions were inadequate for the theatrics of Bible-thumping Methodist preachers who paddled and hiked through central Muskoka in these pioneering times, they denied travelling Christians the last plausible excuse for not packing a Bible.

Most of the plentiful family Bibles accompanying early settlers into the bush were larger because they served, in addition to being a source of moral uplift, as a convenient place to record on the blank inside front and

RIVER TOWN, BOOK TOWN. Pioneers to Bracebridge and Muskoka came with books, and soon took measures to acquire many more. Reading with the accompanying sounds of a waterfall must have been pleasing to this early resident of Matthiasville, upriver from Bracebridge.

back covers the family's marriages, births and deaths. These genealogical records, helpful for researchers today, provided a practical use as well for the Bible dating from much earlier practice.

Like other North American communities settled in the 1800s, Muskoka abounded in Bibles once the settlers came. Contributing to the high incidence of these books of scripture in the bush was the fact that many people took pride in having their own. A gift Bible to a young person marked a right of passage, an acknowledgment by one's parents or elders that a child was now mature enough to be trusted with this greatest of gifts. Of many good ways to foster a child's reverence for books, this was one.

In the Bible presented as a gift to a teenage Hannah Boyer by her grandmother Mary White in 1846, for example, my great-grandmother inscribed the fresh front pages "Hannah Boyer Her Book" over and over again like any proudly possessive teenage girl might do until the empty sheets were all filled with her declarations. That Bible is just one of more than a dozen of my own family's accumulation of leather-bound and

worn Bibles with entries of vital statistics dutifully recorded through generations all the way back to marriages in England in the 1700s, a fraction
I am sure of the total number of Bibles over four generations and many
ancestral branches in Muskoka. The earliest bears an inscription made on
October 23, 1784.

Despite the constraints on the legal standing and economic status of
women in those times, owning "a Bible of One's Own" was a treasured
and even necessary component in a culture where women had a primary
responsibility for religious propriety and instruction. This was definitely
a society where a book and its contents were part of life. Apart from the
keys it offered for unlocking the kingdom of God, a Bible was a symbol of
one's status, carried to and from church services to complete a wardrobe
as proudly as a fine hat and proper gloves.

After 1862 the settlement by the falls began filling up with the places of
worship of a growing variety of religious denominations. Although forms
of racism, often grounded in religious dogma, would also be expressed in
Bracebridge over the years as in many other North American communities, pluralism and diversity, not religious exclusion, would increasingly
become hallmarks of this Muskoka community. This general openness to
diversity was a concomitant feature of a town where a love of books and
an open curiosity and independence of mind were essential ingredients
from the beginning.

There was a practical side to the spiritual side of religion, too. In most
small Canadian villages of the 1860s, and certainly in Bracebridge, religious life, church practices and robust Christian values dominated the
local culture. Those pioneer ancestors of many people still living in
Bracebridge and its outlying areas today had a central place for the Bible
in their lives. In its words they found comfort and consolation to miti-
gate the hardships routinely making up their lot scratching the soil-sparse
Canadian Shield that the Ontario government, with poor information
about soil conditions, had finally opened for agricultural settlement.

The Bible, freighted with so much spiritual mystery and aura as it was,
became a talisman for many early settlers who, in the face of daunting
hardships and haunting fears, could turn to it in a very human way for
comfort. Bush Christians not only felt closer to the divine through scripture and the spiritual presence of nature in its pristine state, but also dealt
with stark edges of survival in ways that for many was confirmation of
God's power.

The views people take of such matters, whether reverential or resigned, is also where freedom of religion comes in. Freedom of religion and interpretation, in 1860s Bracebridge a necessary reality and today a constitutional right guaranteed to all Canadians, is in fact a specific application of a larger liberty, the freedom of thought. This becomes inseparable from the story of books and the role of the library.

The sturdy, enterprising, desperately hopeful folk who carried little in the way of possessions but nevertheless had a place for the Bible and a few other tomes when they arrived in the primitive Bracebridge settlement brought with them the seeds of a literate society where reading would be an intrinsic part of life. Typical of these early settlers' literary troves would also be the works of Shakespeare, John Bunyan's *Pilgrim's Progress* and volumes on history and home remedies, all equally helpful to survival in primitive conditions in the Canadian bush.

The culture in the community was not just possession of books, but the use and enjoyment of them. For some, a Sunday afternoon's reading of scripture in the most formal setting available, such as a front parlour in the homes that had them, was a weekly highlight. For many, during the long winter nights, readings aloud in more relaxed settings around the kitchen wood stove, and from books other than the Bible, also formed an early part of this story. Poems and narrative adventures were especially popular. Many could recite lengthy stanzas of poetry from a seemingly bottomless reservoir of memorized treasures. In the absence of visitors, or latter day radio, television and neighbourhood cinemas, the entertainment to take one out of oneself and beyond the confines of one's immediate place came in the form of the magic passport printed as words on the page of a book. For these Muskoka settlers, mostly from Great Britain, the legacy tales of Christendom and exploits of the heroes of the British Empire imparted, even in these scattered corners and backwoods places, a sense of being part of a grand design, a participant in a global and transcendent order, what Canadian historian Carl Berger called "the sense of Empire." From its earliest days, Bracebridge revolved around books and unfolded in keeping with the images and narratives early residents absorbed from their volumes and applied to their lives.

Literary life, however expressed, played a robust role in late nineteenth century Bracebridge. It was a period of learning and schooling and inquisitive exploration of the mind, of science and metaphysics still seen as two dimensions of a common phenomenon, of printing and poetry,

FIRST THINGS FIRST. In 1869 the *Northern Advocate* newspaper office was prominent entering the main street of the Bracebridge settlement where, two years earlier, Confederation had been joyously celebrated with fresh lemonade, patriotic addresses and repeated blowing up of the blacksmith's anvil with gunpowder, the most spectacular frontier fireworks available. From the *Advocate* building, the first newspaper in the northern districts began publishing in 1869 with the arrival of James Boyer from New York who became its editor, and Thomas McMurray as publisher. The first book to be printed in Bracebridge would also be published from this building in 1871. Three years later, in 1874, a community library would be organized. A year after that, the village would be incorporated.

of touring lecturers and Methodist preachers pressing into the bush settlements, of newspapers and books. Poets would incorporate Latin and Greek phrases into their works, offering no footnote or other explanation of meaning because none was needed for those who read or heard them. The quick-minded and educated citizens for whom messages had not been "dumbed down" but who proudly knew the coded meanings and aspired to higher understanding generally comprehended allusions to ancient civilizations, to the Deity, to the sprites of fairytales or the heroes of myth and legend.

As settlement in the community swelled, the books became as varied as the people arriving. No settler could afford the weight or space for many books, nor could many have known in advance the loneliness of long and isolated Muskoka winters that would only enhance the welcome companionship of a book. By the time Muskoka District was being settled, which as noted was later than elsewhere to the south, a great many people who came, either from the British Isles or the United States, were educated and literate. The problems that drove them to start a new life in the Canadian bush were seldom those of inadequate learning, but more the need to make a fresh start after a setback in life or to seize the opportunity of getting free land and establishing themselves with property the way they never could if they remained in a wage economy. The new settlement drew many who were enterprising, alert and knowledgeable. It would be no fluke that among the earliest creations in town, after a newspaper, would be a library.

While the hermit John Beal was enjoying his quiet reading time up at the north end of town, which at this time was also the south, east and west part of town, unbeknownst to him tourism was getting under way. Tourism in Muskoka's future would always be as important as settlement, and in many ways the two were just different aspects of the same thing, but it set an important keynote that the first tourists were men of books. As well, they also proved that one did not really need a good map to head into the wilderness if their sense of adventure was keen.

In July 1860, two young men in the book publishing business in Toronto decided to strike out into the north country for a week. James Bain, Jr. and his partner John Campbell, both young men of literary spirit, sought adventure during their summer escapade away work. They packed homemade knapsacks, took a gun and powder and shot flasks, grabbed their fishing gear, carried a box for botanical specimens and headed north. When they reached Lake Muskoka where Gravenhurst now stands, Bain later recalled, "not a tree appeared to have been cut along the shore and two Indian wigwams stood on the beach." Their initial encounter with Muskoka was so memorable that these pioneers of tourism in the District returned the very next summer, this time in August.

Entering over the new Muskoka Road, they were swarmed by mosquitoes and black flies which they fought off with handkerchiefs and leafy boughs, and suffered great thirst as their penalty for thinking the cool clear water running in the streams they passed would not be fit for human consumption.

"But at the end of 12 miles," records their literary journal, the first written tourist record of Muskoka sojourners, "we came to a log hut of peculiar construction which we concluded to be Mickey McCabe's tavern." The journal then goes on to describe their encounter with a woman who

MEN OF LETTERS FIRST TOURISTS IN BRACEBRIDGE. Tourism to Muskoka Lakes began almost simultaneously with the first footfall of the settlers when two young men, John Campbell, 18, and James Bain, 20, took a summer break from book publishing and arrived through the bush in 1860. Every summer thereafter the pair brought a growing number of adventurers to Muskoka islands to engage nature and literary interests, to leave the city behind, not bring it with them.

Campbell, Bain, William Tytler and others boated on Thursday, July 30, 1863 to North Falls, fishing and staying at the log cabin "Royal Hotel" before the settlement was renamed Bracebridge. Early in the 1860s they formed the "Muskoka Club" and bought islands in the Muskoka Lakes to become the first of what are known locally as "permanent summer residents." Back in a Toronto photographer's studio, Muskoka Club members Chris Lee, John Campbell, James Louden, W.M. Smith, William Tytler and James Bain posed for this early picture.

Louden was later president of University of Toronto; Bain became founding librarian of Toronto's first public library, pioneer of the Toronto Reference Library on College Street and first president of the Ontario Library Association; Campbell an internationally recognized scholar, author and member of the Royal Society; and Tytler a schools inspector and president of the Ontario Library Association which, with Bain, he had helped establish in 1901.

WILLIAM TYTLER (left). Tytler's diary for the Muskoka Club's July 1863 stay in North Falls gives the first recorded mention of a stage coming to the settlement on the Muskoka colonization road. It was, he noted, "full." Tall, thin, intelligent and alert, Tytler was always up for adventure and often at the forefront of developments, becoming one of the Ontario Library Association's "originals" just as he was one of the "first islanders" of European-settled Muskoka.

JAMES BAIN, JR. (right). Bain was born in 1842 and died the year the Bracebridge Carnegie Library opened in 1908. In between, his remarkable pioneering advances included pure tourism in Muskoka, public and reference libraries in Toronto, and the potent Ontario Library Association, of which he was founding president in 1901.

could not comprehend the fact that they were travelling through the area for pleasure, but who, nevertheless, gave them a much needed drink.

Campbell and Bain returned annually to Muskoka, their party growing in size each summer as the two pioneers of tourism in the District attracted an ever widening circle of cultured people who loved the rugged wilderness, "discovered" Lake Joseph, bought islands, tented and boated, and wrote skits, poems and little operas they performed around their campfires.

Following their 1864 expedition, Campbell, Bain, Tytler and others formed The Muskoka Club. The members of this club, as well as being pioneers in Muskoka tourism, provided some of the earliest written descriptions of the area. The club's constitution set forth the club objects as being "to provide an annual expedition for its members, to preserve the records of past expeditions, and to receive information on subjects of interest to its members."

Both the educated and well-off tourists and many educated settlers following the first founders into the district established the enduring cultural complexion of the Muskoka community. The fact that Muskoka is a crossroads of cultures and values, both Aboriginal and non-Aboriginal, both summer Muskokan and permanent resident, ensured a livelier and more cosmopolitan and pluralistic sensibility than is possible in communities more singularly grounded. Bracebridge was not a hastily assembled mill town or a remote mining community, a resource-based company town or a self-sufficient rural farming centre, but rather an economically diversified and steadily growing community emerging from the bush in the presence of books. Being a place of singular rugged beauty that was also conveniently close to southern Ontario and populous American states, Muskoka attracted players from the high levels of industry and entertainment, commerce and politics, education and religion, sports and arts. In Bracebridge and around the Muskoka Lakes well-written and significant books of the kind scholars and literary critics contend about centuries later, as well as books for entertainment and pleasure, were available and in circulation from the inception of organized settlement and early tourism.

The literary life of this community was planted with the seeds of its first settlement. Books may have been in short supply for those coming through the bush to Bracebridge, but their thirst for them was not.

THREE

Early Library Beginnings

The settlement that sprang up around the cataract where the river races and dances down a ragged split in the precambrian rock was appropriately named "North Falls" to distinguish it from "South Falls," a narrower but more majestic spectacle three miles to the south on another branch of the same river system. This is important because each library achieves its unique institutional attributes by being a particular expression of local culture as well as its custodian. Bracebridge is a river town.

This river and these falls provided the *raison d'être* for the settlement. John Beal was content in 1859 for this rocky barrier and its waterfall to halt his retreat into the wilderness, and the isolated bliss he found here became the foundation of a community that could have grown up in a dozen other locations. Alexander Bailey was happy in 1864 to tap the water power of the falls to turn the grinding stones and mill grain in the gristmill he constructed that gave the small settlement new economic importance. Before long the same water power would drive the engines of additional manufacturing enterprises and provide electricity to the town that helped it entice even more mills and factories. Just as many people who came here felt life would not be much without a book, the town itself would be nothing without the river and its powerful falls.

From the day in 1866 when navigation on the Muskoka Lakes by steamships was inaugurated with the maiden voyage of the *Wenonah* from Gravenhurst to Bracebridge, the town became more important as a pivotal centre for transportation at the head of navigation. Like all rivers throughout the Canadian Shield, the North Branch of the Muskoka also

WHAT'S IN A NAME? This "District Exchange" store, one of a number of Bracebridge retail and commercial establishments with lofty names (others included "The Royal Hotel" for a structure with earthen floors and sod-chinked log walls, a barber shop called "Her Majesty's Old Reliable Shaving Saloon," and a general store named "House of Commerce") showed that Bracebridgites could aspire to grandeur.

Built in 1868, the Exchange had a small addition, seen on its right side, built to house the Bracebridge post office. When granting this post office to the distinctively named settlement of "North Falls," a literary official in the Post Office Department renamed the community "Bracebridge" from the title of Washington Irving's book *Bracebridge Hall*, an unimaginable act of nemesis for the town's propensity to high-falutin' names.

provided a convenient transportation route for shipping logs downstream to lumber mills. The community prospered with the rise of logging and lumber production, but it also prospered because of the steamship traffic. The free-floating logs and large booms made the river dangerous and often unnavigable to the steamboats, so the community got used to rigorous debate over significant issues.

For the kind of future North Falls might enjoy, much depended on good transportation not only by water, but also by road and rail. Because the easiest crossing of the Muskoka River for the colonization road was at the narrows by North Falls, the town increasingly became a crossroads of transportation routes. The community would wait impatiently, however, for the all-important northern extension of the railway, which was delayed by lobbying pressures from the business and commercial interests in the rival town 11 miles to the south. McCabe's Landing, the only flat townsite in Muskoka, was getting its act together as an important transshipment centre at the head of the railway and terminus of the expanding fleet of the Muskoka Navigation Company, and believed the end of the railway in their community was to its best advantage. Fortunately for North Falls, other interests in the country saw a less parochial picture and pressed to extend the railway further into the hinterland and its waiting resources. For the riverside settlement at North Falls, prosperity was assured when the railway reached the town in 1885.

The diversifying local economy and spreading general prosperity took tangible form in the schools, churches, fraternal organizations, sports clubs, agricultural societies and a number of early small private libraries scattered around town.

No community had ever been more aptly named than North Falls. The designation was a tribute to both the northern element of the Canadian frontier and the town's very genesis in the powerful watercourse that flowed through the heart of the settlement. Then, through a symbolic twist of fate, a book changed the town forever.

In 1864, residents in the robustly growing settlement at North Falls sought to take the next step in their progress by opening their own post office. Alexander Bailey, who had come to prominence by building the gristmill at the falls, was pretty much the instigator of these demands and sent off an application to the postmaster general.

The task of reviewing Bailey's letter of application fell to the secretary of the post office, W.D. LeSueur. Quietly reviewing his application for a post office at North Falls, LeSueur saw no objection to naming Bailey postmaster. The man had demonstrated enterprise and appeared to have the sense of responsibility required for such a position. Bailey would get the mail contract and became the settlement's first postmaster.

Then LeSueur paused. He found himself looking at Bailey's letter about postal service at North Falls just as he happened to be reading Washington Irving's novel *Bracebridge Hall*. As a man of literary interests, LeSueur was unusually impressed, for some inexplicable reason, by this name "Bracebridge." He liked it so much he decided to bequeath it to the settlement in conjunction with granting the community a post office. It was within the power of department officials under the Postal Act, in cases where an applicant village sought to have the name of an existing town, to make a change and prevent confusion. This, however, was not the case with North Falls. Not for the first time would an official take a

A RIVER RUNS THROUGH. A view of "North Falls" at the time the village was incorporated in 1875, showing Henry Bird's woollen mill and the wooden bridge across the river. A Mechanics' Institute Library with several hundred books and lectures for its members was already operating.

decision that only made sense from behind his desk in a distant capital and which exceeded his power.

William Dawson LeSueur was certainly a worthy person to name a town that would have such a connection with books and literature through its library. Born at Quebec City February 19, 1840, he "became the most important Canadian man of letters of his generation," according to historian A.B. McKillop. A critic and historian, after 1856 LeSueur also became a top civil servant in the Canadian government. He would continue to pursue his wider interests as well, becoming noted for "introducing a spirit of critical inquiry into journalism and historical writing."[1] Writing widely on religion, science and social philosophy in Canadian, American and British journals through the 1860s and 1870s, LeSueur eventually would turn his special focus to historical writing and political criticism in the 1890s. A critical biography he wrote in 1908 about William Lyon Mackenzie, leader of the Rebellion in 1837 and icon for those honouring Canada's liberal tradition, would become the subject of protracted litigation, which kept his book from being published in this land of freedom of the press and freedom of expression until 1979.[2]

Bracebridge was evidently fated to be more identified with world literature than local geography. Washington Irving, author of this noteworthy book, was a well-known American man of letters of the early part of the nineteenth century. With the purpose of lessening the ill feeling between countrymen of both the United States and England—a hangover from the Revolutionary War—he spent many years in England and wrote much about English life and customs. *Bracebridge Hall* was one such book, but there were earlier references "to the pleasant country home of the Bracebridge family" too, such as in Irving's *The Sketch Book* where his Christmas essays describe pleasant seasonal merriments at Bracebridge Hall.

Irving could never have imagined that his noble quest to foster improved American understanding and sympathy for English culture and folkways in the bitter aftermath of the American war of independence would produce, through the power of the printed word and the serendipitous borrowing of his book from a library by a literary civil servant in 1864, a sideswipe effect causing a distinctive Canadian town to unwillingly forfeit its universally unique appellation. To the book *Bracebridge Hall*, Bracebridge owes its loss of status as the only place in the world named "North Falls."[3]

This change from North Falls to "Bracebridge," an odd structural description seemingly drawn from a road engineer's lexicon, only makes sense in the haphazard workings of our larger fortunes at the hands of

WASHINGTON IRVING published *Bracebridge Hall*, subtitled *The Humorists*, in 1819 using his pen name Geoffrey Crayon. He is remembered as the author who inspired giving uniquely named "North Falls" its moniker "Bracebridge" and gave New York its nickname "Gotham City." Andrew Carnegie, who gave Bracebridge its library, was much taken by the author's writings for unity of English-speaking peoples and is buried in the Sleepy Hollow Cemetery in New York close to Washington Irving.

literature. It perfectly underscores why this town's story cannot be adequately told or properly understood without always tracing back to the role of books.

That one book's impact on the town, however improbable, nevertheless seemed symbolic, for as the development of library services and literary life advanced in Bracebridge the importance of books in making and re-making the community ascended in tandem. Washington Irving's goal had been to write books that would provide an American with a passport to the world of the English and thereby bridge the gulf of ignorance and misunderstanding between them. Almost two centuries later, the Bracebridge Public Library, where books are passports bridging the gaps between the townspeople and the global community, has as its stated objective to provide residents of the town with "access to the resources of information they find relevant to the changes, choices and decisions of their lives." The wording of this goal of the Bracebridge Public Library though typical of generic present-day "mission statements," otherwise could have been penned, and in a sense really was, by American author Washington Irving.

William Dawson LeSueur had introduced a new motif to the rugged settlement of sawmills and horse-drawn wagons traversing muddy roads up and down the rocky hills of this river town. This Canadian place, too, whether its astonished residents liked the new name or not, would now become "the pleasant country home of the Bracebridge family."

CULTURAL STAR. Dr. Samuel Bridgland had barely landed in Bracebridge in
1870 when he stepped onto the stage in a
local drama presentation and from then
on continued to star in the community as
a medical practitioner, Liberal Member
of the Ontario Legislature for Muskoka,
and strong library supporter as a lover of
books.

Following advent of postal service in Bracebridge in 1864, a new source for reading material became mail-order books. A diverse range of volumes from histories and novels and almanacs and medical home-remedies were soon being delivered to the local post office for homes in Bracebridge, arriving from publishers and booksellers in London, New York and Toronto as residents responded to their newspaper advertisements in the *Northern Advocate*, the *Free Grant Gazette* and the *Muskoka Herald*. This inspired a pattern for bringing books to the attention of widely scattered populations and delivering to them upon order that has continued into the present day with the Internet and online book buying. Then, as today, this steadily accumulation of home libraries contributed further to the impact of books on the town.

Mail-order books posed the same anxious uncertainty in the waiting period between order and arrival as mail-order brides, who were also occasionally ordered up in early settlement days. An alternative was provided by local bookstores where readers could make themselves familiar with the merchandise before buying. A further advantage of buying one's books from merchants in town, in addition to supporting local enterprise, was that bookstores could better reflect the reading interests of residents of Bracebridge as the booksellers learned through experience of trade what books to stock. Thus even as they incubated the local book-centric culture, the bookstores also extended it further.

VENDOR TO BOOK LOVERS. Isaac Huber (far left), Bracebridge bookshop owner in 1877, would not have sported his Masonic regalia in the store but appears resplendent in it for this early photograph. Huber's ad in 1879 said "Any books not in stock will be procured as publisher's prices."

MAIN STREET BOOKSELLER. James Thomson (left), of the Henderson & Thomson Bookstore on Manitoba Street, in 1902. The numerous bookstores in Bracebridge from earliest days helped foster, like handmaidens of the Bracebridge Public Library, the town's book culture.

TIME OF THE FIRST LIBRARY. The small Bracebridge community was home to many who had books but wanted to read more. In 1874, around the time of this photograph showing Henry Bird's Woollen Mill, bottom left, and a wooden bridge across the river, bottom right, a number of townsfolk formed a Mechanics' Institute Library, like a co-op, to pool their private collections and thereby increase their reading possibilities.

From early days, retail shops carried books even when there was not enough demand to sustain a stand-alone bookstore. Often books were sold alongside stationery and other complementary goods. Early Brace-bridge bookstores included one owned by Isaac Huber, who later sold his business in 1889 to W.H. McCann when the former moved from selling books to become the first Clerk of Muskoka District Court. John Smith, who had been a councillor and was elected reeve of Bracebridge in 1879 and "took particular satisfaction in performing the many duties" attached to his new office, still needed to make a living and continued his business as another of the town's book dealers—in his case combining the book-store with a shoe store, while his wife had a millinery shop farther along the street.

Two other bookstores in Bracebridge in the 1880s were those of W.H. Colville and Thomas Bros. By 1892, the firm of Thomas Bros., operating a combined bookstore and fancy goods shop, came to be known as Thomas and Booth after Noah D. Thomas went to North Bay to open a store there and in his place Harry Booth, a watchmaker, joined a partnership with G.H.O. Thomas in Bracebridge. Mr. Thomas at the time was also the school principal. By 1905, he would become proprietor of the *Bracebridge Gazette* and project himself into the conduct of local affairs both through his published opinions and a 1934 book *Bracebridge in 1884* recording and interpreting early days in Bracebridge, and his terms on council including as mayor of Bracebridge in 1916–17 and 1926–29.

E.J. Pratt owned a handsome three-storey red-brick structure on Manitoba Street where, on the street-level floor, he operated a bookstore and jewellery business through the 1890s and into the early twentieth century until the building burned in 1902. At that point, Aubrey Henderson and James Thomson, operating The Henderson & Thomson Book Store on Manitoba Street next to Chancery Lane since 1901, took over the stock and business of E.J. Pratt in school supplies and stationery. By 1904 Henderson sold his interest in the bookstore to his partner Thomson.

Schools began operating in Bracebridge in the late 1860s and gradually began to acquire books, which was a good thing because the teacher himself was not always present to instruct the often-barefoot children. James Boyer, himself a teacher in Macaulay Township just outside Bracebridge, wrote that in 1869 the only school in town was a small frame building on the slope of the hill above the Royal Hotel. It was, said Boyer, "a 10 × 12 affair and may have cost $25 to build and furnish." The teacher was an old veteran name Fraser, he explained, "who, on account of his arduous duties, found it necessary occasionally to take a refresher during school hours, and sometimes forgot to return to his duties until well after the time for closing school."

In time, public schooling became more restrictive, as teachers with longer attention spans for pupils and less inclination to support the town's taverns were hired, but they also became more expansive, with growth of public and high school reference libraries to supplement course texts. Bracebridge schools gradually came to acquire worthy library collections of reference works to supplement course texts, and had at least part-time librarians for both public and high schools by mid-twentieth century.

Later, the appearance of private educational services in Bracebridge such as the Northern Business Academy in the 1890s would mean another clustering of texts and course materials.

If first settlers brought Bibles and hymnals for spiritual guidance, a select group was now accounting for more extensive collections of books on

BOOK-CENTRED FAMILY. In the 1890s James Boyer, Bracebridge town clerk and a Muskoka magistrate, holder of senior positions in the Agricultural Society, Methodist Church and loyalist lodges and former editor of the *Northern Advocate*, was engrossed in a book as his wife Hannah worked with her knitting. They had come to Muskoka in 1869, after meeting and marrying in New York City. Their family at the front of their frame home on North Manitoba Street included son George, the youth with the cap on the left, who would become a Bracebridge newspaper publisher, town councillor and mayor, and a strong supporter of the Bracebridge Public Library. At the time of this photo, James Boyer, as a member of the Bracebridge Mechanics' Institute Library, was promoting the idea that it become a "free library" under the Ontario statute passed for this purpose a decade earlier.

religion. The ordained clergy in Bracebridge from the mid-1800s onward had, for the most part, additional selections available from the extensive religious canon. This did not apply in all cases. Itinerant Methodist preachers who travelled to the scattered settlements to preach the word did not pack more than the Bible, nor did early Baptists countenance a much wider spiritual literature. However, the Roman Catholic priest and the clergy of the Anglican and Presbyterian churches matched their intellect and spiritual curiosity with the ecclesiastical texts and religious commentaries in their small but growing private collections.

Besides importing books to the community for use in schools and churches, a gradual building up of private libraries paralleled the town's growth in other areas such as business, sports and physical facilities. From all evidence, a significant number of the early settlers in Bracebridge were people who enjoyed the wide pleasure of books of many kinds. A substantial body of English literature was housed in different homes around town, reflecting a life in which books were integral. Many of these original works continue to occupy shelf space in Bracebridge today, even as the tombstones of those who brought them to town have weathered and grown moss covered. Such personal libraries in the dwellings of townspeople were the first beginnings of libraries in Bracebridge.

In addition to libraries in residences, others were found in the summer homes and resorts around the lakes. Muskoka, since the advent of the railway and steamships, was become famous for its lakeside resorts and the palatial summer homes of American and Canadian plutocrats, who, in the days before automobiles and highways, did not drive fast for a hurried weekend but arrived in style with many trunks and a large staff to spend the entire summer away from polluted cities in the restorative atmosphere of the Muskoka Lakes. Fine boats, good dining and special company were among the attributes of Muskoka magic, and so were books. A number of summer homes held immense libraries, most at least had a number of books about nature, wildlife and water sports as well as novels for dockside reading, while those coming to the lodges and hotels found a goodly supply of titles available for a relaxing read on the wide shaded verandahs.

Specialized libraries, too, were beginning to be established in Bracebridge at a variety of locations under the auspices of local chapters or branches of organizations such as the Masonic Lodge, the Independent Order of Odd Fellows and the Loyal Orange Lodge, fraternal societies with meetings rooms that housed works appropriate to their purposes. The Women's Institute did tremendous work in the communities of Muskoka and shared its books with anyone interested. Initially its books, too, were kept in private homes. The South Muskoka Agricultural Society gathered for the education of its members, and the guidance of its judges at the annual fall fair displays of agricultural produce and livestock, numerous volumes and booklets on crops and livestock, the arts of animal husbandry, soil conditions and climatic challenges. These various scattered libraries, adding specialized depth to the overall collection of books in Bracebridge, were of course being assembled according to the needs and interests of their owners or sponsors.

From the time a printing press arrived in 1871, Bracebridge became home to the first newspaper in Ontario's northern districts. That year Thomas McMurray, the town's first newspaper publisher with the *Northern Advocate*, also claimed the record for first book printed in Bracebridge.

Entitled *The Free Grant Lands of Canada: From Practical Experience of Bush Farming in the Free Grant Districts of Muskoka and Parry Sound*, it contained valuable information about the district and conditions of settlers written up with erudite boosterism to promote further immigration into the District. Much of this book was written by the *Northern Advocate*'s editor James Boyer, some 24 pages of whose original handwritten manuscript still remain, with additional contributions McMurray solicited from several others around Parry Sound and Muskoka districts. Crammed with positive information about the future economic prospects of this region, *The Free Grant Lands of Canada* was pitched to attract newcomers. This book was widely distributed by the entrepreneurial McMurray, who was meanwhile busy building new stores and offices along the main street of town in anticipation of the coming boom, and by government land offices and railway companies similarly seeking to encourage an influx of passengers and settlers for reasons of their own. The free grant lands book did much to promote Muskoka and encourage additional settlers.

For those already in the community or coming newly to Bracebridge, meanwhile, the competitive output of the two newspapers fostered further interest in reading among residents of the town. The second newspaper, the *Free Grant Gazette*, had appeared on the scene and soon publishing wars began to rage between rival papers. The expansion of local printing facilities in turn increased the number of locally written and produced books.

The publishers also depended on libraries for their work. Books, especially of a reference nature, were collected in the editorial offices of both the town's newspapers.

A particular group relying on books were men engaged in the administration of justice and those practising law in its many forms, especially property conveyancing. Early settlers with any hint of legal training found themselves propelled into the forefront of bar and bench, including those appointed as magistrates. Bringing the rule of law to life in the clearings and settlements of the Canadian Shield did not necessarily require the volumes of Canadian and Ontario statutes, manuals of procedure, or published commentaries on the law, but having them at hand helped.

In 1868, the Ontario government appointed C.W. Lount as magistrate for the District of Muskoka and promptly the provincial Department of Public Works erected a building on hilltop land in the centre of town bordering Ontario and Dominion streets. It served Lount as his courtroom and housed other provincial government offices where he also performed services as Crown lands agent, registrar, and administrator for provincial government services pertaining to new settlers. These precincts had need for the bookshelves that Lount insisted be added, and gradually the courthouse built up its library of law texts and bound consolidations of statutes.

The following year, 1869, when James Boyer arrived with his family, he brought a number of law books. Boyer had clerked as a youth in law offices in Stratford back in England, then studied law in New York City and was called to the bar of New York State. He seemed adept at many things and began conveyancing work at Lount's registry office, and before long was also appointed a Muskoka magistrate by Liberal Premier Oliver Mowat who was not unmindful of Boyer's affinity with his political party. His law books were long since crated up, stored in poor conditions, and eventually destroyed, but at the time they too constituted more foundation material for early library development in the Bracebridge community.

In the local legal firmament, it was William Cosby Mahaffy who landed like a literary meteorite in Bracebridge in 1877, arriving to open a much needed law office. Mahaffy was a soulful and intense man of rakish appearance, with wavy hair parted near the middle and a massive waxed walrus moustache covering his mouth, as dramatic as his high white collars and deep penetrating eyes. The man was as consumed by an interest in libraries as he was devoted to the administration of justice. Not mistakenly he saw the two institutions as common underpinnings for the British way of life being adapted to conditions in the town.

Mahaffy was appointed Muskoka district judge in 1888 when the provincial government separated Muskoka from Parry Sound District, making Muskoka its own judicial district with its own judge. Judge Mahaffy held court in the Bracebridge Town Hall until 1900 when the province completed erection of a magnificent courthouse for Muskoka on the site of the earlier court building. Mahaffy happily moved a few doors down the street, since the new courthouse was even closer to his imposing stone

SOLID BEGINNINGS. When William Cosby Mahaffy arrived in Bracebridge in 1877 he bought this stone residence overlooking the falls and Bracebridge Bay. A lawyer who became the first judge of Muskoka District, Mahaffy was an avid champion of library service and chaired the library board through the institution's three transitions as a Mechanics' Institute Library, then the Bracebridge Free Library, and finally the Bracebridge Carnegie Public Library.

home toward the southern end of Dominion Street with its view over the nearby falls. His property ran steeply down to the edge of Bracebridge Bay. The judge would sell part of this land to the municipality early in the twentieth century when it came time to build a new town wharf. The rest of his land remained with his home, a building which today is The Inn at the Falls. During the long years of his occupancy, William Mahaffy's spacious residence, like his law office and later his judge's chambers, bulged with books.

If W.C. Mahaffy's arrival in Bracebridge would prove to be good news on the library front, the landing of Henry Bird in town was equally so. This remarkable entrepreneur of great learning would boost the early Bracebridge community in its formative years, including helping with formation of the town's first library service.

Bird was an exemplar of the high calibre of individuals emerging in the Bracebridge business class. Born in England in 1841, where he learned his woollen milling skills at his father's weaving mills, Bird travelled in his early twenties to Australia then Canada. After working for the Rosamond

JUSTICE AND BOOKS. W.C. Mahaffy, Muskoka district judge and chairman of the library board for decades, did his best to advance library interest and support because in rapidly expanding Bracebridge the early library was often strained beyond its capacity in every sense by the demands for more space and more books.

Woollen Company at Almonte, he bought his own mill on the Conestoga River near Guelph. It was flooded out completely by great rises in the river in 1870, then again in 1871. Business catastrophe was followed by personal tragedy. Henry Bird's wife, Sarah, their three-year-old daughter Elizabeth and six-month-old son were killed. Henry Bird decided to make a new beginning.

Once again, the power of a book seemed fated to play a major role in the town's story. Henry Bird, a man of method and scientific approach, had decided to research where in the wide world he would relocate to make his fresh start in life, including possibly going back to Australia or England. In his researches, he acquired a copy of the book Thomas McMurray had just published that year at Bracebridge, *The Free Grant Lands of Canada*.

COMING SOON, A LIBRARY NEAR YOU. Henry J. Bird arrived in Bracebridge in 1872 to establish a woollen mill and soon began the effort to create a community library. Two years later he and others established the initial library service in Bracebridge through a Mechanics' Institute, a year even before the fledgling settlement was incorporated as a village in 1875.

A NEW AGE. Henry Bird, who in 1874 was one of the leaders in creating Bracebridge's first community library, was a commanding man in many ways. He built a mill whose distinctive "Bird Woollen Blankets" sold in world markets in their own right, and also as the famous brand he made for the Hudson's Bay Company, the "Hudson's Bay Blanket." Bird's woollen mill provided a broad economic base for the town, gave workers steady jobs, and created a continuous demand for wool supplied by prospering central Muskoka sheep farmers. Then he built this eight-sided house on high ground above the Muskoka River with a commanding view over his mill and Bracebridge town. The Bird house, named Woodchester Villa, remains one of North America's best enduring examples from the 1880s of these buildings that embodied a full measure of advanced scientific learning and spiritual understanding. Even at the simplest level, the magic of an octagonal house is its own invitation to think differently about the space we inhabit and, in turn, about ourselves in relation to our surroundings. No doubt astute Henry Bird saw the connection: that is also the magic of the passport provided by a library.

The picture was so rosy it drew him to Muskoka District's capital town. After looking things over, Henry Bird chose Bracebridge as the location for his new mill. The next year he constructed his substantial woollen mill on the upper part of the north side of the town's falls, where there would be no risk of any more disastrous flooding and where he could be assured of plenty of power from the millrace that he himself designed.

Henry Bird was a free thinker who read widely and followed a scientific bent. He had first belonged to the Methodist Church but gave up church attendance and later disassociated himself from any organized religious allegiance. A Conservative in politics, he was the local treasurer of a fund to erect a monument to Sir John A. Macdonald after the prime minister's death, but Bird kept friendships with those of different political views, just as he did not make his religious convictions a matter of contention with others. A careful businessman with a rapidly expanding milling operation, he stayed closely abreast of all developments in the techniques of woollen manufacturing, but beyond that he sought explanations for new scientific inventions generally and wanted their benefits to be enjoyed. He helped Muskoka farmers develop extensive sheep herds, which was to their mutual benefit, since the farmers found raising sheep was easier than trying to grow crops on the rocky outcroppings of the Canadian Shield and Bird benefited from a steady local supply of wool for his ever-expanding milling operations. In time he would serve a number of terms on town council, a political outlet for one of the many dimensions of his creative energies.

With so inquisitive a mind, such a clear desire to help others, and so ardent a commitment to see Canada and his local community develop, it was inevitable that Henry Bird's fascination with literary and scientific subjects would soon become channelled into the formation of a library for the community.

FOUR

Saga of the Mechanics' Institute Library

The year 1874 stands as a milestone for Bracebridge because that year, even in advance of organizing a fire brigade to protect their lives and property, townsfolk brought forth a library. Operating continuously in Bracebridge ever since, library service is thus among the most venerable institutions in the community. It predates even municipal government in Bracebridge. At the time the library was organized, the Bracebridge community was still part of Macaulay Township, which itself had just been organized for local government as a township municipality three years before. Only in the following year, 1875, would Bracebridge become a separate village municipality on its own.

Creating a village library at this early juncture underscores just how important books were to the people of Bracebridge. This major step for a small settlement was another display of the early settlers' confidence that propelled them forward on many fronts, building up the settlement. In a sense the new library even helped give birth to the municipality. In 1875, when the decision was taken by others as to whether these enterprising people qualified to incorporate as a village on their own, the fact that a library already existed in the settlement was taken as an indication of qualification for independent municipal status, yet another example of the way the history of Bracebridge and its library are interwoven.

By the early 1870s Bracebridge had several retails stores, hotels, a sawmill and gristmill, woollen mill, a newspaper, Methodist, Presbyterian and Anglican churches, and provincial government offices to serve the

A PUBLISHER'S PLACE. Bracebridge newspaper and book publisher, promoter and developer, Thomas McMurray enjoyed his handsome residence "The Grove" on a street named after him. The Grove is seen here in 1874, the same year the Mechanics' Institute Library was founded in Bracebridge. McMurray's lovely home with great verandahs was demolished in 1925 by the Board of Education which bought it to build a high school on the site. The school would operate, with many additions including a recent extensive library facility costing some $760,000, until closed in 2007 to be relocated out of town. The Grove stood just across McMurray Street from the small plot of land where town council in 1906 would seek, among many other places, to build the new Carnegie library.

Territorial District of Muskoka. Social life was becoming more organized. The children had a school. Members of the Protestant loyalist society, the Orange Lodge, had a meeting hall. At mid-decade a Roman Catholic priest took up residence in town for the first time. Several more tradesmen arrived every year. Residents around the village enjoyed community entertainments sponsored by their churches. However, not everything was rosy. Newspaper publisher and business developer Thomas McMurray had overextended himself. His financial collapse gave the main street of Bracebridge an unprepossessing look because McMurray's fine brick block of commercial buildings were all closed up, as were a number of other buildings in town. Newspaper contributor and author W.E. Hamilton, taking stock of the community in March 1875, said that circumstances had "knocked the bottom out of the institution of Bracebridge."

Even so, other economic elements at work would help Bracebridge recover. "There was as a general thing much of bustle and life in the village," noted Hamilton, "owing to the lumber traffic and the large number of immigrants on their way to locate on free grants or to pur-

chase farms."[1] How ironic that many arriving had learned of these opportunities through McMurray's promotional book, *The Free Grant Lands of
Canada*, but that in building costly stores and offices in anticipation of the
prosperity they would bring to the town, he had not been able to hold on
just a few months longer. Other risk takers meanwhile, despite their set-
backs, were contributing to the overall expansion.

Apart from the mood of frontier adventure in Bracebridge that accompanied opening new land and the influx of more people jostling together
and all the swirling economic and social energies these activities generated, intellectual excitement was also energizing the community. Hamilton, who had graduated from Trinity College, Dublin, was especially
taken by what he called "a cultured society" in Bracebridge. He enjoyed
the company of Rev. J.S. Cole, the Anglican incumbent in town, a Cambridge University graduate, author of a book on geometry, and son-in-law
of a lady who wrote a noted book on Muskoka published in London, England. The Browning family, especially James B., members of an old family from Newcastle, England, were "thoroughly posted on the literature
of the time" and had travelled extensively before coming to Bracebridge.
Aubrey White, then Crown Lands agent, was "gifted with a phenomenal memory and could tell the names of all the sitting members of all
the parliaments, great and small, of Canada, their antecedents and their
constituencies, together with the dates of the various by-elections since
Confederation." W.E. Foot, the fishery inspector, also from Dublin and
now living in Bracebridge, was an accomplished musician and amateur
actor in demand in the village to take part in concerts and plays. Mr. and
Mrs. W. F. Burden, proprietors of the British Lion, one of four prospering
hotels in Bracebridge at this time, had also been associated with the stage
and provided excellent talent for theatricals in the pioneer village.[2]

The strong local book culture of Bracebridge coalesced with the presence of men and women come from communities with libraries and now
wanting to create one for their use in this fledgling settlement. Bracebridge,
still very much a river town, seemed destined to grow astride Western
culture's wide flowing literary stream as well as along the banks of the
Muskoka.

Forming a community library was the accomplishment of a few key
people to whom books were as essential as bread. One leader in this initiative was the enterprising Henry Bird. The same scholarly research methods Bird had previously applied when scouting the best place in the world
for his new woollen mill, that resulted in him coming to Bracebridge in
1871, now propelled him to research the best way to organize a commu-

nity library that would cut across the religious and occupational distinctions around which a number of smaller specialized libraries had already been started in Bracebridge. He sought a plan for a library that would serve the larger community more generally, while at the same time benefiting through participation and support from the many diverse book lovers of the town.

In the United States, Benjamin Franklin began "lending libraries" in the 1730s, which spread as they filled an evident desire on the part of people to read books. In Britain, the same idea was taken up by a number of groups. One such group, the Mechanics' Institutes, established libraries, held lectures and conducted study programs, and their model of operation spread to Canada in the early 1800s.

Henry Bird completed his studies, looked up, and knew what it would be. All signs pointed to founding a Mechanics' Institute in Bracebridge as the best available vehicle for the formation of a local library.

Others concurred. Bracebridge Public School principal Anthony McGill actively joined with Bird to form the Mechanics' Institute in Bracebridge and continued to be one of the mainstays in the Institute's library for its first half-decade of operation, before going to Ottawa as a deputy minister. By then, William Mahaffy had already been in town a year since opening his law practice in 1877. Mahaffy's arrival was like signing up the library league's top scorer for the Bracebridge team. No one would single-handedly do more to support, maintain and advance library service in Bracebridge for the next three decades than William Cosby Mahaffy. James B. Browning, already noted by Hamilton as being "thoroughly posted on the literature of the time" also joined Henry Bird as a founding member of the Mechanics' Institute Library in town.

Another leading light of the community throwing his support into the library cause was Dr. Samuel Bridgland. It is almost shorter to list the few things that Bridgland did not do, so completely involved was he in every dimension of affairs, from medicine to agriculture, sports and politics, literature and entertainment. Although Dr. Bridgland was not the settlement's first medical practitioner, a distinction going to Dr. J.N. Byers, he arrived shortly thereafter. Bridgland was certainly in Bracebridge by January 1871 when a newspaper account in the *Northern Advocate* reported him as being one of the stage actors in an Anglican concert. The Hall for that performance, according to James Boyer's report offering a glimpse into the vibrant cultural life of early 1870s Bracebridge, "was brilliantly lighted, most tastefully decorated, and filled to its utmost capacity by the elite of the District, while the whole entertainment exceeded our most sanguine expectations."[3] Sam Bridgland was at stage centre from the start, an elected representative whose public offices progressed through the ranks of local school board, municipal council, and Member of the Ontario Legislature for Muskoka. It was a given that in 1874 he would also be a founder of the Mechanics' Institute Library in Bracebridge.

Adding lustre to the Bracebridge Mechanics' Institute Library by serving as its honorary secretary was Aubrey White, the man who, for political matters at least, carried around his own library in his head. Aubrey worked efficiently for years following the library's inception, then like McGill went on to greater things, a local boy who advanced to become Ontario's Deputy Minister of Lands and Forests.

This model for a library in Bracebridge, following British rather than American plans before the 1900s, contributed the foundations to the "library movement" that began developing in the province after 1830. These early Mechanics' Institute libraries provided an organizational structure in a number of communities. They offered a centre at which those with book interests could gather, discuss future plans together, and fulfil their personal intellectual and social interests. Although they were narrower in scope and membership than the later "free libraries," which allowed wider public accessibility to books, the Mechanics' Institute libraries came into existence when there was nothing else, providing an organized start and an identifiable order to book collection and circulation.

LIBRARY SUPPORTER. Aubrey White arrived in Bracebridge from Ireland as a teenager, became a steamboat captain on the Muskoka Lakes, was Crown land agent for Muskoka, rose to become Ontario's deputy minister of Lands and Forests, and died at Chief's Island, a citadel of literary pursuits in Lake Muskoka, in 1915.

A strong supporter of library service in Bracebridge, White was as a member of the Mechanics' Institute Library and for years was its honorary secretary. He carried an extensive personal library of parliamentary and political information around with him—all in his phenomenal memory. A cairn to Aubrey White was erected at High Falls, upriver from Bracebridge, in 1965.

When the province's legislators enacted The Library Associations and Mechanics' Institute Act in 1851, giving the province its very first library legislation, it was really a catch-up effort. The Act gave legal form to what had already been taking place in communities at the local level, where library associations had existed in the province since the early 1800s and Mechanics' Institutes had already been formed in a number of municipalities as a result of citizens themselves importing the model from overseas. The 1851 statute set out some structure related to the incorporation of new Institutes and the continuation of existing ones under the Act should they choose to do so. So light was the government's hand in these matters that it was not obligatory even to conform to these minimal structural attributes. No "mission" or role for the Institutes was addressed in the Act, nor did the statute provide anything regarding the all-important matter of funding, only routine matters of enactment of an Institute's by-laws and the corporate authority of its directors. The enactment of 1851 was perfunctory, a legislative recognition of a state of affairs already existing in several towns. For a library, leadership would have to come from resilient citizens in their own communities who wanted it and set about themselves to create it.

Bracebridge was in advance of other Muskoka communities in establishing a library for the community in 1874. Gravenhurst started its library in 1883, Huntsville in 1885, Port Carling in 1887. Yet none broke new ground. Toronto had established its library in 1831 and Kingston its in 1834, with places like Hamilton and Niagara Falls soon following suit. By 1858, some 143 Mechanics' Institutes had been created in Canada East and West, following this spreading pattern for creating a local library.

Formally, the Mechanics' Institute library began in 1874 when Henry Bird, Sam Bridgland, Tony McGill, James Browning and others took the initiative by creating a constitution and enacting bylaws for the local organization in keeping with the 1851 statute. Then they gathered together some 225 books from the private home collections of members. For the first time in a building separate from peoples' homes, outside the churches and school, apart from the newspaper office and the meeting halls of fraternal societies, Bracebridge had the nucleus of an altogether new institution.

The library was housed in the top floor of the Sam H. Armstrong Building on east side of the main street of Bracebridge. The librarian was Josiah Pratt, described by Hamilton as "painstaking and courteous." In addition to running his jewellery store at street level in the Armstrong Building, Pratt served as librarian for the Institute upstairs.

After the Mechanics' Institute first opened its library doors in 1874, the collection of 225 volumes kept growing as demand for reading material increased. By 1877 a grant of $400 from the Ontario Government helped boost the holdings to 700 books, including the *American Cyclopedia*, which cost nearly $100.[4]

Besides making books available, the Institute sponsored scientific presentations, educational lectures and literary entertainment. Under its auspices lively exchanges were enjoyed as clever wits and well-read critics participated in an affiliated literary debating society. Debates were on literary topics. Henry Bird, widely read and scientifically minded, entertained fellow members with occasional evening lectures on topics ranging from some of his own inventions, such as a new generator, to the latest techniques in the woollen industry.

Because a Mechanics' Institute was a private organization, this meant a member of the public could not just freely stroll into its library and have access to its resources, as would be the case with a public library. A person had to join the sponsoring organization, The Mechanics' Institute, to participate.

In 1881, seven years after beginning operation in Bracebridge, the Mechanics' Institute Library sent two canvassing committees around town to enlist new members and to seek better service for the community. Thus while in theory the Mechanics' Institute Library was a private affair,

LOGS, LIBRARIES AND LINERS. Robert Dollar, Bracebridge lumberman and town councillor, was a member of the Bracebridge Mechanics' Institute and a strong library supporter in the town before setting out for California where he founded the Dollar Line of ocean steamships.

it was by no means exclusive or exclusionary. The members of these canvassing committees gladly signed up anyone in Bracebridge willing to join and pay the relatively modest annual subscription fee of 80 cents.

The committee members also made a point of inquiring closely, as they made their rounds, about any additional services residents of Bracebridge might like to see The Mechanics' Institute provide for the benefit of its members. A number of new subscribers said they wanted a reading room established, following a pattern of other Mechanics' Institutes in southern Ontario. A reading room was not so much a place for using books which members could sign out and take home but for reading the periodicals and newspapers they could not. The Bracebridge library had subscriptions to a growing number of periodicals and newspapers. Following its 1881 survey around town, the Institute promptly established the desired reading room facility, to the satisfaction of its old and new members alike.

The second floor premises accommodated the Institute's circulating library, reading room and a stage for shows. By rounding out the cultural and intellectual dimensions of life in Bracebridge with an organized program, the Mechanics' Institute was initiating a pattern of book-centred activity for the enrichment for townsfolk that would continue in Bracebridge to the present day. Bracebridge was filling up with avid book readers, so the town's love affair with literature blossomed even further. Just as naturally, the growing library had by now pushed the limits of its accommodation. Another over-the-store premises, farther north on Manitoba Street and on the west side, offered more space and the Mechanics' Institute Library relocated there.

Money is important for libraries but the 1851 statute enacted to deal with libraries in the province was silent on the subject of their funding. Any amounts paid were a matter of policy, not a statutory program of entitlement. Shortly after the Bracebridge Mechanics' Institute Library started up it received a provincial grant of $400. Seldom did the municipal government in Bracebridge come up with money to help. Henry Bird, who had done so much to launch the library and support its program through his lectures, was also one of its most consistent financial supporters.

In many respects, the Mechanics' Institutes were viewed as a type of private club, so there were frequent debates over how much public tax revenue, if any, should go to support them. Complicating these debates was the fact that there had been a period of corruption in the 1850s, before

MOBILE LIBRARY. In the twentieth century a provincial mobile library service circulated books into isolated rural areas, and during the 1930s Depression also brought them to Bracebridge. In the nineteenth century, however, Bracebridge had a different meaning for library mobility. The town's first community library, organized by the Bracebridge Mechanics' Institute in 1874, moved from place to place during its periods of growth. The mobile library was housed in various second-floor rooms over these stores on both sides of Manitoba Street, seen here looking north.

Bracebridge was even founded, that tainted the giving of government grants, since some literary societies received a double grant by calling themselves both a "library association" and a "Mechanics' Institute" and applying twice. In reaction, aid from parliament dried up after 1859, which had a crippling effect on many smaller Mechanics' Institute libraries operating in a bona fide manner, and the library in Napanee was among those forced to close. After Confederation in 1867, funding resumed and the annual grant reached as high as $400, which was the situation when the Bracebridge Mechanics' Institute and Library arrived on the scene in 1874 and was able to benefit in this sanitized era of financial support. Part of the new regime also included assigning school inspectors the additional duty of visiting and checking out these libraries and making reports on them.

After awhile, the presence of an established local library might start to be taken for granted. But the loss of the library in Napanee in the 1860s showed that the tide could go out as well as come in. The accomplishment of the library founders in Bracebridge in the 1870s, moreover, stands out because for many other towns, the tide never came in at all.

More than half a century later, a sizeable number of Ontario communities still had no library service. Those without any library, for example, included such centres the size of Bracebridge as Bridgeburg (population 3,521), Kapuskasing (3,819), Portsmouth (2,741) and Petrolia (2,596). Even larger, East Windsor, with a population of 14,251, was without a library 60 years after the citizens of Bracebridge had taken this crucial step.

Just as noteworthy, by this same date of 1931, fully 500 communities around Ontario still had private subscription libraries only, or what came to be called "association libraries," rather than public libraries with free access. These included Huntsville, and towns comparable in size to Bracebridge such as Blind River, Bowmanville, Burlington, Cobalt, Cobourg, Cochrane, Copper Cliff, Dunnville, Haileybury, Long Branch and the one eventually re-established in Napanee, not to mention much larger municipalities like Sandwich with 10,715 people.[5]

By 1887, with the village continuing to grow rapidly, there were more Bracebridge readers craving more books and the chronic problem of inadequate shelf space for all the volumes reared its head again. The Institute needed larger premises to house the library's expanding book collection. Already for several years the Institute had been actively seeking a better place for its reading room.

The members of the new village council, elected on January 1, 1887, were generally all supportive of the library and sympathetic to its plight. Several were themselves keen readers, with home libraries of their own and memberships in the Mechanics' Institute.

Besides, since 1882 when the Ontario Legislature had enacted another statute to deal with libraries, one reflecting the wider sentiments of the library movement that books should be free to all, The Free Library Act offered a different model from that of the Mechanics' Institute. The prospect of more money from the provincial government was an enticement to adopt the structure embodied in the new statute. Bracebridge council seemed to be preparing itself to adopt a far more satisfactory plan for the library. Yet these were also years when the small council of four members facing annual elections could experience rapid, and sometimes complete, turnover in 12-month intervals, so the thinking on council about the library could change direction quickly.

For the immediate term, even while many issues raised by the proposed shifting of the Mechanic's Institute Library into a Free Library remained parts of a floating agenda, there was at least something specific to do. Those connected with the library were no longer happy to intermittently decamp from one premises to move into larger upper floors of an office building. The councillors supported their desire to get a better arrangement and made a fine offer to the Mechanics' Institute members, voting to give them free space in a ground floor room of the large new town hall on Dominion Street. Such a prominent place and greater space for the town's library would signify the importance the community leaders accorded to books and their ready circulation.

Just days later, calamity intervened. A devastating fire swept through downtown Bracebridge on January 27, 1887, which destroyed the post office along with Ellison's photograph gallery, Josiah Pratt's jewellery store, Dr. Bridgland's drug store, and the Independent Order of Odd Fellows Hall on the second storey above it. When the paraphernalia of the Odd Fellows was being carried out of the burning building to safety by the village's now-established volunteer fire brigade, the lid fell off a long narrow box revealing a human skeleton, which caused one fire-fighting volunteer to faint. Then he, too, had to be carried to safety along with the ceremonial trappings and the many books from the I.O.O.F.'s own library. At least the fact the Mechanics' Institute Library had moved several years before from the space above Josiah Pratt's jewellery store meant its holdings were not lost to the conflagration.

In consequence of the fire, Bracebridge's postmaster urgently needed new accommodation and Council was anxious to see routine mail service restored promptly to the community. Councillors voted to rent the available room in the town hall for use as a temporary post office at $8 a month. The rental, equivalent to about $175 in current values, modestly helped the town coffers but did nothing for the cramped Mechanics' Institute Library, which suddenly found itself outranked in the wake of the village's disaster for the space in the town hall. The library remained stuck in its overcrowded precincts since the "temporary" post office continued to operate from the town hall for quite some time. However, the library would in time move into the town hall. Oddly, there would even be a prospect in the future of the entire town hall building becoming the municipality's library. But for now, the crowding continued and the quest for better space resumed.

By the early 1890s, Bracebridge itself had emerged as a going concern in a relatively short span of time. In 1889 it had moved from village to town status. Citizens had elected Alfred Hunt, a visionary who had already displayed initiative in founding a local private bank as the first and only bank then serving Muskoka, to office as mayor. Under Hunt's leadership, Bracebridge installed municipally owned public streetlights in 1892. Townspeople fell in love with their lights, "no longer stumbling through mud-puddles and over stumps in dark streets as they made their way home at night," wrote James Boyer. Two years later, wearing his hat as municipal clerk, Boyer conducted a local plebiscite when the citizens of Bracebridge debated the merits and risks of shouldering debt to finance more electricity services. They voted strongly "Yes" to authorize the town to buy out the power generating plant of a local leather tannery. With this pioneering effort in public ownership in 1894, Bracebridge became the first municipality in Canada to own and operate its own hydroelectric generating and distribution system. Bracebridge then turned to extending electric lighting throughout the municipality, not just along streets for illumination at night, but into offices, factories, homes, schools, shops and churches.

In 1894, Bracebridge also took bold action on another front. Council created a public waterworks system and ran pipes to homes and businesses throughout the town, an engineering challenge on the uneven rocky terrain of the Canadian Shield. Readily available clean water was a major advance for hygiene in an era when fouled water carried cholera, typhoid and other bacterial diseases that devastated populations. Now having taken far-sighted initiatives to provide both low-cost electricity and ample safe water the town surged forward with many new factories.

Bracebridge now boasted two major leather tanneries, the Anglo-Canadian and the Beardmore, and become the largest centre for tanning in the British Empire, with hides even from Argentina. A five-storey furniture factory rose beside the river in the centre of town, drawing on electricity, ample supplies of hardwood, and a growing population of skilled craftsmen. Bird's Woollen Mill expanded its facilities to accommodate machines powered by low-cost electricity, utilizing local wool and exploiting competitive advantage. Bracebridge also became home to a cheese factory, a match factory, boat-building factories and extensive poultry operations, while also expanding its capacity for grain milling.

The town's new prosperity enabled support, in turn, for rapid advancement of first-rank schools, two newspapers, an early hospital, an agricultural society, a choral society, a town band, and other social and cultural

BOOKSTORES, LIBRARY LOCATIONS, phone exchange, photography and newspaper office. The town was alive with culture and communications. Bracebridge photographer Richard W. Ryan, whose shop was on this main thoroughfare, took this mid-1890s picture of the west side of Manitoba Street. Along the elevated wooden sidewalk connecting the stores and commercial establishments, rigorous commerce and lively society coexisted.

The 1890s town pump is at road level, in front of the J. Caisse "Barbering Parlour" operated by handsome Joseph Caisse. Caisse's daughter Rene was a nurse who came into possession of an Indian herbal remedy she dubbed "Essiac," the family name spelled backwards, as a cancer treatment she offered to those with tumours. Based on its apparent efficacy she then opened her widely renowned "clinic of hope" in the British Lion Hotel on Dominion Street, attracting people from far and wide to Bracebridge, as well as having clinic operations in the United States.

After the McEwen Tailor Shop is the Thompson drug store, more loftily known as "The Medical Hall," identified by the men standing in front. This building included the Bell Telephone Company's exchange on the main floor, and upstairs the offices of the *Muskoka Herald* newspaper until it moved to its own newly constructed building on Dominion Street around this time.

Three buildings along, the handsome 3-storey structure was the E.J. Pratt Building. Mr. Pratt's bookstore and jewellery business operated on the street level while the Mechanics' Institute library was in premises above.

Farther along, past Chancery Lane, two buildings beyond the "flour and feed" sign of Hutchison Bros. store, a small structure served as the Bracebridge post office in this era, later as a ladies' wear shop. In the second floor of that building, the Mechanics' Institute library had also been housed in one of its several locations between 1874 and 1908.

amenities. In this increasingly dynamic context, those responsible for the Mechanics' Institute Library and Reading Room endeavoured to keep up.

On October 9, 1890, 500 new membership cards were printed for the Institute. By 1892, the Institute's library had grown to 3,000 carefully selected volumes, besides the many magazines and periodicals, and financially the organization was quite healthy. The work of librarian continued in attentive hands for when Josiah Pratt, who had been custodian of the library's affairs since 1874, was succeeded in this role by 1892, his replacement was "the obliging and painstaking librarian" R.H. Smith. Both descriptions are by Hamilton, who would have had each man under close observation.

In the early 1890s, there were close to 200 members of the Mechanics' Institute in Bracebridge. In May of 1893, the Institute compiled a list of new books acquired by the library and had a pamphlet with this information printed, at a cost of $1.75 for 200 copies, and distributed to its members. By 1896, Henry Bird and Josiah Pratt solicited advertising from local businesses to fund publication of a printed catalogue of all the books in the library.

In addition to the educational meetings and entertainment programs, the members gathered each spring for the annual meeting of the Institute, to elect officers, hear reports, and discuss and vote on that year's issues and proposals. The meetings were advertised in the local papers and generally were very well attended. By this time, the recurring issues at annual meetings, as for the board meetings each month, were the twin problems of cramped space and the increasing strain of operating such an important community service through the volunteer efforts of wearying citizens. In the background was the pressure of the library movement in Ontario, and the idea that libraries should become fully free.

By 1899, the Bracebridge library had been struggling along under financial difficulties and space limitations for long enough that those responsible for the library were looking for help and becoming increasingly desperate to find it. Only the interest of certain devoted citizens, especially Judge Mahaffy, kept it going. That year Francis P. Warne, another local pillar of the library and an enterprising citizen especially active in sporting clubs and railway promotion, appealed in desperation to the Bracebridge town council to take over the library and offer book services to citizens free of charge. Warne's request was refused. Instead, a one-time grant of $100 (or about $2,500 in today's values) was given to the library.

FIVE

Democratizing the Bracebridge Library

After nearly a quarter century of operation, the Bracebridge library service boasted many more books than its original complement of 225 and, despite its several moves, still suffered from a lack of space. However, it offered the quiet communal pleasures of a reading room in which to keep abreast of developments, informative lectures to enrich one's education, and entertaining programs to fill the winter evenings— all supported by voluntary donations, membership fees, and sporadic small grants from either the local or provincial government. The whole enterprise was still, legally, a private club. One had to join the Mechanics' Institute to gain these benefits.

Because the books were not, strictly speaking, free to the public, the Institute's library did not qualify for some of the increasing amount of provincial government financial support that was being provided in the late 1800s as a result of the public library movement's effective lobbying at Queen's Park. As well, there was incentive to change because it had become a struggle to maintain, in the existing structure, library service of a calibre suited to such a book-minded town. Around Bracebridge a growing sense emerged that it was high time to change the constitutional structure of the library. In 1897, the Bracebridge Mechanics' Institute directors accordingly looked into making the Institute a free library, a change they themselves now sought.

Unlike the situation in 1874, when library proponents in Bracebridge cast about for a structured precedent for a community library and chose the Mechanics' Institute model then in vogue, now the Bracebridge library's directors had the provisions of The Free Libraries Act of Ontario to consider. In the decade and a half since this statute's enactment in 1882, other communities in the province had established Free Libraries and qualified for an annual grant from the Ontario Government of $250, an amount worth about $6,270 today, for books, papers and magazines.

In practice, the townspeople of Bracebridge had already made this transition to a "public library" without the formalities. Back in 1881, as noted, the yeasty democratic sentiment in Bracebridge combined with the Institute's need to recruit more fee-paying members propelled a community-wide door-to-door canvass by members of the Mechanics' Institute. In this recruitment drive, not only was everyone in town solicited to join the Institute's library, but their ideas were also actively sought about what would enhance Bracebridge library service. Adding the reading room was the most visible outcome of this survey, as mentioned, but also notable were changes in the library's acquisitions policy to expand the categories and extend the range of titles in existing ones. As a result, the library's holdings came into closer harmony with the needs and interests of the town it was serving, which made the Mechanics' Institute Library resemble more a public than a private institution. A decade later, in 1891, when the *Muskoka Herald* has settled into its new two-storey newspaper building on Dominion Street, it printed an excellent directory and illustrated historical edition that listed the town's 95 professionals, businessmen, officials and merchants, among whom R.H. Smith was identified as "public librarian." By the mid-1890s, the facility itself had come to be referred to in many quarters of town as "the public library." There was, it appeared, a growing inevitability that now only required some formalities to complete the transition.

On Tuesday evening, August 24, 1897, the directors of the Mechanics' Institute Library were moved to a new level of resolve upon hearing a strong appeal for a free library in Bracebridge. Mr. R. Mayes, Inspector of Public Libraries for the Province of Ontario, a true believer in the cause, had come to town to strongly urge the formation of a free library and public reading room. The directors, joined in this meeting at the town hall by a number of other Bracebridgites keen to upgrade library service in town, became more deeply convinced than ever about making the change in the library by the unanimity of thought in the auditorium. Mayes encountered no resistance from his highly receptive audience when he preached that with a Free Library and Reading Room very many more books would be read, that all ratepayers would then receive the benefits of the library, and that the government grants would be increased.

Following Mayes' appeal and some discussion, the directors by vote then "decided a free library would be preferable to the present system."

They appointed a three-man deputation to engage the town council on this matter at its next meeting. One authoritative representative was Henry Bird. The second member of the delegation was Francis Warne, an ardent entrepreneur in the community and an energetic younger director of the library operated by the Mechanics' Institute. Third was Josiah Pratt, owner of a handsome three-storey brick building on the main street which housed his bookstore and jewellery business, and, at one interval, the Mechanics' Institute Library.

However, Mayes' message and the Mechanics' Institute directors' decision had already been directly transmitted to at least part of the council. Two local government representatives in close sympathy with reconstituting the "public library," Mayor Singleton Brown and Councillor Robert Ford, had attended the summer evening meeting in person. Both men tended to common views on issues in the town. According to published records in the town's newspapers which appeared on the street the very day after the meeting, they both "concurred in the opinion that we should have a free library."

This change in status, it was explained to townspeople reading the *Muskoka Herald* that week of 1897, "will mean that the library and reading room, under certain regulations, will be open to all residents over 12 years of age." The issue of children in libraries was its own special controversy. For the time being, the wisdom in Bracebridge was to saw off a compromise at age 12.

Yet, the stumbling block in moving forward now would be getting majority support from Bracebridge Town Council, generally a confident

WARRIOR FOR THE LIBRARY. Francis P. Warne, champion for improved library services and facilities in 1890s and turn-of-the-century Bracebridge, was a treasurer of the Bracebridge library, advocate for converting the Mechanics' Institute library into a "free library" for the town, a municipal councillor and a member of Bracebridge library board. Warne also deployed his high energy into town athletics and plans to build a railway from Bracebridge to Lake of Bays.

and sometimes even a visionary body. Suddenly, a number of councillors inexplicably hesitated to take on the library as a public responsibility. Politics can be funny, depending on the personalities involved. Some councillors were nonplussed to read in the town's newspapers that Mayor Brown already thought the Free Library a good idea, before Council had evaluated the costs and collectively reached their decision. That councillor Ford was on side as well put off some of his fellow council members. Had he and the mayor been opposed, they would have favoured a Free Library.

In such circumstances, arguments have to be found to justify positions already arrived at emotionally. Some council members therefore argued against the proposal on the grounds that the Mechanics' Institute was a free enterprise, a private club rather than a public body, and thus not a proper recipient for public tax revenues. They had missed the point. This view failed to grasp that the proposal entailed the Mechanics' Institute Library and Reading Room changing its status to remove that very hurdle to which objection was being taken. Certainly such a distinction that many on council now seemed intent on making, about private interests not being recipients of public assistance, had been no hurdle whatsoever to the same councillors voting during this same period to extend generous tax concessions, grants, cheap electricity and other enticing benefits to private businesses if only they would locate their new factory in the municipality. Some councillors just seemed to feel more at home dealing with factories and employers than books and educational institutions.

Their reluctance in 1897 to assume the library as an operation of the Town of Bracebridge in turn precluded the Ontario Government from making a significant grant of $250 to Bracebridge had the library been made "free"—that is, openly available to all. So in deciding to save money, they lost money. "Such an attitude seems inconsistent with the commitment already made to public power by Bracebridge," observed local historian R.J. Boyer years later about this quixotic council's library policy, "which made this Town the pioneer in Ontario in municipal water-power electrical generation."[1] The reluctance of some councillors to take over the library was at least offset by pressure from others, including Mayor Brown, to act in the wider interests of the community. A grant by the Town to the library of $100, for the year 1897, was the best that could be salvaged from this reversal of fortunes.

The library by this date had 2,134 books, valued at some $2,500 (a value equivalent to about $62,670 today). Of these, 105 titles had just been recently acquired. During 1897, books lent to readers totalled 5,597 circulations, including 683 borrowings of histories, 74 of biography, 502 on "voyages and travels," 125 books on science and art, 371 of general literature, 20 poetry and drama, 34 in the field of religious literature, a whopping 1,931 works of fiction, and some 1,857 other "miscellaneous" titles. In 1897, the library received $71 in fees, the $100 grant from the town, and $194 as the legislative grant from the province.

Although stopgap measures helped keep library service operating in town, they did not lay the groundwork for a strong future built upon a library as a central institution in what was, by all other standards, an increasingly democratic and robust centre of self-starters. As one century turned into the next, Bracebridge surged industrially and commercially. The town's population was increasing. More schoolrooms were needed. Better services were demanded and steadily provided.

In such a dynamic setting, the Mechanics' Institute Library was falling further and further behind. It could no longer meet the surging expectations of its members for new books and greater diversity in reading materials. Private donations were insufficient to sustain operations and acquisitions. The more generous levels of provincial funding were unavailable due to Council's refusal to take it over and make it a free library that would qualify it for larger grants. It continued legally as a private library under the terms of The Mechanics' Institute Act of Ontario.

In 1899, Francis Warne again intervened with the town council. Though not yet able to persuade its members to support the move to a Free Library, this local library activist managed to get another "one time" grant of $100 from council as guilt money. "At this time the library was beginning to feel its way to larger things," recounted Robert Boyer in *A Good Town Grew Here*, his history of the period. "The Mechanics' Institute had given good service but it was a private enterprise," he summarized, "and those who had so generously given of their means and time to supply the community with good reading could not be expected to continue when the town had grown out of its swaddling clothes."[2]

Councils were elected annually on the first Monday of each year and so early in 1900, on March 12, the library officials met with the new town council to plead for a reasonable response to their increasingly untenable position. Peter Hutchison, who had heard their appeal the year before during his first time on council, had been re-elected. A merchant active in the community through the Sons of Scotland Freemasons in Bracebridge, as an executive member of the curling committee, as president of the Bracebridge Board of Trade and as president of the Muskoka Liberal Association, Hutchison, who would a decade later himself become mayor, was among those who championed the cause of converting the Bracebridge library to a Free Library. Despite his considerable support, the library directors' repeated efforts achieved no movement from council's dug-in position. If opposition to the Free Library idea was council's position last year, why change? Resistance to change is one of the most potent forces in public affairs, and its power is not dependent upon it being logical.

The year 1901 began in Bracebridge with more than just a freshly elected municipal council. Solemn ceremonies in town marked Queen Victoria's death. She had been reigning monarch for as long as most people remembered, so not only was a new century under way but the familiar old "Victorian Era" had ended. Letters home from local boys soldiering in Imperial Britain's stalemated war in South Africa provided eagerly received news of the war. After the transition to a new monarch and apprehension about the fate of Canadian soldiers in a distant foreign war, came the looming library question.

The library directors were now completely worn down by their unending difficulties financing the operation and bringing it to a level of service expected in a town such as Bracebridge. They sombrely gathered in crisis and decided to give up the work entirely. They would make one final effort to persuade the Town to take responsibility for the municipality's library.

So bleak was the situation that even the town's most determined supporter of the library, Judge William Mahaffy, was prepared to throw in the towel. He led a discouraged delegation to meet with Bracebridge town council. Their message was direct and dire: the directors of the Mechanics' Institute were going to give up the library. The Town, if it wanted a library at all, would have to take over full responsibility for it. Things had come to a bleak impasse for a town wedded to books.

This was pretty much the same message as four years earlier, except the library directors were now so fed up that their feelings emboldened them to take the course of bloody-minded brinkmanship. Another change was that four elections had taken place since Bracebridge Town Council turned down the Free Library plan. Make-up of Council by 1901 had changed considerably during the intervening four years of annual elections. Singleton Brown, a supporter of the Free Library proposal, was no longer available to uphold the cause: he had gone missing for three days before his body was found near his farm at Severn River where he had died from a heart attack while walking. The council itself was a smaller body, since in 1899 the office of reeve had been eliminated and the number of councillors reduced to six, elected at large rather than by wards. When Judge Mahaffy and his library board colleagues surveyed the 1901 Bracebridge council, they actually had some reason to hope that Mayor John Thomson and councillors I. B. Aulph, Henry J. Bird, Harry S. Bowyer, Peter Hutchison, John M. MacMillan and Member of Parliament Angus McLeod, who also held an elected seat on Bracebridge town council, would be more inclined to approve this same measure now. The single biggest change in their favour was the presence of Henry Bird on council for the first time, placing him on the other side of the table from where he'd made the pitch four years earlier. Was this a sign of a deeper strategy in play? With Bird and Peter Hutchison, the council now had two highly effective members who were strong library supporters and who between them covered both political parties.

There was another signal as well that Mahaffy's brinkmanship message to council was not so much wild desperation as a coolly calculated strategy to advance the best interests of the town by accepting its groaning need for an open, free public library. The Mechanics' Institute directors had also tapped directly into Bracebridge's grass-roots democracy by circulating a petition among townspeople urging the Town to take over the library. It came back signed by such an overwhelming number of citizens that the elected councillors risked turning down the Free Library plan at their political peril.

Because the measure was so important to the community, and given the depth of concerns councillors believed had underscored earlier council positions, Council in its turn displayed political adroitness and respect for the democratic nature of community decision-making. Since the issue had not been specifically campaigned on in the most recent municipal election, councillors now voted to directly consult the people through a plebiscite. The question was duly voted upon. The news of the ballot count was no surprise. It showed a solid majority in favour.

Town council, on the basis of so much conclusive evidence of popular support for the best possible library service, avoided the ire that would arise in Bracebridge if the library were to collapse entirely. It voted to take over the library. Judge Mahaffy and his many fellow supporters of library service in Bracebridge had played their cards well.

In the end, all this political and governmental activity simply meant that Bracebridge was catching up to the state of mind the townspeople already had about their "public library" and regaining lost ground, relatively speaking, with the recent impressive advances across Canada and the United States as a result of the ever-strengthening public library movement and its rallying cry "Free Books For All!"

Now it was time to press the advantage of momentum. A deputation headed by Judge Mahaffy attended a meeting of Council to ask that the maximum amount allowed under the Ontario statute for free circulating libraries of one-half mill be granted to fund the town's reconstituted library. This would be added to the local tax rate so that, under the municipal taxation system where property assessment and mill rates translate into tax revenue for the town, all those who had called so urgently for a "free" library and voted for it in the plebiscite could now pay for it. Citizens were again reminded that in public affairs as in commerce and love, the enticing word "free" is always a misnomer.

Mahaffy's deputation also sought, for the first year of the library's new operation as the Bracebridge Free Library, a special donation of $50 from the Town. Council voted to approve both proposals.

To round out matters, since the Town of Bracebridge itself was now responsible for the local library, Council appointed a board of library trustees to conduct the library business. The three-member board consisted of Rev. J.M. Leith, T.J. Anderson, a local merchant, and W.C. Shier, the principal of the public and continuation schools. None of them was a member of council. Leith had arrived in Bracebridge to become minister of the Bracebridge Knox Presbyterian Church in September 1898 and promptly set about integrating himself into the community, becoming an executive member of the town's new curling committee within weeks of his arrival. The inaugural trustees of the Bracebridge Free Library thus had good connections into the community through education, church, business and sport. Designating a member of the clergy to be on the library board was reassuring to a number of devout townsfolk and councillors alike, a guiding hand to see that the books available to the public, now that the library was free to all, would be the right kind, assisting moral uplift, not leading to thoughts of an ignoble nature.

Officially, the town's collection of books and their administration became the Bracebridge Free Library on March 12, 1901. Who better than Francis P. Warne, familiar with the business of books and ardent applicant to the town council for money, to be named its treasurer? He opened the library's books of account for 1901 on April 1, showing a credit balance of $5.90. During the year this figure rose through further contributions until it stood at $457.68. Moses J. Dickie, secretary of the library board, ordered a new rubber stamp "Property of BRACEBRIDGE FREE LIBRARY" to mark all the books.

Establishment of a Free Library in Bracebridge meant it would provide library services without charge to all residents in the municipality,

ARRIVAL OF MOSES. After Moses Dickie relocated to Bracebridge from a settlement near Baysville he bought property on McMurray Street from the Presbyterian Church and built a frame house on what had been the manse gardens. This structure later received this distinctive brickwork, becoming unique in town for is artful combination of red bricks from the Bracebridge Brick Works and Beaverton white bricks.

Moses Dickie was a dealer buying and selling hay, then set himself up in the insurance business. Active in local lodges, agricultural societies, municipal government and Baptist church service, he relished reading and became a pillar of the Bracebridge Library, starting a dynasty of four generations of the Dickie family connected with the Carnegie Library and controlling its affairs for years.

which was a significant step since the 1901 census-takers, counting 2,480 residents in the bustling community, noted an increase of 1,020 since the prior census of 1891, almost a doubling in a decade. Open access to the library by all these townsfolk would increase pressure on its resources, but in turn would enable more provincial financial support to flow at last. With Council now having also set a rate of one-half a mill from town taxes to support the "new" library, a precedent had been established from which there would be no turning back from that day to this, generating a reliable if sometimes modest stream of local government revenue for the institution.

Although the Mechanics' Institute in Bracebridge had struggled along at times from its founding in 1874, it never failed to provide reading material for Bracebridge people. Its accommodation was never adequate,

A LIBRARY DYNASTY. Moses Dickie and his family became pillars of the Bracebridge Public Library through four generations. Moses, seated in the centre left of this photograph taken around 1895, holds baby Arthur on his knee. In centre is James Arthur, and next Moses' wife Violet holding infant Wesley on her lap. In the very front, is Hattie, whose proper name was Harriet. She would work closely with her father at the library in many secretarial and administrative positions and then take over from him as librarian in 1915, retaining this position until her marriage in 1934.

In the back row, left to right, are sons Jeremiah (Jerry) and John William, and daughter Sarah. Moses and Violet had eight children; Stanley is missing from this picture.

before it moved into the town hall, its rooms upstairs over stores had made it hard for older members with arthritis to climb to the library, its rooms themselves forever growing crowded as more volumes were acquired and members crowded in to read periodicals. All in all, the Mechanics' Institute in Bracebridge fared at least as well, and in many ways better, than its earlier urban counterparts in such places as Kingston, Toronto, Hamilton and Niagara Falls. In hindsight, moreover, its library can now be seen as an indispensable second phase in Bracebridge's transition from private libraries in homes and clubs. Now in a third phase of evolution, Bracebridge had achieved a Free Library.

The library has passed through its indispensable phases of evolution, from private libraries in homes and clubs, to a Mechanics' Institute library, and now in its third stage of growth into a Free Library. Besides books to borrow and a place to read current newspapers and magazines for free, the library continued to offer entertainments of an educational and cultural aspect as well.

Creation of literary societies and local book clubs in Bracebridge, for instance, was one such intertwining of literature and community life. Three years before the town's library had been taken over as a municipal institution and made free to all, one of the first organized book clubs made its appearance, the Bracebridge Ladies' Literary Society. It then served, by its success in the intellectual and social pleasures derived by its members from their book-centred communions, as a precedent that would guide and stimulate other groups forming for the discussion of books, right down to the present day when some 18 different book study circles or clubs operate in Bracebridge.

The Bracebridge Ladies' Literary Society worked closely with the town library. For example, its members had a hand in the arrangements in 1904 when the library board brought Pauline Johnson, the celebrated

REPRESENTATIVE OF THE PEOPLE. Along Dominion Street comes the stately procession for the funeral of Dr. Samuel Bridgland, long-time library supporter and Member of the Legislature representing the people of Muskoka on the Liberal side. This photograph was in 1903 from Manitoba Street in front of the spot where, five years later, the Carnegie library would be. Sam Bridgland had supported creating a "free library" in Bracebridge under the provincial Free Library Act of 1882 and believed a separate building was needed, as he and library chair Mahaffy had been seeking at the time of his death.

Canadian Indian poet, to Bracebridge just as she was returning from a widely publicized world tour. When Johnson gave a recital of her work the town hall, chosen by the board because it boasted the largest auditorium in the community at the time, overflowed. The literary and cultural event was a success in every respect. The works of Pauline Johnson proved hard thereafter to keep on the shelves at the library because readers avidly borrowed her volumes of poetry.

Before too many years passed, it became clear to those connected with the Bracebridge library that they faced a recurring pattern with a cultural institution in a growing town and a changing world. After finally accomplishing one goal for the library, another need began to loom on the horizon. The change to a public institution for which the town was responsible and to which all people had free access had been important, but despite these successes some of the deeper patterns that afflict the operation of community libraries began to reassert themselves. Space was the most urgent. The town hall was itself growing crowded by municipal government needs as the town kept growing. A new building for the library was needed.

The town's appointed representatives in 1905 on the board of library trustees were Francis Warne and Alfred E. Mundy. Mundy, who would be elected to town council two years later, had just moved with his family to Bracebridge from Trenton in the fall of 1903 as successor in business of James Shepherd's main street store. For his part, Warne on becoming a library trustee had relinquished his position as library treasurer. The treasurer's duties were then added to the responsibilities of the library's secretary, Moses Dickie. The conduct of the Bracebridge Free Library was now consolidated in the hands of one man to a very great extent, because Moses Dickie had also recently been hired as the new Bracebridge librarian at an annual salary of $112.50. With Dickie, a man with no particular training about books or library administration, it was tacitly acknowledged that the town's librarian was principally a custodian of property. Mundy as a council representative on the board was new to town. This gave Francis Warne, as knowledgeable as anyone about the library, an upper hand in influence, but he was so pro-library that he would not be one to provide challenges to Board decisions or the library's management in any exercise of accountability for town council. All in all, those running the Bracebridge Free Library had a fairly free hand, which meant the continuing library board chairman Judge W.C. Mahaffy and the secretary-treasurer-librarian Moses Dickie were firmly in charge. In a way, this autonomy was not in the best interests of the library, for although the

Town had passed a resolution about changing the library's status, nothing indicated that it had really taken on the library as an aspect of local government, the way the schools and utilities were. So the big new need for a proper library building was not clearly seen as a responsibility for the Town. By default, the task of raising money for a new library building fell back to the same men and women in town who had always been the library's supporters when it was operated by the Mechanics' Institute.

The growth problems of booming Bracebridge did not only affect the library. At the school, despite recent completion of an addition, by 1903 the classrooms were again overcrowded. The year 1902 had been a record one for construction of new homes in town. Then in 1903 building activity surpassed those records. All these measurements of progress had direct implications for the library. The library had become free and public, but the premises in the town hall were inadequate. A new building was needed but the town council, especially its grouchier members facing demands for so many other expenditures of pressing urgency for the town's municipally owned electricity system, roads and sewers and water lines into the spreading townsite and new demands for industrial services, saw little chance for finding the municipal funds needed to construct it. The topic, in fact, was not even broached in Council.

A new solution was needed. Literary life in Bracebridge and the town's book-centred culture was alive and well and the community library was a central fixture in the life of the town, but a new library building was needed to accommodate the town's growth. With the town's resources stretched, that could now be nothing more than an impossible dream.

SIX

The Patron Saint of Libraries

No one believed more that a library could be a passport to the larger world than Andrew Carnegie.

In 1848 the impoverished Carnegie family quit Scotland, but fared little better trying to make a fresh start in the New World. Soon 14-year-old Andrew left school to support his family working as a bobbin boy in a factory earning $1.20 for six 12-hour days of hard labour. Life was grim. Then the youth, now as voracious a reader as his unemployed father, discovered a place to satisfy his quest to educate himself: Colonel Anderson's library on Federal Street in their Pittsburgh suburb Allegheny.

James Anderson, who fought in the War of 1812 and afterwards made a fortune as an iron manufacturer, had donated 1,500 books on historical, scientific and religious subjects to the town. "His purpose was to provide a building of knowledge, free of charge, for apprentices for whom school was not an option," explains Carnegie biographer Peter Krass.[1]

"Colonel Anderson opened to me the intellectual wealth of the world," explained Carnegie himself about this experience. "I became fond of reading. I revelled week after week in the books. My toil was light, for I got up at six o'clock in the morning, contented to work until six in the evening if there was then a book for me to read."[2]

Carnegie thereafter attributed his success to these early days with the books in the colonel's library. The information he gained, the lessons he learned, seemed to prove in his own life that such an advantage given to others would make the whole of society better. The colonel's pattern would become a model for Carnegie in several important ways—the wartime experience, earning a fortune afterwards, and giving away books to help others, except in Andrew Carnegie everything was magnified: instead of the War of 1812-14, it was the American Civil War; instead of making of small fortune in iron, it was the world's largest in steel; and instead of donating a few thousand books for hundreds working boys in one city it was a few thousand libraries for millions of people around the world. The power of example in how we lead our lives should never be underestimated, and those of us today who cherish libraries have much to thank James Anderson for.

Carnegie's early experiences and the influence of his family made him a radical. Intelligent and hard working, he saw and took opportunities in the telegraph business, then in the railway business, then in making steel. By age 66 he became America's dominant giant in steel, but in 1901 sold everything to financier J.P. Morgan for $303,450,000 (an amount in present-day values of some $7,413,200,000). In the process, the radical had also become a red-blooded capitalist. That it was not a complete conversion left him torn with inner conflicts.

Scores of books have been written about Andrew Carnegie's evolution, both pro and con. As the man who invented cost accounting, pioneered its use in his railway career, and later applied it to the manufacture of steel to undersell his competitors without undercutting his profit margin, Carnegie the industrial titan offers readers raw intellectual adventure in the world of capitalism as served up in such books as Harold Livesay's well-researched 1975 account *Andrew Carnegie and the Rise of Big Business* and Joseph Wall's trenchant 1970 version recounted in *Andrew Carnegie.* Equally compelling reads are the books by social critics who round out this fascinating Carnegie story by documenting how it was not only cost accounting but also ruthless exploitation of workers that enabled him to gather in his millions.

One of the best books to address these conflicts and contradictions in Carnegie the man is also one of the most recent, authored by Peter Krass in 2002, entitled simply *Carnegie.* The author's great-grandfather had been one of the thousands who slaved in Carnegie's horrific mills and died prematurely helping create all the wealth that Andrew later would lavishly spend to help ordinary working people reach extraordinary destinations by entering "the free republic of the library." Krass ended up convinced that, despite the horrors, Carnegie had accomplished great good for countless millions. Krass found "a titan I both disdain and respect" who was "full of internal conflict and contradiction." This balanced biographer found that Carnegie, both purposefully and unwittingly, had planted seeds for civilization. "While trampling asunder thousands of working men," concludes Krass about Carnegie, "he ultimately uplifted millions of people in the future."[3]

The primary interest of this book, however, is not with the well-documented ways Andrew Carnegie amassed his "tainted" fortune. That moral problem is highlighted by the fact some places like Detroit would not accept Carnegie's controversial money for their library until a decade-long debate had played out, while in Canada the reaction of certain politicians and newspaper editors and their cartoonists was equally scathing. While acknowledging this ethical paradox, our primary need is to understand the basis for the remarkable philanthropy by the "patron saint of libraries," because Carnegie's money was generally accepted despite this moral conundrum faced by its recipients, and because his patronage would transform so many communities, Bracebridge included.

Once he became the richest man in the world, Andrew Carnegie's new obsession was to give away all his money before he died. Carnegie said to university students, "Look upon a rich man and you will never see him smile." He believed it would a cruel legacy to shoulder his widow with such pressures and problems. The solution was to divest himself of the money.

Carnegie first launched his philanthropic enterprises, beginning in 1881, with a library for his birthplace, Dunfermline, in Scotland, followed by two libraries in the United States, one at Braddock and the other in Allegheny, two Pennsylvania communities with which he also had close connections. It was payback time to the community, but it was also a way to show off to folks who remembered the poor kid that he had really made it big. The gratitude of these surprised townsfolk reinforced Carnegie's desire to proceed with more such gifts, but now with a more systematic and less personal approach.

At various stages in his ascent Carnegie had written personal memos about his plans for the future and set out his goals in private manifestos. Now he continued the practice so his "policies" on libraries specifically and philanthropy generally became clearly spelled out in writing. It served Carnegie's purpose for his new philosophy of philanthropy to be widely known, and his documents were published as articles on both sides of the Atlantic. Because he was now so focused on the business of philanthropy, and because he had such a vast fortune to give away, he quickly became an acknowledged authority in the field, and not just to sycophants hoping to cut in on the his largess. Early in the twentieth century multi-

THE GIFT OF READING. Andrew Carnegie slaved long hours for low wages as a youth but found his passport to a larger universe in a library to whose books he and other working boys in the Pittsburgh area had access. "I became fond of reading. I revelled week after week in the books," he said. "My toil was light, for I got up at six o'clock in the morning, contended to work until six in the evening, if there was then a book for me to read."

When Carnegie became the richest man in the world, he gave millions of other people this same passport to freedom and independence by building well over two thousand beautiful public libraries including, in 1908, the new library in the town of Bracebridge, with open access to all.

millionaire John D. Rockefeller consulted Carnegie for lessons on how to give away money like it mattered, just as a century later American multi-billionaire Warren Buffett, in making history as the most generous philanthropist of all time announcing in June 2006 his decision to give away most of his $44 billion, turned to Bill Gates.

These patrons, then or today, all faced the same challenge that governments, once they got into the business of supporting arts and culture and other community programs, likewise encounter: determining whether they are getting value for their money. Evaluating the success of projects intended to produce beneficial change is not easy. Today's leaders in the not-for-profit sector and those responsible for annually giving away billions for educational and charitable purposes constantly grapple with this issue. Is the money doing any real good for the intended beneficiaries? In many respects, the efforts of philanthropists and those seeking to measure outcomes all flow from the pioneering work by the same man who invented cost accounting.

Following the reasoning Andrew Carnegie laid down in his landmark philanthropist's manifesto, the communities that would benefit from his grants in the future no longer needed to be ones like Dunfermline, Braddock or Allegheny to which he had personal or business connections. Rather, a standard formula would require that any recipient community provide free land for the site of the library and collect taxes sufficient to provide on-going funds to operate its new Carnegie library equivalent each year to ten percent of the building's capital cost. Decades before franchising was invented, Andrew Carnegie had come up with the concept for his libraries.

The seminal document that would guide the dispensing of millions of Carnegie dollars first appeared as an essay entitled simply "Wealth" in the June 1889 issue of the *North American Review*. Unlike anything before, this was a reasoned justification for the accumulation of wealth but, even more radical, "a bold and systematic philosophy for distributing wealth" according to values Carnegie considered best for society and the recipients of such philanthropy.

Once someone had accumulated great wealth there were, he suggested, three ways to get rid of it: leave it to the family, give it as a bequest following death for public purposes, or administer it toward good causes before dying. Since he had already decided to follow the third route, he quickly dismissed the first two.

This of course left option three. But for Andrew Carnegie it was not an option so much as a cause. As crucial as it had been for young Carnegie to discover books as his passport to freedom, it is just as important to realize that Carnegie seized upon free access to books for an impoverished working boy as the greatest measure of social justice. It was a principle Carnegie the radical believed so strongly he would now fund it just as earlier he had fought for it when Colonel Anderson's library had been closed to him.

He now asserted with great vehemence that the only acceptable method for dispersing a massive fortune was for its owner to accept his responsibility for it while still alive, to deal with it and give it all away in his lifetime. He became a zealot on the point, and he implored, coaxed and admonished other capitalists who kept acquiring more wealth or indulging themselves with it as they aged, to change their ways.

His essay included examples of the best kinds of philanthropy, ranked according to Carnegie's view of society. He clarified, of course, that giving cash to beggars was worse than a waste; it was counterproductive. Andrew Carnegie believed it was a sin to just give money away to people because getting something without effort would destroy the recipient's character. He was, however, attracted to those who had already worked hard to make it on their own. He saw his benefactions as a reward for initiative already shown, not as an incentive to get someone or something started. When it came to libraries, it mattered very much to him that people in a community had already shown sincerity by trying to do something for themselves, like making their best effort to operate a library against the odds.

He believed the only worthy recipients were those who would help themselves, and reasoned in turn that philanthropy should not be emotional but based on considerations of what would best serve society in the largest sense. This meant, mainly, giving large amounts to institutions that could do some good. At the top of his list came universities, then free libraries, followed by parks and places of recreation to help men improve in body and mind. After this he felt works of art were worthy, both to improve public taste and provide pleasure to those who viewed them. A residual category was for public institutions of all kinds that served to improve general conditions for people—again a requirement that it be an institution.

In a way, Carnegie saw the world of giving akin to his world of making, with the distributing institutions the counterparts to his manufacturing factories. It was a structured solution, but the imperative was real. He always saw how things worked as systems and he dealt with them in very realistic, hands-on ways. So now it was to be the same with systemic philanthropy. He recognized more clearly than ever, as he moved from small acts of beneficence to large-scale philanthropy, or as Krass puts it, "from a retail phase of library giving to wholesale,"[4] the tremendous power of his money.

The reaction to his article swirled across the full spectrum of praise and condemnation, but the owner and editor of *North American Review*, considering it "the finest essay he had ever read," invited Carnegie to proffer a sequel, which he was only too happy to do. He accepted another turn in the pulpit. Entitled "The Best Field for Philanthropy," it appeared in the December issue that same year.

This time Carnegie was even more specific about the guiding criteria for implementation. The principles for giving were clear: it was a disgrace to die rich, and one should not pauperize recipients but instead stimulate members of the community to take responsibility for improving themselves. It did nothing for the human race to indiscriminately help charity cases. Those who were "irreclaimably destitute, shiftless and worthless" should be sheltered, clothed and fed by the government. Carnegie's tough love, combined with laying-off responsibility to institutions of the state, stood in contrast to John Rockefeller who could display genuine compassion for down-and-out folk. Yet these views were commonplace for red-blooded American capitalists of the era. Where Andrew Carnegie got more controversial, because he broke new ground, was in ranking the seven best fields for philanthropy.

This began as an elaboration of his earlier declension from the June article, starting with the top two worthy causes: universities, then free libraries. Regarding the libraries, he reported to readers of the *North American Review* that "The result of my own study of the question, 'What is the best gift which can be given to a community?' is that a free library occupies the first place, provided the community will accept and maintain it as a public institution, as much a part of the city property as its public schools, and, indeed, an adjunct to these."[5]

Moving up into third spot now was the "founding or extension of hospitals, medical colleges, laboratories, and other institutions connected with the alleviation of human suffering, and especially with the prevention rather than the cure of human ills." Public parks were still on the list, but slipped to fourth ranking. The last three were: music halls, public baths, and churches—in that order. Clergy railed against this ranking, but Carnegie as a non-believer considered they were lucky to make his list at all. Churches were sectarian and served only a small segment of the public, he believed, so funding them he considered of limited value.

Having put down his markers for how to conduct beneficial philanthropy, Andrew Carnegie then set about the hard business of dispensing all his wealth in his lifetime. To help him administer the project of reviewing appeals for libraries and deciding which should be funded, Carnegie relied on his long-time personal secretary, James Bartram, and his lifelong financial secretary, Robert Franks

There was no application form as such. People aspiring to get a library, having read articles or newspaper reports of what was taking place, such as John Cotton Dana's 1906 article "How a Town Can Get a Library,"[6] simply wrote in. Requests for libraries came from library boards and clergymen, teachers and realtors, mayors and sundry others who knew that libraries were important or who somehow hoped to get in on the fabulous Carnegie millions.

To cope in orderly fashion with their new philanthropy business, Bartram or Franks would open a file for each supplicant, kept alphabetically by name of the communities hoping for libraries. There then followed more correspondence as Bartram gathered the needed information on the size of the municipality, availability of a suitable site for the new building, the existing library services and facilities in the community, and whether money had already been raised toward the project locally. As they gained additional experience, more information was sought earlier in the exchange of correspondence to ensure only worthy projects got through their screening process.

Bartram, Franks and Carnegie himself were very interested in the architectural plans, for this could be an area of wasted money that had little to do with serving the needs of library users, and it was also important in terms of the philosophy of openness and accessibility of the free public library, including the still contentious issue of whether stacks should be open for patrons to browse through on their own. Carnegie believed absolutely that the republic of the library must be open and free in every sense of the word. In time, Bartram learned by experience that he could save time and frustration for all concerned by producing and distributing a booklet to applicants listing the essential design features required of a Carnegie library whatever the building itself ended up looking like architecturally.

Once the town council had provided satisfactory land, had voted to adopt the requisite by-law committing to pay from local taxes ten percent of the value of Carnegie's gift library toward its operation and maintenance every year thereafter, and once the architect's plans had been approved and contracts awarded for the building's erection, payments for the construction came from New York at intervals of completion.

The thick files of the Carnegie Corporation attested to the early development of a new plan for patronage and philanthropy. The letters, in their rich variety reflecting the human qualities of those who wrote them and the community pressures that made them say what they did the way they did, make far more interesting reading than the preformatted online applications submitted today by a library or educational organization in Bracebridge or anywhere else appealing, say, to Carnegie's wealthy philanthropist successor Bill Gates for money to fund a worthy library-related educational project.

On December 31, 1908, *Collier's* magazine published an interview with Carnegie at a time when the library philanthropy seemed pretty much to be winding down. Included with its interview of Carnegie, the publication gave this tally of Carnegie's patronage to that date: $51,596,903 had been given to construct 959 library buildings in the United States, 329 in England and Wales, 105 in his native Scotland, 86 in Canada, 42 in Ireland, 14 in New Zealand, 5 in the British West Indies, 3 in South Africa, 2 in Australia and Tasmania, 1 in the Seychelles Islands, and 1 in the Fiji Islands. In 1985 when Robert Boyer addressed the official opening of the expanded Bracebridge Carnegie Library, his research led him to state that Andrew Carnegie had given $60,000,000 to build a total of 2,811 public libraries throughout the English-speaking world. Of 125 such libraries in Canada, he reported, 111 were in Ontario. A definitive book on the Carnegie libraries in Ontario, *The Best Gift*, published in 1995 and co-authored by Margaret Beckman, Stephen Langmead and John Black, listed 111 Carnegie libraries paid for in the province between 1901 and 1917, a number that included one addition to an existing library and seven branch libraries in Toronto and one in Ottawa. In 2005 Russell Mackinnon, a member of the Bracebridge Public Library Board, completed his research and wrote an article for *Muskoka Magazine* about

Andrew Carnegie, stating that over a 42-year period, Carnegie had spent $56,162,622.97 building 2,812 public libraries: 1,946 in the United States, 660 in the United Kingdom, 17 in New Zealand, 12 in South Africa, 5 in the West Indies, 3 in Australia, 1 each in Tasmania, Mauritius, Fiji and Seychelles, and 165 in Canada.

Even with all this precision in dollars and numbers, it seems it was hard to keep track of such a far-flung and novel undertaking. So many libraries had been given that few had a definitive count of the number. The benefactor himself saw this process as planting seeds for the future of civilization. The scattering of seed is less about where they land or how many there are, and more about how they sprout and what they bring forth. A number of Carnegie libraries have withered away. Some have been removed. Others would thrive and expand.

"The letters received from parents thanking me for libraries established and telling of the change these have made upon their children are numerous," the patron saint of libraries told *Collier's*. Not only what a library did in a community, but just as important, what it prevented, was emphasized by Carnegie. "If young men do not spend their evenings in the library, where will they be spending them? If the young do not acquire a taste for reading, what will they otherwise acquire?"[7] The old man had gone full circle, seeing again himself in Colonel Anderson's library for working boys reflected in the millions of us who would slip into a Carnegie library after school or in the evenings throughout the twentieth century.

Some critics, including Carnegie's friend Mark Twain, suggested he simply wanted to see the Carnegie name plastered on thousands of buildings to perpetuate his fame. He did not require that his name be used on the libraries and in a number of cases refused requests to do so where it would have been linked with such names as Lincoln and Webster that as an American patriot he considered sacrilegious. Some of his beneficial acts he insisted remain anonymous, such as secretly paying off the debts of Lord Acton in England so his famous library would not have to be auctioned off to settle accounts with the legendary peer's creditors. The renowned "Carnegie Hall" in New York City, originally named by Carnegie himself simply as "The Music Hall," but to which European musicians refused to come and perform because it sounded to them like a cheap cabaret or honky-tonk American show biz palace, was renamed during Carnegie's absence overseas by its New York City directors without consulting him. In total the name Carnegie was used on only about

37 percent of the libraries he paid for. All the same, Andrew Carnegie rightly saw the value of publicity in naming: it gave the example to others, especially the vain and the rich and those wanting to memorialize a departed loved one, of what might appeal to them and in the process support society and advance civilization.

Another criticism of Carnegie's library program was that he paid for the buildings but not the land on which they were built nor the cost of operating them once they were opened to the public. Yet this policy reflected his hard-headed pragmatism that communities had to commit something themselves to be worthy of the gift, that land was usually something any municipality could come up with for little or no cost to itself, and that unless there was on-going local support including the flow of some tax revenue the library building would not last all that long even if build sturdily.

Yet another criticism of his libraries, by H.L. Menken, was that Carnegie did not provide the books to go with them. This criticism of Carnegie's philanthropy, like others that he let pass, missed another important point about the Carnegie library program: he believed that the best people to know what books would be needed and of interest to a particular community would be the people living there. On the four of five occasions when for particular reasons he bent this rule and did fund the purchase of books, another chorus of critics loomed to damn him for trying to impose his views and values on others by deciding what they should read.

Andrew Carnegie's internal conflict between his radical side and his "robber baron" side as a ruthless capitalist was uniquely synthesized when he used his money for philanthropic works among which the free public libraries stand as an enduring centrepiece. His gift of reading to millions who would never have had access to libraries was profound. Architects designed his libraries to implement a program of free access to books by the reading public—a revolutionary idea to those who actually did seek to control what people could read.

In 1900 when Andrew Carnegie was establishing his new "residential library" at his extravagant castle estate known as "Skibo" in Scotland which he had purchased in 1892, he wanted what he was then just beginning to give others with his library philanthropy: access to the great literature of the world. He hired Hew Morrison to buy books so he would have at hand the canon of western literature, specifically instructing him,

"I do not wish rare or curious books or elaborate bindings. It is to be a working library, only the gems of literature."[8]

Among the many volumes in Carnegie's library were works by the American author Washington Irving, including *Bracebridge Hall*. The central mission of Irving was to draw the English-speaking peoples of the United States and Great Britain together, and this resonated with the trans-Atlantic dimensions of Andrew Carnegie's own life and values. At the level of international relations Carnegie was strongly anti-Imperialist, but at the level of humanity and in terms of English-speaking peoples in particular he, like Washington Irving, saw the common elements among all English-speaking peoples and himself lived in both the United States and the United Kingdom. Carnegie envisaged the English-speaking race governing the affairs of the world and promoted this concept tirelessly.

It is unclear whether Andrew Carnegie ever came to the Canadian town of Bracebridge, in the course of visiting his friends at their splendid summer homes on Lake Muskoka, but like Washington Irving, his impact on the community was great. One indirectly gave the town its name Bracebridge through his book; the other gave the town a home for its books through his library. Although this experience of getting a Carnegie library was common to dozens of hundreds of other municipalities, it was Carnegie's link to Washington Irving that forged a unique connection with the Ontario town whose destiny had been altered by the writings of Irving. When he died, Carnegie was buried in the same cemetery as Irving at Sleepy Hollow, New York.

The unusual connection between Andrew Carnegie and Bracebridge did not end there. American cities in the industrial age that followed the Civil War became hellholes, especially in the heat of summer. Polluted, congested, noisy, dangerous and filled with impoverished workers who toiled long hours in grimy and treacherous mills and lived in overcrowded slums, cities like Pittsburgh were places from which those with wealth eagerly escaped to more pleasant settings. America itself offered many such summer colonies for its troubled urban plutocrats, and Andrew Carnegie himself withdrew to such pastoral as well as to his palaces in Scotland and England. Yet to more thoroughgoing North Americans without a pull back across the Atlantic, Canadian venues also became desirable places for respite and genteel recreation with just a quaint touch of being abroad. Beaumaris, a small community on the Bracebridge side of Lake Muskoka known locally as "Millionaires Row," was one of two Pittsburgh colonies in the province for Pennsylvania's "iron kings."

The mystique of the rich outsider celebrities who summered at their colony in Muskoka had become woven into the very being of Bracebridge and its surroundings from the earliest days, and forms a context for understanding the townsfolk's very mixed feelings about dealing with Andrew Carnegie and his "tainted money" to get funds for a library. The annual influx of wealthy and prominent Americans, many of them significant players in the business, finance, education and politics of the United States, was already well established by July 31, 1898, when the *Philadelphia Inquirer* reported some "mid-summer gossip" on how "several well-know gentlemen" from Pennsylvania had gone north of the line to enjoy the pleasures of the "Solid Comfort Club" on Lake Muskoka. Summering in Muskoka was a concept spreading throughout the networks of America's well-to-do.

As a result, Muskoka began to develop its own version of the unique relationships between the stolid year-round residents whose pleasant locale affords a comforting retreat for the wealthy, and those who come to such places to escape the pollution of their mills and pressures of commercial intrigues by which they gained their fabulous wealth in the first place. The layered tensions that play out between the transient and sophisticated rich and the erstwhile locals is a universal story, captured adroitly by F. Scott Fitzgerald's *The Great Gatsby* in one such venue on Long Island on the east coast of America. Another such place was Muskoka, which soon developed more fodder for similar tales than it had artful writers to craft them. Some novels with passages set in Muskoka touch upon the delicate etiquette of mutual dependence and mutual resentment between these two classes, but more resides in local folklore and awaits the telling in books yet to be written.

By the turn of the twentieth century, in any event, a sizeable number of prominent Americans had come to savour the possibilities for escape by transporting their culture into Muskoka's lake district. Not far to the west of Bracebridge, the growing shoreline community of Americans around the village of Beaumaris extended onto the outlying series of islands in Lake Muskoka which offered Americans from Ohio, Pennsylvania and New York just the right mix of security and privacy in this relaxed setting. Ensconced in large summer homes with wide verandahs, winding flagstone paths, extensive gardens and spectacular vistas of dancing waters and majestic pines, these summer Muskokans experienced few restraints in their Canadian paradise.

One of the first really great estates of the era was John Walker's summer place, a Beaumaris landmark of exceptional beauty, nestled in its exclusivity on Buck Island. Its owner John Walker, of Scottish ancestry and a steel man like Carnegie, was, according to the *New York Times*, "one of four pioneer industrialists who blazed the way for Pittsburgh's leadership in the iron and steel industry." "There is no spot in Muskoka," stated the *Gravenhurst Banner* on May 30, 1913, in describing Walker's Buck Island estate, "that equals this place for beauty, the gardens in summer being gorgeous in their loveliness." Walker's expansive summer home included capacity for many guests, with 14 bedrooms in the Great House itself, many consisting of suites with private baths, and eight grand stone fireplaces. Gardeners were gainfully employed tending the prolific spreads of perennials and annuals surrounding the winding stone pathways which, as the *Banner* noted, added to the splendour of this lakeside manor, especially by marvelling boaters as they passed slowly by. The island's private shoreline perimeter of 1,197 feet, with sand coves and sweeping views, offered docking on both windward and leeward sides. Among the many attributes of creativity in Walker's development of Buck Island was a five-storey drying tower that also housed an artist's studio, a house in miniature secretly located in the attic of the Great House, and of course, in special prominence on the main floor of the Great House, his extensive Buck Island library. He had grown up in a family where reading books was a respected priority, his father reading at night when John's friend Andrew Carnegie frequently came over to see his sister Elizabeth and they all talked books and debated Adam Smith and *The Wealth of Nations*. Year after year Walker lovingly added books to his lakeside library, and it was here in Muskoka that he had most time to read.

The list is long and the lore deep about rich Americans summering in Muskoka from first days that railways and steamboats made it possible to reach the pristine peace of the Muskoka Lakes, from Woodrow Wilson, who owned Formosa Island, to dozens of other prominent leaders in finance, commerce, education and politics. One other example alone, however, indicates the significance of "Little Pittsburgh" near Bracebridge, and that was the presence of John Walker's summer neighbour on Squirrel Island, Andrew Mellon. Born in Pittsburgh in 1855, Mellon owned his own lumber company by age 17, a bank two years later, built up a financial and manufacturing empire in steel, oil, shipbuilding and construction, became one of the wealthiest Americans after John D. Rockefeller and Henry Ford, was an art collector and philanthropist, and served his country as Secretary of the United States Treasury from 1921 to 1931 under three different presidents, Harding, Coolidge and Hoover. As befitted a man of such standing, Andrew Mellon had established himself in a majestic island estate where the whole Mellon family summered. His visits into Bracebridge included seeing lawyer Russell M. Best, Q.C., who handled all Mellon's Ontario real estate legal work and from whose law office the distinguished man in casual summer clothes made long-distance business calls, on one occasion telling his agent at the other end of the line, "Offer them $10 million and not a cent more," then hanging up.

The Pittsburgh plutocrats mixing into this central Muskoka community of Beaumaris and Bracebridge did so in a variety of ways, in some respects very down-to-earth and nuanced. People from many local families worked at Millionaires' Row, in all conceivable occupations. Those in service saw the back-story of the rich and famous. Those in trades came to respect the knowledge and practicality of the owners, men who in many cases had themselves started early in life working with their hands and knew what they were talking about when discussing a concrete retaining wall or a particularly challenging plumbing job.

Who could have known it would matter so much for Bracebridge that it had Pittsburgh connections to the "patron saint of libraries"?

SEVEN

Seeking a Carnegie Library

The Bracebridge library had never had a building of its own. Converting the Mechanics' Institute Library to a Free Library made no difference whatsoever as far as cramped facilities were concerned. Not only did townspeople see better libraries elsewhere. Those interested in books and education felt the tug of North America's rising library movement that sought "free books for all" in accessible and attractive library facilities. Those responsible for Bracebridge's library wanted something better.

A new building for the library would be the ideal way to address this need and realize these possibilities, but it seemed beyond reach with only so much money to go around and the booming town bursting at its seams and needing more and better accommodation right across the board. The schools were crammed and overflowing. The town hall, two decades after it had been built, was small for the conduct of municipal affairs, the fire department, the police, and now the library. Operating the library here on prestigious Dominion Street was becoming no more satisfactory than during its earlier migrations into rooms over stores on the main street.

The fact the municipality had notionally taken on responsibility for the library in 1901 in no way solved the issue of space or sense of place. It simply meant the need for new and larger library premises contended for attention and money amidst the town's lengthening list of major public works projects clamouring to be dealt with. A library building was not a council priority. It was not even on the council's agenda.

Yet Bracebridge was a place of self-starters. Supporters of the town's library began to raise funds privately for a proper new library building. The usual sources for funds for a building were members of the organization that wanted it, the governments that raised taxes from the municipality and were responsible for it, and local men of wealth who owned a mill or factory. Any source would do.

One of the determined supporters of this initiative was Albert Ecclestone. The successful owner of a plumbing business at the south end of the main street near the railway tracks, Ecclestone was an ardent supporter of the Bracebridge library. He was such a voracious reader, in fact, that in his household everyone knew not to put a good book they were reading down because he'd grab it. The large Ecclestone house at the north end of John Street was fully insulated with a large collection of books.

Ecclestone began plowing the Bracebridge community for money but found the ground hard and stony. "He decided to ask John Walker," recounted Ecclestone's daughter Eva.

Millionaire John Walker, as already mentioned, summered in Muskoka. He was one of Andrew Carnegie's trusted friends and earliest business associates, ever since their first deal together buying the Kloman iron mill in 1872 when Carnegie began his long series of triumphs over Pittsburgh's iron and steel aristocracy that would eventually see him emerge with the largest operation of all, U.S. Steel.

It was as a plumber in Bracebridge that Ecclestone had first met Walker, when he built and then maintained the extensive plumbing works at the American's summer estate on Buck Island. Both were practical and hard-headed men, one a major player in the competitive big leagues of American iron and steel, the other successfully operating a small town plumbing business. They respected one another and enjoyed conversations together. The steel tycoon and the plumber, both book lovers and pragmatic men of business, in fact became friends. Walker had an immense library at his island home, as did Ecclestone at his residence in town, and the two men would mention books to one another. On his return to Muskoka each season, Walker visited Ecclestone at his main street store in Bracebridge to catch up and discuss projects. Although his Pittsburgh staff always called the locals to line up employees and support services before each annual return, Walker personally called Ecclestone to say when he'd be arriving so the two could meet. The Ecclestones at Walker's invitation picnicked amidst "the magnificent guardians" on Buck Island, as daughter Eva enthusiastically remembers, and the Walkers occasionally visited the Ecclestone home on John Street. At the end of the 1902 summer season, Susan and John Walker came by to say farewell to Flora and Albert for another year as they headed back to Pittsburgh for the winter, "delivering a large assortment of beautiful cut flowers and perennials from their Buck Island gardens" for the Ecclestone's John Street home.

"We're talking about raising some money for a new library," Ecclestone told Walker. "But I'm afraid if we just go with the money we can raise around town, it won't be much of a library."

"Andrew Carnegie is giving money for entire libraries," replied Walker after a thoughtful pause. "That would be a lot simpler. I'll put in a good word for Bracebridge. You want to write him a short letter, tell him what is proposed, and just make a request for the new library. Probably it's best for the chairman of the board to write. It could go right to Carnegie's secretary. I'll give you his address in New York."

But it took library chairman W.C. Mahaffy most of the winter to get around to writing the letter because of divided views in Bracebridge.

Although the idea of seeking a Carnegie library for Bracebridge never formally came before town council for two more years, it was discussed a great deal around town as a tantalizing proposal, and the topic was always on the agenda in the chambers of the town's two newspapers. D.E. Bastedo and G.W. Boyer at the *Muskoka Herald* supported the idea of getting a Carnegie library. Their paper was the Tory sheet in town. George Thomas at the *Bracebridge Gazette* opposed the idea of "getting something for free." His was the Grit paper. These men and their papers battled on, both Thomas and Boyer advancing their journalistic causes and political interests by election to town council, and each in time serving as mayors of Bracebridge. But in the crucial years between 1902 and 1908, when the library became an increasingly contentious Bracebridge issue, George Thomas was already on council and in the ascendant with a better-financed paper and a more dominant personality, and the town's rival publications were intensively participating in developing opinion as well as reporting it.

The problem was that a Carnegie library building was simultaneously coveted but controversial. The reason the new building was coveted was obvious. Hard-pressed library supporters in Bracebridge, and in Gravenhurst too, where there was interest in getting a Carnegie library once it was learned Bracebridge was thinking about it, sought to break free from their struggles in providing library service. Weary of operating their town's libraries from upper floors over stores and scrounging needed money to buy books or subscriptions to newspapers and magazines, the library boards in both communities could appeal to Carnegie to lift them into a bigger league.

The controversy stemmed from the fact that the $303,450,000 Carnegie received when he sold his steel empire to J.P. Morgan was all "tainted money" in the eyes of many, including knowledgeable Muskokans. For complex motivations of his own, however, Carnegie was now fully prepared, even anxious, to give away his millions. His early radicalism was in him still, along with his robust capitalist's spirit, and with the blood of thousands of working men on his money, this man who was not a believer did at some level reconcile himself to his internal civil war between the radical and the capitalist by devoting the rest of his life and his money to world peace, libraries and other acts of selfless philanthropy to uphold society and advance civilization.

Now, potential recipients had to do some reconciling of their own. A few municipalities like Detroit ascended to moral high ground and refused for years to accept the steel monopolist's money, but elsewhere, in places like Bracebridge, local leaders intent on finding non-local funding for local improvements saw their chance only in terms of pragmatic necessity and application of the town's municipal development strategy. If young Carnegie had discovered what he called "the free republic of books" and was now inspired by his own experience to give the same gift of reading to others, perhaps the solution to this ethical dilemma of dirty hands doing good works was to go forward concentrating on good works and overlook the past without excusing it. If Carnegie with his fabulous wealth could make his dream come true, not just in places where he lived or owned a mill but wherever there was a need, couldn't others in places like Bracebridge also make their dream for a better library come true, too? It was a rare moment in the history of the world. Carnegie had more money for this astonishing project than any government, anywhere, has ever spent on libraries before or since.

As the pros and cons of seeking money from a man deeply reviled in many quarters continued to be thrashed out in Bracebridge, other communities in Ontario already began getting their free libraries from Andrew Carnegie. The rush was on, despite misgivings about laundering money. News reports of a number of these developments ran in the *Bracebridge Gazette* and the *Muskoka Herald*, which served to prod Bracebridgites by showing how they were missing what others were getting. Eight municipalities in 1901 had been catapulted into first-rank library status, including Collingwood, Stratford, Guelph and Ottawa. By 1902 the list expanded with 12 more municipalities in the province, including Lindsay, Smiths Falls, Brampton and Brantford. Some of these towns now in the "have" category were not far from Muskoka, nor any larger than Bracebridge. The list for Ontario in 1901 totalled an impressive $229,000 worth of Carnegie libraries, and the dozen library grants in 1902 added up to $279,900. Then another dozen Ontario towns and cities got Carnegie libraries the following year. Why remain a "have not" town any longer? This miracle of a new library might as well happen here, too.

Through the winter the Bracebridge Library Board discussed applying to Carnegie for a library building as Albert Ecclestone strongly advocated. Nothing ventured, nothing gained, pretty well summed up the emerging attitude. The fact Bracebridge town council had not actively taken up the matter, even though the town's library had in some sense become a municipal institution in 1901, reflected for better and for worse the practical autonomy with which the library board continued to operate.

On their own, Albert Ecclestone, William Mahaffy, Moses Dickie, Francis Warne and a few others came to the view they should seek a Carnegie library. The advance of 1901 to status as a "free library" now needed to be consolidated in a new, purpose-built structure. Had not Carnegie himself proclaimed the very essence of a free library? "There is not such a cradle of democracy upon the earth as the Free Public Library, this republic of letters, where neither rank, office, nor wealth receives the slightest consideration." Such a democratic sentiment fitted with the spirit of Bracebridge, certainly as represented in the local vanguard of the public library movement by men like Francis Warne and Albert Ecclestone. If Carnegie saw a library as a democratic institution and was prepared to fund one in so natural a home for it as Bracebridge, surely that now mattered more than how the man first got the money he was now lavishly distributing. In Bracebridge as elsewhere, people found is easy to persuade themselves about being deserving of a coveted gift.

On March 9, 1903, Judge William C. Mahaffy, District Judge of Muskoka and chairman of the Bracebridge Library Board, strode uphill a hundred paces from his large stone home at the south end of Dominion Street overlooking the falls and still-frozen Bracebridge Bay, sat down at his large desk in the new Muskoka District Courthouse on Dominion Street, picked up his steel nib pen, and scratched out a three-page letter to Andrew Carnegie's private secretary, James Bartram, at 5 West 51st Street, New York.

"Dear Sir," Mahaffy began. "I beg leave to apply on the part of the Town of Bracebridge in the District of Muskoka, Ontario, Canada, for the amount of $5,000 to build a Free Public Library in the Town." It was that easy.

Mahaffy paused, his legally trained mind now contemplating the law of contract and the ping-pong process of offer and acceptance, not to mention the etiquette of appealing for a gift of money from a stranger in another country, then scratched out an odd second paragraph in the affected manner of speech of his day: "Under the extraordinarily kind offer of Mr. Andrew Carnegie for these purposes I presume no apology for this request is needed."

Judge Mahaffy then went on to sketch, for his intended reader in bustling New York City, how this correspondent was himself in an equally robust, if smaller, centre of expansive prosperity. Bracebridge, Mahaffy informed Bartram, "has about 3000 inhabitants, perhaps 3500, and is rapidly growing. For this growth the wonderful water power rights in the Town is responsible and now that this power is being intercepted people are awakening to the fact that the Town is surrounded with magnificent water pumps which will one by one be used and make this Town a very large place."

Turning to the central matter at hand, having argued his preliminary case, the judge explained to the gatekeeper of the Carnegie funds how the existing Bracebridge library "was made free just two years ago and since then we have added 600 volumes to it and considerably increased its conveniences. In 1901 we lent out 5,400 volumes, in 1902 we lent out 7,400, so the increase in use is encouraging. We have over 2,600 books valued at selling price at over $1600." Judge Mahaffy stated authoritatively that the Board was thinking "seriously" about obtaining "the sum of $5000 from Mr. Carnegie's beneficence, if possible." He added that "our Council have no doubt of the Town's willingness to expend $500 annually upon the maintenance of the building" and confirmed that "there will be no trouble about giving the site."

These were early days in developing the skills or even the proper form required to align a supplicant's desire with a benefactor's criteria, so Mahaffy ended his initial salvo to the Carnegie Foundation with this appeal: "Will you my dear sir have the goodness to advise me just what to do to enable us to secure the sum mentioned from Mr. Carnegie's bounty and very much oblige me."

Thus opened a protracted process. Half a decade would pass before books were placed on the shelves of a Carnegie library in Bracebridge. Even then it was a miracle the facility had been built at all.

AN INSPIRING PUBLIC BUILDING. Muskoka District Courthouse was built in 1900 by the Ontario Department of Public Works at the corner of Dominion and Ontario streets in central Bracebridge. Here Judge W.C. Mahaffy held court and wrote letters to Andrew Carnegie.

The building had a transforming effect. First, getting a new courthouse paid for by a senior level of government was a revelation in itself since Bracebridge had been paying its costs for administration of justice until then. Secondly, the courthouse inspired many Bracebridgites to realize that large organizations at a distance, such as the government of Ontario for this courthouse, the government of Canada for a post office and armories, and the Carnegie organization of New York for a library, could enhance the appearance and functions of the town through the building of really impressive public buildings otherwise far beyond the town's own financial means.

The new courthouse from which the chairman of the Bracebridge Library Board dispatched his appeal to New York in the winter of 1903 was itself one example among a growing number of how the town could build itself up with financial help from beyond the community's own limited resources.

Fifteen years earlier, in 1888, Muskoka and adjacent Parry Sound district to the north had been set up as a single judicial district, but within a decade Muskoka's own identity became more firmly established when the two were separated in 1898 and Muskoka made a "compact and united district" on its own. Then for the next 12 years the town of Bracebridge provided, at its own expense even though the cost of administering justice in the province was meant to be for the account of the provincial government, a courtroom, judge's chambers and other conveniences for the judicial precincts. This generous underwriting of another government's responsibility reflected the "can do" attitude in Bracebridge being applied to ensure proper provision of facilities for administering justice. It also was another manifestation of a strong democratic instinct pervading

CAMPAIGN HEADQUARTERS FOR PHILANTHROPY. In this library of his 91st Street mansion in New York City, Andrew Carnegie orchestrated breathtaking acts of funding libraries and world peace with more money than most governments could muster. Despite the town of Bracebridge's fumbling attempts to meet Carnegie's only two requirements—providing some land for the free building and agreeing to pay $1,000 a year for its operation—the "patron saint of libraries" would persevere. Bracebridge has since benefited from his library in the town for a century. *Carnegie Library of Pittsburgh*

Bracebridge to take charge of things locally. Still, the town had other uses for its money and was jubilant when the Ontario government began construction in July of 1899 on the district courthouse in Bracebridge, paid for by the government of Ontario. When the doors of the two-storey red brick architectural gem opened for the administration of justice a year later, a "jubilation" took place in the form of a banquet at the Queen's Hotel on June 20, 1900, gathering together some three dozen notables including the mayor, the judge, magistrates, the member of the legislature, members of council, doctors, local businessmen, lawyers and the sheriff. The mood was buoyant, uplifted by speeches on the "Progress" theme highlighting the importance of good public buildings in the capital town of Muskoka, for which the splendid courthouse now set the new high standard.

The new courthouse was not the only example. Other large organizations with resources to draw on had similarly arrived in town to build factories of all kinds. The clues were clear: the community could go ahead, with the help of outsiders. As this lesson sunk in, this model was becoming increasingly well established. Bracebridgites progressed by following a two-pronged strategy: preaching to outsiders the advantages of locating their business in town, and then following up with actual inducements and benefits to forge a partnership with them for mutual economic advantage.

By the time Mahaffy wrote Bartram in March 1903, this pattern had already developed to cookie-cutter perfection for promoting the town to outsiders. One began by tantalizing people by referring to the electric street lights, the health and sanitation of pure water piped throughout the municipality, good schools, many churches, a robust and diversified manufacturing sector, local farms with fresh produce, transportation by rail, road and water, and a strong retail section in town offering the latest in everything from ladies' fashions to books.

In that particular department, of course, things were indeed booming in this town that loved books. Not many communities of 3,000 had a Free Library bulging through its walls and three well-patronized bookstores. The thriving book culture and all it represented was intrinsic to this larger view that was part of the Bracebridge state of mind. The only thing still missing from this scene of earthly paradise was a proper library building.

The letters between Bracebridge and New York stretched over so many months they would display well as artifacts in an exhibit about the invention of the typewriter early in the twentieth century. Exchanges with the Carnegie organization began with Judge Mahaffy's pen-and-ink letter in 1903 as chairman of the board and ended with cleanly typed correspondence in 1916, which Hattie Dickie pounded out for her father Moses as secretary of the board on the library's Oliver typewriter. In between, the transition was ragged, reflecting the gradual uptake of a new technology and a transition in the skills and preferences of those corresponding.

Besides the technology of communication, there was the matter of the culture within which this correspondence was being conducted. Today someone in a Muskoka municipality who seeks a financial contribution using the online application form of the Bill and Melinda Gates Foundation is light years away from Judge W.C. Mahaffy sitting down to his desk in Bracebridge in 1903 to hand-write a letter to someone he did not know in New York City asking for $5,000 to build a new library, not just because of the contrast in technology or dollar amounts, but in the culture itself.

Today we know the world of philanthropy differently and every sports team and cultural group is expert in the art of getting grants and winning corporate sponsorships. In 1903, when Mahaffy made his awkward request from Bracebridge, thousands of others were penning similar appeals to Andrew Carnegie from all across Canada and the United States and around the world. Going through the archival records of the Carnegie Corporation today is to see both ends of these exchanges of correspondence back when a completely new form and culture of philanthropy was being born. There was no form to fill out, no etiquette about the matter, and little in the way of formal criteria for qualifying. Some made businesslike proposals, others were like family letters about the library, many exuded a mixture of pride in their community and desperation at the state of the community's library, and not a few, including Mahaffy in one letter, managed to misspell the name of the patron saint of libraries. Some just boldly demanded the money they felt was their due.

Turning to someone you did not know, who did not know your community, who lived in another country, and who indeed was controversial because he was a prominent capitalist who owned not a local mill but once the largest steel corporation in the world, was pioneer's work.

W.C. Mahaffy's opening appeal, to judge from the thick files of the Carnegie Foundation, was representative of others pouring in to Andrew Carnegie and James Bartram. Like Mahaffy's first letter, many entreaties were a mixture of boastful claims about the worthiness of the community awaiting a Carnegie library; evidence of preparedness, which in Bracebridge's case had been described both in terms of the pre-existing book culture of the town and of the local council's compliance to Carnegie conditions; and emotional ambivalence about how to actually pitch the appeal for funds.

In this last category, Mahaffy's wording was no more awkward than most. For example, another town the size of Bracebridge was Bradentown, Florida. From there, Mahaffy's counterpart, president of the library board Mrs. P.J. Bachman, testily wrote James Bartram that, "We seem to have been unable to make the situation regarding our present library clear to your corporation." Echoing the dilemma of Bracebridge and hundreds of other supplicants for Carnegie largesse, Bachman explained: "Our town has outgrown not only our building but our books. While we have been able to supply good fiction, we have not been able to buy reference books, and if you had heard our high school boys and girls make an appeal to our virtue at a public meeting before the election in December, when the question of a Public Library and the amount of taxation sufficient for same were to be voted on, you would realize how much our children feel the need of good books."

Andrew Carnegie had a rule of thumb about the amount of money he would give for a library that correlated to the size of a municipality. So James Bartram placed Bradentown and Bracebridge, regardless of what amount they asked for, in the same $10,000 category. This is why Mahaffy's request for $5,000 was doubled by New York, where they had learned from experience by this time constructing new libraries in Canada and the United States how much money was needed for a building of the calibre they desired.

Judge Mahaffy, finding himself uncertain and having no human contact with either Carnegie or Bartram, opted for a voice of grandiloquent obsequious that perhaps only those in the legal profession could achieve. As for Mahaffy's boosterism for Bracebridge, while reflecting a bit of Chamber of Commerce optimism for the future, it was quite modest alongside the bold assertions being made to Carnegie by many American towns concerning their singular importance and indeed uniqueness on the planet.

Seeking a Carnegie library took more than just a wistful desire for books and a building, more than a promoter's craving for an elegant central building to enhance real estate values and attract new businesses to the community. Getting a Carnegie library was serious business. Both as earnest money and with a long-term view, Carnegie required the municipal council in question to commit irrevocably to tax the local citizens enough every year to pay a full ten percent of the cost of the library for its ongoing operation. For a $100,000 library, a town would have to pledge $10,000 annually in perpetuity. This stipulation alone thinned the ranks of applicants.

Many towns applied for the money. Yet even more did not. It largely depended on how strong the book culture was in a particular community. And of those who did seek the philanthropist's funds, many were turned down. There were towns Carnegie refused because he considered them too indebted already and did not want good money following bad. Some applicants, it turned out as Bartram dug into the facts, already had adequate library facilities. Also, as Peter Krass notes in his biography of Carnegie when reviewing reasons some applicants never made it, he would not pay if another rich benefactor in the community could. Nor did he give "to state libraries, state historical society libraries, and proprietary or subscription libraries because they had access to alternative funding." Had Bracebridge not converted from a Mechanics' Institute Library to a Free Library, for instance, it would have been automatically disqualified by these criteria.

Not every town got what it wanted, and some that were initially well advanced in the application process forfeited their free library due to "fumbling management of the library request," which pretty much is the fate that seemed to be awaiting the town of Bracebridge.

Many months after Mahaffy's March 9, 1903, letter of solicitation for Carnegie funds, it was clear the new library would not appear as swiftly as first fantasies had suggested might be possible. No building site had even been chosen. Although Mahaffy had intimated there would be no problem providing the land, when explaining to Bartram that the town supported the move, fully two and a half years passed and the matter had still not formally come before Bracebridge town council.

Telling Bartram the town was ready to comply with Carnegie's conditions had to be based on conversations with councillors, because they had certainly not passed a resolution to this effect. In a small town everyone knew what was going on. The judge worked three doors along the same street from the town hall in the courthouse, and lived only a couple doors beyond that. Moses Dickie, the librarian, lived two and a half blocks from the town hall, where the library was operating. The judge often appeared before council to deal with various matters or was being requested by council to do certain things for judicial administration, but he was also personally engaged throughout this very same period in a prolonged negotiation to sell the town a parcel of his land that ran right down to Bracebridge Bay. At this time Dominion Street ran straight down a very steep hill to the river and the steamboat wharf, which was located near the outlet of Bracebridge Bay. The town wanted to build a new wharf at the head of the bay just below the falls, and needed to buy some of Mahaffy's land in order to do so. They were talking all the time.

Over the 32 months between the date Mahaffy opened his correspondence with Bartram about the library and the first motion passed by council on the subject, it is inconceivable that the chair of the library board would not have broached the topic of suitable land for a new library with the town's political leadership. Still, and most oddly, nothing happened during all that time. Mahaffy was often before council, but all that the minutes record relating to the library during this period of presumed preparation for winning the nod from Carnegie, were Judge Mahaffy's annual appearances to make his appeals of despair, seeking an increase in the mill rate from one-half to three-quarters in support of the library, or alternatively a grant of $100, to keep the beleaguered operation going.

On Monday evening, November 13, 1905, the Carnegie matter came before the Bracebridge Council as an item of business for the first time. With the mayor absent for this meeting and councillor Sam Bowyer "voted to the chair" in his place, council heard Moses Dickie, appearing as a representative of the Free Library Board, "ask support of council for the proposition of the Board to obtain a grant from Mr. Carnegie." He explained that it was necessary for council to grant a free site and guarantee 10 per cent of the amount granted for maintenance. Councillor George W. Ecclestone, Albert's brother, then moved, seconded by Councillor David Sweetman, "that this Council grant a free site and guarantee 10% of the grant for maintenance of the proposed Carnegie Library." The motion carried.

Now it was time to find some land, hardly a problem in a new town on the vast Canadian spread. With recurring pressure from the library board to get moving, town council turned its attention to a suitable location for the desperately needed new building. The first place considered was the recently created Memorial Park in the centre of town. This would have meant filling in the open space of a fairly elegant central park with a structure that would end the new park's brief existence to memorialize the recent South African-British Empire war and the young men of town who died fighting the self-defending Afrikaans "Boers" or Dutch farmers who lived there. However, it did not take long to register with the elected councillors that Memorial Park was a non-starter as a site for the new library.

One of its own members, councillor and newspaper publisher George Thomas, was among those leading the charge to kill the idea, and not just because his majestic home on Kimberley Avenue at the intersection of Manitoba Street (today a restaurant) overlooked the park. He sensibly opposed filling in the newly created park with buildings. It had only recently been cleared of its houses and shops by a fire that levelled the whole block except for Harry Boyer's marble works at the south end, which Boyer then relocated farther south on Manitoba Street, making the park area even larger. Vigorous protest against using the park sent town councillors scurrying to find a different location, although their initial instinct to place the prestigious new library in an open space within a park-like setting was inspired. Unfortunately, that townscape concept became a casualty after this opening skirmish.

Months had been lost. It was time to start again.

The next site to be proposed came as a matter of sheer inspiration as councillors sat around their cramped council chamber in the Bracebridge

NO PLACE FOR A LIBRARY. Memorial Park, created in the centre of town on a large triangle of land after shops and homes in this block burned at the turn of the 20th century, memorialized the British Empire's war against Dutch homesteaders in South Africa in which young men from Bracebridge fought and died.

In the picture above the Park is seen from Kimberley Avenue looking east to stores and residences on Manitoba Street. The townspeople, seen assembling in the park for a public event, protested vigorously when town council proposed building a new Carnegie library on this very spot. Below left, Memorial Park is seen from the other side, looking west to Kimberley Avenue, with cannon and bandstand. The third view, from the north end looking southeast down Manitoba Street and south along Kimberley Avenue, shows the band shell in the middle. Townspeople and G.H.O. Thomas of the *Bracebridge Gazette* protested infilling the Park with a new Carnegie library.

Rather than having a library built in it, the park continued to enrich the cultural life of Bracebridge in other ways, such as Monday evening concerts in the summer by the Citizens' Band, readings by famous Canadian authors such as Bliss Carmen in the 1920s as part of Canadian Chautauqua's program to bring culture to the people, the Muskoka Arts & Crafts shows until they outgrew the space and moved to Williams' Park by the river, and Robert Munsch overflow events with kids from the public library in August 1997.

Council's initial sound instinct to site the library in a space with lots of room around it got lost in the ensuing controversies.

Town Hall. The building was an imposing red brick two-storey structure on Dominion Street, but it had been built in 1881 when the town was smaller. There had been some thought that despite all the other buildings needed, expenditure for a new and improved town hall would be justified. Suddenly, it all seemed to come together. Council would sell the town hall in which they were meeting to Mr. Carnegie so that he could then give it back to Bracebridge as its free library. They could then use the windfall either to build a new town hall in the style of Gravenhurst's prestigious Opera House, which everyone in Bracebridge envied, or perhaps just move into an industrial site outside town. With enthusiasm, they voted to set the price for Bracebridge Town Hall at $6,000, more than double what it had cost 25 years earlier. With a smug smile about this masterstroke, they prepared to once again best Gravenhurst while serving Bracebridge.

The wrinkle with this deal, however, was that the books were already in the town hall. After the post office relocated from its temporary accommodation following the fire that destroyed the earlier post office facilities back onto the main street, the library moved into the Dominion Street municipal premises. This brazen idea to sell Carnegie the Bracebridge Town Hall would only work if he didn't realize that effectively nothing would change in Bracebridge regarding the library facilities as a result of his "beneficent" payment. The town fathers were in effect attempting an elaborate scam on the American millionaire.

It was with deep consternation, therefore, that they read this swift response, dated January 22, 1900, and addressed to Mahaffy, from Carnegie's personal secretary, James Bartram:

Dear Sir,
Yours of January 6th and schedule received. If the town has a town hall which they have no use for and which they propose to turn over for the library building, there is no need of Mr. Carnegie's assistance.

This was a clear message. It not only disdainfully rejected the proposed purchase of the existing municipal building but intimated as well that with so many other applicants for Carnegie funds he would deal with municipalities taking the venture more seriously than Bracebridge. Overnight, the prospect of getting any Carnegie library at all, let alone a new town hall in the bargain, had evaporated.

The library board members became as apoplectic as their phlegmatic natures would allow. Such news from New York meant it was time for immediate back-pedalling. In desperate hope of keeping the prospect for

TOWN HALL LIBRARY. Bracebridge town hall, constructed in 1881, was indicative of the high building standards of the frontier town and reflected a belief on the part of the town fathers that as you build, so you become.

In the early 1890s a room in the Bracebridge town hall was offered rent-free as a place for the overcrowded Mechanic's Institute library to relocate its collection. As a central public place in town, this was ideal for the Institute's library, but because the Institute itself was not legally a public entity some citizens objected to assisting a "private" organization in town's facilities.

The Town's initial offer of space in this building was delayed, however, when fire on Manitoba Street destroyed the post office and council decided, instead of giving the space free to the library, to rent it to the post master in the emergency. In time, the post office returned to the main street and the Bracebridge library was housed in this building until the end of 1907.

a new library alive, Mahaffy sent a letter in which he tried to save the situation. He wrote that the "Mayor [had] intimated the willingness of the Council to give the site of the present Town Hall, free, and the building at a considerable reduction," but hedged his bets by adding, "our Board considered this as an extra offer over and above a free site which the Council stand ready to make good without any building whatever." He went on to defend the town hall proposal: "My idea was simply to lay the matter before you sir for your consideration if you thought it would affect a saving, why it would make the grant so much less and please the Town quite as well, the whole matter being subject to your architect's plans and ideas at any rate."

As well as confusing the issue of what the town proposed, Mahaffy further complicated things by stating that the mayor had not been informed about the offer and that there was division within the library board regarding the suitability of the town hall for the library: "I did not go into the matter with the Mayor as all our Board were not desirous of acquiring the Town Hall and thought before saying anything about it you should express your approval."

He concluded by stating, "The Town Council no doubt wishes to build a new and larger Town Hall, hence their willingness to overdo their part. There is talk now of getting the Government to turn over the Town Hall into a Post Office, the old one being now too small. However, this idea is merely a suggestion aside from the free and unencumbered site and may be dismissed without changing our status in the least."

William Mahaffy's quick correction only made matters worse. He perplexingly explained that somehow the town wanted both the town hall proposal and a new structure to go ahead. The town hall would be offered

"TELL THEM THEY HAVE NO NEED OF MY MONEY." James Bartram worked closely with Andrew Carnegie as his secretary. Here he records a letter as the pioneer philanthropist dictates. When Bracebridge council offered on January 6, 1904, to sell Carnegie the town hall, saying it would make an ideal library, a snappy reply from Bartram in New York on January 22 stated simply, "If the town has a town hall which they have no use for and which they propose to turn over for the library building, there is no need of Mr. Carnegie's assistance." *Carnegie Library of Pittsburgh.*

as a free site, even though money was to be paid for it by Mr. Carnegie. The land for a new building would still be provided. The town hall already offered to Carnegie was also being considered for a post office. Acquisition of the town hall "would make the grant so much less" even though he had asked for $5,000 and the town wanted $6,000 for the building. All this should have been enough for James Bartram to close the file on this town up in Canada.

However, the people of Bracebridge can be forever grateful that James Bartram was blessed with patience, that through Andrew Carnegie he had heard from his supportive friend John Walker that Bracebridge was a most deserving case, and that Bartram extended to others the kindness Andrew Carnegie showed to him. So he sat down and wrote another letter to Mahaffy. Addressing the suitability of the town hall for use as a library, Bartram stated: "If the building is not good enough for municipal offices and town hall, it is not likely to be good enough for a library. However, you give no particulars. We should have photograph of the building and plan showing the accommodation, also particulars of cost of the building and of the site separately and how much the Council wish to realize on the building."

This solicitous letter from Bartram, so different in tone from his prior missive, sent the Bracebridge crew into months of activity on the evident indication that the town hall proposal was, indeed, still viable. While these further efforts aimed at selling the Bracebridge town hall to Andrew Carnegie would turn out to be a hugely misguided waste of time, at least the lines of communication with New York were still open.

This is where things took another inexplicable twist. It was almost as if a second file was being opened. Ignoring the earlier negotiations, the town of Bracebridge simultaneously started along a parallel track to get Carnegie money, as if the town hall proposal had never been made. On November 13, 1905, the Bracebridge town council passed a resolution confirming its commitment to providing a site for a new library and support for its maintenance should Carnegie agree to provide a grant of "$15000 or less" for its construction.

This was about how things should have been proceeding in the normal course, except that council had now tripled the amount originally requested by Board Chairman Mahaffy.

How odd, though, that William Mahaffy would then, as if his first letter of March 1903 had never been written, nor his previous letters about the town hall proposal ever been sent, next sign such a letter as the following, dated January 6, 1906, and addressed to Andrew Carnegie himself:

Sir,

The Board of the Bracebridge Public Library do hereby respectfully petition you, Sir, in response to your most munificent offer of assistance to Public Libraries, for a grant to the Public Library at Bracebridge, Ontario, Canada.

The Board have conferred with the Municipal Council of Bracebridge on the subject and found them unanimously in favour of soliciting your kindly aid for this purpose to the amount of between $10000 and $15000, for the erection of a Library here.

The Council has undertaken to give the Board the deed of a capital site for the Building as soon as your consent to the grant shall be obtained, and also to furnish the necessary ten per cent annually, of the amount of the grant, for the maintenance of the Library and Building up to the sum of $1500.

Bracebridge is the District Town of the District of Muskoka and the seat of the law courts. It is situated on the Muskoka River and is the great supply centre for the tourists on the Muskoka Lakes, and a favourite rendezvous for the tourists through the season.

The population is over 3000 and steadily increasing and it is a very busy and prosperous town.

The Library here was formerly of the pay kind, but about five years ago was made free, under the Ontario Act, since when it has gone forward with immense strides and is wonderfully patronized and frequented by the people generally, and though it has twice changed its location, for larger premises, it is now again crippled for want of space, and in dire need of a whole building to itself to meet the constantly growing demands upon it and there is now no sufficient accommodation to be found for it in the Town.

Should this petition be favourably entertained by you, Sir, the intention is to begin building as soon as proper plans could be obtained and sanctioned by you.

Herewith is transmitted a resolution of the Bracebridge Council supporting this petition.

We take advantage of the season sir to wish you many happy returns of the same

and are, sir, yours very respectfully,
the Bracebridge Free Library Board,
W.C. Mahaffy, chairman
Moses J. Dickie, secretary

This businesslike letter could have served as a model for all such appeals. Its clarity of purpose, succinct presentation of the necessary information, and cordially upbeat tone made it seem that someone in Bracebridge had been taking the courses of Andrew Carnegie's unrelated namesake, Dale Carnegie, who at this same time was teaching North Americans how to win friends and influence people through clear and confident communication.

The very next month, however, the council was again walking down the other side of the street, with its alternate proposal about the town hall. On February 12, 1905, the town clerk recorded that the town was willing to grant the town hall site to the library board for free and the building itself for a sum of $6,000. At one point $8,000 was proposed, then $7,000.

James Bartram simply chose to accept that the library and municipal leaders of Bracebridge were a mixed-up lot who were promoting different proposals for a new library on different days. In his next letter to Mahaffy, Bartram asked: "Will you kindly explain how it is that an effort has been made to sell a building costing $5000 twenty years old to Mr. Carnegie for $6000? I don't believe you would get $1000 for that building in Bracebridge over and above the value of the ground on which it is built."

Rather than discerning that Andrew Carnegie's right-hand man was nonplussed by this effort to put one over on the great benefactor, the Bracebridge folk who still zealously held to the idea that the town hall should be fobbed off as a library only tried harder to justify what, to James Bartram, was indefensible. What could turn the tide better, they thought, than an appraisal? Accordingly, Alfred Hunt, the town's assessor, produced a letter stating that the town hall building had a value of $7000, and that the site a value of $1500.

This was a valuation provided to support the interest of the Town of Bracebridge prepared by the assessor employed by the Town of Bracebridge. How anyone seriously thought such a document could do anything but annoy the Carnegie people from whom they were seeking a free library is puzzling, as is the fact that Judge Mahaffy even chose to forward it to Bartram. Not only did he do so, but he also combined it with an extended letter pleading his fullest case yet for the town hall proposal, as if he had not written his utterly different letter just five weeks earlier. It is thought that individuals may have split personalities, but this is evidence of a municipality in that condition.

His letter certainly made clear that Judge Mahaffy had himself now become an advocate for the town hall option, which only confounded the prospects for Bracebridge ever getting a Carnegie library, since it was really no option at all. Despite his solicitation of support for the "Town Hall" library from "a great many" inhabitants around town and his suggestion that this was a "good business" for Carnegie, the kind of retrofitting of existing buildings, even if done with plans prepared by the Carnegie-approved architects from Lindsay or Berlin as Mahaffy suggested, was not at all the program being rolled out from New York under Andrew Carnegie's library philanthropy. A definite idea about the design, look and function of a modern library called, under the Carnegie plan, for new purpose-built structures. Money was not the issue. What mattered was the design of the library, and also not trying to take old man Carnegie for a ride.

Although those in Bracebridge pursuing the cause of a new library were aware of grand libraries in the larger cities of the world, had seen pictures or even visited a few of them, they evidently just could not envisage such a structure in the local context, even though it could be theirs for the taking. A narrowness of vision constrains many who find themselves in elected office, a perspective reinforced by complaining electors reluctant to give up their money in taxes. The result is frugality in public spending. Such a condition is particularly prevalent in smaller communities where the tax base is small. For council to think about the Bracebridge Town Hall as a building for the library was in one sense an advance because it was a handsome building, even if in another sense their motives were dubious to say the least. However, even to the extent this town hall proposal might charitably be viewed as progress, it was now out of step with what was happening with libraries.

A different and larger view was emerging about the architecture and public purposes of library buildings, an outlook that entailed social engineering along with structural design. Library buildings constructed "the right way" could help transform society, inspiring and moulding patrons by their physical attributes just as the books they contained could uplift and redirect their lives intellectually. This second, larger "library culture" was the one embraced by Andrew Carnegie and his personal secretary Bartram, who administered the funding applications for libraries with a strong hand to see this advanced approach translated into communities all over North America. The celebrated cadre of "Carnegie libraries" would not have been created if all that the Carnegie millions had been spent on was retrofitting old town halls and similar structures.

Not just Bracebridge but a few other places, too, tried to fob off existing buildings on Carnegie, as if any place with room for bookshelves could serve as a public library. Like Bracebridge, they appeared to appreciate neither the very specific requirements for buildings built uniquely to facilitate the many functions of a library, nor the diverse needs of those who work in them and use their services. Andrew Carnegie believed in the importance of freedom and open accessibility of a public library, including the ability of readers to stroll through open stacks and browse randomly at what was available.

This goal, in order to be reconciled with the fact that budgets of smaller libraries had money enough for just one librarian, and also with the well-founded fear of library administrators that open stacks would lead to stolen books, was to be achieved by new thinking from architects. Carnegie libraries adopted design principles that enabled a single librarian to supervise the entire operation from a central position at her circulation desk, with sightlines that enabled her to keep the whole operation in view, with open-stacks that allowed patrons to roam and find books on their own.

In major cities around the world battles raged between designers and users of libraries, with many interests and values contending with one another as new thinking and radically different library buildings took shape. Issues about children in libraries, for instance, were similarly addressed through revolutionary designs in the buildings as much as by policies of exclusion. The Carnegie millions were clearly aligned on one side of this historic battle over the nature of such important cultural institutions and marked a turning point in the democratization of the "public" library. This meant older buildings designed for utterly different purposes, such as Bracebridge Town Hall, were non-starters.

Big principles like those just mentioned about the goals of public libraries and architectural design to achieve them do not exist in the abstract. They only take form and acquire meaning in specific application on the ground in real people's lives and neighbourhoods. That is why the nature of the library building for Bracebridge, if it was to be Andrew Carnegie's funds that paid for it, was not a minor detail. It entailed fundamental choice about structured access to civilization's culture by the people.

In Bracebridge the search continued for a suitable site for the new library, while Bartram in New York was becoming increasingly exasperated trying to get a straight answer on the real value of the town hall. More efforts yet ensued to advance the town hall library proposal in trying to get a handle on the value of the building. The report by Alfred Hunt, the town's assessor, only stirred up the muddy waters.

Mahaffy, rather than calling it quits and moving on to simply get a nice new library on a fresh piece of vacant land, in accordance with the other track on which he had been simultaneously dealing with Carnegie, called on a dozen different contractors to supply him with written valuations that might be crisper. After rashly sending a note to Bartram defending Hunt's letter, Mahaffy finally seemed ready to concede the point and recognize that Carnegie was not going to be duped into paying for the town hall when other assessments contradicted Hunt's view. The ever-patient Bartram then threw Mahaffy a lifeline. Still trying to find light at the end of the tunnel, Bartram again clarified how little was really required to get a splendid new library for free:

March 24, 1906

W.C. Mahaffy
Chairman Library Board
Bracebridge

Dear Sir,

Responding to your recommendations on behalf of Bracebridge—
If the City were by resolution of Council to maintain a Free Public Library, at a cost of not less than One Thousand Dollars a year, and provide a suitable site for the building, Mr. Carnegie will be glad to give Ten Thousand Dollars to erect a new Public Library Building for Bracebridge.

Respctfly yrs,
Jas. Bartram
P. Secty

Although Bracebridge council had already passed resolutions to this effect, it did so once again.

With matters dragging out as some Bracebridgites continued to flog the stillborn proposal for the town hall library in the forlorn hope they could yet bring it to life, others realized they should look around for a different parcel of land somewhere central in town.

This was when all eyes turned, not onto the building itself for the new library, but a patch of land behind the town hall. On Monday April 9, 1906, Moses Dickie appeared before council "to urge on the library scheme," reported the *Gazette*, because "time is getting short and something must be done soon." Dickie said that if council was "not disposed to buy property for the library then the board was willing to fall back on council's proposition of the ground immediately back of the town hall." This land hidden away was also at the rear of commercial buildings on the main street, room enough for a jail and an alleyway for deliveries to the shops, but hardly for a new public library, although, amazingly, the librarian himself contended "all that was required was 35 x 35 feet." His idea was "to have the stacks of books down stairs and the reading room in the upper part. The librarian will have his office immediately at the entrance to the stairs."

This prospect of open access to the stacks concerned several councillors, one saying he thought it "a funny way to allow the citizens to go down and handle the books as they please." Librarian Dickie, however, assured them "this was the up-to-date method in vogue in many libraries."

Open access to the books was a given with a Carnegie library, but to even get one, the two primary conditions of Andrew Carnegie—that land be given and money provided for the library's upkeep—first had to be met. Opinion on these was divided and feelings ran high.

On the need to provide the financial commitment, George Thomas launched a major attack. He wondered "if the town was committed to this library scheme" and said he did not believe council "had any moral right to commit the town to $1,000 maintenance for all time to come." He said the town already gave "almost that amount" and added, "according to law the library is entitled to a rate of ¾ of a mill." These were contradictory arguments, for if the town was already giving at the level he objected to, what was his objection to saying it would continue to do so—especially if getting a $10,000 building needed for Bracebridge was part of the bargain. It was odd to question the "moral right" when he himself noted that a legal right already existed by statute for the library to get money at these levels. It was odd, as well, for the man heading the property committee looking for a library site to seek to prevent a condition precedent for the library being fulfilled. These positions mattered, because Thomas had vote on council and voice in his newspaper. Henry Bird, at this meeting in April 1906, simply answered Thomas by saying he "considered the library offered an education second only to that of the school and financial support should be continued." Thomas would not relent, however, and the repercussions would create problems for the next decade,

On the need to give land for the building, Councillor Bird strongly objected to giving the land behind the town hall. "There is no saying when it might be required," he objected. Rather than this unimaginative option of using land behind the town hall, Bird invited council to turn its sights elsewhere. He "had a plan whereby a piece of land that could not be utilized for anything else would be quite suitable."

Two blocks to the west of the town hall, where the Knox Presbyterian Church stood at the corner of Quebec and McMurray streets, lay an odd piece of property right in front of the church. This tiny triangle of steeply sloping land, formed by the intersections of Quebec and McMurray streets and Tanbark Hill, was referred to locally as "the gore," using the Old English term for a triangular parcel of land.

Councillors in general "seemed favourable," reported the *Gazette*. Librarian Moses Dickie liked it: it was only two doors from his home. Councillor Henry Bird liked it: he was accustomed to building on slopes. Councillor Thomas even liked it, provided a new library constructed on the gore also include a gymnasium and public baths. They all considered it central, but Bird additionally noted that "as most of the reading was done in the winter time, a large bulk of the fourth ward citizens could cross the river on the scows and reach the building in no time." Their excitement about this new proposed site for the Carnegie library had allowed their imaginations to detach from reality. The small gore was available land because to this point it had wisely been considered unusable.

George Thomas, as chair of the property committee of council, was directed to investigate and make a recommendation to council. They seemed intent. The resolution authorized him to employ a surveyor and take legal advice on the matter.

It is almost a cause for wondering what Bracebridge's leaders thought the new library, any library for that matter, would really be like. George Thomas, following up in his newspaper on April 19, urged town council (of which he was a part) to "Remember the Gym" and observed that a place of recreation such as a modern gym could "go very well hand in hand with the reading room. Any why not? One is for the upbuilding of the body and the other of the mind." He was talking about a building to be constructed on a small triangular slope that at its largest would be approximately 37 by 40 feet. That would be some gymnasium and reading room, for the 3,000 people living in Bracebridge, not to mention the books that might also go in a library. However, there was more. Thomas also exhorted his readers and urged town council to ensure that a base-

IN THE SHADOW OF THE STEEPLE, NOT. Knox Presbyterian Church at the corner of McMurray and Quebec streets is what library patrons would have seen, had Bracebridge council succeeded in landing the new Carnegie library on the tiny triangle of land bounded by McMurray and Quebec streets and the Tanbark Hill road after three of council's earlier proposed sites had been rejected. The Carnegie organization in New York and a vociferously outspoken group of townspeople protested using this tiny, steeply sloping site, although G.H.O. Thomas, writing in the *Bracebridge Gazette*, proposed seriously that, if built here, the library should even include a gymnasium and public baths. Eventually, the library was instead built were it stands today. As for the church, it was later bricked, subsequently destroyed by fire on January 25, 1931, then replaced by the present structure.

ment be constructed in this library for public baths and saw "no reason they could not be run in connection with the library here."

The property committee recommended the site. Town council passed a resolution on May 3 approving the transfer of the parcel to the library board. Again the town was in an uproar, with protests that the size was too small, the slope too steep, the angle too restricting of design, and generally, that it was a very ill-conceived idea.

A few days later, however, board chairman Mahaffy transmitted the good news that a site had been chosen to Andrew Carnegie. An exasperated Bartram replied to this proposal: "Sir, The amount of land described is inadequate for the purpose of a library." Had he known about its shape and slope, Bartram might have used a stronger adjective than "inadequate." Bracebridge was slipping steadily closer to the edge of rejection for a Carnegie library.

Fortunately, there is only so much land within Bracebridge town limits. By the law of averages, council was bound to hit upon a location eventually that Bartram and the townsfolk would approve of, and this it did by looking north of the town hall to where Dominion Street intersects Manitoba Street, the principal thoroughfare. On the west side of this angular intersection lay a large area of open land. How it escaped earlier consideration for the library is beyond all speculation.

Before Memorial Park was created, the triangle of land formed by the junction of Manitoba Street and Kimberley Avenue was quite large. It has long since been minimized by buildings filling in the south part and the widening roads and sidewalks encroaching on its other two sides, but in its early years it was big and had a wooden octagonal bandstand with a conical roof and a flagpole flying the Union Jack among its features. The area was alive with entertainment and became known as "the Broadway of Bracebridge." There was even more to this central section of town that earned it that designation. Across from this triangular town square was "quite a big field," as Redmond Thomas, son of George Thomas, recalled in his 1968 book *Reminiscences* published in Bracebridge by the Herald-Gazette Press. This "very large space" was "rented out from time to time to such visiting activities as the merry-go-round and the medicine shows." The merry-go-round was a big steam-powered affair that ran on a heavy circular steel track. The medicine shows coming to Bracebridge were presented in this field at night on a wagon or small stage by the light of coal oil flares.

The usual show, as Thomas reminisced, "was put on by an entertainer, generally a burnt-cork coloured man, whose program was jokes, songs and banjo music and who was sometimes assisted by the spieler. Between numbers the spieler gave his pitch to sell his medicine products—maybe a wonderful oil made from his own secret formula, guaranteed to be the best thing in the world for humans, horses and harness. Those spielers were marvels of smooth loquacity." But once the Memorial Park was created at the end of the war against South Africa, the bandstand was moved up the street to it and that brought down the curtains on "Broadway." The area "was no longer a prestigious location for outdoor entertainment." The merry-go-round then operated closer to the Grand Trunk Railway by which it travelled from town to town, the medicine shows moved to hotel yards, and as an outdoor entertainment area this open place in central Bracebridge "was already dead by the time the present Carnegie Library came into use in 1907 on the former field."

There was, in other words, a huge area of land readily available for a

LOCATION, LOCATION, LOCATION! Bracebridge town council passed many different resolutions in 1905 and 1906 about the library site and the town's degree of financial support for the facility, some at cross-purposes with others, one the opposite of Carnegie's two basic conditions, trying to square the circle in its efforts to get money from Andrew Carnegie for a town library.

In the front row of this picture of the 1906 Bracebridge council are (from left) town clerk Alexander C. Salmon, Mayor Peter A. Smith, councillors Henry J. Bird and Fred Sander. Across the back are councillors George H.O. Thomas, George W. Ecclestone, Samuel H. Armstrong and John Thomson.

UNNECESSARY AND EXTRAVAGANT. Town council frequently displayed reluctance to spend money on the Bracebridge library, but this did not necessarily mean the citizens' representatives were opposed to book culture in the community. Some councillors were just tight-fisted about everything. One of many examples of this came in 1906, the same year council's pusillanimous instincts were jeopardizing Bracebridge's chances for getting a free Carnegie library. When this bridge over the river connecting the centre of town to the Hunt's Hill ward replaced an earlier wooden structure, still visible in this photograph, the recorded attitude of a couple of council members was that building a new bridge to replace the low wooden one was "unnecessary and extravagant."

large library with spacious grounds to heighten the elegance of the town, and it had been there all along during the three years of looking. Yet once the tiny hillside gore which councillors Henry Bird and George Thomas favoured had been rejected, they both turned against the next proposal to use the flat, available, plentiful and open space in the centre of town.

Bird would resign. Thomas for his part would now argue in his newspaper that just giving the $1,000 a year to townspeople and letting them buy their own books would not only be smarter but also save the hassle of looking after an unnecessary building. And in his other instrument of local power, the council chamber, he now sought to prove he had been right all along that "you never get anything for free." He opposed the Carnegie requirement for ongoing financial support of the library, at $1,000 a year, as "exorbitant."

At a special afternoon meeting on Tuesday, June 19, 1906, the day finally arrived for Bracebridge council to rescind its previous grant of the gore to the library board and instead grant a bit of this large open space fronting on the main street of town. Councillor George Thomas stayed away. Councillor Samuel Armstrong moved "that in view of the unsuitability of the site given to the Library Board for the Carnegie Library, this council grant to the said Library Board a portion of lot 39 Manitoba Street West now owned by the corporation and consisting of the north easterly corner of the said lot with a frontage on Manitoba Street of 40' and extending back from the said street 50', and that the grant to the Library Board made on May 3, 1906 be and the same is hereby annulled." Councillor Fred Sander seconded the motion.

At the end of all this effort Bracebridge, the community that had created its first library even before it had been incorporated, a municipality on track to get a modern and stately library for free, the town that had displayed such progressive government in the recent past creating an electricity system to serve the people, could not now rise to the occasion in providing any element of those three attributes for a library site to serve the people. The major new public building, and all the space and services it would require around it, was to be, if this small-minded measure even passed, crammed onto a lot no larger than the combined cemetery plots of the councillors.

The resolution carried on a recorded vote with only a minority the seven-member body actually supporting it. Three councillors, Sam Armstrong, Fred Sander and John Thomson, voted in favour. Mayor Peter

SHORTSIGHTED LEADER? Peter A. Smith, manager of Muskoka Leather Company, was mayor of Bracebridge from 1904 to 1906 at the height of protracted intercessions with Andrew Carnegie over a series of improbable sites for a new library in the community. The town ended up giving a lot only 40 by 50 feet for a major new public building, already a problem at the time and an even more aggravating one a century later.

Smith withheld his vote. Councillor Thomas was absent. Councillor George Ecclestone, Albert's brother, abstained, and councillor Henry Bird voted against. Even this minimum level of support for the library from the now generally reluctant and hostile council was only to give the library board an inadequate lot for a major public building, although there was plenty more available land owned by the town in this open space previously used for visiting circuses and other civic sport.

Once council had acted, board chairman Mahaffy wrote to Andrew Carnegie informing him of the next proposed site for the library, but based on experience now simply transmitted the information without comment or pleading. This time the Carnegie people in New York agreed about the land.

Architect George M. Miller of Toronto, then at the height of his professional career designing and consulting on buildings for the Massey family such as Massey Hall and the University of Toronto's Hart House and Lillian Massey Building, was awarded the commission for the Bracebridge Carnegie library. Having travelled over so much empty land to get to Bracebridge, he looked with disbelief at the minuscule lot, 40 by 50 feet. More room was needed for such a public structure.

On July 9, 1906, Moses Dickie re-appeared before council, thanking them again for the site on Manitoba Street, but explaining that the building would be 50 feet deep and that "the piece granted would cramp the library board for room." It was moved "that the Free Library Board be given an extra 20' on the rear of the lot" and the motion carried with four votes. Henry Bird, now obstinate, voted against. George Thomas, miffed, absented himself from the meeting.

This small piece of property, seen as "cramping the board for room" within the first few days, and causing an appeal for more land within a month, was a severe problem for building at the time. The library was constructed to the full 40-foot width of the lot, never to be graciously set off by grounds the way lovely public buildings with space for gardens and walkways, lawns and benches, can enhance the appearance of a community and give citizens a pride of place. Bracebridge town council of 1906 bequeathed a sour legacy to the town. Despite far more available land at the site, which the town owned, the library was cramped in its initial 1907 design and construction. The land had not expanded by the 1980s when the town was bigger and enlargement of the library building was severely constrained. The legacy of the town fathers of 1906 continues undiminished today, when further expansion of the library is required.

But why commit municipal sabotage just one way if you can do it twice? Councillor Thomas also moved, and council passed, a resolution that the town pay an annual amount to support the library "not to exceed one thousand dollars annually," which was a back-door way of actually paying very little. The council that tried to foist a used town hall as a new library was a council that now passed a resolution to do the opposite of what they had explicitly undertaken to do. The Carnegie folks spotted this subterfuge and sent correct wording from New York, and council passed yet another resolution, this time to conform to their agreement. The annual grant to the library was never to be *less* than $1,000.

Wherever they were located, the Carnegie libraries boosted library service for millions in ways that would not otherwise have happened. Andrew Carnegie's concentrated largess in a relatively short time-frame exceeded anything municipal governments with their local library boards could accomplish or even in most cases dream about. Nor was it a program any state or provincial government with its modest operating grants to existing libraries had either contemplated or could afford. The approximately $60,000,000 flowing from the Carnegie Corporation to cover the capital costs of newly constructed, purpose-built libraries would be close to $1.5 billion in today's currency.

At last, $10,000 of that amount would make its way to Bracebridge.

EIGHT

Building a Carnegie Library

While it is true that a Carnegie library was only a building—Carnegie did not supply the books or pay for staff—it was much more than just bricks and mortar. It was a structure that came with a philosophy of free accessibility and cultural ennoblement incorporated into its very design. Invariably a Carnegie library also became a prominent edifice of inspiration on the local landscape. Libraries under Andrew Carnegie's patronage vied with other public institutions like churches and banks being constructed in this early twentieth-century, pre-war era, and usually outdid them. They were all built to the highest standards. Any place is improved by the presence of books, but these public citadels would improve both the books and those who came to read them by their atmosphere of integrity and grandeur.

Toronto architect George M. Miller, born in 1854 and in sole practice since 1886, was in his early 50s and at the height of his prominent career when he received the nod from the Carnegie Corporation to design the new Bracebridge library. Exuding an abiding personal interest in the buildings he designed, Miller was keen to accept his professional responsibility for directly overseeing details of construction at all stages. In this, his fastidious perfectionism was its own reward. Many of the structures he designed in the provincial capital are today listed in the *City of Toronto Inventory of Heritage Properties*, including the Gladstone, Havergal Ladies College, City Dairy and Stables, and Wycliffe College Chapel. He was responsible for modifications to Hart Massey's house and for the plans of the Lillian Massey Household Sciences Building at the University of Toronto. Miller served also as consultant for Massey Hall. His commis-

READY FOR A LIBRARY. Two views of Bracebridge give a sense of the physical town around the time the Carnegie library was being built to enhance the cultural town within. The five-storey Hess Furniture Factory in the right foreground of the top picture, and the Bird Woollen Mill in the foreground of the bottom scene, highlight the industrial side of the community.

sion for the Bracebridge library came mid-way through these prestigious Toronto projects, and the Bracebridge library would reflect the same high standards and quality. Indeed, the Bracebridge Public Library would come to be designated in time as a heritage building. Interestingly, it was the only Carnegie library he designed.

On September 5, 1906, the contract to build the library was entered into. William C. Mahaffy and Moses J. Dickie signed for the Bracebridge Free Library Board. In August, the library board received and reviewed

George Miller's plans for the new structure, then voted to approve them. Contractor Henry Oscar Appleby of Bracebridge agreed to the terms specified. He would provide all materials and workmen and build the structure "agreeable to the plans, drawings and specifications" prepared by Miller. For the entire project (except for the heating system, a separate contract) Appleby would receive $9630 in "money of Canada." Henry Appleby agreed to finish the job and leave the grounds "clean and clear from all refuse by April 1, 1907."

A projected completion date the following spring left plenty of time to put up a public building. Two decades later, for instance, the town's new high school would be started in the spring of 1925, with cornerstone laying ceremonies on June 3, and ready for classes in September.

George Miller's specifications of labour and materials required for the erection of the library building in Bracebridge reflected not only his perfectionism but also the imperative of Carnegie libraries to represent the highest expression of civilization's possibilities. Attention to quality touched every element.

In addition to written specifications running to 33 pages, a full set of enlarged and full-sized details for both interior and exterior work "as required in properly carrying the work into effect" were furnished by Miller to the contractors from time to time as the work proceeded. It was a contractual condition that all his drawings, written instructions, figures and details "must be carefully and accurately followed." The entire construction project was to be "executed in the best, most substantial, secure and workmanlike manner" with all materials used throughout to be "of the best quality of the several kinds."

When George Miller submitted his specifications for the building he also provided a printed roster of firms supplying the contracting trade— from plumbing and heating contractors to painters and carpenters, metalworkers and glass manufacturers, stair builders and sign-makers—more than 45 "approved" suppliers in total, all from Toronto. No information remains about which of these subcontractors Appleby engaged, although Bracebridge had its own strong roster of skilled tradesmen and building supply merchants by this time. At least a few local contracts were given for the library work. The slow progress of construction was smugly attributed in some quarters around town to the ways of city people.

When it was finished, the building and its entire works were to be "delivered up in a perfect and undamaged state without exception." Such a

ARCHITECT FOR BRACEBRIDGE LIBRARY. George M. Miller, born at Port Hope in 1854, taught at the Mechanics' Institute in Toronto in the early 1880s, then took up the practice of architecture in 1885. His neoclassical structures included the Lillian Massey Building at University of Toronto, Havergal College on Jarvis Street in Toronto, and the Toronto General Trust Building. He was consultant on the Massey Hall on Shuter Street in Toronto, and the Gladstone Hotel on Queen Street. Elsewhere across Ontario, Miller was architect for the Canadian General Electric Building in Peterborough, the Macdonald building at Ontario Agricultural College in Guelph, and in Whitby, both the Ontario Ladies College and the House of Industry.

Miller was in his early 50s and at the height of his prominent career designing major buildings when he got the commission for the new Carnegie library in Bracebridge, whose construction he closely supervised. Today the library is one of the town's seven designated heritage structures, having benefited from restoration in 1984–5. George Miller would be pleased if he could see the library today, though someone would have to explain computers to him. *Park Bros. Studio, Toronto, and University of Toronto Rare Books Collection* compass setting in the direction of perfection was intended to enable the building to reach its destiny as a pivotal institution uplifting citizens to achieve their fullest potential.

It is worth taking note of how the work was to progress because the construction standards, materials and methods at the turn of the last century provide insights into the evolution of building since. These details are also the back-story to award-winning architect Brian Chamberlain's design to double the Carnegie library facility while retaining its architectural integrity 80 years later, when he would repeatedly emphasize how well the original structure which he was restoring and adding to had been designed and built. Solid libraries built to last were what Andrew Carnegie took pride in. When he spoke at the official opening of one of his libraries in New Jersey, whose steel and stone structure evoked permanence, he asserted, "We believe in the future so we build to last." Yet as that case would illustrate, a building is only as good as those who care for it, and by 1970 it was an abandoned wreck. A cumulative scandal is the number of Carnegie libraries that did not make it through their first hundred years, succumbing to industrial-grade additions, disposal for other purposes, or simply destruction beneath the wrecker's ball. It was a fate that, at several intervals, seemed even to await the Bracebridge Carnegie library. One of the things that saved it was the quality of the building itself.

The quality of the building was something that Miller was a stickler about, and his detailed specifications for it extended to the foundations, since firm foundations would be requisite for any enduring institution. The contractors were directed by Miller how to "protect the foundations from frost"—a Canadian reality. In excavating the basement area for foundation walls, footings and drains, the architect's drawing showed the various lengths, depths and thicknesses "necessary to ensure solid foundations" and "also to admit of one foot gravel between wall and clay bank." Once the site was excavated, Miller added a requirement, in addition to the standard drains he'd provided for in the plans, to add a "four-inch white drainage tile at bottom of wall all around and connect with drain." Out of sight was not out of mind. "All drains to be laid with first quality, sound, well-glazed Tile pipe, laid with uniform and sufficient grade, firmly bedded and well jointed in Portland cement. All joints to be made perfectly gas tight, smooth and level inside."

Even at this early stage, Miller regularly left his offices in Toronto and hopped the train up to Bracebridge to supervise Henry Appleby's progress. If eventually progress on the project slowed, it was no punishment for Miller to find himself travelling to the celebrated Muskoka tourist district for an extended period during the best months of the year.

In Bracebridge, Miller would meet the town's drain inspector to ensure the grading, bedding, jointing junctions and traps of the drains were "in strict accordance with Town plumbing by-laws," that all branches to down pipes had been brought up to within 18 inches of grade line, and that all necessary bends, junctions, up-turns, taper pieces and elbows were properly connected before directing the connection of drains into the street sewer and ordering them covered so the next stage could begin.

Building up the exterior foundation walls and footings, together with footings of interior brick walls and piers, required use of "good, sound, large flat bedded stone" with all footings to be "of extra large stones." The angles in the walls had to be "especially well bonded." Miller directed the masons where to place a damp course of felt and pitch all around inside and outside walls.

The exterior face of the stonework was coursed with "square rock faced stone with pitched joints" and laid in coloured mortar and pointed. He checked to see that the walls were flushed up solid with mortar, the interstices filled in with stone chips and spauls, and that everything had bonded together successfully. All this so-called rubblework had to be carried out, he insisted and inspected, "perfectly plumb, level and true, with all interior and exterior faces well flushed up and pointed." In addition to the close watch by Miller and the town's building inspectors, routine inspections were also daily carried out from the sidewalk by citizen supervisors who watched with interest and amazement the structure gradually taking shape above ground at the top of Queen's Hill. With an active Masonic Order in Bracebridge—indeed, one with its own library—it is probable that Miller's high standards for stonework and masonry met with approbation. The library's door would face East.

The brickwork came next and here the traditions of the red brick town were fully honoured. Of all Bracebridge public structures, only the post office and armouries constructed for the government of Canada a half-block south on Manitoba Street a decade later would exceed the quality and standards of this library. The new Carnegie building was certainly on a par with the recently constructed courthouse, and of better intrinsic quality than the imposing town hall.

At the library, all cellar brick was extra hard clinker type, while the walls, flues and chimneys were made of "sound, hard burnt red stock bricks" laid in the same coloured mortar that was used for the stone foundations. Each brick was well soaked in water before being laid, and was laid in a full bed of mortar with end and back joints flushed up solid with mortar, "the whole carried up and out perfectly plumb level and true, and in every respect of labour and materials done in the most efficient and workmanlike manner satisfactory to the architect." Ensuring that the bricks were both cool and wet when laid meant they would not absorb moisture from the mortar, thus allowing it to harden properly.

With the masonry and brick work completed, the masons were directed to "well bed and carefully back up behind all cut stone sills, well bed in general all framed and timbered work, bed and point in lime and hair mortar all door and window frames, and point up under all stone sills, heads and string courses." The hair mixed in with the mortar, provided either from horses or Bracebridge barbershops, was standard reinforcement for plaster.

All exterior arches were constructed with "neatly gauged brick." All window lintels, whether wood or stone, that spanned more than five feet, were required to be supported by relieving arches. Steel stanchions or supporting posts for the building itself were set in concrete foundations and carefully constructed pad blocks.

For added strength, the entranceway porch had three pieces of railway iron embedded in it during construction. The building had only this one front entrance, up the long steps from Manitoba Street. It would require more deaths through fires in public buildings before building codes would be enacted to require more than a single means of egress. Only in 1967 did the Bracebridge Public Library gain a second door.

Many Bracebridge red brick buildings appeared more solid than they were. Built of wood with a brick veneer, they all had a chance to burn over the years as the town underwent a series of disastrous fires that, as in so many other communities including Bracebridge's two sister towns of Gravenhurst and Huntsville, wiped out big sections of the main street. The Carnegie library, however, would be less vulnerable, not only because it was free standing, but because it was built with far less wood and more stone and steel.

The cut stonework of the library building was "selected first quality Ohio stone, uniform in colour and free from all defects, with tooled faces." The keystones, tooled to face and sides, had to be "tailed in 9 inches to wall," while all windows had cut stone sills with exacting specifications, including being "tooled on upper face with proper wash seat and drip."

Steel work would provide the supporting skeleton for the library. Here again, detailed specifications governed the length and sizes of caps, brackets, gussets, plates, angles, cleats, flanges, sills, bolts and rivets. Once Miller inspected this steelwork to ensure that it was "perfectly plumb, level and true and securely and rigidly fixed," as well as all cleaned off and painted with one coat of "good oil colour."

Now the carpenters and joiners could move onto the site. Like all other tradesmen on this job, they found detailed instructions awaiting them, too. Miller had specified that all timber had to be "of good straight grained hard pine, sawn die square, thoroughly seasoned, and free from sap, shakes, large loose or dead knots, and all imperfections impairing its strength and durability" and satisfactory to him. For the ground floor, the joiner was directed to use "the best description of black ash, clear and free from all imperfections, thoroughly seasoned, and all to be smoothed with the hand plane after machine dressing." The basement would be finished in white pine for painting, and the window sashes pine painted white.

Constructing the library's vaulting and arching, which would add so much to the elegance of the expansive interior of the library, was also the task of the carpenters. Based on his methods that made his buildings such a success with the public in Toronto, he created seven pages of detailed architect's directions for floor and ceiling joists, specifications for strapping the walls for plastering, rules about trimming around all openings, directions for constructing the sloping roofs and building access ladders to the roof, orders about erecting posts carrying trusses, not to mention regulations for building air shafts and a dumb waiter. The basics of floors were provided, so that all floors not concreted would be laid of a ⅞-inch pine underfloor, topped with tongue-and-groove selected maple or birch flooring, all "blind nailed" on angles at the side so no nail heads would show. More elegant touches, which would come to be among the library's celebrated features, were his designs for cornices, lunettes (small lights to the roof), the winding main staircase and balustrade, and the "goods slide" made of teak.

The reading hall and vestibule would have a panel dado (the part of a pedestal of a column included between the base and the surbase) three and a half feet high with moulded capping, all of black ash. There were also hardwood square columns and wall pilasters. These were all built on pine backings and cradlings, and either plugged to walls or wedged up and around steel work.

Part of the contract price covered hardware that the contractor would install, but again to reflect the standards of a Carnegie library and the refined tastes of an architect to the Masseys, George Miller himself would select. Quality would extend to every detail: window pulleys, weights, cords, fasteners, lifts, pull down plates, pull down hooks and poles, hooks and eyes, door hinges, butts, bolts, locks, fasteners, door stops, turn style, dumb waiter gearing and rope, transom butts, transom lifts, counter, cupboard and drawer hardware, hat and coat hooks. The carpenter could choose the nails himself.

The roof of the library certainly continued Miller's high standards. The whole of the sloping parts of the roof were covered with the best Canadian slate. As always, the specifications made clear how to install the pieces of slate: "with 3" lap, double course at eaves, well and securely nailed with heavy slating nails laid on one ply of No. 1 felt." Galvanized iron was used to cover the roof or deck over the porch and vestibule, as well as for eavestroughs, down pipes, ridges and flashing. Although as an architect George Miller embraced the culture of the Carnegie library movement, he had not embraced the climate of the town of Bracebridge where the building he designed was to be built. As time would soon enough reveal, his roof design was inadequate for the snow loads and ice formation in a community on the Canadian Shield, different conditions than those experienced by his other structures created for southern Ontario. Snow accumulated above the portico entrance and had to be regularly shovelled off, not an easy or convenient manoeuvre. Ice build-ups and water back-ups gave rise to leaking inside and falling chunks of ice outside, problems that endure, despite several renovations, to this day.

The library's smooth inner wall and ceiling surfaces, across which leaking water would sometimes run in winters and springs of the future, would be achieved by rendering "the whole of the outside walls from top of stonework to underside of roof boards with a good thick coat of mor-

SAMUEL H. ARMSTRONG was mayor of Bracebridge from 1889 to 1890 and again in 1907 when the Bracebridge Carnegie Library was under construction.

FINE DETAILS. Interior views showing architectural details: the balcony (above), Georgian window over entrance doors (below), and plasterwork and moulding (bottom). These are still intact a century later.

tar." Specific instructions were given by Miller for the artistic details that were the hallmark of fine plaster work—the cornices, caps, vault ribs and angles—still visible today enriching the style and feel of the vaulting interior.

The installation of the glass in the windows represented the finishing stages of construction. All windows, including the fanlights, were to be glazed with 26-ounce clear glass. There were some notable exceptions, such as for the front and vestibule doors, which would present greater measure of solid elegance with ¼ inch plate glass with 1½ inch bevelled edges. All glass was required to be "of the best quality of the several kinds, free from all blemishes, and well bedded, braded and back puttied." The glass in doors had to be "especially well put in with stops and felt."

It was time for painting. All the dressed woodwork of the library, both inside and outside, was to be "well knotted, primed and stopped" then given "three full bodied coats of white lead and linseed oil paint" of approved tints. The whole of the woodwork had to be sandpapered before each coat of paint. The areas with hardwood finish had to be "filled, shellacked, then rubbed down with fine sandpaper, then hard oiled two coats, and well rubbed with pumice stone and oil."

With the electrical wiring for the library, although the position of lights was shown in Miller's plans, the architect was the least specific of any instructions given, saying only that the building "is to be wired to suit the system of lighting at present in use in the town." The building was to be "wired complete by the contractor, including everything necessary to make a successful electric light wiring installation, such as wires, cutouts, insulators, switches, etc."

Such specifications stand in stark contrast to his highly detailed directions for concrete work, steel structures and carpentry, a sign both of Miller's relative unfamiliarity with the technical side of the electricity revolution and the rapid pace at which it was developing new applications. He enunciated a principle or two, such as "All wiring to be done so that the loss of voltage on any circuit will not exceed two volts when all lights are burning." He was clearly deferring to the expertise of electricians to know how to achieve these concepts in practice.

The overall impression given by the new library building in Bracebridge was similar to that offered by other pre-World War 1 public buildings in Ontario and in many of the Great Lakes and New England States in this era—a blending of a variety of architectural styles and attributes. "In the wood and plasterwork could be seen Greek revival," points out architect Brian Chamberlain, who took charge of the building's complete restoration in the mid-1980s. "The outside of the building was Romanesque," he added, "with some Georgian flavour thrown in."

The Carnegie Corporation in New York released payments for the library in stages to match progress in its construction, which eventually spread over 14 months. The first draft for $2,000 arrived November 1, 1906, with subsequent payments received as $2,250 on December 31, a further $2,250 on June 26, 2007, the fourth of $1,500 on November 4, 1907, and the final draft of $2,000—bringing Andrew Carnegie's total to $10,000—on January 24, 1908. The value of the $10,000 to Bracebridge in 1907 would be about $221,300 in present-day dollars.

The treasurer's final entry shows that the full cost of the building came to $11,840.36. The difference of some $1,840 had to be picked up locally. The Bracebridge folk were, however, not entirely above seeking some topping-up money for extra charges. On March 28, 1908, Moses Dickie, wrote to Andrew Carnegie:

Dear Sir,

I am instructed by the Bracebridge Free Library Board to write you to say that in our final settlement with the contractor he presents claim for $200 for certain changes that had been made by the Architect in detail work and which consumed more Labor & Material than at first intended and which had not been made known to the Board until the final settlement and after all moneys had been appropriated. The Architect also concurs in the claim, and we are now asking if you will supplement your very liberal grant with a bonus of $200, the amount claimed by the contractor.

We are now in occupation of Building which is beautifully situated and is the pride of the Town. We have been told that we have the prettiest Library in Ontario, and as soon as we have the motto in front and the snow is all away from the building we will have a Photo prepared and sent you together with a suitable acknowledgement by the Board for your liberality in giving us such a comfortable and beautiful Library Home.

Hoping to have your favourable consideration, I remain your obedient servant.

Moses J. Dickie
Secretary & Treasurer
Bracebridge Public Library

PIVOTAL POINT. From the opening of Bracebridge Carnegie Library in 1908 until 1967, this is the view all librarians had of the main library hall and entrance if looking straight ahead from the central circulation desk. The design of libraries a century ago, when open stacks were being introduced, ensured that from a central position the librarian, who usually worked alone in small libraries like this one in Bracebridge, would have sight lines to all areas. This photo was taken after 1967 "renovations" took out the circulation desk, removed the central staircase to the lower level, and added hanging fluorescent lights.

Perhaps not surprisingly, the letter went unanswered. Andrew Carnegie had kept his side of the bargain. Had the local work proceeded on schedule, it might even have come in at the estimated cost. Elsewhere around North America, many Carnegie libraries being built in this same period were constructed on schedule to the exact dollar, a number exceeded the budget, and a few came in under the estimate. Andrew Carnegie's gift made all the difference to Bracebridge. Without it the town would never have had such a library. Having to make up $200 in the large scheme of things is something a more gracious recipient might have been embarrassed to pursue. The silence was an elegant response.

SILENCE! The Carnegie Library opened very quietly in 1908. One of the most imposing structures in Bracebridge, this splendid gift from Andrew Carnegie began operation without public notice or any fanfare whatsoever, to avoid the controversy stirred up especially by G.H.O. Thomas of the *Bracebridge Gazette*. Moses Dickie, librarian and secretary-treasurer, achieved the world record for a minimalist opening of a new public building. As a result, those planning an anniversary to celebrate the opening of the building had plenty of scope in choosing a date.

The front entrance to any building holds promise of what lies within, but for a library, especially, the steps, pillars and entranceway are particularly important for establishing a requisite sense of respectful dignity for books, reading and learning. Here, too, George Miller provided direct guidance for the front of the Bracebridge library whose entrance steps and the coping to the side were constructed of "fine Portland cement concrete." Above the entrance was to be a tooled stone tablet measuring two feet by two and a half feet, and eight inches thick, "with projecting face and small moldings around edge, and sunk lettered, average 8 inches, as follows:

PUBLIC LIBRARY
ANNO. 1907 DOM.

The architect's specifications, approved by the Carnegie staff, clearly required that the date the building was erected be shown. This, however,

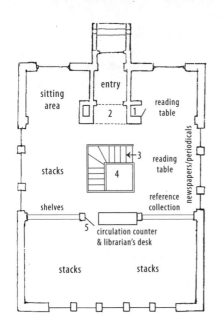

BRACEBRIDGE
CARNEGIE LIBRARY 1908

Main floor

1. hidden ladder to balcony
2. balcony above
3. wooden staircase down to offices, boardroom, work area, boiler room, storage
4. stairwell, open to below, enclosed by wooden balustrade
5. counter-height swinging gate (oak)

0   5   10 ft

COUNTERPOINT TO CARNEGIE LIBRARY. In 1908 this new public school in the Fourth Ward of Bracebridge opened with great celebration by the children and their parents on the east side of town. The school would close during the 1930s Depression when mills and factories shut down and the population of Bracebridge diminished. Today it is home of the Bracebridge branch of the Royal Canadian Legion, where the small military museum from the Bracebridge library was lodged in 1967 when the library's display cases were removed in "renovations." Back in 1908, in contrast to the jubilation over the new school, the controversial new Carnegie library opened with neither a whisper of publicity nor a single word of welcome.

was a problem. When the stone was fabricated in Bracebridge for $35 by Harry Boyer, who had learned his stone-cutting skills in New York City as an orphan, he did not follow the stipulated specifications in one important detail: the date was omitted. Construction had dragged on for so long that the line "Anno. 1907 Dom." was quietly dropped, on explicit instructions from Moses Dickie, so as not to make the lapsed year the butt of further jokes when it would be installed prominently on the front of the building sometime in 1908.

Dickie, who by this time as librarian and as secretary and treasurer of the library board, had in the eyes of the community become closely personified with anything connected to the library. He had already taken all the ribbing he cared to on the streets of town about "When's that new library going to be ready, Moses?" Editorial writers in George Thomas' *Bracebridge Gazette* had even commented, not kindly, about the slow

"PUBLIC LIBRARY" NAME STONE. Bracebridge Granite and Marble Works, where Harry Boyer cut the naming stone for the new Bracebridge "Public Library" for $35 but omitted the date specified by the architect because delays in the library's construction had become a sore point to the *Bracebridge Gazette*. Boyer, at left in doorway, learned his trade as an orphan in New York City. He operated this works with sons Sam and Harry at the juncture of Manitoba and Dominion streets near the present library. They also cut the stone plaque with the names of the library board members at the time the new Carnegie library was built, seen inside the ground-level entrance today, which G.H.O. Thomas of the *Gazette* criticized in print for being ready before the building was.

ONE STEP FORWARD, TWO BACK. It was good that townspeople could enjoy the impressive new Carnegie library building on the main street of Bracebridge in 1908 because by the end of the same year a December 28 fire decimated many fine buildings in the downtown commercial district, a block from the library. *Redmond Thomas/Brenda Cox Collection*

progress. Every month or so an update on construction progress, or lack thereof, was featured in the *Gazette*.

Local historian Robert Boyer, when reviewing the move of the town library's 3,080 books into the new Carnegie facility sometime in early 1908, would remark in one of his hallmark understatements that "a remarkable lack of ceremony attended the event."

Moses just wanted to quietly start up without drawing attention, so gradually he just moved in and gradually got operations under way. Every now and then in the quiet of evening he'd carry another box of books over from the old library premises. People might not really remember how long it took to build, or embarrass him any further, if no opportunity was given for them to draw attention at an official opening ceremony.

The Board members did not seem to miss the fuss. They were satisfied that Harry Boyer's Granite and Marble Works had chiselled up another stone for the library, this one a plaque with their names all on it. The grey stone engraving is still at the entrance of the library today, so everyone can be reminded that the library board in 1906 consisted of chairman Judge W.C. Mahaffy, members Peter A. Smith, Alfred Hunt, F.P. Warne, James Whitten, J.M. Ballantyne and H.J. Bird, Sr., with Moses J. Dickie being secretary-treasurer and librarian.

Yet at the material time, when the long-awaited new Carnegie Public

Library was finally ready for its special consummation with the townspeople in their endless love affair with books, no music played. There was no event to mark this historic milestone. There were no notices or advertisements in the newspapers. There were no speeches. There was no ribbon to cut. There was no special cake, nor fruit punch. The national anthem was not sung. No clergy were on hand to bless the library, its noble purpose, and all who work in it or come to discover the true joys of learning therein. The town of Bracebridge, at some uneventful moment in 1907 or 1908, set a world record for achieving a new essence of minimalist ceremony. Just gradually, unobtrusively, the quiet workings of a town library began to occur at the new premises and in time it just seemed to everyone that like a fairytale castle it had always been there. This was the magic.

NINE

A Library through Times of War and Depression

From its prestigious accommodation in the new Carnegie building at the crest of Queen's Hill on Manitoba Street above the business section of town, Bracebridge Public Library and everyone connected with it in 1908 settled into a new groove.

The naming stone above the library entranceway, like a trumpet sounding a higher keynote, made clear this was a *public* library. For the first time in the town's library service, the term "public library" was officially in use, making known it was an institution for all. The term "free library" remained in use too, since its adoption in 1901. Either way, free or public, the connotation was the same. What is more, for the first time all townspeople knew they had a library because they could physically see it as an entity on its own.

What they saw was impressive beyond anything before in Bracebridge's love affair with books. The library's exterior was pleasing to the eye, properly squared and well-pointed stone walls rising to a height above ground, the upper walls above that of red brick, with numerous gables and windows. Similar to the overall impression given by other eclectic turn-of-the-century public buildings in Ontario and many of the Great Lakes and New England states of this era, this building displayed a variety of architectural styles and attributes. In the wood and plasterwork could be seen Greek revival, while the outside of the building was Romanesque with some Georgian flavour thrown in. A photograph of the building, taken as promised to express thanks to Mr. Carnegie in New York even though no record exists it was ever sent or received, was soon

TOWN WITH A LIBRARY. At the time the Bracebridge's Carnegie library building was built, this was the view south down Queen's Hill and Manitoba Street from the middle of the road in front of the library, well before the town's main thoroughfare was paved in 1928. The third building on the right of this photograph, centred between two utility poles, is one of several that housed the Mechanics' Institute Library on its upper floors after 1874.

on proud display everywhere, adorning post cards and featured in newspaper stories about milestones in the progress of the town.

Emotional uplift rewarded anyone who climbed the stairs, passed between the upper pillars and through the vestibule into the open space of the main library hall itself. Here lofty walls and very high ceilings of pure white, huge windows and numerous electric lights gave an ethereal impression to send one's spirits soaring. Yet there was reassurance here, too, coming from the elegant warmth in the fine ash woodwork and panelling, the highly polished furniture, and the oak counters, tables, book cases, and balustrade around the central stairwell, all finished in the natural grain of the wood. A visitor's eyes, taking in the straight lines of shelving and the four library tables in the reading room, saw in such clean symmetry a place where the playful human intellect itself might become more ordered as well.

Behind the librarian's counter were eight book cases, ranging tall and straight and running out toward the back wall. Six of them had double-sided shelving, two were against the side walls. All held books and had good aisles in between. The shelves did not seem well lighted, but the row of large windows at the rear provided some help. Moses Dickie, a very careful, painstaking and efficient individual, could tell anyone who

142

asked that these shelves now held 3,808 books, but had space for 7,000! If books could liberate people, on these spacious shelves books themselves had now found freedom after years of tight cramming in the library's previous quarters. Everything about the new Carnegie library heralded a new openness.

The stairway to the lower level carried into a boardroom where a good heavy carpet on the centre of the floor and new chairs of deep comfort awaited members of the library board and their next meeting. The extensive space down here afforded lots of room for storage, although just now the main thing being stored was furniture from the old library.

Because patrons could now look for books themselves, as a result of the Carnegie policy requiring "open stacks," it meant the library for the first time was a self-service centre. Library patrons no longer had to request and wait for the librarian to fetch the books and bring them to the circulation desk for checkout. Early on, Andrew Carnegie had subscribed to the liberating school of thought developing at the end of the nineteenth century that in libraries, the more people could do for themselves, the better. The fewer the staff needed, ran the logic, the more financial resources would be freed up to spend on books. This principle transformed big city libraries, but was less relevant in a one-librarian town. Staffing the Bracebridge library was simple. Moses Dickie was in charge, assisted by his daughter Sarah. Books were occasionally damaged and some were stolen, but supervision was close. Patrons could freely browse through the stacks, but the only way to leave was by passing right beside the librarian's counter, where there was a bit of control in the form of a low-level swinging oak door. The library was open during all days of the week but Sunday, during the mornings and afternoons, and on Friday evening.

Space limitations had intermittently hobbled library service in Bracebridge during the three preceding decades, but that would not be a problem in the foreseeable future. Indeed in this spacious new library, because books did not even begin to fill the shelf space available, a sense of more complete occupancy was achieved by displaying a number of books face out. There was no need to cull the collection in 1908. Ample working space also awaited students and adults at desks in the reading room. Each of the four tables on the main floor area designated as the reading room could accommodate nine persons, so that 36 people could be seated at one time.

The circulation of books in 1907 had been 9,359, and in the new premises that number climbed well over 10,000. Books, several newspapers and a number of magazines and periodicals were available to read on the premises. The library owned an encyclopedia, atlases and a number of other reference books, all of which had to remain in the building. Most of the books, however, could be signed out for up to two weeks at a time.

No system for borrowing books from other libraries was in place in 1908. The Bracebridge Public Library's operations pertained primarily to the books and publications it had under its own roof. In this sense it was very much a freestanding institution whose fortunes, and resources, depended on those running it. Additions to the collection of Bracebridge library came principally through donations and purchases of new books. Once the board had set the amount available for acquisitions, the librarian decided what books to buy.

The Bracebridge Library Board, which Judge W.C. Mahaffy chaired, consisted of Peter A. Smith, Alfred Hunt, Francis P. Warne, James Whitten, J.M. Ballantyne and Henry J. Bird, Sr.

The budget for this inaugural year in the new building was $1,000. Expenditure items included $10 for water, $85 for light, and $100 for coal. While the fuel would have been bought under a private contract, the town was charging one of its own institutions for municipally provided water and electricity. Another budget item was $25 for insurance, which was placed by the library's resident insurance broker, Moses Dickie. For his caretaker and librarian services for the year, Dickie was paid $500. An amount of approximately $250 was available to purchase books, newspapers and magazines.

Not only was the issue of space solved, but the earlier financial challenges facing the Bracebridge library now appeared to have been overcome as well. As a free public library since 1901, it qualified for larger provincial grants than had been the case when it was still a private library operated by the Mechanics' Institute. Having a reliable source of operating revenue certainly helped for budgeting purposes. Financial support from the town council, which had previously been no more than grudgingly sporadic at the best of times, would now be provided in perpetuity in the amount of at least $1,000 annually, thanks to Andrew Carnegie's agreed-upon funding formula.

The effort at public outreach by the library was minimal. The town was small and people who cared knew where the library was and what it was for. If anything, more mention of the library was made in advertisements in the town newspapers by others, such as the weekly ads for M.J. Dickie Insurance prominently yet simply giving its business address as "In the

Library," or merchants like John Burke "The Clothes Man" advertising his business location as "Opposite Public Library." People in Bracebridge knew where to find his store. The new library building that was launching the town and its book culture into a higher orbit for the new twentieth century had also quickly become a landmark and reference point in the community.

Bracebridgites continued to live a life stimulated by their book-centred culture. The Bracebridge Literary Society was flourishing even more by 1908. A couple years later, the "Great Library Contest" of 1911 demonstrated the explicit link between library and community service organizations in Bracebridge. The contest prize? "An elegant library of many volumes of books contained in handsome sets of shelves!" It could be won by the church, lodge, or society whose members produced the greatest number of "votes" in buying from 13 participating local businesses, ranging from hardware and pharmacy shops to the Lyceum Theatre and the *Muskoka Herald* newspaper and printing shop. This town-wide competition, which reinforced the high standing of books in town, began in September 1911 and ran until January 1912. Enthusiasm for this library contest was whipped up by prominent coverage in the *Muskoka Herald*, not surprising since the newspaper's editor, George Boyer, was its principal organizer. When all the votes based on purchases were counted, the winner of the "elegant library" was the Independent Order of Odd Fellows.

It said a lot about a town that books and shelving to hold them would be made the prize for a public contest, that many congregations and community clubs encouraged their adherents and members to participate, and that one of the town's newspapers would conceive and promote this initiative. Such signs underscored why the new Carnegie Public Library was in a community where it would not only be welcomed, but could play a very significant role going forward.

If suitably bookish, the town was also very British. Many immigrant men in senior positions still spoke with English accents. Even for those born here, the culture made its imprint: Bracebridge was part of the British Empire, the Union Jack flew overhead, books by English authors enjoyed pride of place on the library's shelves, and the loyalist societies had no difficulty mustering large parades through its main street. When war drums beat, Bracebridge would pour out its volunteers to "rally to the side of the Mother Country" and swell the ranks of those enforcing the might of the British Empire.

By 1908 one such war was over and military artifacts from the South African battlefields were gathered almost like a shrine in the library's special display cases. By the end of this first decade of the new library's life in the year 1918, the same cycle would have been again repeated but more dramatically than ever as the world's order of civilization would be shattered and the British Empire's strength permanently undermined by four years of calamitous war. Then more instruments of death—a Gatling gun, grenades, rifles with bayonets—could be added to the library's military archive of "the Great War," while the names of many more dead young men of Bracebridge could be added to the honour roll to accompany the earlier sons of Bracebridge killed in the Boer War (eventually all these names would be engraved on a cenotaph up the street in Memorial Park).

That still-awaiting future would include not only the cataclysmic Great War from 1914 to 1918, but a roaring time of prosperity and excess in the Twenties, then a brutal economic depression that scourged Canadian society from 1929 to 1939, followed by yet another six years of what Adolf Hitler's propaganda minister Joseph Goebbels in Germany called "total war" from 1939 to 1945. That conflict, in turn, would end only to usher in nuclear weapons and an ideological Cold War that would paralyse the world for the next half century after that. History, as we see in this chapter covering the period from 1908 until the 1960s, would generally place the local library at the calm centre of these many storms, a refuge for those seeking diversion from despair or pursuing self-education about the fearful conduct of human society.

At the start of these years of upheaval, the library was under steady guidance from the Dickie family. Nothing had changed on that front, not in the slightest detail. Even the rubber stamp Moses Dickie bought in 1901 to mark the books "Bracebridge Free Library" had not been replaced with the advent of the Carnegie Public Library, and would still be in use marking new acquisitions with the same "Free Library" impression into the 1930s. In a world of change, the Bracebridge Public Library stood apart.

"The library without Mr. Dickie would be as the cage without the songster," smiled George H.O. Thomas in the *Bracebridge Gazette*. The Dickie family had become indispensable to the town library, as much a part of the place as the solid stone foundation of the building itself. To help him with

AWAY FROM BOOKS AND BUSINESS. Long-time Bracebridge public librarian Moses Jones Dickie, handsome with a distinguishing white beard, on front lawn of his McMurray Street home in early 1920s. Wife Violet is second from the right, with son Stanley in wheelchair. Stanley sustained serious World War I injuries overseas and died because of them in 1922. Moses, born in 1844, died three years later in 1925, age 81. *Dickie Family*

his many different tasks at the library building, Moses hired his daughter Sarah. Years before, when John W. Dickie and his wife moved from New Brunswick to a farm near Brantford, then later continued north in 1871 to claim free Muskoka land in McLean Township near Baysville, where they promptly gave their name to Dickie Lake, they could not have known they would also bring forth a family dynasty in library service. Their son Moses Jones Dickie, born May 2, 1844, was in his mid-forties by the time he moved from Dickie Lake into Bracebridge in 1888, and it was good for the town that he came.

Moses became a director of the Muskoka Agricultural Society, an active member of the Independent Order of Odd Fellows and the Sons of Scotland, then for good measure joined the United Workmen. He was appointed a Justice of the Peace, dispensing speedy justice in police court and issuing marriage licences any time of the day or night, because that's the way it was in Bracebridge. By 1891 a general directory of the town, published by the *Muskoka Herald*, listed Moses Dickie as "dealer in hay, etc." He prospered buying hay from farmers and selling it into the lumber camps where teams of horses built up strong appetites pulling highly stacked loads of logs all winter. That same year Moses paid masons to

MOSES DICKIE SET A PATTERN. Moses Dickie took an active part in the life of Bracebridge, as a local entrepreneur and businessman, certainly as one of the key players getting the Carnegie grant for the new town library, and unquestionably in the operation of the library thereafter. Dickie was elected to town council in 1892 then re-elected in the three successive annual elections. He was a member of the Independent Order of Foresters, Sons of Scotland, the United Workmen, and the Bracebridge Mechanics' Institute. Moses Dickie was no stranger to the Baptist Church on Quebec Street, where this photograph was taken. He was a deacon of the church and the Sunday school superintendent for more than a quarter century. That he and his family were so closely entwined with the Bracebridge library for decades, while he was also extensively involved in community affairs, set a pattern for library governance as something of a self-regulating operation with little interference from or connection with the formal municipal government. *Dickie Family*

brick his home on McMurray Street using Beaverton white brick, the first used in Bracebridge, making him a man to stand apart even though he was becoming ever more closely entwined with community life in the town.

By 1892, when lumber baron James Dollar became mayor, Moses was elected to council as one of the two councillors for Ward II, and was re-elected in 1893 when Alfred Hunt, owner of the local bank, became mayor. He was re-elected in 1894, when the council followed up the plebiscite decision of 1893 for the municipality to acquire its own electric plant and extend lights throughout the town. Councillor Dickie ensured his son William got the job that year of going throughout town signing up people for the new electricity system being run by the municipality. With Bracebridge beginning its third decade as an incorporated municipality in 1895, Moses the good provider was again re-elected to town council.

In addition to the spread of electric light in Bracebridge, Moses was engaged in distribution of spiritual light to young Baptists in their small grey-brick church on Quebec Street as well. He was a deacon of the church and ministered to its active congregation of young people in his capacity as Sunday school superintendent for over 30 years. Not only the Good Book, but also good books in general, commanded Moses Dickie's interest, which was both cause and effect of him becoming increasingly active in the local library. Although rendered half-blind in boyhood when, while walking though the bush a branch hit him square in one eye, this impairment did not diminish his great love of books. Despite being a man of limited formal education, Moses Dickie had a retentive memory for whatever he read with his one good eye.

Bracebridge was clearly a highly active and enterprising community, but a small town all the same. This meant individuals had to play important roles in many different organizations at the same time, partly because their interests pulled them into it, but partly also because there were just not enough people to do all the things that needed to be done. The cross-involvement Moses Dickie had in all these community organizations, though remarkable, was simply typical of the era and the community. At this time Moses Dickie also started up an insurance business in Bracebridge. All the while he was secretary-treasurer of the Bracebridge Library Board, and by 1906 had become town librarian, too.

His contributions to Bracebridge were not a solo effort, however, because the next generation of Dickies, following their father's example, was also becoming active in the community, in a variety of ways. Son William had moved to Burford, but returned in January 1913 as a speaker at the Farmers' Institute. Son Stanley in 1912 was among many young men from Bracebridge volunteering for the 23rd Regiment which went up to Parry Sound for training camp during September that year. By 1913, now as a corporal in Company C of the regiment, Stanley travelled with many others by special train to drill in the Canadian Army camp at Niagara-on-the-Lake. That same year, Hattie Dickie, who was now helping her father with his work at the library in a secretarial capacity after her sister Sarah had moved on, sang in the chorus for a musical dramatization of the Bible story "Queen Esther" directed by the Methodist Church's choir director, George W. Boyer. The performance ran for two nights in February and was attended by the largest audience ever yet to fill the town hall.

Despite being an enterprising man well connected in Bracebridge and a good reader of books who was increasingly becoming "Mister Library" in town, nothing in Moses Dickie's background particularly trained him for librarian service. In many peoples' eyes, the job was primarily one of custodianship, of the building as much as about the books and their read-ers. Although not trained as a librarian, his disposition and experience with the Baptists' children served him well in this role. Redmond Thomas, a son of G.H.O. Thomas, recalled from his first encounters inside the library that the librarian "was always kind and patient with small boys who did not know what they wanted except a 'shipwreck story'."

Yet help was on the way. These were still early days of library organi-zation at a provincial level, but things were moving quickly now. It had only been in 1901 that the same James Bain who in 1864 had arrived by boat in Bracebridge as a pioneering tourist in his early twenties and subsequently became a permanent summer resident of Lake Muskoka, delivered his inaugural presidential address to the first Ontario Library Association conference in Toronto, outlining an ambitious agenda for mobilizing public opinion and library activism. The inspiring leader of the province's libraries "looked forward to new lines of work, to vast increase in the number and sizes of our libraries, and to extension in every direction which aims at their true end—the mental advancement and cul-ture of the people of this province." Within the decade Muskoka Dis-trict had been grouped by the new Ontario Library Association into a "Public Library Institute" with the five counties of Haliburton, Victoria, Peterborough, Ontario and Durham. This arrangement would help the Bracebridge library exceed anything it could do on its own.

Moses Dickie began attending the Institute's conferences, which helped him to develop administration and procedures for the library that he and his daughter had been operating, up to now, without any training or even good examples to emulate. More than just yielding lessons about better practices in library administration, however, Dickie found that participating in the work of the Institute also fostered personal relationships with other librarians. As his activities in Bracebridge already made clear, Moses was someone who fulfilled himself participating in organizations. So he eagerly travelled over to Lindsay for the 1910 central Ontario "institute" that year.

The librarians gathered in the Lindsay Public Library for morning and afternoon sessions on Friday, February 25, taking the opportunity to stay the weekend and expand librarian relationships. Appropriately, given the Institute's make-up, the focus of the conference was on "topics of special interest to small libraries." Ontario's inspector of public libraries, W.R. Nursey, shared his observations from a governmental perspective dealing with libraries small and large throughout the far-flung province. Then the former president of the Ontario Library Association, B.A. Berlin, took up the topic but from the vantage point of libraries themselves. Dr. George H. Locke, chief librarian of the Toronto Public Library, rounded out the program by inspiring those from small libraries when he talked informatively about life in the big leagues.

The organization of such events was a good indication of the administrative structure developing in Ontario to support and develop libraries. The government of Ontario endorsed the importance of such librarian gatherings, so under the Public Libraries Act the Department of Education paid the expenses of one delegate from each library in the zone to attend.

Growth of this librarian network continued steadily with regular gatherings. Those returning each year felt more and more part of a cohesive social group. In the summer of 1912 when the Public Library Institute's members arrived in Bracebridge for their fourth annual conference, the town hosted a social outing for the two dozen visiting librarians, including Ontario's inspector of public libraries Walter Nursey and secretary of the Ontario Library Association E.A. Hardy, aboard a Lake Muskoka steamboat. The other librarians present from Muskoka were Mrs. E. Trimmer of Huntsville and T.M. Robinson of Gravenhurst. Being a good host paid off. That year the central Ontario librarians elected Moses president of the Institute.

Although Moses Dickie may not have appeared to be such a zealot of the library movement as others like Francis P. Warne of Bracebridge, his steady performance delivered results for the local library. Not all librar-

ON THE MOVE. Southbound train at the Bracebridge Grand Trunk Railway station, seen in the year the Carnegie library was built in town. In 1914 this crowded civilian scene was dramatic and different, as uniformed soldiers from Bracebridge and central Muskoka paraded here to ship out to war in Europe, including the librarian's son, Stanley Dickie. Stanley would die from injuries after returning home from the war in a wheelchair. *Brenda Cox Collection*

ies succeed and most have their ups and downs over the cycles of history. So steady performance on the ground was essential to the staying power of the library as an institution, which was something Andrew Carnegie, a most realistic optimist, stressed in his 1897 "Gospel of Philanthropy."

Even as Moses Dickie's health gradually began to fail, he remained determined to carry on with the library. He had been so central to its life that he now saw himself as indispensable to its successful operation. From 1910 onward his daughter worked closely with her father in the library, learning its protocols and procedures to such an extent that she was becoming as entrenched herself in the library as he was.

On July 23, 1914, Canada's Prime Minister, Robert Borden, and Lady Borden returned to relax in Muskoka, just as they had done the summer before, and booked in at the queen of all Muskoka summer lodges, the Royal Muskoka Hotel on Lake Rosseau. The Bordens attended a regatta and the prime minister delivered a couple speeches in Port Carling in which he described the pleasure he and his wife took in a vacation from political life in "the world-famous Muskoka District with its scenery of the finest and the beautiful homes of the hundreds who spend their summers on these lakes." One week after arriving in Muskoka, however, just barely getting into the books he had brought with him to read, Robert Borden received a telegram that ended his dreamlike vacation. The prime minister "left Muskoka rather hurriedly on the evening of July 30 for Ottawa," the *Bracebridge Gazette* reported on August 6, "on account of the looming war clouds." Soon a recalled Parliament would vote Canada's declaration of war on Germany.

A few days after the war began, Bracebridge men were in uniform under orders from the 23rd Regiment to join their unit for the formation of the first Canadian contingent. On August 14, amid patriotic music, cheering crowds and tears, 24 "gallant boys" paraded down Manitoba Street past the Bracebridge Public Library, led by the Bracebridge Citizens' Band, to the train station "where a great crowd had assembled." That wet winter they trained with other Canadians on Salisbury Plain in England; in February 1915 they crossed with the First Division to France, and by April they were into heavy and murderous battle in Flanders near Ypres.

As soon as that First Contingent had left Bracebridge, the raising of

THE WAR REACHES BRACEBRIDGE. The Great War transformed the world and Bracebridge did not escape. These soldiers marching on Manitoba Street pass the library en route to war, which became their different passport to the world. By the ragged end of it in 1918, some of these men would return home, take part in family and community affairs, and enjoy the library. Others did not. Instead their names were added to the honour roll, later chiselled in the cenotaph erected in Memorial Park after World War II. The town library, apart from acquiring more books dealing with the subjects and objects of war, also expanded its encased collection of weaponry.

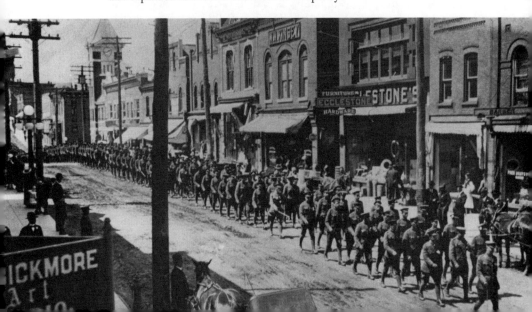

the Second Contingent got under way for the 23rd Northern Pioneers Regiment. Enthusiasm for the war was still running high in this British-loyal town. More young men in Bracebridge volunteered than the specified numbers required. On the evening of October 31, 1914, this second large group of sudden soldiers was sent off from the train station by another immense crowd. Meanwhile, a number of local groups had formed to support the war effort, including a Bracebridge Branch of the Canadian Patriotic Fund. Farmers were called upon to increase food production and promptly five carloads of potatoes and oats were sent from Huntsville, Utterson and Bracebridge railway stations for the war relief effort, although one Muskoka community decided instead to send its foodstuffs for the benefit of poor people in Toronto. Foresters in Muskoka were urged to supply timber for all uses from pit props to trench work because Britain's supply from the closer Baltic countries was cut off by Germany's shipping blockade in the North Sea. Henry Bird's woollen mill accelerated production for rush orders to provide blankets for Canadian, British and French soldiers.

As the war lengthened, so did the lines of men leaving. A very long column of young men from Muskoka now uniformed as soldiers in the 122nd Battalion marched from Memorial Park south on Manitoba Street, down the hill to the train station instead of up the steps into the library, on their way to the all-consuming Great War in Europe. Librarian Moses Dickie's son Stanley was among them. Elsewhere, Andrew Carnegie, whose other greatest act of philanthropy in this period focused on world peace, was beside himself.

In the aching years of warfare that followed the initial exhilaration in 1914, the new library in Bracebridge provided a counterpoint to the overshadowing military campaign, as did libraries in other communities wherever Andrew Carnegie's well-ordered philanthropy rolled out a different campaign intended to uplift people and honour civilization. By 1917, amidst the blighting turmoil of this war between Europe's imperial powers, the Russian Revolution succeeded in bringing the Communists to power in one of the world's largest countries. Societies everywhere had become unhinged from the values and theories that had previously held them in a stable order. The twentieth century, the bloodiest and most war-ravaged yet, had arrived with unanticipated vengeance.

Even when revolutions are under way, small details still need attention. In the global scheme of things just how Hattie Dickie was classifying the books at the Bracebridge library in these tumultuous years may not have ranked as noteworthy, except that within the world of libraries the introduction of "the Dewey Decimal System" was itself revolutionary. Public libraries everywhere were shifting to this new way of organizing information about books so that they would have a common code for identifying them.

New York State librarian Melvil Dewey, whose zealous penchant for organizational efficiency had led him to invent a great breakthrough in organizing paperwork, the "hanging vertical file" that began transforming office operations and bureaucracy from the start of the twentieth century, was equally intent on bringing to the chaotic diversity of libraries the same quality of order for all their books. Dewey worked out ten broad categories and many topics and sub-topics within each, and then developed a code consisting of numbers and letters, known as "call numbers" because that is how a book under his system would then be called or identified. The call number assigned to each book could then be universally recognized, just as the more recent International Standard Book Number or ISBN is a universal and unique identifier for each particular title. His system was comprehensive and could accommodate anything written. It was a computer-like program devised before the computer had been invented, and in some ways anticipated and even helped those working to make the computer's structured organization of information possible.

Having developed the Dewey Decimal System through the 1890s, this high priest of simplified order then toured librarian conferences across the United States and Canada to tout its breakthrough efficiency and profound ease of use. Before long, Dewey Decimal was being implemented by public libraries everywhere. When Dewey next applied his simplifier's approach, it was to clean up the English language, which the Americans still used. Back when Noah Webster had been devising his dictionary, he had come to the view that Americans would be too confused by the intricacies of British spelling and so simplified it. Now Dewey picked up the same cause, resolving to carry it further. He found strong supporters, including President Teddy Roosevelt, Andrew Carnegie and Mark Twain, and they agreed to drop the "u" in words like "neighbour" and tidy up the end of words by cutting out the silent "gh" so that "straight" became "strait." Dewey changed his own name Melville to Melvil and would have preferred Dui for his surname. Carnegie urged James Bartram to the new style, so "have a building" became "hav a bilding" and for awhile Bartram's letters to those seeking a free library, including several received in Bracebridge, looked like they had come from an unschooled person.

However, his system for cataloguing books, a timely advance that enabled librarians to cope with the increasing number and diversity of titles, proved more successful over time than his foray into cleaning up the spelling of words.

Moses had first learned about Dewey's classification system at the inaugural meeting of the Public Library Institute in 1909. When the Institute gathered in Bracebridge for its 1912 conference, his daughter Hattie sat in with her father for the session on book classification. Everyone present was closely interested in whether, and how, to apply the Dewey Decimal System for his or her collections of books. They became better informed when Patricia Speriman of Toronto read a paper on Dewey's system to those gathered in the Bracebridge Public Library. On August 1, 1912, G.H.O. Thomas pronounced on the matter, informing his readers in the *Bracebridge Gazette* that, "This system is recognized as the best known system on classificating [sic] books in a library, small or large."

For those more interested in what books the local library had than how the librarian kept track of them, the *Muskoka Herald* reported on February 24, 1916, that a stock-taking of the Bracebridge Public Library's holdings in 1915 showed there to be 49 philosophy books (plus 1 on philosophy for juvenile readers), 191 religion, 150 sociology (plus 18 for juvenile), 3 on philology, 254 natural science books (plus 34 for juveniles), 144 "useful arts" (with 8 more for juveniles), 28 fine arts (plus 4), 321 literature (7), 337 history (27), 225 biography and travel (27), and 1,983 fiction (plus 629 juvenile fiction works). That represented a sizeable 800 books for juvenile readers, while the total of "adult" books across all categories was 4,264.

Those three books classified under "philology" would have dealt with the study of literature touching on grammar, criticism, literary history, language history, systems of writing, and, says Webster in his dictionary, "anything else that is relevant to literature or to language as used in literature." In short, philology embraces literary or classical learning. It encompasses historical and comparative linguistics, traces how language serves as the vehicle of literature, and studies how human speech sheds light on cultural history. If works of philology were not in a public library, wherever would they be found?

In the second year of the war, work at the library officially passed into new hands with the hiring of a librarian to replace Moses Dickie. However, continuity was assured because it was Hattie Dickie, who in 1915 simply took over these duties her father had been carrying for well over a decade. No competition for the librarian's position was held. Moses simply interviewed his own family. The library board, of which he remained both secretary and treasurer, quietly approved. As a single woman living at home, Hattie Dickie would not be paid much, just several hundred dollars for the entire year. The move only strengthened the Dickie family's grip on the Bracebridge library as it passed down a generation.

Hattie would effectively run the Bracebridge Public Library for a full quarter-century, first during those five years prior to 1915 as her father's increasingly self-reliant understudy, and now for two more decades stretching into the future to mid-December 1934. Between 1915 and 1920, she would even take over the additional responsibilities of secretary-treasurer of the library board, about which she had also learned everything working closely with her father. By 1920, that part of her load would be transferred to a new secretary-treasurer, but of course still a member of the Dickie family: Hattie's brother Jerry.

What Hattie knew about the library she had learned witnessing her father's experience dealing with the strains of transition, first during the protracted negotiations between Bracebridge and the Carnegie Corporation; then, the gnawing embarrassment sparked by the grand vituperations of local newspaper editor G.H.O. Thomas over the delayed construction of Andrew Carnegie's great gift to the town and Moses Dickie's apparent responsibility for that; and, after 1908, the patterns of establishing new library routines and procedures. What she did not understand she could always ask about, downstairs at the library or at home over the dinner table, because her father was never far away. Throughout the piece, Judge W.C. Mahaffy's continuing role as chairman of the library board further suggested normalcy and stability at the Bracebridge library.

Moses Dickie remained on the premises, continuing to operate his insurance business from the lower level of Mr. Carnegie's building. He was handy to answer Hattie's questions, deal with policy issues and library correspondence, but by this time shovelling snow and feeding coal to the furnace in winter, or cutting the tiny patch of library lawn in summer, and other heavy lifting, had passed to his son Jerry.

A solemn atmosphere characterized library etiquette under Hattie. The young Baptist woman who still lived at home looked around the impressive library and took her high mission most seriously. Silence was not only golden, but also enforced. During her long reign at the library, a couple generations of Bracebridge youth would be schooled in the necessity of hushed tones, akin to reverential whispers in places of worship at all times and in every part of the library. Fred Hammell was just one of many local youngsters disciplined in library etiquette after "speaking above an august whisper in the august aisles between the rows of books." As he summed it up years later in his *Muskoka Sun* column, when he himself was the chairman of the library board, "A quick visit from the custodian left the culprit mute for a considerable time after the confrontation."

Problems worse than noisy boys were looming for Bracebridge Public Library.

Despite what had appeared to be a sound financial footing for the library, as a result of the $1,000 minimum Bracebridge was legally obligated to pay as part of the deal for getting a $10,000 library building, the persistent campaign by G.H.O. Thomas against this provision was succeeding, to the detriment of the library and the town.

Thomas' campaign was not a one-day affair. Nor was it narrowly confined. He fought on two fronts and leveraged them both to great effect as both a town councillor and newspaper publisher. His opinions ran throughout the news columns of the *Bracebridge Gazette*, but his biggest shells where lobbed from a front-page featured column entitled "Comment" and signed by his initials, G.H.O.T.

Councillor and columnist George Thomas had railed against the $1,000 provision on and off for a number of years on the pages of his newspaper. In council, when Thomas first moved a resolution to gut this $1,000 condition, he even succeeded in getting council to pass it on May 3, 1906. It stated that the town would "hereby guarantee 10% of the sum granted by Mr. Carnegie for maintenance of said library, which sum at no time to exceed $1,000." That could mean any amount down to and including zero dollars for the library. Only the vigilance of James Bartram in New York caught the Bracebridge council's duplicity. On May 31 the council again passed the required resolution, one hopes with red faces, this time with wording sent from Carnegie's office to clarify that the payment by the town from taxes to the library would be "not less than $1,000 a year." Having yet again seriously jeopardized getting a free library, council convened itself to make matters right. It explicitly confirmed that in accepting the donation of a library, the Corporation of the Town of Bracebridge "does hereby pledge itself to comply with the requirement of said Andrew Carnegie" and that for the amount "of not less that $1,000 a year" the annual levy "shall hereafter be made upon the taxable property of the said Town sufficient in amount to comply with the above requirement."

Lawyer or not, that is clear. The annual amount from the town must be at least $1,000 and it must come out of taxes. George H.O. Thomas was a member of Bracebridge town council when this was enacted. It was done at a special meeting of council. It was done using wording sent from New York. It was formalized in every way imaginable, signed by the mayor of the town, Peter Smith, signed by the clerk of the municipality, Alexander Salmon, and sealed with the corporate seal of the Town of Bracebridge. It was all done, moreover, to expressly reverse the resolution Thomas had got through council earlier the same month. Did he not notice any of this?

Thomas seemed a little crazed on this point. At the council meetings he challenged the Carnegie library scheme even as he was chairing the property committee's search for a suitable site. He was writing in his newspaper about the extra features, such as a gymnasium and public baths, that he contended needed to be added to a new library, even as he was challenging the basis for getting the library in the first place. He seemed on some days to go along with the idea that it would benefit Bracebridge to have a library, but then through the *Gazette* ran his opinion that the

THOMAS FAMILY HOME. This fine large residence at the north end of Kimberley Avenue at Manitoba Street overlooks Memorial Park and was built in 1897 by George Thomas a block from the school where he was principal. Seen holding the verandah railing, with other family members present, Thomas was a forceful presence in local affairs and at turns served Bracebridge as school principal, merchant, publisher of the *Bracebridge Gazette*, councillor and mayor. His son Redmond Thomas continued his father's tradition as editor of the *Gazette*, was also Muskoka magistrate and author of local history, and lived in this home until his death in 1973. The place today is a restaurant.

MEN OF THE GAZETTE. E.F. Stephenson, early editor of the *Free Grant Gazette*, is seen with his family (above). When Duncan Marshall (above left) came to Muskoka organizing for the Liberal Party in 1903, he bought the paper from Stephenson, then changed its name to *Bracebridge Gazette*. The days of free grant land were over and he also wanted to suggest the Liberal cause had a modern voice for the new century.

The *Gazette* at the time was stirring up Bracebridgites against getting a Carnegie Library, with G.H.O. Thomas (bottom left) writing trenchant columns to develop the paper's opposition to getting "something for free" and playing off sentiment against Carnegie's "tainted money." Marshall, having advanced Grit purposes as best he could, then sold the paper to Alfred McIsaac (middle left) and moved on, leaving Thomas to shape local opinion.

George Thomas had come to Bracebridge in 1882 to be school principal. Later he gave up that position to be a full-time merchant as owner of a stationery and jewellery business. In 1906, in partnership with Harry Linney, a Bracebridge man in the insurance business, Thomas bought the *Bracebridge Gazette* from McIsaac. The following year Thomas became sole owner, editor and publisher, reassuring readers that the paper would continue a "strong Liberal line."

PROMINENT NEWSPAPER. The *Bracebridge Gazette* published for a number of years early in the twentieth century from a section of the Bird Woollen Mill building beside the town falls.

citizen's of Gravenhurst and Collingwood were now going through the same "disease" of "wanting something for nothing" that afflicted residents of Bracebridge. He asserted at council that the elected body "had no moral right" to impose a $1,000 financial obligation on the town in perpetuity, yet contradicting himself by explaining that such an amount was already going to the library anyway and that indeed there was a statutory obligation to pay it. He championed as the very best possible library site the impossible sloping patch of triangular land by the Presbyterian church, but after it was rejected out of hand by James Bartram on behalf of Andrew Carnegie and the site on Manitoba Street selected instead, first he did not come to council to vote for it, then later wrote expansively in his newspaper on February 6, 1908, that "surely no better location was ever found for a Public Library." G.H.O. Thomas resembled Stephen Leacock's man who "mounted his horse and rode madly off in all directions."

After the new library was up, open and operating, Thomas walked past it every day. Even so, he still proposed in the *Bracebridge Gazette* new plans of how better things would be without it. Instead of the town having saddled itself with the need to pay $1,000 a year to maintain the place, he argued it would have been better to get no library at all. This was strange, was it not? He spread lots of hypothetical alternatives to the library before his devoted subscribers, at least some of whom might have wondered why he bothered since the building was now a reality.

One of G.H.O.T.'s plans was to use the $1,000 a year to buy schoolbooks for the children. Another was to give $1,000 each year to townspeople, instead of the library, so they could buy books, "the great majority of which can be bought in large quantities, new at $10 a hundred," which meant "there could be ten thousand books bought and given away per year." "On a basis of 500 families," continued this author of a plan to take Bracebridge back to its pre-library status of 1874, "that would mean that 20 books, of just as good reading matter as the Free Library popular books, could be given outright to every family in Bracebridge every year. In ten years each family could have a nice library of 200 books, perhaps not the same books they would read from the Library but just as good. A good point in connection with this plan is that it would induce people to take care of the books."

George Thomas may not have been the most clear-thinking or stable person on the council or at the helm of a weekly newspaper, but he was determined. In that very same edition of the *Bracebridge Gazette*, he floated

NEWSPAPER SUPPORT. The *Muskoka Herald* newspaper and printing office relocated from second floor offices on the main street to the new "Herald Building" on Dominion Street beside the town hall in 1891. The Conservative-minded *Herald* was a strong supporter of local library service. The *Herald* printing shop received orders for library cards and a catalogue in 1898 listing all the books in the town's Mechanics' Institute library for distribution to its members. The paper's editorial office housed its own considerable collection of books, part of the town-wide scatter of small libraries.

a gross untruth when he stated, "At the time the Library was first suggested it was very generally understood that the $1,000 was to be made up of all revenue, including government grants. Now we are told the town has to raise the whole thousand, independent of outside support."

The very opposite was "generally understood" by all concerned, as documented from William Mahaffy's very first letter in March 1903 seeking a Carnegie library, on through seven separate resolutions of Bracebridge council passed over a three-year period, and even in Thomas's own previously published writings that acknowledged the nature of

MEN OF THE HERALD. David Edgar Bastedo (bottom right) was publisher and editor of the *Muskoka Herald*, as well as sheriff for Muskoka and a school trustee in Bracebridge. Bastedo had purchased printing press and fonts of type from the defunct *Northern Advocate* to start the *Muskoka Herald* newspaper in Bracebridge

George W. Boyer in 1906 became editor of the *Herald* and, as an ardent Conservative, supported the appeal for Carnegie Library funding while George H.O. Thomas, ardent Liberal and editor of the *Gazette*, grew increasingly opposed. Boyer was away from town during the First World War, serving as an officer in the Canadian Army in France and suffering badly burned legs that affected his walking for the rest of his long life, but returned to take up local affairs, including strong support for the Bracebridge Carnegie library, through the newspaper, municipal politics, and a number of agricultural and loyalist organizations in which he held senior positions for years.

the obligation for the $1,000—which was the very reason, after all, that he was, he said, opposed to it. Now shovelling fog over Bracebridge's clear legal obligation, he began a process in the pages of the *Gazette* to get people thinking that what was true was not, and that what was manifestly false was "generally understood" to be true.

Mendacity of this sort often pays off. From that first article in the early weeks of 1908 through a repetition of his line over the years, G.H.O. Thomas turned the tables. He persisted in achieving, behind the scenes administratively, what he had not been able to do openly with his resolution that the town's yearly payments "not exceed $1,000." From the opening year of the Carnegie library in 1908, the Town of Bracebridge charged the library for both water and electricity, services provided by the municipality, even though Bracebridge council in 1901 had already made the library a municipal institution. Councillor Thomas had also calculated that because no municipal taxes were levied on the library, this had a value of $168 a year, which was deducted from the $1,000. By 1909, the town of Bracebridge had begun reducing its payments to the library by offsetting what the library received from the provincial government. By 1911, even the library fines that borrowers were paying on overdue books were being tallied by the town of Bracebridge and subtracted from payments to its library. Councillor Thomas could take smug satisfaction. He had bested the hardest of all bargainers, Andrew Carnegie.

On March 14, 1916, Moses Dickie as secretary of the library board appeared before Bracebridge council to plead for "an advance of $250 to meet immediate expenses." On July 24, 1916, Dickie was back before council "asking for a further advance on account of library maintenance." By September 12, 1916, Dickie applied to the town "for a further advance to the library board on account of the levy" and council voted to authorize the town treasurer to advance a "sum of $100 to the library board on account of the levy for maintenance." On November 14, 1916, council received a communication from the library board asking for a further advance, and on motion by councillor Francis Warne council authorized "the sum of $150 be paid the library board on account of the levy." Could nobody see what was happening?

Some 15 years earlier, Warne himself had experienced the identical predicament when he appeared on the other side of the council table, trying to keep the financially threadbare library afloat in a sea of indifference and unspoken hostility from Bracebridge council. Yet now, neither this long-time champion of the library cause, Francis Warne, nor anyone else on Bracebridge council dealt openly with the cause of the library's constant appeals for emergency funding. The outspoken publisher of a weekly newspaper who sat among them intimidated an entire municipal council.

When the rival newspaper in town, the *Muskoka Herald*, rose to the occasion and pointed our the drawbacks inherent in this situation, the next issue of the *Gazette*, on December 10, 1914, featured a "Comment" by G.H.O.T. at the top right-hand corner of the front page, most prominent spot in the paper: "After lying comatose a long time the *Herald* wakes to say 'If Bro. Thomas were Constable, Magistrate, Prosecuting Attorney, Grand Jury, Petit Jury and Judge, justice would be properly administered.' This apparent dawn of intelligence in the *Herald* is a hopeful sign."

By 1916, the now pathetically weak library board, being pummelled behind the scenes, appealed to Carnegie for moral support. Moses Dickie sought an interpretation to help counteract this newest phase of the Bracebridge municipality's corner-cutting. On February 21, 1916, Andrew Carnegie's secretary, James Bartram, at the offices of the Carnegie Corporation at 576 Fifth Avenue in New York City, opened a letter from Bracebridge, dated five days earlier:

Dear Sir,

I have before me a copy of the Resolution passed by the Town of Bracebridge dated the 31st day of May 1906, and presume that you are in possession of a copy as well, which I would be glad to have you refer to. I wish to write you in connection with the maintenance of the Public Library here, the funds for which were generously provided by Mr. Carnegie, and to secure from you an opinion on a matter which would probably be a great help in solving a difficulty which is at present giving our Board considerable concern.

According to the resolution the Town pledges itself to support the Library at a cost of not less than One Thousand Dollars a year, but if you will look in the report sent in sometime in August 1915, you will see that they have practically fallen short of this amount every year since the Library was built.

They contend that they do not have to give the Library One Thousand Dollars, but deduct the amount granted annually from the Ontario Government, the monies raised by the Library itself, also all taxes for light, water and local improvement.

This places the Library on a limited amount for salary, new books and the improvements they may wish to make, and this we think altogether unreasonable. I understand that there are other Libraries placed in a similar position and if there could be any chance of compelling the Town to keep up to their agreement we would like to do so.

We intend taking the matter up with the Council in the near future but in the meantime would like to get your opinion as to exactly what Mr. Carnegie intended when he donated the money, which might aid us materially in our endeavour to place our Library on a better footing. No Public Library in these days can subsist on a bare Thousand for all expenses, and we have always contended that the Town is wrong in withholding the difference.

I would be very glad to hear from you in this matter.

Moses J. Dickie,
Secty, Public Library Board

Moses promptly received back the ammunition he needed. This letter was dated March 6, 1916:

My dear Sir,
Your favor of February 16th received. If the Town Council provides a thousand dollars a year for carrying on the library and spends not less than that amount annually for the purpose, it fulfills the condition imposed by the letter of promise. When the letter was given, however, it was assumed that the Town would levy a tax to produce a thousand dollars a year for carrying on the library and that such items as 'fines' would supplement the thousand dollars.
YVT
Jas. Bartram
Secty

Bartram had simply reiterated what was plain on the face of all the documents and the prior resolutions on public record in the minute book of the Bracebridge council. Bracebridge got a $10,000 asset and all the benefits that came with it, which otherwise the town had no hope of enjoying, and in exchange $1,000 a year was the legal consideration the municipality was obliged to pay toward the library to keep it operating. One might think that perhaps dire straits brought on by wartime had created an overriding justification for temporary retraction on such obligations, but that was not the case at all. This practice of the Bracebridge local government to cheat its own library out of the money it owed it had begun long before the outbreak of war in 1914.

As much a concern here was the weakness of the library board to assert its right to the money. The matter had dragged on for some eight years. The town had cut by one-fifth the amount it was legally obliged to pay. In 1915, the library received $800 rather than $1,000 from the town. These seem trifling amounts today, but the annual budget for the library was just over $1,000 in total, so this cutback was a severe reduction that obviously was playing havoc with its operations. The difference of $200 was more than Hattie Dickie's librarian's salary for the entire year. Beyond the money, however, this pattern of municipal practice for more than a decade and a half, from council inexplicably rejecting the 1898 plan to create a "Free Library" to the town's unconscionable welching on its contractual obligations to support the library from 1908 onward, revealed an attitude that was crippling the local institution.

Andrew Carnegie had imposed the 10-percent rule precisely to prevent this problem, knowing that the ongoing operation of a facility needed steady long-term funding. His approach to philanthropy, his well-thought-out plan for the business of benevolence, required that it be conducted in a systematic manner through institutions with staying power, such as incorporated libraries with boards and municipal corporations with accountable elected councils. Carnegie had not been giving away libraries to make friends. He had been doing it to uphold learning, enhance freedom and enlarge civilization. He was a hardened businessman who drove his agenda for free access to the greatest number of books by the greatest number of people, by using his leverage in the situation to require "earnest money" from local governments wanting a library building that exceeded what they otherwise would likely ever pay for the local library. He was serious about this. Cumulatively, through more than 2,000 Carnegie libraries, this policy had a transforming beneficial effect for the large general public. Carnegie knew some municipality might cut corners and be unscrupulous in meeting its side of the bargain, and the Town of Bracebridge was unbecomingly proving him right.

Just as the library opened sometime in 1907 or 1908 with no notice or fanfare, so the town unobtrusively went about deducting amounts from what it was legally obligated to pay. Although most of the public debate in Bracebridge over the Carnegie library had been about its location there was, as Robert Boyer recorded in his history *A Good Town Grew Here*, "a select minority to argue against putting $1,000 a year on the tax rate to support the Library as required by Andrew Carnegie." The sentiment expressed by that minority had not gone away. It had simply gone underground, waiting for a chance to resurface.

Bracebridge's written agreements in correspondence and resolutions passed in council were one thing. Yet something even more than money for the library was forfeited here, something that resembled the town's honour.

Meanwhile, the world was still locked in war.

The 1915 annual report Hattie Dickie compiled for the Bracebridge Library Board to submit to the Ontario government showed circulation for this mid-war period of some 12,949 volumes, a significant growth since 1908. The town's demonstrated appetite for fiction especially continued unabated.

Perhaps novel-reading had even become an escape from the dire reports flowing from the barb-wired and mud-mired trenches in France and Belgium, although even this alternative to the fearful and gripping newspaper stories did not offer a guarantee of respite. Novels dealing with the War, part of the propaganda effort, appeared on the library's shelves. In 1917, H.G. Wells' *Mr. Britling Sees It Through!* became enormously popular because Wells captured the grief and trauma of the times. If most books borrowed were fiction—some 11,262 circulations—the rest divided about equally between the other classifications. All told there were 626 borrowers using the public library in 1915, or about a fifth of the town's total population, and on average they each borrowed 20 books that year. The library clearly was fulfilling an important role in town.

That year the library had revenue of $1,003.65, most from governments ($808.29 from Bracebridge Town Council, $139.05 from the Ontario government) and the rest in fines. Spending in total during 1915 was $948.46. This included $26.25 to repair the building, $5.50 on additional equipment, but most money went to purchasing 181 new books, paying subscriptions for three daily and five weekly newspapers and 20 magazines, and paying Miss Dickie her modest wages. In the donations columns, three additional magazine subscriptions had been given to the library that year. On the financial records, the new library building and its furniture were carried at a value of $10,074.75, while its contents of books were valued at $4,755.34.

With the approach of another winter of mud, cold, hunger and death, the European's called off their four-year slaughter on November 11, 1918, a truce that would hold for 20 years. The soldiers still alive, many wounded, returned to Bracebridge. The town would be devastated the next year by the Spanish Influenza epidemic that claimed some 18 million people worldwide, including a proportionate share in and around Bracebridge. The town was always part of the larger world.

By the start of the 1920s, however, the community was likewise beginning to share in the world's return to prosperity and its exuberant effort

SOLITUDE IN THE STACKS. This inconsequential area of the library may look spartan, but it, too, provided a passport to new places. The row of windows across the back gave light where patrons examined books of interest from the stacks running, on the right, to the circulation desk. The relative privacy of this space let cautious or younger users peruse books they might hesitate to check out for fear of having the librarian look sternly across the top of her glasses.

to overcome the deprivations of the recent past. With the library Andrew Carnegie had given to the people of Bracebridge at its centre, literary life began to unfold as pleasantly as a stroll along one of the town's maple-canopied streets in the dappled sunlight of a long summer afternoon.

Just as the Muskoka Club of John Campbell, James Bain, William Tytler and other literary and musical men and women had earlier fused literature, drama, spiritual studies and closeness to nature in their summer encampments on islands in Muskoka's lakes, a follow-on development had been the Chautauqua movement that began in New York State in the late 1800s and spread through the United States and Canada with a strong presence in Muskoka. The Muskoka Assembly of the Canadian Chautauqua drew Canada's great literary figures such as Bliss Carmen to Bracebridge in the 1920s, where they gave public readings from books, a story fully recounted by poet, English professor and Muskoka summer resident Sylvia DuVernet in her book *Muskoka Assembly of the Canadian Chautauqua Institution* published in Bracebridge in 1985.

In this decade, more titles continued to steadily arrive at the Bracebridge public library, the library continued seemingly unchanged under Hattie Dickie's dispensation, and people of Bracebridge, if shaken by new conditions, still found comfort and insight in the familiar groove of their love affair with books.

With relatively few cars in Bracebridge in the late 1920s, traffic in residential areas was light to non-existent. Jerry Dickie and George Johnson one sunny day backed out the long driveways at the sides of their respective McMurray Street homes. Both drivers looked up the street, then down. Seeing no moving vehicles in either direction, they each simultaneously accelerated out onto the street, right into the back of the other's car in a loud rear-end collision that broke the placid summer silence. Rear-view mirrors were not added to automobiles until a few years later, following their invention by a racer at the Indianapolis 500-mile race, since in racing as in life it is always good to see what is gaining on you from behind.

George Johnson had been hired to come up to Bracebridge in 1925 as principal of the new high school, a few doors away from where the Dickies lived. He bought "Westlawn," the large former home of member of the legislature Dr. Samuel Bridgland, and moved in with his wife, Lillie, and their three daughters directly across McMurray Street from the Dickies. Not many months had passed when one day the local public school inspector provided an unintended lesson for the children in a Monck Township school he was inspecting by collapsing and dying on the spot. Johnson was not slow to act. He decided he would rather inspect schools than be principal of one. Getting around to the scattered Muskoka schools would give good opportunities for fishing. Once appointed by the provincial Department of Education, Johnson's neighbour Dickie suggested he might find the library a suitable place to maintain his office as the new school inspector.

Now, the two men sheepishly surveyed their damaged cars, just one more episode in the common fortunes of the Dickie and Johnson families. Neighbours on the same street, active worshippers in the same Baptist church, they had since become closely connected in an integrated pattern centred on the library. Jerry and George by this time both worked from offices in the lower level of the Bracebridge library building, one as insurance broker, the other as school inspector. George had taken the space

LONGEST-SERVING LIBRARY BOARD CHAIR. George S. Johnson became high school principal in Bracebridge in 1925. The school is seen in the background as he is found happily in the garden behind his rambling "West-lawn" home. In the late 1920s he became a member of the Bracebridge library board. By 1933, Johnson became chairman of the board and served in this position into the 1960s, a longer stint for one person at the helm than even Judge W.C. Mahaffy's extended tenure.

there at Dickie's suggestion because they both understood the Department of Education would pay rent, which would provide a needed source of revenue for the library board. The nature of their work involved being intermediaries who intelligently applied pre-established criteria to different local cases, insurable risks and Muskoka schools. They both reported to out-of-town entities, the insurance companies and the Department of Education. Since this work entailed being out of the office much of the time, and since neither man generated work requiring more than one person on a part-time basis, they shared a secretary at their adjacent offices, and usually she was the daughter of one of them. Being a man with a university degree, an educator who had been both teacher and school principal, George Johnson seemed a natural to join the Bracebridge Library Board. Dickie asked the obvious question, and Johnson gave the only correct answer. There was now justification for them to use the comfortably spacious boardroom on the library's lower level, too, since in a small

HOME OF LIBRARIANS. On the west side of McMurray Street between the public and high schools, "Westlawn" was the first brick house in Bracebridge. Constructed for Dr. Samuel Bridgland, a pharmacist in town and member of the legislature representing Muskoka, Westlawn became associated with library work. Bridgland was an ardent book man and library supporter. It was the same with George S. Johnson and his family, who moved into Westlawn in 1925 when Johnson came to Bracebridge as principal for the new high school just doors away.

Johnson would serve for three decades as chairman of Bracebridge Library Board, and his two eldest daughters Patricia and Genevieve would have continuous close connections with the library including as librarians.

town where everything flows together and people wear many hats, who could say where library board responsibilities took up or left off?

It was inevitable, the way things were going here, that Johnson would be drawn the last step into the Dickie fold. Once on the library board, by 1933 George S. Johnson had become its chairman. He would hold the position for more than 30 years. Jerry Dickie, for his part, would serve as secretary-treasurer of the Bracebridge Library Board for over 35 years, never relinquishing the position right up until the day he died in office in April 1958. The two men would become such entrenched parts of the operation that few considered making a change, especially since Jerry Dickie's and George Johnson's increasingly long memories of prior developments assisted more recent arrivals on the library board to understand the prudent way experience had taught to handle things.

For a significant stretch of the twentieth century, then, Bracebridge Public Library would run forward on cruise control. Such continuity would cause *Herald-Gazette* senior reporter Lou Specht, looking back on this period from 1962 when writing a story about the local library for Canada Library Week in April that year, to conclude his overview by suggesting, "Little else can be said about this Library, for with the exception of staff changes and the increased numbers of books and other attractions, little else has been altered. The building still looks the same as when it was built, although the exterior was painted in 1952, and an oil-burning unit has been installed."

At the end of the 1920s the stock market, home to wildly inflated values as everyone from secretaries to travelling salesmen learned the game of buying company shares on margin, crashed. In the United States, banks failed. The financial crisis spread. Businesses closed and governments sought to fight the deepening economic recession and protect their own country's industries and the jobs they provided by imposing high tariff barriers. A prohibitive U.S. tariff against Canadian lumber ended the export of wood to the American market. Sawmills at Bracebridge closed. Loggers in the woods were left without work. Orders for goods fell off and manufacturing plants around town cut back or closed altogether. The remaining leather tannery in Bracebridge, once the largest in the British Empire, closed. People moved away and the town shrank. The Ward IV School, proudly opened in 1908 at the same time as the library, closed.

Canadians would grind away throughout the 1930s. In Bracebridge as elsewhere a heightened interest in the books of the library was to see what explanations they offered for the bleak predicament. Nuance was no longer being sought, for the thinking and actions of the world were shaping up along bolder lines. The failure of capitalism was bringing into vogue the ideological alternatives of communism and fascism. Freethinking democrats would be in for a long, hard time ahead.

Hattie Dickie carried on through it all. Then in 1932 she received two major surprises. First, she learned from Pittsburgh lawyers settling the estate of Muskoka summer resident John Walker that the millionaire business associate of Andrew Carnegie had made a bequest to the Bracebridge Public Library. This was news to her, although Albert Ecclestone, as his daughter Eva Shields recalls, had been told quite some time before that his friend had included this provision in his will. Walker even had bookplates printed in the United States for this purpose, to formally indicate the provenance of all the books in the Bracebridge library that would have come from his shelves on Buck Island.

Back at the end of summer 1902, when his Bracebridge friend Ecclestone asked about financial support for a new library in town, Walker gave him the contact information for Carnegie's personal secretary James Bartram, just then involved with the second year of Carnegie's philanthropic project of funding new libraries in Ontario. Thereafter, Walker's representations on behalf of this Muskoka town encouraged those admin-

CULTURES IN TRANSITION. Bracebridge public library, required to embrace many transitions in culture and technology, was itself sometimes a silent witness of the limits of technology in the face of nature, as with this 1930s winter rescue of a stranded car by a team of horses.

ALONE NO MORE. Hattie Dickie held the position of Bracebridge librarian from 1915 to 1934, when she married and retired. *Dickie Family*

istering the Carnegie money to have needed patience. That enabled the increasingly improbable Bracebridge deal to struggle forward from early 1903 to 1907. Now, in 1932, Walker's third contribution to the Bracebridge library materialized, and once again it did not take the form of money, but something infinitely better: books!

The news Hattie received that the still roomy shelves of the Bracebridge library would now be filled with 2,400 additional books from Walker's private collection brought her special joy. What librarian would not welcome more books? Townspeople who used the library were astonished. Getting such a major acquisition in the depths of the Depression when there was little money for buying new books was a genuine blessing.

Some "gifts" could be a problem if their donors only saw the local library as a handy dumping ground before Bracebridge had used bookstores or a Salvation Army retail shop to receive such donations. This posthumous gift from John Walker, however, was altogether different. These books were quality editions of classics, biographies and good fiction, virtually all in excellent condition. On top of that, books from a private library of one of the plutocrats of Millionaires' Row at Beaumaris carried a special caché in Muskoka. If some patrons of the Bracebridge library in the future 1990s did not want to read books that had been handled by prisoners at the town's satellite operation at Fenbrook Institution, in the 1930s many in town experienced the same phenomenon in reverse, positively keen to turn the same pages that had been touched by the fingers and eyes of a remarkable millionaire. Books may carry special qualities beyond the words printed on their pages.

Hattie's second surprise was altogether different. In through the front door of her library with John Walker's books walked love. Joe Oatley of Beaumaris was an Englishman. As groundskeeper out at the golf and country club near Millionaires' Row he had developed good ways of being pleasant with people while getting things done, earning a reputation for reliability among the Americans who owned the club. When it came time to move Walker's many boxes of books from Buck Island to the Bracebridge Public Library, the executors of his estate in Pittsburgh simply followed the deceased's detailed instructions. John Walker, always a careful man who liked neatness and order, had not left the fate of his prized books to chance. The executors telephoned Joe Oatley and

JOHN WALKER'S SIGNATURE AND BOOKPLATE. Close business associate of Andrew Carnegie and pillar of the Pittsburgh steel community, John Walker summered on Buck Island near Bracebridge and had promoted a Carnegie library for the town to his Bracebridge friend Albert Ecclestone as early as September 1902. When the American millionaire died three decades later, his bequests included some 2,400 quality books from his Buck Island estate to the Bracebridge library built with Carnegie money he had had a role generating.

Bookplates to designate his donated books as "Presented to the Bracebridge Free Public Library by the late John Walker" had been printed on quality linen stock in the U.S.A. The volumes also bore his own signature, and were stamped "Property of Bracebridge Free Library" by librarian Hattie Dickie, as shown in this reproduction from the novel *Mr. Keegan's Elopement* by the American Winston Churchill.

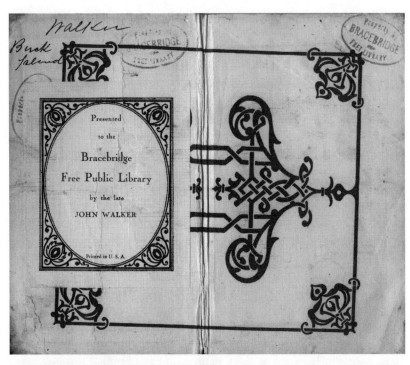

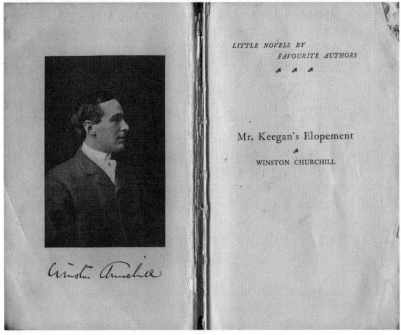

he proceeded to implement the agreed-upon plan. Hattie Dickie, who did not golf had never been at the country club, met her future husband for the first time under the most favourable conditions: he was bringing the librarian the biggest single acquisition of volumes in the Bracebridge library's history. Hattie married Joe Oatley in December 1934.

Surprised by this happy turn in her life, Hattie unexpectedly found herself ready to give up marking books with Mr. Dewey's code, stamping them with the old "Bracebridge Free Library" stamp, and being a scold to other people's children after more than two decades of doing all three. She now invoked the ultimate rule in her book of library etiquette: female librarians, like female schoolteachers, should be single. The rule was already being broken elsewhere, but Hattie was not one to challenge society's norms.

The big news around town was that Hattie Dickie had finally relinquished the position of Bracebridge librarian.

Patricia Johnson, a recent university graduate with a strong record in English literature whose zest for life obscured her lack of training in administrative skills, landed the job right away. As the first librarian in Bracebridge to have a university degree, she was familiar not only with the local library which she had frequently used since coming to town in 1925, but also with the operation of McMaster University's library and its programs. As well, it helped Patricia that she lived across the street from the Dickies, worshipped with them in the same Baptist church, and had a father who was chairman of the library board.

Hattie's departure from the library at the end of 1934 also meant the loss to the Dickie insurance and library operation downstairs. Even as librarian, she had still helped out in various ways with those tasks. So the arrival of Patricia in her place upstairs was one-half of a plan that saw George Johnson's daughter Genevieve slide into a complex role downstairs at the same time. She would work for him as school inspector and also as Mr. Dickie's administrative secretary in the insurance agency. Since both men, moreover, were also in charge of running the library through their positions as chairman and secretary-treasurer, respectively, Genevieve soon became indispensable as the one person who knew the status of everything.

Both Patricia and Genevieve Johnson, who had grown up in different parts of Canada from Saskatchewan to Northern Ontario and who had gained the additional sense of a wider world by living three years in

Hamilton while studying at McMaster University and earning their Bachelor of Arts degrees, were now back living in small-town Ontario under the parental roof once again. Patricia Johnson's pay as librarian was $50 a month, or about $1.60 a day. Jobs were scarce in the Depression, so even this modest remuneration was appreciated for work to be had. Expenses were low because like her predecessor, Hattie Dickie, Patricia still lived with her parents. Only 22, she was the town's youngest librarian.

In March 1935, librarian Johnson secured 40 books from the Ontario Department of Education's travelling library for four months. Ontario's travelling library services were provided to remote and rural areas lacking their own libraries, but during the 1930s the Education Department, knowing how the Depression was imposing crippling budget restraints on established libraries in small towns, extended the service to them. "The local library is fortunate in securing the loan of these books," wrote edi-

THE BEAUTIES OF A BOOK. When Lillie Johnson came to Bracebridge where nobody knew her, she decided to make a fresh start and gave up dying her hair dark. It had turned completely white when she was a young woman, giving an ethereal quality to complement her angelic voice with which she melted men's hearts as she sang inspirational hymns. Here Lillie sits with her first-born daughter, Genevieve, behind her, as both look upon the page youngest daughter, Stephanie, is reading. To the right is the middle sister, Patricia. By this time the two older girls were being treated like twins, often appearing in similar clothing such as these same striped sweaters, look-alike hairstyles, and being called "Paddy" and "Patsy." They would go to McMaster University together. In time both would even share the same job as town librarian, Patricia for four years and Genevieve on an interim basis for four months.

tor Robert Boyer in a front-page story in the *Muskoka Herald* on March 28. The collection on loan included some adult fiction and juvenile interest books, but the majority were non-fiction, such as Lawrence's *Revolt in the Desert* and Toronto newspaper columnist J.V. MacAree's *Fourth Column*. "Since it is impossible for the Board to expend more than $25 a year on non-fiction books," he noted of the economic reality of the times, "the present arrangement brings many attractive volumes for the use of readers."

Johnson also received a special gift for the Bracebridge library in 1935, an oil portrait of the patron saint of libraries. In his day Andrew Carnegie did not seek to make shrines to himself through his gifts of libraries or other buildings like the music hall in New York City or the international peace palace for the World Court in The Hague. By 1935, however, a new generation in charge of the Carnegie Corporation in New York decided a fitting way to honour the hundredth anniversary of Andrew Carnegie's birth was to send each library a portrait of its donor, and so librarian Patricia hosted a festive event that November to hang it on the library's walls. Over the following decades, Carnegie proved to be lively, moving all over his library, sometimes even taking refuge in the storage area. As Abigail van Slyck notes in her book *Carnegie Libraries and American Culture*, "Although these portraits still hang in many Carnegie libraries, library officials have had difficulty finding appropriate places for them in the reformed library." By the centenary of his library in Bracebridge, Andrew Carnegie would look out again from a prized position in the main library hall upon young people at computer terminals.

Patricia's love of literature and her strong sense of community made her happy in the role of librarian. Yet after a few year she began to feel the walls closing in, not to mention her uncertainty about marriage to the local newspaper editor to whom she rewardingly supplied her weekly "Library Corner" column with a pleasant visit every Monday. He was one of several suitors. Should she escape? Patricia sought and got a teaching position away from town, and at the start of September 1938, resigned as librarian. An independent woman, she packed her own car with books and clothes and motored south to teach modern languages French and Spanish, classical languages Latin and Greek, as well as English Literature, to the students at Newmarket Collegiate Institute.

With Patricia leaving, the next development was a sure bet: Genevieve was named librarian, at least on an interim basis, on the recommendation of their father George Johnson, still chairman of the library board. For those approaching the circulation desk in Bracebridge Public Library, whether finding Patsy Johnson or Paddy Johnson, two women of similar outlooks, similar appearance and common experiences as McMaster University graduates, it sometimes seemed to be a distinction without a difference.

Behind the scenes and inside themselves there were real differences, but Paddy's distinctiveness was invariably muted. This sister was the one expected to conform to the pattern of the other. The two were not twins, but had been raised as if they were. Their younger sister, Stephanie, was allowed to dance to a different tune and become herself. The separate lives of Paddy and Patsy, however, were woven so that in many ways they increasingly appeared as one. Her elegant and enchanting name "Genevieve" was changed in practice to the more pedestrian "Paddy" by the very parents who first named her, to now be better paired with her sister Patricia's abbreviated nickname, "Patsy." It continued like that for years, living not in her sister's shadow but in her image. She became librarian only after her sister had moved on. For the few happy months she had the position of Bracebridge librarian, she dutifully took up writing the "Library Corner" column for Bob Boyer's *Muskoka Herald* by following her sister's format.

It turned out that Genevieve's time as librarian was only an interim term after all. The men downstairs, her father and Jerry Dickie, discovered they could not get along without her. So Genevieve left all the books and the people and open airy space and dramas of a public place, and went back to the lower level of the library into her secluded office to resume being Paddy. The exhilaration she briefly felt in autumn was replaced with the steady comfort of administration by winter. In Genevieve's place came Winifred Richards as the new librarian of Bracebridge, before Christmas of 1938.

Winifred was a Bracebridge woman, married to Archie L. Richards, and the couple lived on McMurray Street, across from the Dickies and two doors away from the Johnsons. The close control of the library operation was not exactly being forfeited. Winifred, who was fairly stout and always whispered, quickly learned the routines of the library and carried them attentively.

Hiring single women living with their parents, as in the cases of Hattie and Patricia, meant the board did not have to provide much pay. By now hiring a married woman for the first time, the board was not being motivated by a new spirit of equality to intentionally reject the idea that women could only be librarians if they were single. Instead, still struggling with very limited funds, the board simply accepted it could continue paying low wages to a woman who would be supported by her husband.

ON THE HOME FRONT. George and Lillie Johnson, with daughter Genevieve between them, are joined in a garden of Westlawn by their expanding
family in the early 1940s. On the left are Patricia and her husband, Robert
Boyer, editor of the *Muskoka Herald*, with their daughter, Victoria. To the
right are Stephanie and husband, James MacNaughtan, with baby David. Jim,
home on leave, would soon depart for service overseas with the Canadian
Army and see action in liberating Holland. Bob had just enlisted in the Canadian Army as well. George Johnson was still chairman of the Bracebridge
Library Board. Patricia and Genevieve had both completed turns as Bracebridge librarian.

Through the Depression of the 1930s and the cataclysm of a Second World
War, Bracebridge Public Library advanced like a stately ship, steady and
sedate amidst rolling swells of economic change and confusing under-
currents of social upheaval. The lack of change in positions at the library
during the grey Depression years seemed of a piece with the mood in
the community generally. In 1938, at the same time Patricia Johnson was
leaving town, Mayor McBride was acclaimed for a third straight term in
office. There had not been an electoral contest for the office of mayor for
more than a decade.

By 1930 the integrated Dickie role in the insurance agency, library
maintenance service, and administration of the public library as secretary-treasurer of the library board had been fully taken over by Moses'
son, Jerry Dickie. In time, this nexus of library affairs and insurance busi-

ness would pass down another generation to his pharmacist son, Cecil W. Dickie, Phm.B. Cecil was associated with a remarkable drug store on the main street of Bracebridge. It had first been established by Dr. Samuel Bridgland, who cut a wide swath through the community soon after landing in Bracebridge in 1870, a strong supporter of the local library and Liberal MPP for Muskoka from 1888 until his death in 1903. Then his brother Harry Bridgland, Phm.B., took over the pharmacy while also serving as sheriff of Muskoka. The store was operated by Harry Everett, one of whose fellow employees was Gerald Dunn, Phm.B., who went on to establish Dunn's Pavilion at Bala and put the tiny Muskoka lakeside community on the North American map by booking the continent's top big bands like the Dorsey brothers and musicians like Louis Armstrong every summer for years. Harry's son Robert E. Everett, Phm.B., would eventually take over the operation but go on to further fame as a talented artist, in time donating a valuable collection of his work to the Bracebridge library. For a place that was selling drugs and under-the-counter condoms, smokes and paperback books, it was almost as important a local institution on the main street of Bracebridge as the library itself.

A fourth generation of Dickies also had connections to the library, but by mid-twentieth century the dynasty had effectively run its course.

ANOTHER CULTURAL CENTRE. Complementing the library, Everett's Drug Store was one of several places in Bracebridge selling current magazines like *McCall's* and *Maclean's*, newspapers and popular paperbacks, as well as sodas, smokes and pills. Gerry Dunn could make a fine ice cream soda too.

GENEVIEVE JOHNSON. The eldest daughter of Lillie and George Johnson, she was nicknamed "Paddy" and spent her years supporting prominent men like school inspectors Johnson, Gordon McIntyre and Fred Hammell at their office in the library building, while also handling the administration of the Dickie's insurance business from the same premises, as well as attending to many matters for the library board. A university graduate, she also was the town librarian briefly in 1938 and secretary-treasurer of the board for two years.

Cecil's son Ted would learn to climb the "secret ladder" in the wall to reach the portico and small balcony over the front entrance to shovel off the accumulating snow and chip away the treacherous ice before it backed up water into the library. Ted, in a family tradition back to his great-grandfather, also took his turn cutting the tiny library lawn in the summertime. His sister Jo Anne Dickie, too, had a special connection to the place, running the shortcuts from McMurray Street to the library carrying her grandfather Jerry a mason jar or thermos with soup for his lunch, once he was too old to walk home for the noon meal. Through four generations, one or other of the Dickies generally knew the state of every brick in the library building and the status of each book on its shelves.

Jerry Dickie's secretary, Genevieve Johnson, was even more familiar with the operational work of the library because she had been writing most of the letters and making many of the telephone calls about library administration for several decades, and because her own father with whom she continued to live was himself the long-serving chairman of the library board. When Jerry died, few were surprised that, as a newspaper account put it, "Miss Johnson was prevailed upon to fill the breach."

But when Genevieve Johnson had put in two years as secretary-treasurer of the library board, this accomplished woman who also served as treasurer at the Baptist Church and was a founding member of the Bracebridge Business and Professional Women, had finally had it. She found herself imploding from the inescapable and omnipresent nature of her cloistered responsibilities at the library upstairs and the Dickie insurance business and her father's school inspector work downstairs, at home, across the street, and at the small Baptist church in between that she passed four times daily. There was no escape from any of it. Could one escape? Her sisters had both married and moved into the adventure of raising families, which she could witness but not experience. Her close women friends came for visits from southern Ontario cities, but these companionable times were infrequent. Genevieve Johnson was wedded to her unending and overlapping responsibilities overseen by her father. When George Johnson retired as school inspector, his replacement, Gordon McIntyre, simply slipped into the same chair in the same office in the lower level of the library building, where Genevieve Johnson carried on as his secretary. Constrained by patterns she had not created for her life, this valiant, intelligent and sensible woman in March of 1960 requested a leave of absence for reasons of health.

Today we honour the idea of arms-length relationships and excoriate nepotism in our institutions on the basis of good public policy. This newer ethic, however, also serves individuals who need space and freedom. The departure of the Johnson sisters from their key roles with the Bracebridge Public Library, though two decades apart, and even Hattie's unexpected escape to marriage, helped end the era of close control at the library and usher in more open management and leadership. When Genevieve stepped away for awhile in 1960, her father George S. Johnson soon found it was time for him, too, to relinquish his long tenure as chairman of the library board. He had held the position in an unbroken period in office from 1933 to 1960. That coincided exactly with his daughter Paddy's years there, and makes clear who was really running things at an operational level.

The apparently seamless continuity had come at a price, and not just for "Paddy" Johnson. One can only speculate about what gains and losses for the wider Bracebridge community resulted from failing to get "new blood" into these key positions at the Bracebridge Public Library—chairman of the board, secretary-treasurer, librarian—which were all nestled within Dickie and Johnson families for decades on end. Nepotism, or the hiring of one's own family members, looked different in small town Canada in the first half of the twentieth century than it does today. Not only were family businesses the norm, with brothers, sons and other relatives sharing the venture, but a number of public and semi-public positions in such offices as magistrate, newspaper editor, police chief, school principal, librarian, library board chairman, town councillor and more were occupied with little change for years. The second half of the twentieth century would be different. More rapid turnover in positions and a new sensibility to conflicts-of-interest would contrast to the public ethics of earlier decades. Yet while celebrating the benefits of more advanced concepts of public interest, one cannot help but take note of the simultaneous demise of "loyalty."

Paddy Johnson returned and continued as before. When Gordon McIntyre retired as school inspector his successor was Fred Hammell, the noisy kid in the library who had grown up to become a teacher and write royalty-paying textbooks on mathematics. Now that he was school inspector operating out of the library office, he would soon also become chairman of the library board as the pattern held. The common connector was Hammell's administrative secretary, Paddy Johnson.

Even before the end of the war, however, librarian Winifred Richards was ready to move on. In 1944 the board hired Hilda Leake as her successor. After Hattie Dickie's decades-long run at being librarian, it seemed by comparison the library was experiencing a rapid turnover. Was this normal, or was there something inherently wrong? Certainly by the 1940s the pay had increased, even though Hilda Leake could, the board assumed, count on the support of her husband, Major Frank Leake. Her annual stipend was now $780.

In 1945 the world war ended, first in Europe and then in Asia. Canadians had been in it from the very beginning to the bitter end. This war included conflict of ideologies, with fascism pitted against communism and liberal capitalism, and competition of technologies, with radar and atomic bombs contending against transcontinental rockets and heavily mechanized warfare. The people of Bracebridge recovered and adjusted, building a cenotaph in Memorial Park to honour the dead and living in palpable resolve to build something different and better than they had known over the past decades of war and depression. It could become a time of shared prosperity. Much, much deeper, it was a time of promise.

Hope rose in a new context. All illusions were gone. Lillie Johnson, wife of the library board chairman, clipped and pasted her scrapbooks that chronicled the developments: the front page photographs of the corpses of executed top Nazi officials that the world needed to see to know the deed was finally done following the world's first "war crimes" trials at Nuremberg in Germany; the photographs and descriptions of the concentration camps where the murder of millions had been organized like a sadistic industrial process; the charred field of dust that had been the Japanese city of Hiroshima; the signing of the treaty in San Francisco to create the United Nations Organization; the new movie releases and news of the stars from Hollywood; happenings from the world of arts, drama and the churches; the reports from the *Muskoka Herald* and *Bracebridge Gazette* of soldiers returning home to Bracebridge. The new mood was optimistic realism.

The small Canadian town was now part of the larger world more than ever. The many frontiers of this "brave new world" demanded that townspeople know what was going on, that they be free and responsible, that they address the global challenges which a liberal society preserved at great cost through yet another war now faced in new forms everywhere. The Bracebridge Public Library was more important than it had ever been.

Powerful wartime forces of industrialization in Canada had created demand for more skilled technicians and for scientific education. Expansion of national public information services, including documentary and educational films, combined with greater air travel and automobile use, were boosting mobility throughout the country and breaking down isolation between the regions. In Bracebridge as elsewhere in English-speaking Canada, a mood of nationalism took hold based on pride in wartime accomplishments and optimism for the future. Even before the battles of the world war ended in 1945, planning for post-war Canada was under way. In Ottawa, economists planned Keynesian fiscal policies and Canada became the first country to implement counter-cyclical fiscal policies based on John Maynard Keynes' ideas that were the reverse of what governments had attempted during the Depression, because Canadians were determined those conditions would be repeated "never again." Sociologists devised government support programs to provide a basic level of economic welfare and personal security for all. Committees of lawyers drew up provisions for a new United Nations Organization. In 1943 a new Canadian Library Council was incorporated.

The impacts of the Second World War, notes Harry C. Campbell in his 1969 book *Canadian Libraries*, "gave emphasis to educational innovation in Canada and served to lift library services to a different level."[1] Benefiting from the surge of nationalist feeling at war's end, the library council sought "to spur on new library services and librarianship in Canada."

Hilda Leake really knew books. She read widely and with a keen mind, and enjoyed talking about new titles with those coming regularly to the Bracebridge library, just as these patrons found it refreshing to find a librarian who was more than a checkout clerk in a grocery store. The library in this period acquired a sense of class, as well, because this thin librarian with a pretty face and a lovely personality was an elegant woman.

Just what new books those would be at the Bracebridge library was no longer the result of the librarian alone making the selection, as it had been in Hattie Dickie's day. Members of the library board now read books to recommend whether they would be worthy additions, or in some cases, never find a place at all on any shelf of the Bracebridge Public Library! This role had taken on importance during wartime censorship being in force in Canada. One of the keenest members of the board for this assignment was the daughter of G.H.O. Thomas, Shelagh, who was married to Russell M. Best, Q.C. She would, her daughter Brenda Cox recalls, "read a book a day." Once she was shocked to find her husband enjoying *Lady Chatterley's Lover*. She was only part way into D.H. Lawrence's 1928 novel when deciding the explicit treatment of the adulterous affair between a sexually unfulfilled upper-class woman and the game keeper on the estate owned by her wheelchair-bound husband was just too much. It landed in the wastebasket. That is where Russell soon discovered he could reliably locate the best reading material.

At the end of World War II, when the Bracebridge library suddenly suffered a significant and seemingly inexplicable drop in the circulation of its books, Hilda Leake understood what was happening. Her librarian's annual report to the library board explained: "The return of many servicemen to their homes has meant that fewer women have time for reading." The post-war baby boom, with many new children for the schools and readers at the library, was on the horizon. By 1947, Hilda Leake had decided it was time for her to return from active duty at the library to her own home front with the Major at their home in Milford Bay.

Hilda's replacement was Emma Fryer, who became Bracebridge librarian that same year. Emma Hyunga, whose family was of German origin, had worked as a young woman in an office job at the Beardmore Tannery, then up and left Bracebridge. Some years later when the wife of Charles Fryer of Bracebridge died, he turned to Miss Hyunga, who had since become a nurse. She returned to Bracebridge and they were married.

Although Fryer's children did not take to their new "mother," the patrons of the library found her pleasant and efficient. While the fact she was short posed a problem re-shelving books on the high stacks, there was no difficulty at the circulation desk because she had a little platform behind the high oak counter to stand on. As one whose Germanic instincts and previous office administration experience showed, Emma conducted the affairs of the library in a routine manner. She was small, matronly and quiet-spoken, but firm. She lived nearby on Kimberley Avenue.

At this time Sybil Jackson, who would in time become Ontario's first female sheriff, had just moved with her family to Bracebridge from Hamilton and frequently visited to library to borrow books. "The library was not a complicated place in the 1940s and 1950s," she recalled. "You just went in, looked through the books until you found some you wanted to read, and Mrs. Fryer smiled and signed them out."

This was pretty much how Andrew Carnegie envisaged it should be. He did not fancy the tendency toward administrative bureaucracy creeping into libraries, nor the notion that librarians required special courses. "As for library training," wrote James Bartram during a confrontation in 1915 with Alvin A. Johnson, an economics professor from Cornell University who had been commissioned by the Carnegie Corporation to make a study of the operation of all the Carnegie libraries, "Mr. Carnegie never believed in it. He believed in having books where anybody could get hold of them. A librarian's business is to hand out the books. That doesn't require a long, expensive training."

Emma Fryer continued from 1947 until the early part of 1956, when she retired during the winter.

Betty Reid took her place as Bracebridge librarian on March 1, 1956 and saw the operation through into the sixties. Her annual salary was now $960, an increase of $847.50 over the 55 years since Bracebridge's librarian was at the helm of the reconstituted "Free Library" earning $112.50 for the year. A pleasant and approachable woman, Betty was down to earth, practical about the books, sharply opinionated and quick to act on things. Her husband, Harold, was a popular caretaker at the high school.

The demand for books was growing at Bracebridge Public Library in the fifties, another facet of the post-war economic boom. So Betty concentrated especially on reporting to the Bracebridge community about "new arrivals." In addition to listing the titles and authors, she would often add a descriptive phrase about the work. She astutely tied books to events in the community or cycles of the seasons, seeking to underscore the relevance of reading to life. For instance, her January 24, 1957, "Library Corner" column observed that "the seed catalogues are arriving" in peoples' homes from the nurseries, "so here is a partial list of some of the books that may help you in planning your garden" then listed more than half

END OF AN ERA. Built in 1881, the Bracebridge town hall succumbed to a stubborn fire that started late one afternoon in December 1957 and by midnight had destroyed the historic structure. The chagrined Bracebridge Fire Brigade, housed in the same building, were unable to prevent even their own fire hall from burning down. The kid watching this conflagration, barely discernable through the second-floor window of the adjacent Herald-Gazette building just several yards away, is the author of this book.

Apart from housing the council chambers, municipal offices and theatre on whose stage local citizens had enjoyed many notable productions over the decades, the town hall at one time was home to the Bracebridge library.

That winter night's fire destroyed this building, so long a hub at the centre of the town, but a special noble quality in Bracebridge as expressed in the town hall's emblematic style of architecture disappeared into the smoke that night, too. Hastily a squat yellow-brick box with aluminum-framed windows would replace what had been an open town-centre courtyard and red-brick structure of proportion and artful design—the advent of a discordant industrial-style design that thereafter spread over the public buildings of the municipality, and within a few years would even taint the venerable Carnegie library building.

a dozen, from *Green Thumbs* by Fillmore through *Home Vegetables and Small Fruits* by Duncan to a book highly appropriate for gardeners on the rocky Canadian Shield, *Natural Rock Gardening* by Symons-Jeaune. Making a list of new books in the library the mainstay of her column proved problematic when none came in ("When the end of the week came and no new books had arrived to report, I tried to think of something to chat about that would be of interest to you—after all, I must not disappoint my public!") or came locked in a shipping box ("The box from the Traveling Library arrived. Its contents are still a mystery to me though, as the key had not come at the time of writing.")

A librarian like Betty Reid was never without something to say, however, and could always be counted on for sensible advice pertaining to living the good library life. "Why not get the Library Habit?" she asked in one column, going on to explain that "If you set aside a definite time each week to visit the Library, you will find yourself reading all those books you had intended to read." Betty could seldom refrain from chasing those with overdue books, so added a concluding benefit that flowed from getting the Library Habit. "Also it is usually the intermittent reader who forgets to return the books on time and the result is a fine."[2] She could always work this point in.

In another column, for example, proudly reporting on the fact that during the year 1956, not only had circulation at the Bracebridge Public Library increased by 1,830, but that "the increase in adult non-fiction alone is more than half the overall increase." However, as to the cause of this worthy advance in serious-minded reading, "I am sure that a lot of the credit should go to you," she thanked her readers, "for getting the books back so promptly and giving others a chance to read them."

Not everyone coming to the library sought books, however, or was part of the general pattern of economic prosperity. On March 22, 1957, a thief gained access to the library through a basement window during the night and made off with $71.50 in cash and some stamps, garnered from the petty cash box in the office of M.J. Dickie and Son and the librarian's collection of fines from overdue books at her desk upstairs.

During these years Betty Reid had the good fortune to be assisted by Agnes Tough, and in 1963 when Betty retired as librarian, the town of Bracebridge had the good fortune to have an assistant librarian like Agnes move seamlessly into the role. Not only was she totally familiar with the library and its operations from the first day she became chief librarian. Agnes Tough was a sophisticated woman well equipped to remain calmly and intelligently in control as the sixties arrived with far-reaching cultural changes.

Among early initiatives, the Canadian Library Council sponsored microfilming early Canadian newspaper files, started a publications program, and agitated for creation of a National Library. As well, noted Harry C. Campbell in *Canadian Libraries*, the council took a deep interest in Canada's "cultural reconstruction" after the war by encouraging programs for the assimilation of new Canadians, sending information about Canada overseas, and expanding social assistance in the form of adult education and programs in community centres.

These initiatives through the Canada-wide community of libraries of which Bracebridge Public Library was a part would gradually take their own shape at the local level as the character of those in charge of the library interacted with the circumstances in which they found themselves. At the national level, Canadians got a National Library in 1953. Some of the expansion envisaged by the Canadian Library Council, as bold in its own way as the program James Bain had outlined a half-century earlier in his librarian's manifesto at the birth of the Ontario Library Association in 1901 before two world wars and a global economic depression. Once again, just as the Ontario Library Association benefited the Bracebridge Public Library early in the twentieth century, this new wave of progress would be manifested in Bracebridge, too, in time. New library talks, community outreach, and educational materials came soon enough. The new technologies for storing and retrieving information would only materialize later, however, for example in 1993 when under librarian Ann-Marie Mathieu the library would begin microfilming 120 years of Bracebridge newspapers. But that work would, as the Canadian Library Council anticipated, be a good record to preserve. The microfilming was important because many of those archival records would later be wantonly trashed.

It was also valuable because those pages recorded week by week how the town's Carnegie library was evolving, and that itself was the story of the town.

TEN

Everything Old is New Again

A marvel of spacious design in 1908, Bracebridge's bulging public
library by the 1960s badly needed a makeover.

The long economic recovery of the post-war years found Bracebridge
thriving and its population growing again. Cultural changes brought
about by liberation of women with the Pill, music with Soul, and art
without inhibition, all accompanied by upheaval from an American war
in Vietnam and continuing threat of global nuclear annihilation were
among many forces touching and stirring the lives of Bracebridgites.
New demands faced the library. People wanted to make connections and
understand what was going on. They were doing so in fresher ways, in
greater numbers, than ever before. The attractive building on Manitoba
Street remained reassuring, but it needed more than external grandeur to
keep pace with the deeper currents now moving through society.

The quality of Andrew Carnegie's original library structures meant
they would last a long time. If they could be adapted to changing conditions, their communities would be able to exude pride in these heritage buildings by the early twenty-first century. That was precisely the
problem, however, the tipping point for many of them. Sooner or later all
these buildings needed to be updated if they were to have a future.

In Bracebridge as elsewhere, the challenge facing library boards and
municipal councils looking to expand an early twentieth-century Carnegie
building to serve much larger populations in different ways was stark: do
we retrofit a rigidly built structure to provide more room as well as level
access and elevators, or do we start from scratch?

Bracebridge provides, here again, a specific case study for the cauldron

STEADY AS SHE GOES. In the 1960s, senior writer for the *Herald-Gazette*, Lou Specht, said, "not much has changed at the library" over the years since 1908. This shot, taken from across Manitoba Street, pretty much substantiates his thesis. For a long stretch in Bracebridge it seemed the observation of Alexander Hamilton was being taken to heart: "That which is not necessary to change, it is necessary not to change." However, the stately exterior of an unaltered building belied the evolution of the library as a vital institution in the community and a revolution in librarianship taking place inside.

of controversies that such library renewal projects universally raised in other towns and cities as well. Amazingly, this particular example even demonstrates two radically different approaches to the same expansion option. In another of those unique Bracebridge twists, the town did it not once, but twice, on the same building! The first round in the 1960s was followed by a second in the 1980s and the town's experience in both would highlight for all time the distinction between "renovation" and "restoration."

The way the Carnegie buildings like the one in Bracebridge anticipated future growth was by creating space surplus to existing requirements when built. As more books and additional staff arrived in the future, they could simply fill the empty shelves and occupy the waiting available space. Yet such a growth strategy could only work for a finite time. Then would come the travesty of "culling" books from a library to cope with bulging shelves. This practice, an artless admission of failure though justified by senior people whose arguments are as empty as they wish their shelves to be, had set in at Bracebridge Public Library by the 1960s. Teaching by example, the library associations served not only to promote "best practices" but sometimes also the worst ones, too, persuading librarians that what they instinctively knew to be wrong, somehow wasn't. Until there was added shelf space, however, and as long as more books kept arriving, what other options did they have, these queens of cast-offs wondered unimaginatively, especially in a rigidly built Carnegie castle? Out the books kept going, at ten cents apiece and sometimes free. The Bracebridge library like most of the rest needed to install revolving doors and rename its collection a rotation.

A later generation of architects would develop modular construction designs making it easier to extend buildings physically when the need to do so arose, but they were not the ones who, at the vanguard of their own times, had drawn up the blueprints that James Bartram in New York signed off on. The Carnegie library's solid stone and brick walls, the fixed and relatively narrow entrance at the top of a long flight of concrete steps, the sculptured space of vaulted ceilings and the craftsmanship details in wood panelling were the very things that made Carnegie libraries, in Bracebridge and elsewhere, hard to expand or even alter.

Their unyielding strength was a principal factor in a number of them being demolished. In Guelph, Ontario, Andrew Carnegie's magnificent domed library building, completed in 1905 at a cost of $24,000, stood as an elegant feature in the so-called Royal City. A photograph of it even adorns the front cover of *Free Books for All*, Lorne Bruce's excellent history of the library movement in Ontario, chosen no doubt for being emblematic of the noble Carnegie vintage libraries. Yet less than six decades after it had been built, on the morning of Monday, December 7, 1964, a demolition contractor's steel wrecking ball smashed through the majestic dome. Then it proceeded like a vandal to demolish the rest of Guelph's Carnegie library.

As the twentieth century advanced, the possibilities facing the Carnegie libraries and other public buildings from that earlier era were three in number. One was that followed in Guelph, where the old building was obliterated. This idea had a few strong supporters even in 1960s Bracebridge.

A second option was to leave the building standing but convert it to non-library purposes while relocating the library to new facilities elsewhere. One of the places this "solution" was implemented was the city of Barrie, 60 miles south of Bracebridge, where in 2001 the original Carnegie library was converted with a $6.5-million reconstruction and addition of a new wing to create 27,000 square feet of floor space and then reopen as the MacLaren Art Centre. Another place this would be done was Gravenhurst. This option would come to also be strongly advocated in Bracebridge, by an even larger number of people and, most important for appearing to seal the fate of the 1908 building, by the town council itself.

The third choice was to renovate and expand the existing building. This third option carried its design risks, as Orillians south of Bracebridge discovered when their original Carnegie library was hidden by a modern addition of brick and glass. Only by a remarkable interaction of character and circumstance did this option, risks and all, become the town of Bracebridge's path for giving the 1908 Carnegie structure its badly needed makeover and a new lease on life.

In 1908 the spacious new Carnegie library with shelving for 7,000 volumes easily accommodated Bracebridge's collection of 3,808 books, with so much extra room that librarian Moses Dickie had ample space to display books face out upstairs in the library and operate his insurance agency business from the lower level of the building downstairs, and still have accommodation left over to rent to the Department of Education for public school inspector George Johnson's offices. Even by 1951 there was still plenty of room in the building for the new school inspector Gordon McIntyre to continue sharing the lower part of the premises with the Dickie insurance operation and share as well the secretarial services of Genevieve Johnson, who worked half days with each employer in their adjacent offices.

This unusual arrangement for a library, only possible because of all the surplus space created at the outset as a strategy to deal with later growth, had contributed to the emergence of close control, like a local Family Compact, over library operations in Bracebridge. The different elements under this same roof were all of a single piece, because aspects of the library's operations upstairs continued to be interwoven by much more than shared premises. Dickie and Johnson were both involved with the library board and her father was still its chairman. As well, the state of libraries in the public schools being visited by Gordon McIntyre was a subject of mutual interest with Emma Fryer, librarian upstairs in this period. The school population had been greatly increasing. At the end of World War II 660,000 students were attending elementary and secondary schools in Ontario, a number that had now doubled by the mid-Sixties. Related to this was an impressive building up of school libraries begun in the 1950s by Ontario's Department of Education. Thus how the town library and the school libraries now complemented each others' resources and coordinated their services was important as a matter of program and policy for these twin educational institutions, the central Muskoka schools and the Bracebridge library, and those running them. Even by the end of the decade, in 1959 when Fred Hammell replaced Gordon McIntyre as school inspector, he could still move into the same accommodation in the basement of the library.

Then the Sixties arrived.

The Bracebridge response to the now urgent space problem came in two waves. The first was certainly the easiest: because the downstairs space was finally required for expanding library services, the non-library users were ousted. That had always been the plan of the originators of the building. Both the school inspector and the Dickie insurance business began looking for new premises, no member of the Dickie family was any longer running either the library or its governing board, Genevieve Johnson retired, and George Johnson stepped down as board chairman. The chaos of the Sixties worked its own rules for renewal.

The second wave would take longer to break, but it was coming: an addition at the back of the 1908 structure to house a new stairway to the lower level, and create a new side entrance to the building that would enable the library space inside to be reconfigured in a more functional manner for the times—most notably, the incorporation of a children's library.

The idea for a children's library originated with Dr. William Monk. A skilled surgeon and talented musician, a man of intense sensitivity and focused temper with a strong interest in the arts, Bill Monk made an effective appeal to his fellow members of the library board in proposing a children's library. Certainly the times warranted it with the growing number of youngsters. Not only had the number of school-aged children doubled since the war, but the percentage of younger people was also growing in relation to the total population. Board chairman Fred Hammell knew the library situation intimately, having operated from the premises as school inspector until having to leave due to overcrowding. As a teacher and principal and school inspector, with four daughters of his own, Hammell was quick to grasp the full implications of Monk's suggestion. With Fred Hammell's genial leadership and Bill Monk's persistence, the board persevered until Bracebridge council agreed to make the library's expansion a centennial project to commemorate a century of Canadian Confederation in 1967. By dressing up the plan for the library's inevitable makeover as a centennial project, the proposal would achieve a celebrated status in the community and significant funds from senior levels of government hoping to offset Quebec separatism by an over-the-top celebration of the 1867 constitution that united four provinces. Andrew Carnegie was no longer available to send Bracebridge a big cheque for its library, but the Canadian and Ontario governments would be acceptable substitutes now.

The architects who won the bid for the project were Salter & Allison of Barrie, who had been sprinkling central Ontario with new schools of the late-Fifties and early-Sixties look that celebrated rectangular forms and low-maintenance materials. The contractor whose tender was accepted for the building was Bert Taylor of Bracebridge. The project got financial support for construction costs, as anticipated, from both the Canadian government's centennial commission and the Ontario government's Cabinet Centennial Committee. Strong library supporter and local MPP Robert Boyer was a member of the Ontario committee responsible for approving municipal centennial projects; he made sure the Bracebridge library expansion got its grant. Although senior elected officials publicly celebrated this money flowing from different levels of government as "co-operative federalism" at work, behind the scenes the additional planning and conforming to regulations it entailed really meant additional concentrated efforts from the library board. How much easier it had been when Andrew Carnegie just mailed a cheque.

News notes in the Bracebridge papers kept the community aware of construction progress. On February 16, 1967, the *Herald-Gazette* reported that "during the past weeks construction work made a good start at the Public Library. The familiar stairway in the centre of the upstairs floor has been removed, providing extra space in the reading room. Work on the children's department, which will be located on the ground floor, is also proceeding well."

By March 9, the paper reported that "The new $19,780 cement block Centennial Wing at the Bracebridge Public Library, at present enclosed by sheets of heavy plastic to ward off the cold, appears to be right on schedule as the teams of workmen concentrate on the interior work of the children's department. The new wing extends to the west of the area formerly occupied by the offices of school inspector W.F. Hammell and Dickie Insurance Agency. Work was held up temporarily by heating installations, but last week the men were busy laying insulation and making a start on the interior finishing. The former stairway connecting the downstairs area and the main floor has been removed and covered in."

By May 18, 1967, the *Herald-Gazette* could happily report with front-page prominence: A New Era of Library Service. "Signifying the importance of books to Bracebridge, as communities all across Canada selected special projects to commemorate the first 100 years of Canadian Confederation," noted the paper, "the town made its official centennial project an addition to the Public Library."

With great ceremony the expanded facility had been opened on a spring Saturday afternoon, May 13, 1967, in the presence of a number of *boutonnière*-wearing officials and private citizens, many dressed in 1860s period costume to honour the era of Confederation. In a year when more scissors sliced through more ribbons at more official openings in Canada than ever before or since, this honour fell to long-serving member of the Bracebridge Library Board, W. Reginald Kirk.

In conducting the ceremonies, chairman of the library board Fred Hammell spoke of "the co-operation between town council and the board in realizing this worthy accomplishment as Bracebridge's centennial project." Other speakers represented governments contributing money to the enlargement and renovation of the library. Gordon H. Aiken, MP for Parry Sound-Muskoka, spoke for the Government of Canada; Robert J. Boyer, MPP for Muskoka, for the province of Ontario; and Mayor George Parlett for the town. Ray Smith, as director of the Algonquin Regional Library, of which Bracebridge Public Library was a part, brought greetings. Dr. W.J. Wright, chairman of the town's centennial committee, praised the occasion and all it stood for in a town where the library was so important.

"The choice of a children's library as the town's project is excellent in the sense that such a library is counted as part of our educational system at a time in Canada's history when education more than ever is the most

NEO-INDUSTRIAL STYLE. The symmetry of design and quality of construction in the original 1908 Carnegie library building was accentuated by this artful concrete block addition in 1967. Built to house a stairway and entrance for the new children's library on the lower level of the original building, it epitomized the Industrial-Grade Revival style of public buildings flourishing in Bracebridge at mid-twentieth century.

The dormer on the rear slope of the roof of the original building (top photo) provided light and ventilation to a substantial attic above the stacks.

important area of public responsibility," said Boyer in his address. "The times we live in have changed and continue to change at a rapid rate, and education today must follow new directions. For instance, no one is doing his job today in the same way as 20 years or even 10 years ago." Picking up on Dr. Monk's sentiments, which had spurred this project into being in the first place, he concluded, "These are the young citizens for whom we must provide adequate facilities in our schools and universities, costly though this has become. A library is part of our educational system, and the children's library section represents thought for the future in instruction and enlargement of the minds of the young people in this community it will be serving."

Chief librarian Agnes Tough and assistant librarian Margo Armstrong were both introduced. So were members of the library board and town council and their spouses. It was a happy day in Bracebridge. Here as across Canada a new exhilaration of pride and national hope in this Centennial year was loosening the usually staid ways of Canadians. Once elderly and rake-thin Reg Kirk, his toupee neatly in place for the occasion, had cut the white ribbon across the new ground-floor doorway, a large number of buoyed-up Bracebridgites thronged over the threshold "to examine the bright and commodious rooms for reading, browsing, book-selecting and story-telling."

A well-staged picture taken that afternoon for the newspapers showed town councillors Norman Harkness and Duane Miller being helped to "select books from the shelves of the adult department, which now has increased space available" by junior assistants of the Bracebridge library Linda Sieber, Sharon Raeburn, Margaret Mitchell, and Lori Watson (who was pinch-hitting that Saturday for her sister Cheryl, another regular assistant, away competing in a school field day).

Following the speeches, refreshments provided courtesy of the town were served by spouses of library board members, as one reporter noted, "from the large table which occupies the space for many years the location of that architectural oddity—the central stairwell."

The renovated and extended lower level of the building, now reached by straight stairs that looked cleanly modern with functional steel hand-rails, had overhead fluorescent ceiling lamps and muted beige and off-white tones. A coat of light greyish-blue paint to the door, stairs, reading table and eight straight-backed wooden chairs added an attempt at colour. Display shelves featured books on stamps and stamp collecting together with specimens of postage art since Confederation. A wallboard displayed pen-and-ink sketches and biographical summaries of prime ministers since 1867. A sense of the improbable was achieved by four large rifles starkly mounted against the white wall behind the circulation desk of the lower level. Those unfamiliar with the lore of the Bracebridge Public Library would not have realized this incongruous display of firearms was an attempt to extend the legacy of the library's earlier display of war trophies from battles fought by local boys as soldiers of the British Empire in South Africa, France and Belgium. The character of that display had, like the building that housed it, been lost in the renovation. Yet the rifles, now more openly available, awaited like stage props their future moment in the drama of the Bracebridge library.

In a lead editorial "A Project Completed" following the opening, editor Robert Boyer of the *Herald-Gazette* focused on the "initiative and persistence" of those who had just given Bracebridge "a fine Children's Library, our official Centennial Project, now duly open and serving the young generation of our town." In a view that clearly expressed the consensus of Bracebridge, it was considered "eminently suitable" as a project for the Canadian centennial because "it restores and more adequately uses one of the town's fine old buildings, at the same time as it looks to the future through the added facilities for the education of children.

"Often our old buildings must be torn down to make way for the new," continued this same editorial, "and often they are torn down when they might be restored and continued in service. There are not many buildings in town now that present the original appearance planned by our founding citizens. In some cases we are thankful for the change. Sometimes changing situations, or the disaster of fire, has made the removal necessary. But, where restoration can be achieved, it is good to see that concerned citizens work for it."

Such sentiments were genuine, but in retrospect seem to have been spoken like hopeful words at a wedding banquet intended to hide the error of a fundamental mismatch. In this case, the noble project of an expanded and renovated library had been wedded with a rogue architectural style for public buildings that was on the ascendant in Bracebridge. To even call it a "style" invests the perfunctory mindlessness of construction in Bracebridge in this period with a higher classification than is warranted.

The turning point came late in December 1957. When fire destroyed Bracebridge Town Hall, a special noble quality in the town, as expressed in the 1881 building's emblematic style of architecture and red brick construction, disappeared with it in the ascending sparks and smoke of that

DOORWAY DOWN. The 1967 renovations removed the wooden central staircase to the lower level, and replaced it with this doorway leading to the new metal stairs beyond.

ABSTRACT BLACK AND WHITE. A Bracebridge art student was motivated to create this abstract work in the 1970s which, hanging in the grand hallway, greatly enhanced the lines and look of the renovated library's entrance, revealing the soulful relevance of fluorescent lighting and concrete blocks.

NEW HUB. Circulation desk in lower level of library after 1967 renovations. Stairs down and narrow entrance into lower level seen at rear left of photo.

black winter's night. In early 1958, a squat yellow-brick box structure with aluminum-framed windows hastily replaced what had been an open town centre courtyard and red-brick structure of proportion and artful design. Mayor George Parlett and the town council only emphasized, with a sense of alarmed pride, how quickly they had put up the new building.

Thus was ushered in a discordant industrial-style design that began to spread over the public buildings of the municipality. The public school on McMurray Street, rebuilt in the new standard of the day, was no more capable of giving inspiration than a perfunctory office building or factory, neither its materials nor its design fitting with its setting. Next door to the mundane building that replaced the town hall, the two oldest generations of the newspaper Boyer family contracted to have their 1891 red-brick Herald Building "modernized" by covering it over with white stucco. The next initiative to destroy the streetscape on this principal avenue in Bracebridge took place on what had been the spacious front of the 1900 Muskoka District Courthouse. Here in the 1960s the provincial government affixed a box-like addition of unmatched brick and discordant windows to the heritage courthouse, crowding right out to the sidewalk. There would, bleakly, be many more examples, from a new fire hall to additions to the high school.

By 1967, when it came time for the addition to the Carnegie library, the new "Bracebridge style" had become commonplace in all senses of that word. Although grandly touted locally as "the Centennial Wing," it was just a concrete-block bunker.

MID-WAY EVOLUTION. This 1970s interior view of Bracebridge Public Library captures a stage in its evolution between the 1967 renovations and the 1985 restoration. The original entrance from Manitoba Street is at the front, in the centre of this photo.

The suspended fluorescent lights have been added, the open central staircase to the lower lever removed. Original oak bookshelves have been joined by metal filing cabinets.

In keeping with the town's mid-twentieth-century approach, part of this 1967 centennial project also included "renovation" which took the form of removing several heritage features of the 1908 building. This was happening in many older private homes around town and in earlier commercial buildings in the community at this time, as a new ethic of efficiency and comfort developed against the tableau of human imagination frozen by fear in the spreading twilight of the Cold War and articulated in sterile design. The now-prevailing sentiment was captured in the *Herald-Gazette* reporter's description of the Carnegie building's central stairwell as "that architectural oddity."

After 1967 came a truce in culling because enlargement of the library's useable public area again permitted more shelving for books. Where rotation now picked up, instead, was at the head librarian's desk.

During her five-year tenure beginning in 1963, sophisticated and shrewd Agnes Tough had not only imparted a rigorous intelligence to the mood in the town library itself, she had also matched the library's physical expansion with activities extending its reach into other institutions in the community. She worked with Bracebridge's Danny Poland, a local hockey star who had progressed through his service station business to become a supervisor at Beaver Creek Correctional Camp south of town, so that inmates could visit and use the library's facilities. She became closely connected with the high school, too, collaborating with librarian Diane Clipsham and later Gerry Murphy in development of a first-class school library, and holding orientation sessions at the public library for members of the student library club. After she retired as Bracebridge librarian in 1968, principal Kenneth Black in August 1969 offered Agnes a dream job. Compared to her former position she earn more money, get a pension, have fixed hours, and enjoy intelligent engagement with bright teenagers in their own school environment. As town librarian she had seen the library successfully through the upheavals of the 1967 expansion. Now Agnes Tough could continue the library work of the community in a different venue.

In 1968 it was Kay Cave who replaced Agnes as librarian. Kay continued the library's operation in its expanded set-up through a period of adjusting to the layout of the reconstituted facilities and the reconstructed views of the Sixties, before retiring several years later in 1972, a year prior to her husband Alick Cave's death. Mary Jorgensen, a warm, gracious human being, was next up as Bracebridge chief librarian, bringing good experience with her following prior employment in libraries at Toronto and North Bay. Like her two predecessors, Mary retired after five years, to be replaced by Eugenie Smith, a woman with strong interest in heritage and an instinct to the dramatic which had led her toward a career in acting before she was attracted to library work. Gene would be at the library's helm through important changes over the next five years—personal when she met and married chartered accountant Barry Graham and became a mother, and also institutional, when the town that so recently had celebrated enlargement of its library once again awkwardly found itself re-enacting the same play.

In the fall of 1979, Glen Schroeder, a tall soft-spoken mathematics teacher at the high school who had become chairman of the Bracebridge Public Library Board, met with Bracebridge town council to discuss a proposal to enlarge the library premises. Only a dozen years had elapsed since the library's expansion.

Schroeder's idea received a great deal of consideration by the surprised councillors. Some were just not library-minded folk, but all of the elected representatives were troubled to receive a proposal they had not antici-

HEAT AND LIGHT. The original library's vaulted ceilings are seen in this view toward the south wall. A century of adaptation within this same space shows different attempts to create a desirable environment in the library. The original electric lights were lamps on the tables, and the large windows offered natural light during daytime. In 1967 fluorescent lights seen here were suspended into the hall, brighter light at the cost of aesthetic value. In 1985 they were replaced with more discreet tubular overhead lamps.

Ceiling fans, seen here, were added to circulate the heat in winter down into the large chamber. Several decades before, the coal furnace with hot-water radiators had been replaced with an oil-burner. The old building had been very cold in winter and took a long time to heat up. Today, horizontal slat blinds cover these windows and are drawn most of the time, protecting the computers from too much heat from the sunny southern exposure.

pated would be back on the town's agenda for several decades. At their regular council meeting on October 10, councillors worked through the issues and ended by directing the library board to "look into the feasibility of choosing a new site for the public library." Suddenly, in Bracebridge, it was Option Two for what to do with an old Carnegie library.

However helpful they had been at the time, the two initiatives in the mid-sixties of taking over all remaining space in the Carnegie building exclusively for library purposes and of expanding the facility itself had not created enough room for longer-term needs. Culling was back. The library was on a trajectory towards cramped quarters once again. "There was limited space," Fred Hammell, chair of the board at the time of the 1967 changes, would write in a retrospective view many years later, "simply because the amount of money for that Centennial Project of building the Children's Library was, relatively speaking, quite small. As a result, it was only a matter of time until the Library Board was faced once more with the need to expand."

The town council was interested in "the construction of a new building to provide this service" instead of "putting an enlargement onto the existing old building." Specifically, council had in mind a piece of land the municipality owned a couple of blocks northeast of the Carnegie library, a property at the corner of James and Ann streets across from the Bracebridge Memorial Community Centre. A curling rink had stood here, but now the site was being used as just another of the town's parking lots. The sub-plot in this drama was that certain councillors wanted a new library building because they thought it could incorporate a senior citizens' centre, echoing the multi-purpose idea of a community building espoused by town councillor G.H.O. Thomas who in 1907 wanted a gymnasium and public baths added to a proposed new Bracebridge library.

Council suggested that the board "carry out a brief study in order that the projected needs of the Bracebridge community for library services for the next several years will be known" to give councillors "a better idea with respect to what will be required in a new library building." Such information would benefit the entire community, of course, not just its elected representatives. Additionally Council, again echoing G.H.O. Thomas, seemed mindful of a wide constituency it believed would not want much tax money spent on a library and passed the buck, or the responsibility for raising the bucks, back to the library board. Could it, Council asked, "make certain enquiries of the possible success of a fund raising campaign in order that the Municipal portion of the construction costs may be paid through this method"? In other words, could the board do the council's work, could it help council sidestep its responsibility to come up with the money? In moments such as this, the positive value of Andrew Carnegie's firm-handed philanthropy only grew clearer as the longer light of history continued to reveal the unabated attitudes of municipal councils towards libraries. Municipal council chambers were seldom places of deep pockets, long vision, or high-mindedness.

Council's response had not at all been what Bracebridge Library Board members expected. Overnight everything had shifted from an addition for the venerable Carnegie building to an entirely new structure in a different location. Glen Schroeder would not continue to chair the board.

However, some other board members, thinking they had no option and even wondering if the new approach might not have the greater merit, assiduously took up the challenge. Librarian Gene Smith began requesting different agencies and companies to provide an outline of feasibility studies and the cost of making them. Their responses, however, indicated that these organizations needed terms of reference for a new library before they could proceed. The task was, at each turning, becoming bigger and more complex.

Getting money to proceed was a real challenge for the board. Raising money for a library was much harder than for a hospital, yet Bracebridge council had tasked this volunteer body that was supposed to be running the town's library to now become major fund-raisers as well. Although the Bracebridge Public Library had notionally become a municipal institution in 1901, it remained like an un-adopted orphan of the town. Orphans go where they have to. At this time community organizations had begun to tap gambling proceeds to get them out of dire financial straits. Taking its cue from the town of Lindsay, to the southeast of Bracebridge, whose public library had been the first in Ontario to receive a "Wintario" grant, the Bracebridge board turned to the Ontario government's money-laundering Lottery Corporation. It had been cosmetically named "Wintario" to make the state-run bilking operation of generally lower-income Ontarians more political palatable.

John Raynor of the Lottery Corporation informed the board that Wintario would pay half the cost of a feasibility study for the new Bracebridge library if satisfied with its scope and need. He noted, as a minimum, that the group carrying out such a study should be different from the eventual building contractor so that they would present an "unbiased" report. Even getting free money apparently came with strings attached. Wintario was now yet another party to whom the library board had to provide information and criteria.

The Board dug into its assignment more deeply than ever. After much discussion it decided that among the points a feasibility study should address would be the projected population and economic growth in Bracebridge, an examination of the existing library to get a complete picture of services currently being offered, and a projections of the town's future needs to help decide what new services should be offered. The Board also decided to determine both the cost of expanding the library on its present site and of a new building on a different site. In keeping with the sentiment coming much more strongly now from seniors groups, several councillors and the editorial columns of publisher Dr. Edward Britton of the *Bracebridge Examiner*, it would also consider the shared and joint use of a building, in order to gain "maximum value for facility dollars." Another component that needed to be clarified would be the cost of operating a new facility if it were built, like the original Carnegie building, bigger than current needs required to accommodate future growth.Some board members feared that "oversupply could carry a long-term penalty." Finally—and this consideration brought the board back to where it had started—it needed to firmly establish what might happen if the project was delayed or cancelled.

While some of this information was what any good board would need anyway, it was equally clear that this project was starting to get unwieldy in addressing future unascertainable situations. To get a clearer sense of essential criteria for proceeding, the board members got advice separately from Albert Bowron and Henry Campbell, two individuals experienced in the library field, on how to carry out feasibility studies for new libraries. Bowron, who had conducted many such studies, had credentials that impressed the Board. He suggested a number of points to consider, and his first few ideas corresponded with what the Board had already realized about the need to anticipate the community's future growth, taking a complete look at present services offered, what services were in fact being used by members of the community, and the size or scale of these operations. Then he suggested it would be valuable to compare the Bracebridge library's services with those of other libraries in the region, an idea that would lead to a most comprehensive if time-consuming canvass of several dozen other Ontario library operations. Bowron especially focused the Board on a clear-eyed comparison of the costs of relocation versus the costs of an expansion at the present site. He also urged consideration of other possible sites, in addition to the one increasingly favoured by town councillors at James and Ann streets. Turning to capital costs, Bowron urged the board to get quite specific about the size of the facility it needed for the services it wanted to offer. For example, would it need 6,000 or 7,000 square feet? He pointed out that approximate costs at that time averaged $70 a square foot to complete, excluding costs for the land on which the building would be erected. He also stressed the need to be clear about on-going operational costs of the library, whether in a new building or at an expanded version of the existing facility. With that approach, Albert Bowron informed the Board he could produce a feasibility study in three months, sooner if needed, and that his fee would be around $3,000 with another $500 for expenses.

The second person with whom the Board next explored the way forward, Henry Campbell, was a librarian who at this time was already doing a study for library facilities in the Georgian region. Essentially, he would look into the same points already mentioned by Bowron, could do it in about six weeks, for a fee somewhere between $4,500 and $4,800.

Word quickly spread about the prospects of a new or expanded library in Bracebridge through the grapevine of consultants and architects. When librarian Gene Smith sent out additional feelers at the end of October on behalf of the Board, they triggered letters of inquiry and expressions of interest from those looking for work. She also hit the phones. On November 7, 1979, R.M. Allison, architect and planner in nearby Barrie, wrote to the library board following Smith's telephone call to him on October 31 when she'd explained consideration was being given to relocating the library to a new building. As Allison noted, his firm was "well known in the area" and he had been responsible for the design and addition to the Bracebridge and Muskoka Lakes Secondary School. Allison offered to do a feasibility study and absorb the cost of doing so "into the overall architectural fee, should we be retained to design, tender and supervise the project"—which was pretty much the problem of bias John Raynor of Wintario had averred to. Whether absorbed or paid outright, Allison calculated the cost for the feasibility study of "relocating the library to a new site" would be $750 and it could be done a month.

The momentum for a new library in Bracebridge was becoming unstoppable. Then nature intervened to save the Carnegie building.

The library roof was leaking. Though built to high standards, seven decades had taken their toll. Water and ice damage in the spring of 1980 made nature a participant in the town's advancing "new library" proposal. The deterioration of the old building dramatically changed the whole direction and momentum of discussion about a new library facility, as board members who had been contemplating whether "oversupply could carry a long-term penalty" if a prospective new library were built too big were suddenly brought up short by the immediate reality at the existing building in which they were meeting. Here there was real and present danger of water damage to the library's contents and imminent risk of injury to people outside the building.

By the late 1970s, roof problems were being assessed by individuals calling themselves "roof system consultants" and the library board tapped the services of one such firm, Kingston & Powell Ltd., of Sutton West, Ontario. Ross Kingston came up to Bracebridge and checked out the roof. In keeping with the terminology of his trade, this consultant euphemistically described the problem as "moisture intrusion" at the library. His general examination of the roof revealed that all the slate shingles were in a state of deterioration. Pinholes, fractures, and missing shingles were part of the problem. Over the years, repairs had been made as needed, generally by inserting metal under the shingle tabs, and in one section of the roof by replacing the slates with asphalt shingles. In a number of places, his inspection showed, metal flashings were also deteriorating. The flat roof at the rear part of the building was "heavily ponded," noted Kingston, and due to this condition he was "unable to determine the condition of this roof area" but his general impression was "that the roof is not good and lacks the intended life expectancy."

His report, dated July 18, 1980, on the "Bracebridge Public Library Roof System," also added some more distressing news: the front flat roof "is a mineral surface finish with the granules shedding and in process of deterioration"; at the wall junctions, "the membranes were improperly flashed" and the roofing "is open allowing the present leakage"; the brick chimney was "in poor condition and required pointing and repair"; metal cornices required "securement and caulking"; eavestrough was "either missing, damaged, and should be replaced throughout and/or where it is needed"; in various locations, walls required pointing and windows caulking.

Since few board members or anyone else ever got up onto the roof to see for themselves, they had to rely on the report of the consultant. He had certainly reached a clear conclusion: "It is the writer's opinion that the roofing in general should be replaced and it is not in the Owner's interest to attempt further repairs." Three recommendations were made. One was that the slate shingles and metal flashings be removed and replaced using 210-pound asphalt singles, including a substantial starter strip to reduce chances of ice backups. A second was that a new roof system be installed on the front flat using the existing mineral surface roof as a base, and properly installing membrane and metal flashings at all junctions. Third was that all necessary pointing and caulking to brickwork be done, and eavestroughs installed where necessary.

This focused all available attention back on the state of the existing structure. It was clear something had to be done. It was certain it was going to cost money.

Then, as if this happy conspiracy of dire elements was not yet enough to make sure the "new library" idea would get sidelined by the new urgency, the ante was upped further. Bracebridge resident Peter Bird, reading the Kingston & Powell report, saw much greater liability awaiting the library board than flowed from mere moisture intrusion. Peter J. Bird, P.Eng., a grandson of the founder of the famous local Bird Woollen Mill and of the Bracebridge Mechanics' Institute Library and who later was a town councillor at the time of the original construction of the Carnegie library building, had himself followed his grandfather's propensity toward engineering and was now principal of Bird Engineering Ltd. in Bracebridge. Peter had commissioned Kingston's report on behalf of the Bracebridge Public Library as soon as the board contacted him about the leaking roof in the spring of 1980. In an August 8, 1980, letter to librarian Gene Smith, Bird said "the geometry of the roof system over the front entrance" had to be improved, that "the geometry or the drainage of the flat roof over the new addition" made in 1967 had to be corrected by installing "proper roof drains" and doing "remedial work to metal flashings," and that with the possible exception of the newer flat roof over the addition, "all existing roof surfaces should be removed and replaced with new." Additionally, Bird noted that fairly extensive re-pointing of brick and stone masonry was required to provide a weather screen for the walls.

Then he added the clincher: "The chimney must be re-pointed as it is about ready to fall down." It was his engineer's professional opinion that if the recommended repair work was "not done immediately, extensive damage to the interior of the building will result." He concluded by noting, "There is also the possibility of serious personal injury if the chimney collapses or if a large piece of plaster falls from the high ceiling." The only relief was minor: because the roof system was "found to be so badly and obviously deteriorated," said Bird, sending a lower invoice than his quoted fee, "the inspection task was less onerous."

This grim news about the library's dangerous deterioration played right into the debate in town over what to do about the library. For those familiar at their own homes, businesses or cottages with the destructive

BALANCING BETWEEN OLD AND NEW. The engaged mood of Bracebridge Public Library, circa 1981.

powers of water through the roof, it was not hard to see how a brand new building suddenly held greater appeal than ever over yet another round of repairs to an ageing structure. Yet to those who valued the heritage building and the attractive focus it provided in the centre of a town, the need for major action to save the unique Carnegie library suddenly became all the more urgent. Thus the deteriorating 1908 building, suffering some additional problems because of the 1967 changes to it, seemed simply to harden both side's resolves and give them additional ammunition. And that is how the stalemate would have dragged on, had it not been for another new element to change the debate and derail the "new library" proposal.

A different chairman of the Bracebridge Library Board was unexpectedly in place. Robert Dolphin, an air force pilot during the war and an entrepreneurial businessman since, had just retired to Bracebridge and found himself in a dream where he was miraculously sitting in Glen Schroeder's empty chair on the library board. In what still seemed like a surrealistic turn of events, Dolphin got a phone call one Saturday night from Gene Smith dramatically reporting that water was dripping all over the registration desk. She no longer had enough pails to catch it all! What should she do?

As men always do when responding to an emergency and rescuing a lady in distress, Dolphin scrambled like the old air force hand he was and with councillor Aubrey Glass, ever conscientious about his responsibilities as a Bracebridge councillor and member of the library board, the pair did the best they could hauling tarpaulins and spreading them over everything to protect their library against the intruding moisture. The more the rain came down that night, the higher Dolphin's resolve rose. "I was fed up with water leaking in," he declared looking back at that turning point, "and all the other building issues."

Robert Dolphin's ascent to the chairmanship of the Bracebridge Library Board had been a surprise to many, but most of all himself. Shortly after moving to Bracebridge from Toronto, he got a phone call from town councillor Harold Dawson about an up-coming meeting of the Board. Dawson, an electrical contractor, was also council's representative on the board, in the term before councillor Glass took over. Dolphin turned up to the meeting, a newcomer in town, curious to see what it was all about. His only prior library experience before that night had been as a patron of the North York Public Library. It turned out the Board was going to elect a new chairman. Within a few moments of taking his seat Dawson nominated Dolphin and he was promptly elected. Now an astute businessman with an entrepreneur's inventive flair would bring change to the local scene.

Whatever might eventually happen to the library, as a consequence of the current discussions and debates in town about a new library building, the town council and the library board were concerned about immediate perils and public liabilities. By August 19, 1980, the first quote on the job had come in from A&G Roofing, operated by Audia Roofing Corp. Ltd. of Orillia, offering to do the work for $12,900. By October 29, M&T Roofing Contractors of Midhurst, Ontario, tendered a much lower bid: they would do the same job for $3,066 with a five-year guarantee. That was the end of the slate roof on the 1908 building.

It was also the start of serious thinking about restoring the rest of the structure. Something had snapped the thinking about public buildings in Bracebridge, at least in Bob Dolphin's mind. The concrete block structure at the rear of the library was seen in a harsh light as inadequate, ugly, and poorly built. Gene Graham continued to rush around with her pails whenever it rained heavily outside, catching the flow that "poured like an open tap" inside. One of the inmates from Beaver Creek who was at the library repainting the stairs – the board found it financially advantageous to use convict labour – was knowledgeable about weaknesses in building structures and helped her locate the source of the problem. It confirmed what Peter Bird had observed about "proper roof drains" needing to be installed in the 13-year old Centennial Wing, leaving some to ask about the building standards applied to the 1967 addition.

"Various suggestions were made concerning the problem," recalled Fred Hammell at a later date in his *Muskoka Sun* column. "Some believed that the building should be wrecked and a new one constructed on the same site. Others were of the opinion that the property should be sold and a new location sought. Some hoped that any addition to the Library would include a new centre for the Senior Citizens. Through it all, the Library Board maintained that the old building should be kept and an addition conforming in style to the original be constructed. And finally, that position prevailed."

Hammell's "through it all" reference was one of those retrospective overviews trying to summarize a lot of history in a single phrase. The board members had only come to resolutely believe in keeping the old building and replacing the earlier addition with a new one that respected the 1908 Carnegie structure's architectural integrity, after having first being blown off course by town council and then by experiencing individually and collectively the moment of truth that they were responsible for a heritage building that was deteriorating. Sobered also by the serious implications of attempting to put up a new library building, the little miracle of Bracebridge that occurred in 1980 was the board's breakout from the town's somnambulistic culture of civic architecture that had settled in from the Sixties onward. Bob Dolphin was the spark. "I fell in love with the building," he recalled in January 2008. "It was centrally located, just like Andrew Carnegie wanted, on the highest promontory in town. I was determined to keep the location."

Even so, it is one thing to have the dream, another to turn it into reality. The prospects for achieving this brighter dream were not exactly great. The Town of Bracebridge still wanted the library board to raise the money to upgrade one of its municipal institutions, at whatever location—a different standard than it applied to the schools or the hockey arena. Librarian Gene Smith, who had now become fully immersed in the project, worked with Dolphin researching how other towns comparable to Bracebridge conducted fund-raising campaigns for their libraries.

To the southeast of Bracebridge, Lindsay's Carnegie library, which was five years older, was in great need of an extension. A fund-raising goal of $165,000 had been reached and exceeded but only through a huge effort that included a garage sale and a book sale generating $800, and a young person's walk-a-thon netting $1,500. Jars for coin collecting were placed in stores. Buttons were manufactured and sold. Hasty notes illustrating old Lindsay buildings fetched more money. A five-minute slide show about the need and plans for the library expansion was presented at tea and coffee hours held two or three times a week at the library. Out-of-town businesses were canvassed, but with little response. It clearly took a lot of effort.

To the north of Lindsay, in Fenelon Falls, some $30,000 had been attracted for that town's library at this time using a number of techniques: canvassing door-to-door, letters to former residents, local women's wear shops donating receipts from two fashion shows, the local theatre giving one day's box office receipts, the compilation and sale of a book of local recipes, sale of hasty notes printed from sketches owned by the library, book sales, money contributed to "Library Fund" bottles placed in local stores and businesses, Canadian Tire donating cash for redeemed Canadian Tire money, sale of crafts donated by local residents, a donation pledged from only one foundation although many had been contacted, and a bequest of $4,500. Again, a lot of work by a lot of people.

The town of Elmira, whose Carnegie library had been built five years after Bracebridge's, provided Dolphin and the board with yet another example of diversified, try-anything-and-everything fund-raising for the local library. In this case, the decision to expand the Elmira library was made just the year before, after two public meetings were held at Woolwich Township's request so that the amount of public support could be assessed. The public meetings indicated that many people were definitely in favour of the project and were willing to form a fund-raising committee committed to raise one-third of the projected $60,000 cost of the building. This confirmed what Dolphin instinctively knew about the importance of proceeding only with strong community support. The township council agreed to provide a matching third of the cost, and applied to Wintario for the remainder, which was another reminder to people in Bracebridge of the growing importance of provincial gambling revenue as a back channel for project funding by which the province's libraries helped launder the Lottery Corporation's money.

Smith compiled and the Board studied many of these examples, all of which showed that for their position to "prevail," as Fred Hammell characterized it, could not entail a passive approach. The Elmira example, one of two dozen examined, showed how a wide-ranging, long-term engagement would be required. The Elmira committee raising the money for its library sought as wide a representation as possible, including businessmen, bankers, representatives of local service clubs and community groups, teachers, religious leaders, housewives, and students. Under the committee's direction many specific projects took place: a door-to-door canvass (which turned out to be more time-consuming and less profitable than expected, except from a publicity angle); solicitation by letter, followed by a direct personal contact, of all industries and businesses in Elmira; convincing each service club such as Kiwanis, Lions and Jaycees to make the library one of their projects for the year, with the result that each club undertook a major donation to the fund and provided manpower for each canvass as well; obtaining the support of each bank and trust company in town, especially since many banks have an unwritten policy allowing them to contribute one percent of the financial goal to a local community project. As well, Elmira turned to mail solicitation of businesses such as suppliers, fast food outlets, and liquor stores headquartered outside the town but which did business locally. Foundations were approached. Personal letters went out to former residents of the area. The community was divided into groupings such as "professionals," "teachers," "local store owners" and "industry" so that members of the fund-raising committee could then be assigned a specific number of names on the list to contact. In addition, raffles, sales, and film shows all brought in some money, although these too, euphemistically speaking "were more valuable for their publicity value." Publicity in fact was seen as critical for the Elmira fund-raising initiative, and the committee worked to get as much newspaper and other media coverage as possible. They erected a giant thermometer on the library and kept it there until the campaign donations reached the top—a device already used in Bracebridge while raising money for the addition in 1967. They plastered Elmira with posters. They sold buttons, candy and notepaper. They spoke at as many community meetings as possible. They put displays of the proposed library building in store windows. They sought to thank everyone in as public a manner as possible for their donations and help. They made a point of including the local newspaper editor as a steering committee member in charge of publicity. In the end, they provided a great model for others, and an eloquent reminder of why Andrew Carnegie's philanthropy had been such a gift.

The Bracebridge library board members now realized they were not alone. Many communities around Ontario were being driven into inventive fund-raising campaigns for the sake of their local libraries. Many faced the same problem as Bracebridge, coping with century-old Carnegie libraries. Their experiences illustrated what was working, and what was not. Aurora, a hundred miles to the south, was a comparable town in several respects including a population of 15,000. How it had just raised $105,000 for its public library was reviewed. Another town was Dundas which, just prior to this period when the Bracebridge library board began seriously studying the cash-coercion craft, had entered the field with mixed and curious, though generally successful, results. Much about the Dundas model commended itself to Bob Dolphin. A long-standing member of the community closely connected to the library had been appointed fund-raising chairman, and a former library board member became his assistant. The two of them personally approached industry, businesses and individuals in Dundas, Hamilton, and surrounding areas, to contribute to the fund. The calibre and standing in the community of the persons appointed to this committee demonstrated just how important it is to have individuals with personal acquaintances in industries and businesses. The two members had such connections, and it paid off. Where they did not, an introduction to the contact person for the prospective donor was arranged. A letter outlining the library plans was sent to community service organizations and a number of foundations. This resulted in several donations from foundations, and though these were rather small, one notable exception in this fishing expedition was striking a foundation created by a bequest which specifically mentioned the Dundas Library in the benefactor's will, resulting in a single donation of $80,000. However, this only let the municipal council off the hook. As the Dundas librarian noted, "Because of this donation the Board decided it could probably raise two-thirds of the Wintario grant, rather than one-third. Consequently, all we received from the Town of Dundas was $25,000 on a $270,000 expansion."

A number of these elements would be paralleled in the Bracebridge campaign.

Getting the money in, by whatever means, was only half the equation. The other half was spending it. The cost of a new library in the 1980s loomed large in the growing Bracebridge debate about what to do with the overcrowded facility built nearly three-quarters of a century earlier for a town then one-quarter its current population. When the first estimate of $835,000 to $850,000 was floated, it was pointed out to board chairman Dolphin in an editorial by Dr. Edward Britton, publisher and editor of the *Bracebridge Examiner*, that he should be "more realistic."

To generate a better picture of the actual cost to enlarge the Bracebridge library, Dolphin decided to start by looking at recent specimens of library construction in other Ontario municipalities. The one that he saw in Oakville, Ontario, impressed him more than any other. An architect named Brian Chamberlain had designed it.

By this stage the momentum in town seemed clearly swinging back to Option Three, restoring and expanding the existing building. If council was so disowning of the matter, it could hardly expect to get the new building it wanted with a built-in senior's centre now that the library board to which it had handed the whole project was newly resolved to restore and expand the Carnegie library.

First had come the idea to fight for the old building. Second had come the architect named Chamberlain as the one seemingly destined to handle the assignment. But everyone still needed a budget. What Bracebridge could get would depend a lot on whether it had $500,000 or $2 million to spend on the library, and with Dr. Britton at the *Bracebridge Examiner* as the town's worthy successor to G.H.O. Thomas at the *Bracebridge Gazette*, everyone knew there would be a close eye kept on getting value for money. So those in Bracebridge coming to grips with the costly choices facing the town carefully reviewed statistics, collected by Grace Buller of the Provincial Library Service, on new public library buildings constructed in Ontario since 1970. Some 17 new public libraries had just been built in Ontario in Bracebridge's category, ranging in book capacity from 5,000 to 150,000 volumes. They showed what Bracebridge could expect to face in a new funding commitment.

The 125,000-book Burlington Public Library, with 3,630 square feet, cost $664,939 or $22.61 a square foot in 1970. With a staff of 7 professionals and 34 non-professionals, it served a population of 92,000, had reading room capacity for 165, meeting room capacity for 200, and parking for 100 on its two-acre lot. The Preston Branch of the Cambridge Public Library, with capacity for 50,000 books in its new 1973 9,600-square-foot facility, cost $260,000 or $27.01 per square foot. With a staff of eight, the library served 16,500 people, had parking for 10, meeting rooms for 100, and reading room for about 60. The Dundas Public Library, with 32,000 books and 9,000 square feet on two floors, and a staff of 20 serving 17,000 as well as some county residents, cost $330,847 or $36.76 per square foot in 1970. With parking for 10 on the small 110- by 120-foot lot, the building had reading room seating for 36, and meeting room for 40 in one venue and 75 in another. And so it went, page after page of specific information about the Albion Branch of the Etobicoke Public Library, the headquarters of the Georgian Bay Regional Library System in Barrie, the Terryberry Branch of the Hamilton Public Library, the King Township Public Library, the Byron Memorial Branch of the London Public Library and Art Museum, and more. What stood out, once again, was that while all libraries are the same, each is unique. Every one that the Bracebridge board cared to examine had special features. All clearly had made it a priority to provide meeting rooms and plenty of parking, but the distinctive variety in importance of such features as study carrels, reading rooms, film collections and cozy arm chairs was clear, even rising from pages of statistics.

During this exercise, while the Bracebridge library board was getting together its firmer estimate of the cost, a rare opportunity arose for the town to reacquire for $50,000 the gas station property it had sold off decades earlier adjacent to the land-locked library. Acquisition of this land would create many new possibilities for the library. Spirits rose. But the sentiment of council was against laying out that kind of money. No deal materialized. So the plan was reworked and a revised budget of $585,000, with an additional $30,000 for contingencies, agreed upon. Now there was a basis for moving forward with "more realism." Then followed further discussion of the numbers with council and the town's financial administrators. In 1981, it was agreed. Bracebridge Public Library Board received approval from Bracebridge Town Council to go ahead with a $555,000 project to restore and expand Bracebridge's Carnegie library.

Architect Brian Chamberlain was emerging as Ontario's leading specialist in libraries. After what he had seen of his work in the design of the Oakville library, Dolphin was interested in retaining Chamberlain's services but knew his board needed some reassurance if the work was not going to be openly tendered. As it turned out, a Bracebridge architect, Hank van der Meulen, who had designed many homes around the expanding town and was highly respected, had been a partner of Chamberlain's. He vouched for him. On July 14, 1982, town council authorized the library board to engage the architectural firm of Brian Chamberlain and Associates to draw up plans. Chamberlain was retained.

Before long he had prepared a model of what the expanded building could look like, giving Dolphin the perfect thing for a series of "show and tell" sessions around town, starting with the municipal council. Letting people see what was possible as an outcome was the best way, using the "lateral thinking" approach, of envisaging where you wanted to end up and then working back from there to the present to determine the best route to reach the goal.

Brian Chamberlain and his staff worked closely with Dolphin conducting research about the building's original appearance. Both men felt passionately about the value of fine old buildings in present times. They also shared the code of the air force, for Chamberlain too had served aloft, including as a pilot in the RCAF's famed Snowbirds show team, and now as a reservist flew helicopters and owned his own airplane. Getting from his office in Burlington to Bracebridge did not require booking a ticket, just filing a flight plan. "A good deal of information was found in *The Best Gift*, a book about the Carnegie libraries across Ontario," reported the *Bracebridge Examiner* about their joint mission to now restore the Bracebridge library building with authenticity. No doubt this helped somehow, but as the definitive publication on Carnegie libraries in Ontario this fine book by Margaret Beckman, Stephen Langmead and John Black remarkably has neither photographs nor any description of Bracebridge's Carnegie library.

ARCHITECT TO TURN THE TIDE. Brian Chamberlain of Burlington became the award-winning architect for the mid-1980s restoration of the Bracebridge Carnegie library, which included a major expansion so it could continue to provide service to the community equivalent to its original standards but adapted to a much larger town, new technologies, and new thinking about human physical access and building structures.
Since the Bracebridge project, Chamberlain Architectural Service has become the architect of choice for many other library buildings, including the new Gravenhurst Public Library.

Chamberlain Architect Services staff also worked closely with the library board in exploring government grants available for the project, a field in which they were expert from other library buildings the firm had designed, and helped arrange special fund-raising projects.

One of the most novel fund-raising features of the Bracebridge campaign, not copied from any of the other town whose methods had been studied, was the sale of bottles of Andrés wine bearing the label "Bracebridge Library Edition." Bob Dolphin had a friend with Andrés winery and

BETTER THAN A SKETCH. If a picture is worth a thousand words, this scale model of the proposed restoration and expansion of Bracebridge's 1908 Carnegie library was even better for helping people see the potential and donate money to make the model into a full-scale reality. What held special appeal, in a disquieted town where public buildings had sunk to an industrial-grade functionality, was the way architect Brian Chamberlain honoured the aesthetic integrity of the original building. When the restoration and expansion was complete, Chamberlain would win the design award from the Hamilton chapter of the Ontario Association of Architects for his achievement in maintaining the original building's historic appearance.

the two dreamt up the plan of selling special label wine in local liquor stores. The head of the Liquor Control Board of Ontario, when Dolphin first met him in his thick-carpeted Toronto office, simply said, "We don't allow that." Not prepared to abandon anything that could bring in money to restore the library, Dolphin did not understand any part of the word "No." He mounted a mini-campaign within the campaign. The LCBO relented and gave the green light. At this time the unique idea of using a wine label to promote a cause, the restoration and expansion of the Bracebridge Public Library, had never been done before. Nor would others be allowed to do so. When the Ottawa Public Library wanted to copy Bracebridge's example, the LCBO refused permission. "That was a real jewel in the crown," enthused Dolphin. "This gave us a high profile. Visitors from the United States would buy it by the case." The wine was promoted actively in Bracebridge for three years, from tent cards on restaurant tables to prominent displays right beside the cash registers in the LCBO. The special label wine created a lot of excitement for the campaign. The label on the bottle featured Chamberlain's drawing of the restored library.

Everything Old is New Again

IN VINO LIBRIS. A unique fund-raising appeal for the Bracebridge Carnegie library restoration and expansion was the sale of a special "Bracebridge Library Edition" of Andrés red and white wines. Library board chairman Robert Dolphin was told by the LCBO chairman "We don't allow that." Dolphin persevered. For three years the wine sold steadily at the Bracebridge liquor store on Manitoba Street, generating some $25,000 for the Bracebridge library. Ottawa public library wanted to copy the idea but could not get clearance. Only Bracebridge had pulled it off. The stylized image of the library for the label was drawn by Brian Chamberlain, architect for the 1985 library building renewal.

THIS WINE IS HOT! Library board member Dee Glennie happily holds a bottle of Andrés "Bracebridge Library Edition" red during a visit to the winery with Mayor Jim Lang and library board chairman Bob Dolphin.

Borrowing from the example of other Ontario towns that had recently been fund-raising for their libraries, the campaign executive for the Bracebridge Public Library Restoration-Building Fund was a high-powered group. The premier of Ontario, Hon. Frank S. Miller of Bracebridge, Muskoka District's MPP, was its honorary chairman. Honorary treasurer was Kenneth Veitch, town clerk and avid local history archivist. The general chairman for fund raising was Robert J. Boyer, the former MPP and newspaper publisher, while Dr. Robert M. MacIntosh, president of the Canadian Bankers' Association who with his family "spends as much time as possible" at his Hilo Island summer home on Lake Muskoka near Beaumaris, was active as a highly effective chairman of fund raising from corporations and foundations. Jim Perrin of Orillia, made famous by his daughter Jacquie who went on from being Miss Dominion of Canada to an on-camera career in television, devoted much time and effort from 1982 to 1985 working with the committee to raise the money.

Boyer's letter as general chairman of the campaign, sent by the many hundreds over these months, enclosed a brochure that outlined "the history of Bracebridge's present 'Carnegie' building and the overall plans for restoring this historical structure and at the same time providing modern library services for all residents both permanent and seasonal including much needed facilities for the handicapped." He then explained that the total cost for the work "is an estimated $650,000. With the allowance for special grants, we must raise $350,000 from the public sector in order that this long overdue historical renovation and addition can be completed." Like all construction projects, the library cost seemed to be a guesstimate that changed as things progressed, and Boyer's reference to the campaign goal of $650,000 was up from the $555,000 the town had approved a couple years earlier.

"Andrew Carnegie never lived in Bracebridge," stated one of the campaign's ads, "but his philanthropy and interest provided us with our present library." The ads showed Andrew Carnegie looking intently from the page, close-up and resolute, eyes meeting the reader's. "In 1908 Andrew Carnegie Donated a Library to Bracebridge" said the headline. "Now ... It's Our Turn!"

"A lot has changed in the past 76 years," continued the message. "Library use has increased 79 percent in the past five years. Our collection of books that are enjoyed by everyone from preschoolers to seniors, permanent and seasonal residents has expanded from 3,800 volumes to 20,000." Noting that the space to contain them had not grown, however, the ad explained, "Redevelopment of the library with an addition to double its size and restorations to the existing building has begun. Your donation in needed to the library's $350,000 Restoration-Building Fund to complete the project. You may live in Muskoka for only part of the year but we want you to feel the Bracebridge Public Library is yours while you are here. Your contribution today is as important as Andrew Carnegie's was back in 1908."

The slogan for the campaign, used with the Brian Chamberlain sketch of the building that also appeared on the wine labels, was "The little library ... that's growing!"

The library board itself was particularly strong in this period, small in number but large in reach and dedication. Mary Dee Glennie, Dan Brooks, Bruce McPhail and town councillor Aubrey Glass were inspired to new heights by the imaginative and unrelenting drive of Robert Dolphin as board chairman.

The town's connection with "Little Pittsburgh" remained as important as ever for the library. After Dolphin spoke about the project for some two hours by telephone with president Kelly of Pittsburgh-Mellon, he was told, "I'll put it before the board, with a recommendation for $50,000." The money came through.

On March 4, 1983, Ontario's Minister of Citizenship and Culture, Bruce McCaffrey, approved a $200,000 grant from the province to restore and make and addition to the Carnegie library.

By raising much of the money in their community to support expansion of the local library, Bracebridge citizens were showing commitment to the cause and making tangible their belief in the importance of self-education. As their passport to a full range of global experiences just down the street, they knew the local library was well worth the effort.

Yet this indispensable adhesion between citizens and their library, so essential not just for a library but for any institution to endure over time, can also be seen in the less flattering light it sheds on the avoidance syndrome of municipal councils when it comes time to pay for libraries. Andrew Carnegie was a tough-minded Scot who understood the necessity of forcing municipalities to pay for the on-going operation of any library he built for them. While many towns and cities agreed, because the prospect of a handsome new building in the centre of their community without immediate cost appealed to them, others balked even at that, as Bracebridge had previously done despite the town's legal obliga-

SUPPORT FOR THE LIBRARY. Member of provincial parliament for Muskoka, Frank S. Miller, obtained $60,000 of provincial lottery money towards an addition to the Bracebridge library and presented it to Board Chairman Robert Dolphin outside the library. Several dozen service organizations in town, and hundreds of business corporations and individuals beyond, also presented cheques in connection with a mid-1980s expansion. Like this picture that ran in the *Herald-Gazette*, presentations were prominently reported with photos in the Bracebridge newspapers to foster a sense of honour bidding so organizations and individuals might outdo one another in contributing to the total amount needed of $350,000 for the community's library.

tion, because payment each year of 10 per cent of the capital cost of the building was more than they wanted to pay for the luxurious frippery of books.

The keenness of municipal councils across Ontario and certainly in Bracebridge to lay off library costs to others in the 1970s and 1980s showed this sentiment was still strong. Why spend local dollars, anyway, if a distant benefactor was prepared to do so? For a brief shining moment early in the twentieth century Andrew Carnegie appeared when Bracebridge needed a library it would not pay for, and now his latter-day counterpart was Wintario. Frank Miller of Bracebridge, when serving as

A PORTAL TO THE LIBRARY ITSELF. The 1908 Carnegie library in Bracebridge was constructed in accordance with building codes, both provincial and municipal. A century ago no level access was required, nor even more than one means of egress from a public building of this size. The door at the bottom left of this picture, on the south wall, was only added in 1967 when "renovations" to the building meant it had to comply with a standard that allowed people a Plan B if they were in a burning building. Until then everyone going into the library building, including people doing insurance business with the Dickies or school business with the Muskoka public schools inspector, went in the upper level front door and down the inner staircase, which certainly allowed better premises control. The 1985 restoration work entailed many upgrades, including an elevator between the floors for those needing its use.

Treasurer of Ontario, referred to this multi-million-dollar pot of lottery proceeds as "the government's mad money." A fund that could be used for special projects, it had its own rules for who got the money—a measure of Ontario's enduring awkwardness as a puritanical instinct meshed with gambling and gaming which after all had been a criminal offence until governments decided to get into this game of fleecing people. The millions of dollars scammed from generally lower-income citizens, as Ontario NDP leader Howard Hampton demonstrated in his master's thesis about this "tax on the poor," were not paid into Ontario's consolidated revenue fund to be deliberately allocated according to public priorities between schools, health care, roads and other spending programs. Instead, the separate Wintario fund segregated the money and made people feel wholesome as they accepted the ruse that the Ontario government was not really doing a bad thing with publicly run gambling, especially when the money was going to worthwhile projects like community libraries.

The exception became the new norm. Local groups keen to apply for Wintario grants were encouraged to do so by their spending-averse municipal councils. Bracebridge would apply for, and get, $100,000 of Ontario's "mad money" for its 1980s public library.

As architect Brian Chamberlain found when redesigning the Bracebridge library in the 1980s, the work areas of staff are the most complicated parts of the whole library set-up. Those employed in a library may find a space designed with little thought to how they would function week-in, month-out. The layout of the premises and access to its supporting resources can affect the efficiency of employees, the operation of library services, and the morale of all concerned. By spending a great deal of time with library staff and interviewing them where they worked, he gained understanding of their needs. The resulting plans sought to accommodate facilities so they maximized effective interaction between various staff members and between staff and the library's patrons.

How the library functions as a distribution centre, a role not perhaps often considered by many users of a library, is also important to the layout of the premises if efficiency is desired. The arrival of new books and periodicals, the processing and shelving of these additions to the collection, the arrival and shipment of borrowed and lent items through inter-library loan, the departure and return of books signed out by patrons, the special shipments of books to shut-ins and to Bracebridge's smaller satellite libraries in the seniors residences or at the prison, are among the main elements of a daily handling operation at the library.

Clustering similar functions can be a great benefit for both staff and users in the design of the library. Having related collections in close proximity is part of the logic inherent in a well-organized library, although the themes around which one might group books and other resource materials are as wildly diverse as the topics of the works themselves. Good design helps reduce the costs of inefficient organization, and even curtail the interruptions by patrons requiring directions to the washrooms or photocopier. All this thinking went into the plans and is now on display today in the finished result.

Both Bracebridge papers discerned and expressed the new consensus that had formed in Bracebridge around Option Three.

"The old building has become inadequate for the surging demand," said Judith Brocklehurst in the *Herald-Gazette*. "Books, on shelves too tightly packed together, are hard to reach. The library has to go out of the building to put on the plays and shows. There's a magnificent collection of magazines and newspapers but no special place to relax and read them. Old and handicapped people find the stairs impossible to climb. They feel, rightly, that they are part of the community too, that they need the Library's services more than most, not less." Despite these problems of the existing facilities, Brocklehurst continued by noting its enduring strengths. "The Library is still an important community place. Our grandparents read their books here. Back then, the Library was giving them concerts and lectures, too. Then, as now, the Library was a nice downtown place to meet a friend: 'See you at the Library!' A part of everyone's life. As you go in the door, you bring history into the present. You can sense the ladies in button boots and kid gloves who walked sedately in there. We've always been proud of it. That's why the decision was made not to scrap the old building nor to turn it over to another purpose."

"The project involves restoring the original appearance of the building," reported the *Bracebridge Examiner*, "while doubling the space available through an addition that maintained the historic appearance. The Bracebridge Public Library is an important part of community life, not only as a focal point for reading, learning and community events but because of its unique architecture. The community has been pulling together to raise funds to restore it to its original appearance."

Construction began in December 1983, was substantially complete by August 1984. The restoration gave breathing space, an open airy atmosphere, more book stacks, a children's area, good circulation space, and a room for reading periodicals. The project would also fill two other much-felt needs: proper access for disabled and elderly users, and adequate work areas and office space for staff. Yet all this was happening in a building that was not losing the flavour of the past. Brian Chamberlain's plans incorporated similar materials, including Bracebridge's signature red brick, to those used building the original library during 1906 and 1907. He exercised enormous care to preserve the traditional style of the original Carnegie library, which he described as "an excellent building, very well built."

PROGRESS. The picture above, during the 1984-5 restoration and expansion of Bracebridge Public Library, shows where new construction of a side entrance at ground level replaced the concrete block box addition of 1967. The original building had only one entrance at the top of many stairs, potentially a problem in case of fire, and a barrier for people unable to mount steps. Below, interior work is under way in the space that would become the new home for the adult circulating collection.

An official opening date was set for the start of a national holiday weekend, Friday, May 24, the next spring.

"It is with great pride and enthusiasm that the Bracebridge Public Library Board," wrote its chairman Robert Dolphin in letters of invitation to a wide circle of library supporters on May 1, 1985, "requests the pleasure of your company at the Official Opening of the newly restored and enlarged Bracebridge Carnegie Library by His Honour, the Lieutenant-Governor of Ontario, John Black Aird, at 11:30 in the forenoon, Friday, May 24th, 1985."

"Included in the Official Opening ceremony," continued Dolphin, "will be the formal dedication, in perpetuity, of the 'Patricia M. Boyer Children's Library' by Patrick Boyer, MP, the son of Robert and the late Mrs. Boyer. Mrs. Boyer was not only our librarian some years ago and initiated many of our children's library services, but was one of Muskoka's most outstanding citizens in her service to the community."

On the sun-filled spring Friday morning of May 23, 1985, Ontario's Lieutenant-Governor motored into Bracebridge from his Muskoka summer residence near Port Carling to deliver a congratulatory address. Then in a double-scissors ceremony he and Mayor James D. Lang officially cut the ribbon in two places to mark yet another advance in the evolution of the Bracebridge Public Library. Beaming at their side was librarian Nancy Jones, brighter than ever under intense sunlight in her white suit, along with Robert J. Boyer and Anne Miller.

Mrs. Miller appeared happily relaxed to the public, although she was preoccupied. The reason that her husband, Frank, Muskoka's MPP and now premier of Ontario, was absent from this event was that his minority Progressive Conservative government was losing its first vote in the provincial capital at the same time the ribbons were severed. During breaks in the ceremonies, people listened discretely to car radios in the parking lot tuned to the drama of the voting at Queen's Park. The new library facility for which Ontario's premier Frank Miller had been honorary chairman opened just as his government began to crumble.

Andrew Carnegie was not physically present, either. Yet he was in this place more than anyone else. His connection with Bracebridge, a town he never visited in person although the Ottawa Carnegie Library was accorded the rare distinction of his visit for its official opening in 1906, had always been through books. So nothing could have been more fitting at these Bracebridge opening ceremonies than the moment Joseph

THE HAPPIEST CUT OF ALL. Ontario's Lieutenant Governor John Black Aird and Bracebridge's Mayor James D. Lang cut the ceremonial ribbon at a sunny official opening of the restored and expanded Bracebridge Public Library on May 24, 1985. Watching attentively, from the left, are chief librarian Nancy Jones; Robert J. Boyer, editor and historian, former Member of the Legislature and chair of the fund-raising campaign; and Anne Miller, wife of Member of the Legislature for Muskoka and Premier of Ontario, Frank S. Miller. As a long-time summer resident of Muskoka, His Honour spoke enthusiastically for many patrons who benefit from the library's services during the summer months. Member of Parliament Patrick Boyer then spoke indoors to officially open "The Patricia M. Boyer Children's Library" which honoured his late mother and the town's former librarian.

Dufton of the Bracebridge Rotarians stepped forward and presented library board chairman Robert Dolphin, for the town library's collection, a copy of a book written by Andrew Carnegie and signed by him.

On August 22, 1985, the Bracebridge library board issued a press release announcing that it had completed a review with architect Chamberlain of the final costs for the addition and restoration. The project had not only been completed ahead of schedule, said the board, but below budget since some $8,500 of the contingency fee had not been spent. The board "was even more pleased with what the architect achieved in blending 'the old with the new' facilities that the library now provides."

Restoration of the Bracebridge Public Library would earn Chamberlain Architect Services the 1989 Design Award of Hamilton's chapter of the Ontario Association of Architects.

Despite this revival of interest in ancestral and heritage elements of the community, Bracebridge, although the capital town of Muskoka District, has not yet established a public archive, with the unfortunate result that many irreplaceable records have been lost and more are poorly stored and unavailable for research. Even the minute books of the Bracebridge Public Library Board, last seen in five bound leather volumes for the period up to the 1970s, have vanished without a trace.

To its credit, Bracebridge Public Library during the years of Bob Dolphin's chairmanship began "The Muskoka Collection." It is not an archive as such, but it is the best publicly accessible resource for historical records in town so far. Today it is housed along the south wall of the original main library hall, in a number of glassed-in wall cabinets.

For a municipality where tourism is important, the Muskoka Collection is another of many attractions, bringing people to stay in the town while engaging in research utilizing this unique resource at the local library. The publications held here date back to the 1800s. In 1993, the library began microfilming 120 years of Bracebridge newspapers, starting with the very first copy of the *Northern Advocate* published December 14, 1869, in Parry Sound before the newspaper was relocated by Thomas McMurray to Bracebridge in 1870.

The value of the Bracebridge Public Library having commenced this collection, as it will be when the municipality itself establishes a proper public archive, is that it gives people possessing rare materials and unique records an appropriate place to lodge them. Like a baseball diamond in the middle of a cornfield, "If you build it, they will come!" In 1994, for example, Dr. Robert MacIntosh, who had assisted the library a decade earlier with corporate fundraising for the expansion, donated 89 items to the Muskoka Collection, worth $7,000.

The library restoration of 1985 did not only reinstate for the town its architectural integrity, but with the Muskoka Collection inside the building it began to preserve the deeper story of how all this came into being in the first place.

Other things were going on inside the library, too. The whole aim of the restoration and expansion had not, after all, been to just have a fine building, but to create as board chairman Dolphin often put it, "The best library in Muskoka" and as several other observers have noted, "The best community library north of Toronto."

By 1985 the collection now included some 21,000 books, of which more than 3,000 were paperbacks. Subscriptions existed for 58 magazines and 9 newspapers. The popular young adult collection had more than 1,000 paperbacks. In the vertical files, organized by subjects, the library now maintained up-to-date pamphlets and clippings that were proving especially helpful as a resource to public and high school students and those doing research for books. University calendars also formed part of the library's collection. New book acquisitions in 1984 had totalled 1,835 works, of which 795 were paperbacks. Most recently arrived titles were conveniently stacked in a "new books" shelf in the adult library for patrons on the lookout for new works, a quest assisted by a "new books list" and a "bestsellers list" on a bulletin board beside the circulation desk. This list also showed books that were on order.

By 1985, one in three town residents had their own library card, reported the *Herald-Gazette* on May 22, 1985. In 1984, the paper added, some 66,535 print items were loaned by the library, which "averaged about seven items borrowed per resident in town."

A number of other examples of the Bracebridge library's operations in the year of the 1985 addition further demonstrate ways the place had evolved over the decades and was interwoven with its town. One was a special lending service operating for shut-ins who could not get to the library. From a list of volunteers, Anna Crawford of the library staff established matches with immobile individuals. The volunteers then selected and delivered books to these off-site patrons, and returned some days later to picked up the borrowed books and exchange them for others. Discussions helped clarify the reader's interests, and provided a welcome human and intellectual link to the wider community.

"Talking books" were another innovation. These were audio tapes on which the mellifluous tones of accomplished readers, often famous actors, rendered a reading of an author's entire work, bringing to the ears of blind or illiterate townsfolk a tale they would otherwise not hear. After she went blind, Lillie Johnson, wife of the long-time chairman of the Bracebridge Library Board and mother of two of its librarians, delighted to discover that her life-long love of books need not end. During the many darkness hours spent thereafter with talking books from the Bracebridge library,

THE CARNEGIE STYLE. Andrew Carnegie's nearly three thousand libraries were built in a style to evoke the nobler purposes of civilization, and this rear view of the 1985 addition to the Bracebridge Carnegie library shows it was possible to maintain harmony and symmetrical balance with the original 1908 structure. Relocating the entrance, seen beneath the flags, to street level at the side of the building made access easier for users of wheelchairs, walkers and baby carriages, which was an advance on the earlier structure. Installation of an elevator further enhanced accessibility for those unable to readily climb stairs. Also, with ample parking at the back of the building, the walkway along the south (right) side of the building makes the library more easily accessible from all directions—as many like to get to the library with the least delay or detour—yet another acknowledgment of changing times since 1908. Such greater functionality clearly did not require sacrifice of the Carnegie style or the building's aesthetic integrity. *Russ Mackinnon*

Lillie completely "re-read," as she put it, the entire body of Shakespeare's plays and sonnets. By 1985, the Bracebridge library had over 100 talking books in its collection with access to thousands more through interlibrary loan. For people whose disability prevented them from reading printed pages, the library could still be their passport to a larger world.

By the mid-1980s as well, "large print books" had become another feature added to the Bracebridge library's collections, a boon to those of failing eyesight who could no longer read regular print because their arms were just not long enough any more.

"Storyhour," begun in the 1930s on Saturday mornings for children

BRACEBRIDGE PUBLIC LIBRARY 2008

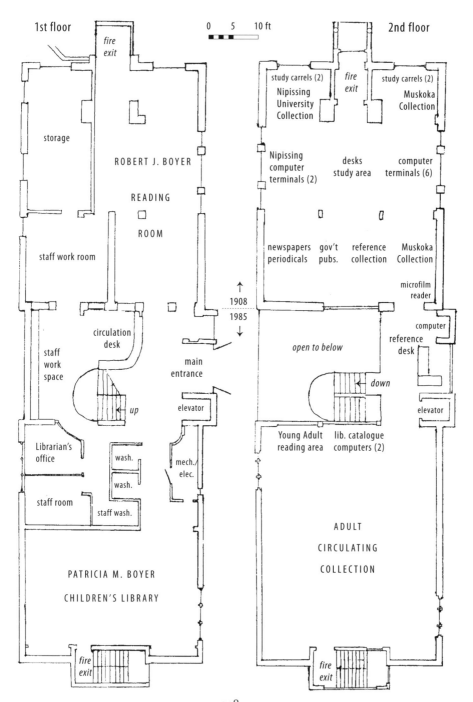

1st floor

2nd floor

0   5   10 ft

fire exit

storage

ROBERT J. BOYER

READING

ROOM

staff work room

staff work space

circulation desk

main entrance

up

elevator

Librarian's office

wash.

wash.

staff room

staff wash.

mech./ elec.

PATRICIA M. BOYER

CHILDREN'S LIBRARY

fire exit

study carrels (2)

Nipissing University Collection

fire exit

study carrels (2)

Muskoka Collection

Nipissing computer terminals (2)

desks study area

computer terminals (6)

newspapers periodicals

gov't pubs.

reference collection

Muskoka Collection

microfilm reader

1908
1985

computer

reference desk

open to below

down

elevator

Young Adult reading area

lib. catalogue computers (2)

ADULT

CIRCULATING

COLLECTION

fire exit

RENOVATION OR RESTORATION? The original 1908 library building was the subject of an "addition and renovation" in 1967. This concept was revisited in 1985, with a "restoration and expansion." Can you spot the difference?

over 10, had evolved by 1985 into a program offered three times a week during the school year to introduce preschoolers and their parents to the library and its books. Some parents familiar with the library wanted their children to be introduced in this pleasant fashion to the place and its ways. In other cases, however, the Storyhour program was serving to bring adults into the library for the first time, too.

Inter-library loan services by 1985 had become a major service enabling patrons get books, periodical articles, census materials, old newspapers and other printed resources not in the Bracebridge library's collection. Computerization of inter-library loans now allowed Bracebridge librarians to draw from materials in the library's own "region" within one to two weeks. If the material had to come from further afield, such as Vancouver or St. John's, it might take up to a month but the material would be made available. As well, with two week's notice, the library in 1985 was now able to borrow through inter-library loan both 8-millimetre and 16-millimetre films.

The expanded and renovated Bracebridge Public Library of 1985 offered an elevator and ramps so that the whole library was accessible to those using wheelchairs or walkers or otherwise unable to use the stairs. The main entrance had been relocated to a street-level access (with automatic doors added in 2004). To use the elevator, patrons simply obtained a key from the circulation desk. Other benefits of increased space included eliminating the problem of overcrowding of the collection of books, using the new program room for educational, recreational and cultural activities, and achieving, as chief librarian Ann-Marie Darling put it, "more complete, easy contact between staff and readers."

Chief librarian Darling at this time also prepared and circulated statistics with considerable enthusiasm. Drawing from the 1985 Ontario Public Libraries Survey, she reported that, "in all areas of service the Bracebridge Public Library experienced tremendous improvement as a result of the new facility. Also, the Library is now seen to be performing at higher levels than the 1984 provincial standards established for libraries with comparable populations." One of the impressive gains included 1985 circulation rising 15 per cent above its 1984 level, which averaged out to better than 8 loans from the library per person in town for the year. Three other 1985 comparisons with prior year 1984 showed library membership up 39 per cent, reference requests up 56 per cent, and annual library uses up 27 per cent. "The citizens of Bracebridge," she concluded, "truly appreciate their new library!"

QUIETER DAYS. This view, though the picture was taken after the 1967 renovations, more closely captures the mood of the earlier sedate edition of the Bracebridge Public Library.

The big events in the evolution of Bracebridge's Carnegie library as one of the town's principal democratic institutions easily eclipse smaller details, such as the saga of the library's rifles and the story of its stairs.

The 1967 Centennial renovations closed up the splendid central staircase to the lower level of Bracebridge Public Library. This also spelled the end for a remarkable display of weapons and military artifacts in glass-front display encasements in the stairwell walls. Wide-eyed boys studied these battlefield trophies for hours, in the days they were still there to mesmerize us: a Gatling gun with its belt of bullets for rapid machine-like firing, rifles and handguns, grenades of various designs, iron spikes to impale horses hooves, straight swords, curved swords, wavy swords for eviscerating an enemy, bayonets, drums, the leopard skin apron for a drummer, shells of many calibres, photographs of the uniformed gallant soldiers, badges and medals and shoulder flashes, a compass and a whistle, field glasses, pamphlet-sized booklets of Orders and Regulations, and of course, a small Bible. Many of these items were removed to Branch

161 of the Royal Canadian Legion in Bracebridge, itself now housed in the red brick schoolhouse in Ward IV, which opened the same year as the Carnegie library and operated for 30 years. A few of the religious relics in the case were transferred to St. Joseph's Roman Catholic Church in town.

However, implementing a misguided decision to symbolically "honour the past," four of these Canadian Army rifles were retained at the library and mounted on wall pegs behind the circulation desk adjacent to the children's library. Patrons ignorant of the provenance of such prominently displayed firepower were puzzled. Had they mistakenly stepped into the local armouries? Did Bracebridge Public Library have frontier-style enforcement of its policies on overdue books or about silence on the premises?

The Ontario Provincial Police, alert to situations in the community whose policing they had now taken over from the former Bracebridge constabulary, were aware of the rifles and one day an officer appeared at the library, handing librarian assistant Keitha Boyer a list of four serial numbers and a special marker with instructions to invisibly mark the rifles for the program to register firearms. The police and those creating Canada's national long-gun registry, anticipating future scenarios of theft and acts of crime, had not imagined some of the infinite other possibilities.

Gene Smith, who had begun in drama and had been heading toward a career in theatre before diverting into librarianship, had not forsaken all her earlier instincts. One day, reaching down one of the rifles, she began a demonstration which had instant theatrical impact on patrons and staff throughout the library. So remarkable was the chief librarian's performance that an early review of it spread at lightning speed to the chairman of the library board.

Not wishing to be too late for the crucial action scenes, Robert Dolphin arrived short of breath at the library but then, in a strange turn of the plot, this member of the audience suddenly entered the action by removing all four of these stage props from the premises and delivering them forthwith down the street to the mayor of the municipality. His Worship Jim Lang was himself disconcerted upon looking up from his desk to see the chairman of the town library entering his office in a state of agitation without prior notice and a full clutch of weapons.

He paid close attention to Dolphin's words as he noisily placed the firepower on the mayor's desk and announced, "You are the chief officer of this municipality. You can be responsible for these. They have no place in a library and will never be there again!"

That was really, really the end of the armament display in the local library.

The central staircase, whose demise was indirectly connected to Mayor Lang starting a gun collection that henceforth puzzled people who saw rifles on the walls of the council chamber, was itself memorable as a structural attribute of the original building. Even a kid reporter would reach for some phrase like "architectural oddity" to remember it once it was gone and the hole in the floor covered over.

The stairwell was square, or a rectangle very close to square, while the stairs had winders of radiating treads at the bends but otherwise consisted of straight runs. The stairs were inescapable. Entering the front door, which was the only entrance to the Bracebridge library, they were a feature at the centre of the main hall. Getting to the circulation desk you walked past them, and looked down. Going to the reference section meant being close. There was no escaping the open mystery they provided, the architectural feature they created with their surrounding rich wooden balusters and railing, with the sense they gave of there being "something more." A house with a staircase has a different atmosphere of possibilities than a single-level bungalow or an apartment. Just as the ceilings in the library rose high the stairs opened to a depth below and both together epitomized the human character's range of potential on any given day.

Staircases in a library, a place intended for exploration and imagination, have a magical force all their own. From Jacob Bronowski's *Ascent of Man* to the descent into Auerbach's cellar in Goethe's *Faust*, our culture is alive with the gradations of experience, real and symbolic, literal and allegorical. These stairs in the Bracebridge library led down, a bit mysteriously, to some place where important things were happening. This was evident because people descended and came up with serious intent going to deal with an insurance matter or a school inspection issue because that's where Dickie Insurance and the Public Schools Inspectors offices oddly were to be found.

This added a significant presence to the Bracebridge library, a phenomenon at the heart of the place that had nothing to do with books. Nor did the magnetic feature of this central staircase, the weaponry displayed from its stairwell walls. But both added to the intensity of a young person's experience here, making this place unlike any other. Take away the central stairwell to the lower level of the Bracebridge library? You might as well remove the plot from a novel.

The 1985 restoration of Bracebridge Public Library achieved a magic outcome, by reinstating a featured central staircase once more in the heart

of the enlarged new building. However, since the entrance was now at ground level, these stairs went up. To complement the new staircase's theme of ascendancy, they are surrounded by wide open space and are an almost luminous white, a perfect airy counterpoint to the earlier stairs descending through darker colours into more enclosed space. Just because everything old could be new again, did not mean it had to be the same.

In the spring of 2003 hammers began ringing and dust started rising as a demolition crew tackled the ground floor of the Bracebridge Public Library to dramatically alter the appearance of the reading room.

Since 1888, a place to sit with magazines and newspapers and browse at leisure had been an important feature of Bracebridge library life. That year the town's first reading room had been added to the original Mechanics' Institute Library in response to urgings from townspeople. For a long run of decades following the opening of the Carnegie library in 1908, the need continued to be met with a spacious reading room on the main floor. It was equipped with large racks holding newspapers on wooden rods, making them easier to display and harder to steal. Several large hardwood tables provided expansive areas for spreading out one's reading materials. In an era when banks were like cathedrals and solemnity pervaded most public buildings, the reading room of the Bracebridge library had a wooden and brown tile floor, not carpeting. The seats around the tables were hard and straight-backed, not soft or easy to slouch in.

With the 1967 restoration, and then again with the major expansion and restoration of the building in 1984 and 1985, the reading room had been transformed. Advent of computers in the library in 1990 meant the "reading space" again took on a different character. By 2003, it was time to make "everything old new again" and provide better facilities for those who come to the library not just to sign out books but to stay and read.

The library's chief executive officer Jill Foster explained this process of renewal to the *Bracebridge Examiner* on June 11, 2003, saying it would create a more inviting and practical space for library users. "The heritage character and graceful architecture of the library building are integral to our view of the Library," she stressed, describing it as "the brick and

EVERYTHING OLD IS NEW AGAIN. Jan Pitman's dramatic image proves how the determination of library chairman Robert Dolphin and the artistic integrity of architect Brian Chamberlain could give Bracebridge a preserved heritage building as a fully contemporary library.

stone grande dame of Manitoba Street. It sits at the crest of the hill as a monument to an era when form was not a slave to function and building design was as much an art form as an engineering project." With this view in mind, she explained, "the makeover of the Reading Room will hearken back to the early days of Muskoka."

The aim of the renovation, she said, would be to improve the comfort level of the space that is the primary area for reading current newspapers and magazines, chatting with friends and accessing the large print and "talking book" collections. Mixed neutral tones of brown, green and cream had been chosen for the new carpeting, wall colours and fixtures, and the existing shelving would be re-faced to complement a few new units to be installed. Pendant lights would replace the ribbon lighting.

Three distinct yet adjacent reading areas were in the works for the long ground-level room running the full east-west length of the original 1908 building. One was a cozy nook with comfortable seating under the window at the far end to house magazines. The centre area would include a large study table in the centre of the room, and be a meeting place for the library board. The third area, closest to the entrance door, would feature a club chair grouping by the new fireplace.

"If the reading room's new look succeeds as planned," said Foster, "it should become a warm and welcoming space that invokes a sense of early twentieth century Muskoka, when the building was originally constructed."

Some rearrangement of materials came with upgrading of the reading room. While the popular large print and "talking book" works would remain in this space for easy access, videos were relocated to the children's library in the case of junior videos and to the non-fiction stacks on the second floor in the case of adult titles.

Feature walls in the reading room now could showcase the library's small but impressive collection of paintings by local artists, such as those donated by Robert Everett. The quilt resembling a bookshelf used for fund-raising could also hang against the south wall, where patrons could seen on the spines of the cloth facsimile books on its fabric shelves the names of those for whom a donation had been made to Bracebridge Public Library. As Foster told the newspaper reporter, "the Reading Room will marry subdued nostalgia with comfortable efficiency in one visually arresting space."

When the work was finished it was time for yet another official opening at Bracebridge Public Library, the building that had originally opened without one. Ribbon-cutting was now out, however, flame-lighting in.

ROBERT J. BOYER READING ROOM. On August 23, 2003, chief librarian Jill Foster officiates at a well-attended public opening of the new reading room in the Bracebridge library. Victoria Billingsley donated some $77,000 to create the comfortable space for reading papers and books, two of her father's steady occupations. Vicki's brother, Patrick, complemented her tribute to their father by writing a biography about him, *A Man & His Words*, published to coincide with this event. Their sister, Alison, had earlier helped their father publish his book *Bracebridge Around 1930* in 2001. In good fun, librarian Foster presented the 91-year-old book lover with a personal copy of Jack London's *The Call of the Wild*, one of the novels librarian Hattie Dickie would not let him read when he was 12. Boyer enjoyed the humour in finally getting the prohibited tome from the Bracebridge library, the boy's story about a dog.

"With a hand-held remote control, Robert J. Boyer lit dancing flames in an electric fireplace to officially open the reading room named in his honour at the Bracebridge Public Library on the afternoon of August 23, 2003," reported Walter Franczyk in the *Weekender* on August 29, 2003. Surrounded by friends, family members and colleagues, "the retired newspaper editor and veteran Muskoka member of the provincial legislature, was remembered as 'a man of words'." The newly renovated reading room was a gift to the community by his daughter Victoria Billingsley. "It was important to her," explained librarian Jill Foster, "that her father be remembered for the many contributions he made to the library over the years."

BOOKISH EDITOR. Forced by the economic depression of the 1930s to leave high school, Bob Boyer became editor of the *Muskoka Herald* at age 19. He then continued his own lifetime education program, a book always on the go and never far from hand. Here he reads during the summer of 1941 just days before enlisting in the Canadian Army. Then his wife Patricia, who had been Bracebridge librarian from 1934 to 1938, took over as *Muskoka Herald* editor for the duration of the war, ensuring intelligent editorial support for the town library. For 17 years from 1955 to 1971 Robert J. Boyer represented Muskoka in Ontario's legislature and served the province as first vice-chairman of Ontario Hydro while continuing as editor of the *Herald-Gazette* (in 1955 the Boyer family had purchased the rival *Bracebridge Gazette*). After Boyer returned to "private life" he opened a bookstore on the main street of Bracebridge, started two more newspapers, wrote and published local histories, chaired the fund-raising campaign for the addition to the library, and read a thousand more books.

Bracebridge librarian Jill Foster presented Robert Boyer, then in his 91st year, with a copy of Jack London's novel *The Call of the Wild*, the book librarian Hattie Dickie would not let him borrow in his childhood because she considered it, from the title alone, unsuited for a juvenile. He appreciated the gesture and the humour it involved, but never read the gift boy's book he had wanted 80 years earlier. By this time Hattie Dickie was gone and he was into racier fare.

Finding the occasion "more intimate" than he'd imagined it would be,

Boyer said to the gathering that "one prime purpose of a special reading room is to encourage more reading. Families long identified with newspaper publishing, such as the Boyers, recognize the value and importance of a growing population of readers and writers."

Victoria Billingsley was "thrilled to see so many people at the opening," noting that the Boyer family now had generations five and six using the Bracebridge library. Herself chair of the Inuvik Library Board in the Northwest Territories, Billingsley paid tribute to her father by drawing on the title of his 1975 book *A Good Town Grew Here*, a history of Bracebridge from its inception to World War I. "A good town grew here," she said, "so too did a good man." Mayor Scott Northmore thanked the library board and volunteers for their help during the construction period which transformed the space into the attractive wood-panelled reading room with fireplace, and thanked Victoria "on behalf of citizens of all ages." Robert Taylor, chair of the board, also said the trustees appreciated the opportunity presented by Victoria Billingsley, the total amount of whose donation for the renovations exceeded $77,000.

It was to be Vicki's last visit to her hometown. A year later she had succumbed to ovarian cancer, and a year after that, Robert Boyer was dead. Born in Bracebridge in 1913, he had been editor of the family-owned weekly newspaper, the *Muskoka Herald*, a job he held throughout most of his working life, including while serving for 17 years as MPP for Muskoka. He wrote 12 books, mostly about local history. After retiring from the Ontario Legislature he led the mid-1980s campaign to finance the addition to the Bracebridge Public Library, an expansion that included a children's department, which at the suggestion of Ruth Tinkiss was named after former librarian Patricia M. Boyer who had started the Saturday morning "Children's Hour" program during her tenure as librarian from 1934 to 1938.

The Robert J. Boyer Reading Room and the Patricia M. Boyer Children's Library now stand like bookends on either side of the library foyer. His story is preserved in a biography written by his son, entitled *A Man & His Words*, published to coincide with the official opening of the Robert J. Boyer Reading Room with copies given to all attending the August 23, 2003, event. The book portrays the importance of books and the local library in his life, and how as the young editor of a local newspaper from age 19 he had come to know the attractive 22-year-old librarian who each week dropped by with her column "Library Corner" for his newspaper. After they married, the Bracebridge Public Library continued to be of central importance in their lives, where today each has their own "library corner"—one for reading, one for children, which is about as perfect as anything can get for a memorialization.

Introduction of computers was beginning to transform the library. The major new lease on life for the Bracebridge library by the physical restoration and expansion of its facilities was being accompanied by a less evident change taking place to link the services which this contemporary library could provide. Just as the government-issued passports still looked the same but became qualitatively different with the addition of a bar code enabling a border official to instantly check world records, so too the library as a passport was being renewed for the computer age.

In September 1984 the first significant change began, when interloan service was improved with installation of a computer terminal. This was part of a project to link family libraries in the Trent region, of which Bracebridge was a part, being initiated by Ontario Library Service. "This computerized interloan system allows us to access considerably more materials than was possible using Algonquin Region's manual and microfiche interloan system," explained chief librarian Nancy Jones, who had taken over as chief librarian from Gene Graham in 1982.

By early 1990, Nancy's successor, Ann-Marie Mathieu, was demonstrating for the Bracebridge newspaper photographers the new computers that arrived in January and which, she said, with six month's training of staff "would mean that the entire operation of Bracebridge's public library would be fully computerized."

The following year, Bob Dolphin's daughter-in-law Evonne Dolphin at Packard Bell Electronics in Mississauga helped secure a donation from the company of its FORCE 1 personal computer and printer to the Bracebridge library. The gift was worth $3,800. Although Dolphin had stepped down as chair he continued as a member of the board until retiring in 1995. His successor as chair of the library board, Elspeth Wood, organized a reception at the library to thank the Packard Bell officials and inaugurate the new computer service, again as with the 1985 opening on a Friday afternoon, May 24—evidently the Bracebridge library's preferred way to begin a national holiday weekend.

The introduction of computer technology streamlined many control and records maintenance aspects of the library's operations, although the physical handing of books and documents would remain an essential task to also be performed. "If we didn't do this," said Dolphin, referring to the library's total computerization in 1990, "we would have had to increase the library staff. This not only slightly reduced the number of library staff, but was more efficient."

Libraries, in Bracebridge as elsewhere, were laboratories mixing tradition and innovation, from Dewey's Decimal System to computer technology, introducing methods that led to entirely new levels of performance. On August 7, 1991, the Bracebridge library became the first public library in Muskoka to implement a fully automated management system for its collection.

Just four of the many ways computers transformed the Bracebridge library are seen in the examples of government documents, research interests of library patrons, the stale-dating of certain library holdings, and the attractiveness of Internet access bringing tourists and a new generation of young people into the library. Government reports are especially important to Bracebridge Public Library because it has been a selective depository for Government of Ontario and Government of Canada

INTRODUCTION OF COMPUTERS. A transforming change to Bracebridge Public Library during its lifetime has been the extension of computer technology. Embracing the advances made possible by computers was as essential for renewal of the library as the physical expansion of its facilities. Ann-Marie Mathieu, chief librarian during this era of transition, engages the library's new computer system in January 1990, telling a reporter from the *Bracebridge Examiner* it would take six months of staff training on the new equipment before the Library would become fully automated.

documents, with new materials arriving each week. Over the past two decades, however, this steady flow has been reduced to a trickle as government documents are now made more widely and swiftly available online instead. The convenience and advantages of this electronic library are real for librarians and patrons alike. From the library's perspective, it also reduces pressure on ever-crowded shelf space. Yet with the benefits come one drawback: unlike a government report that physically forms part of a local library's collection and can be looked at whenever one is interested in doing so, the central agency posting a document on the Internet can simply remove the record if for some reason it no longer wants the public to see it. For example, in Ontario a report on the reorganization of Ontario Hydro was on an official website but disappeared, from one day to the next, at a time when a major reorientation of the electricity utility was underway and certain issues and recommendations in the report created potential embarrassments for the powers-that-be.

Research interests have noticeably changed with advent of the Internet, reports librarian Nancy Wilson. Nancy holds a Master's degree in library science and was hired in 1982 by the Bracebridge library board and over this intervening period of the library's computerization has been able to track changes. In the days prior to the Internet, for instance, she found herself processing requests in two large groups: Essiac and family genealogy. The Bracebridge library had created a number of copies of an "Essiac Package" consisting of several dozen articles and contact information gathered in a clear plastic bag and loaned to the many interested people as a reference source. Often these people were at a great distance, and the package would be sent to them and later mailed back. Those were also the days before the secret Essiac "formula" had been disclosed. People called Bracebridge library from around the world, pressing for the secret in the hope of saving their own life or that of a loved one. Since advent of the Internet, however, requests about Essiac have dried up completely. Now everything about nurse Rene Caisse's "tea" that cancer patients want is readily available anywhere in the world online: information about Rene, about the herbal tea, the formula itself, companies making and selling the brew, people and organizations to contact, and even a digitized copy of Donna M. Ivey's thoroughly researched book *Clinic of Hope: The Story of Rene M. Caisse and Essiac*. Over the same period, however, requests Nancy receives for information about family history have kept steadily pouring in, with the pace even picking up as more retired people with additional time on their hands excavate their ancestral roots.

While the Internet has generally given books a new lease on life, espe-

A NEW ERA. The above scene in this 1970s version of the library is the same spot as in the 2008 version below, but the central wood-framed supporting pillar in both pictures shows how much has changed. In the interval, the 1985 restoration and expansion have introduced a natural brightness, computers have arrived, and the people have changed. The oil portrait of Andrew Carnegie has re-emerged into prominence because of the brighter contrast in the library today. *Jan Pitman (lower photo)*

cially those in the out-of-print and used categories, certain genres of work have been disappearing because they are overtaken by Internet information. Women's health books are a notable example. Research and new developments in the many illnesses and medical conditions unique to woman are now fully reported and daily updated on thousands of websites, many of them specifically dedicated to a particular disease. With the easy availability of current specific information, and the ability to search different sources and alternatives online, the printed books rapidly become dated. They are less and less borrowed, more and more culled, as the new age of publishing in this field is electronic.

A sidewalk sign in front of Bracebridge Public Library advertising Internet Access@Your Library brings in many tourists during the summer, and is a year-round draw for patrons of all ages. The price is better than an Internet café, too, if one costs out the price of a library mem-

IS THIS BOOK IN THE LIBRARY? Once librarians at the circulation desk, asked about a particular title, would either answer from memory or check the card catalogue. If the library had the title, it was then necessary to see if it had been checked out. If it had been, it was then necessary to determine when it would be returned, to advise the patron in quest of the book. Since the complete computerization of Bracebridge public library in 1990, staff at the main circulation desk respond to such inquiries with stunning speed. Even better, two computer terminals in the library are dedicated for searching the holdings so a patron can let the keyboard do the walking through the electronic catalogue. This helps, too, with tracing the whereabouts of books between the main library and the Fenbrook satellite operation.

Here Barbara Forth of Bracebridge has used her library card to gain access and is now focused on all the treasures available in the Bracebridge collection. When one has a Bracebridge library card and thus an access code, the library's holdings can also be checked remotely on-line through the library's excellent website. *Jan Pitman*

HARD-WIRED FROM INFANCY. Mary Jo Pedersen of Bracebridge holds her daughter Nevaeh ("heaven" reversed) while checking things out at computer in the children's library.

Some people quip that kids now are born with a computer chip built in, but it's more likely that starting early and experiencing the ubiquitous technology as the normal way to do things is the reason. Young people as of this date increasingly communicate with one another through text messaging and posting messages on The Wall of their friends facebooks, thinking that emailing is for old folks.

Wendy Nicholson, librarian at Bracebridge and Muskoka Lakes Secondary School, herself only 24 years-old, marvels at how students in her Grade 9 introductory library training course know so much about computers. "They teach the teachers, and teach one another," she smiles. *Jan Pitman*

bership against the charge in commercial operations providing Internet access. Instead of mailing postcards from the Bracebridge post office next door, patrons can send emails or post messages in their friends' facebooks. The Bracebridge library is integrated and integrating in the new age.

Remaining connected, however, is a challenge because of frequent upgrades in systems and equipment. The issue was displayed, at one interval in this repeating process, in January 2002 when a review of the library's computer operation, conducted by Muskoka Computer Centre, showed the "current library technology out of date." Total cost to replace the system reflected the fact that Microsoft no longer supported the library's operating system. Its Dynix system was then running on an old Bull server, and because Bull was no longer in business, parts would be increasingly hard to obtain should the server fail. Anticipating these kinds of problems, the library board in 2001 had prudently earmarked $25,000 for the project.

"Another reason for upgrading is security," explained Geoff Plummer, director of Muskoka Computer Centre, to *Weekender* reporter Matthew Sitler on January 25, 2002. "Public access to workstations needs proper controls to be in place to safeguard the systems, and the library as well." Failure to do so could result in unwanted and expensive litigation, he added. "Staff report frustration and lots of holdups and delays," Jill Foster explained to a Bracebridge council administration and finance committee meeting at this same time. By this date, the library's two computer networks were supporting a total of 17 workstations. One network serviced internal library needs, the other provided public access to the Internet.

A sure sign that the new age of computers had arrived at Bracebridge Public Library came in 2001 with launch of its website. Designed by SellWithPictures, a website company operating from Burk's Falls north of Bracebridge, www.bracebridge.library.on.ca is an exceptionally attractive, informative and easy to use space on the Internet, a new portal through which to access the library's holdings, learn about its history and current programs, make use of the library's online services, and make contact with the librarians.

The home page is updated daily. There is modest but appealing use of sound. For the year 2008, a special feature on the website outlines nearly a dozen activities and events for the library to celebrate the centennial of the Carnegie building. A regular events calendar displays information on current and up-coming library related activities. General information "About the Library" has its own page, as do specific services such as Library Catalogue and Your Account, Public Internet Access, Search Online Resources, Adult and Special Services, Kids, Teens, Inter-library Loan, Local History and Genealogy, and Wireless@Your Library. Links are provided to Helpful Websites and to the Town of Bracebridge website. For specific inquiries, there is also an Ask a Librarian page.

The website and this "virtual library" presents an accurate impression of the quality and high level of service at the building itself at 94 Manitoba Street in Bracebridge, with artful pictures of the library interior making one feel present wherever in the world they may be.

The passport itself has now become the library.

ELEVEN

Librarian Dynamics, Dynamic Librarians

Over 135 years the Bracebridge community's organized relationship with its books has been in the hands of a dozen and a half different librarians. Each librarian's personality, character, and extent of librarianship training have translated rapidly into how the local library operated because the Bracebridge library was relatively small and its role in the community unusually large.

While the library's evolution might reflect how an individual librarian or a particular library board responded to shifting relationships between themselves, not to mention with governments, library organizations, librarian associations, local schools, changing technology and the library's diverse patrons, it was also true that both the library's and the librarian's roles were themselves evolving as all this took place. The whole scene has been highly dynamic, marked by continuous activity and frequent change.

Three attributes of early Bracebridge library service provide a starting point to measure this change. First, the library was largely a gentlemen's affair. Bracebridge's first librarian in 1874, Josiah Pratt, who also operated a jewellery store in the building, was described by a library user as a "painstaking and courteous librarian." Whether helping someone find the right diamond or a book that met their particular need, Pratt was attentive and helpful because he liked to be close to people. The transition to Free Library status in 1901 made no difference in its male complexion. R.H. Smith, identified as the Bracebridge "public librarian" after 1890 even thought the library was still technically a private operation of the Mechanics' Institute, had moved to town in 1888 to engage in bee culture. Moses J. Dickie, who became librarian in 1903, had been a homesteader in the Muskoka bush, then a dealer in hay, before taking up the insurance business.

So the second attribute is contained in the first. Not only were men in charge, but they were men who had not been trained to operate a library. A library in Bracebridge would be very much what they made it, drawing on experience from their own fields of endeavour and applying ideas from other Mechanics' Institutes. Selling wedding rings, making honey or brokering insurance contracts, combined with a strong interest in books, ability to deal with the public, and experience in business, is what qualified individuals for library duty in Bracebridge into the twentieth century. Nor was this out of step with a prevailing attitude, to which Andrew Carnegie subscribed, that a librarian's job was simply to hand books out to people who wanted to read them.

A third feature of the early library's operation is that it was a one-person affair. For the sole individual handling all duties, checking out books was the least of his concerns. Shovelling coal into the furnace or snow off the front steps, or lugging heavy boxes of books, suggested it was desirable to have a male in the librarian's role. Late-Victorian Muskokans now viewed heroic efforts and physical stamina of pioneer women as a primitive condition of the past. Progress meant "the fairer sex" had been liberated from much drudgery and hard work. Bracebridge newspapers ran advertisements for household equipment and devices to save women time and labour. Electric lights, electric irons and electric stoves replaced labour-intensive coal oil lamps, stove-top irons and wood stoves. Finally, an equitable division of labour meant women could enjoy the new leisure with adequate time for such higher virtues as literature and music. This promising trend seemed to be confirmed by formation of the Ladies' Literary Society in Bracebridge in 1898.

Then something deep shifted and women began to overthrow and dominate this male world of librarianship, just as they had replaced men in nursing and teaching, and moved into other roles as store clerks, office secretaries and industrial workers. In Bracebridge, where women have occupied the librarian spot exclusively for almost a century now, it would be satisfying to know that a deliberate decision was collectively made by the entire community on such an important matter of equality. However, as sometimes happens with social progress, change unfolded in a more haphazard fashion. When Moses Dickie's daughter Harriet started to

HARRIET DICKIE. singular librarian. Hattie Dickie worked with her father, Moses, running the Bracebridge Public Library for a number of years before becoming librarian herself in 1915, the first woman to hold this coveted position in Bracebridge since the beginning of library service in the community in 1874. She relinquished the post of librarian to marry in 1934, an era when female librarians and schoolteachers were expected to be single.

help her father with secretarial and administrative tasks downstairs in the library building where he operated his insurance business, very gradually she moved to help with some of his other duties upstairs as well. What she learned about the library was what her father Moses taught her from his own experience, not from any special training, at least in the early years.

Following formation of the Ontario Library Association in 1901, however, this began to change. Meetings with other librarians introduced the Dickies to new ideas about the conduct of a library and its operations, and Moses himself rose through the ranks of the regional library association to become its president. Hattie Dickie's ascendancy to the position of town librarian can rightly be claimed as a step forward for women seeking wider roles in the community and an expansion of their rights and civil liberties. Bracebridge now had its first female librarian two years before women could even vote in Ontario elections. No man has held the librarian's position since.

The twentieth century advanced, and so did the training and qualification of librarians. In its first decade of operation, the Canadian Library Association made good headway developing publications, organizing topical conferences and meetings, providing advice, and running a clearing-house for questions and issues confronting libraries and their staffs. The Association sought to enhance the professionalism and economic status of librarians through salary scales and pensions. In 1921 the Dominion Bureau of Statistics in Ottawa began publishing an annual report *Survey*

PATRICIA JOHNSON: children's librarian. Patricia Mary Johnson, who graduated from McMaster University by age 19, in 1934 became librarian when long-time holder of that position, Hattie Dickie, opted for marriage. In the midst of an economic depression positions were as scarce for university graduates as they were for everyone, but Johnson's father was chairman of the library board and the Dickies were neighbours and fellow Baptists. The young woman who enjoyed dramatic play with children emphasized introducing children to books at the library and began a Saturday morning "children's book... hour." As a natural writer, the new librarian also began writing a weekly newspaper column, entitled "Library Corner" that has continued, with some changes of name and many successor librarian writers, in the local press ever since.

of Libraries in Canada and for the first time librarians and library boards could readily compare their library with others. In 1927 McGill University established Canada's first one-year library school training course for librarians, followed in 1938 by University of Toronto's and a decade after that by the University of Ottawa's degrees in library science. Lorne Bruce, in his history of the library movement in Ontario, portrays a shift from "well-intended but amateur local librarians" to those with better training and stronger professional credentials.

It took awhile, however, for those behind the librarian's desk in Bracebridge to be stamped with such credentials. In 1934, Hattie Dickie's successor, Patricia Johnson, had a university degree, was specialized in literature and languages, and was quite familiar with libraries, but was not trained to run one. Emma Fryer, who came after her, was a nurse. Mary Jorgensen had worked at the library in North Bay. Agnes Tough had been a newspaper reporter in northern Ontario. Keitha Boyer, who worked at a bank in Toronto before starting at the library in 1967, was asked by board chairman Fred Hammell if she would like to be librarian one time when the post fell vacant. "No way!" she replied, though she was flattered to have been asked. She demurred, she explained, on account of "not having the educational training" she knew the position now required. Until the

AGNES TOUGH: librarian at the top of her class. Many in Bracebridge had come to the position of town librarian with little prior workplace experience or special library training, but Agnes Tough's seasoning as a reporter for the newspaper in Kirkland Lake, where she is seen (above left) working in 1953, involved a researcher's instinct and perseverance in "getting the story," skills that later helped her assist patrons track down what they were after in the Bracebridge Public Library.

She was at once worldly yet quizzical. As for the librarian's renowned look of withering penetration over the top of her eyeglasses, Agnes Tough was at the top of the league.

In the mid-1960s Agnes Tough received the first prisoner patrons to the Public Library when Danny Poland of Bracebridge, a corrections supervisor at Beaver Creek minimum-security penitentiary, brought them into town for books they could not get in the institution's limited library. This Bracebridge innovation was a foretaste of things to come. In 1998, a satellite operation of the Bracebridge library was opened inside Fenbrook, a medium-security institution, adjacent to Beaver Creek, southeast of town.

At the original oak circulation desk of the 1908 building before it was removed in 1967, Agnes Tough (above right) with her friendly aloofness or air of skilled professionalism imparted a constructive high-mindedness to the library. These ennobling qualities, combined with her own experience as a mother, helped Agnes Tough give reassuring guidance to students at Bracebridge and Muskoka Lakes Secondary School where from 1969 she enjoyed her role as assistant librarian.

GENE SMITH: part-time, full-time librarian (left). From 1977 to 1982, Eugenie Smith was chief librarian. Unlike Hattie Dickie, who retired upon marriage in 1934, Gene went the opposite direction, marrying chartered accountant Barry Graham and thus appearing in the records also as librarian Gene Graham. Told when starting it was part-time work, Gene soon asked about the low-paid position, "What part of running a library is part time?" During her tenure, staff remuneration was improved, financial administration services taken over by the town so librarians could concentrate on core library activity, cultural programs centred on the library maintained, and the vast project to restore and expand the Bracebridge library launched.

NANCY JONES: librarian of new accomplishments (above right). When Nancy Jones became chief librarian in 1982, she was the first chief executive officer of the town's public library to hold a Master of Library Science (from the University of Toronto), and the youngest (24) to be town librarian since Patricia Johnson in 1934 (age 22). With high academic qualifications and some practical library experience at the Aurora public library, she would preside over the massive restoration project and a construction program to more than double the library's size—while the library continued operating in the midst of it all. In fact, circulations even increased during the hectic disruptions.

1980s, Bracebridge's diverse librarians painted from a broad pallet but none had dipped their brushes into the lustrous science of library operations to do so. Among other reasons, the library's low pay scale was not likely to attract the highly qualified.

Nancy Jones, arriving in 1982, was the first Bracebridge librarian with a master's degree in library science. She only stayed three years, but piloted

ROBERT DOLPHIN: exceptional leadership. Robert Dolphin smiles in his last days at Indal Products Ltd. in Toronto before he and wife Ruth moved to Bracebridge. As a youth he canoed and boated all over Muskoka, served gas and waited tables at Dunn's Pavilion in Bala, and was keen to return. Barely had he arrived in Bracebridge when he became chairman of the library board. Without his determined leadership in the following years, the restoration and expansion of the Carnegie library in the 1980s would not have taken place.

Dolphin ran the library board "on parliamentary procedures," as he called it. Every meeting began with an agenda he and the librarian prepared with contributions from other board members. He had been dismayed to discover no controls and no system for financial records, the library not even issuing purchase orders. Librarian Gene Smith was immersed in myriad administrative matters. "Let the town handle administration," declared Dolphin, and the town began preparing payrolls for library staff. "The library is owned by the town so we should let the town administrators deal with its business administration while we concentrate on our mandate and try to run the best library in Muskoka." He hired the first librarian with a Master of Library Science, started the Muskoka Collection, and initiated the library's computerization

the transition to the enlarged library in 1985. In that time she also made a large impact, carrying into action ideas from her training, with regular staff meetings, innovations in policy and procedure, negotiating better pay for employees, and representing Muskoka's libraries in the amalgamation negotiations for a reorganized library region. She was even attentive to the details of updating technology. In 1909 Moses Dickie acquired an Oliver typewriter for Hattie; in 1983, Nancy Jones acquired an electric typewriter for staff member Audrey McNabb.

MOVING TIMES. In 1985 the books at Bracebridge public library were handled many times, in part because of a boost in circulation as more people came by more often to marvel at the restoration project and borrowed books in the process. The reason all books got handled a lot, however, was the need to keep moving them around to accommodate construction. The empty shelves behind Keitha Boyer, Nancy Jones, Anna Crawford and Audrey McNabb indicate yet another boxing and moving of books completed by the dedicated library staff.

Nancy Jones' three successors, Ann-Marie Mathieu in 1985, Jill Foster in 2001 and Cathryn Rodney in 2006, all arrived with master's degrees in the field, as well as other university degrees and, in the case of the latter two, prior experience running libraries as well. The trend Lorne Bruce described, of "well-intended but amateur" librarians being replaced by highly trained and well-qualified ones, had become another attribute of the Bracebridge library.

Meanwhile, staff was growing. From the mid-twentieth century the solo operation of the library had also, like its maleness and librarians unschooled in the arts and science of librarianship, become a thing of the past. By the late 1960s, chief librarian Agnes Tough was assisted by Kit Boyer, wife of surveyor Ted Boyer and school board trustee, and by Margo Armstrong, wife of a retired Anglican priest. In the 1970s, the numbers increased, with the librarian's support staff including Kit Boyer,

ANN-MARIE MATHIEU: librarian with panache. When Ann-Marie Mathieu (right) became Bracebridge librarian in 1985 with the spectacular expansion and restoration of the library freshly completed, this university graduate with several degrees and talent in musical performance and drama brought a flair for publicity and community awareness to project the institution and its services ever further. Her tenure was a time of change in a many respects. Mathieu, whose surname itself went through changes from Darling to Peachy to Mathieu, and who happily experimented with different hair colourings, may have left the impression for some that there was a rapid turnover in the CEO's office at the Bracebridge library, but in fact she held the position longer than most town librarians, and showed no waning of commitment when compromised circumstances in 2001 caused her to relocate to the west coast.

In this typical scene, where Ann-Marie Mathieu's talents for media attention kept giving the local newspapers photo opportunities about the library, employee Lis Rainey holds a bouquet of flowers Mathieu has just presented in appreciation for Rainey's 25 years of service at Bracebridge public library.

Audrey McNabb, Verna Hawn, Lis Rainey and Anna Crawford, as well as students coming in to help shelve books. By 2008 staff increases resulted in some 14 employees at the library. Uniformly, these positions have been, and are, held by women.

Gender imbalance arose from the usual factors, including the valued skills women brought to library tasks that require attention to detail. The fact most jobs at the library were part-time made it easier for women to balance family and workplace duties. The low rate of remuneration was also a factor. Dedicated women carried the work of the library, since men

JILL FOSTER: librarian with the saint of libraries. In 2005 Bracebridge's chief librarian Jill Foster stands angelically with the saint of libraries. The oil painting of Andrew Carnegie holds pride of place in the restored and expanded building. During Jill Foster's half-decade as Bracebridge Librarian from 2001 to 2006, she promoted literacy through a number of programs, directed a major enhancement of facilities with creation of The Robert J. Boyer Reading Room and re-development of The Patricia M. Boyer Children's Library, and looking ahead, initiated plans for a worthy celebration of the centennial of the town's Carnegie library in 2008. *Russ Mackinnon*

were interested in full-time, better-paying jobs. Audrey McNabb earned $1,177 during 1975, $1,582 for 1974, working part-time six or eight hours a week. The hourly wage in 1976 was $3.20, which rose gradually each year, getting to $7.16 a decade later, and $10.84 ten years after that in 1995. The money was enough to pay one or perhaps two full-time employees, which might have attracted a male candidate needing higher income. Yet the work, broken into a greater number of part-time positions, seemed to suit the women who applied for them, a pattern that still remains.

The library's staff was also becoming more highly trained in new technologies and methodologies, which was important because information in a library can only be put to profit and enjoyment if it can be retrieved with east.

In his day, Moses Dickie typically listed the books he had selected for

CATHRYN RODNEY: chief executive of the library. In 2006 she became head of Bracebridge library staff after wide competition for the now coveted position. Holding an honours degree in English and drama from University of Western Ontario, she also earned a master of library science degree in 1985 from Western's school of library and information science. Seasoned in a complete range of library operations with the Guelph public library from 1987 to 2006, and before that with the London and Waterloo public libraries through the co-op component of her master's university program, Rodney also worked from 1981 to 1983 as a store manager for Epic Bookstores in Elliot Lake. Her personal interests from tap dancing to baseball and music to stained- glass work speak to her well-rounded life. Her experience as a parent and the facilitator of a parent training program called "Making Connections" and promoted through school councils make her especially attuned to the significant children's component of the Bracebridge library.

In addition to responsibility for the Bracebridge Public Library and its satellite operation at Fenbrook prison, with a budget of $625,000 and a staff of 14 as well as many volunteers, Cathryn Rodney took up her position just in time to oversee the 2008 centennial activities commemorating the opening of the Carnegie library in 1908, and to advance the planning for the library's next stage of expansion to keep it in phase with its growing central Muskoka community and the increasing demands for library services. *Jan Pitman.*

the library and updated the record by adding new titles at the bottom as they arrived, in what came to be called an "accession list" or "book catalogue." Also, typically, he shelved the collection of books by placing them in relative clusters by topic. Oversized publications always restricted

INSTINCTIVELY WELCOMING. The modern atmosphere of Bracebridge public library following the major 1985 expansion is one of brightness, seen in the white walls and glass-supported circulation counter, but also conveyed by the staff of the library as seen in these smiles of the library's office manager and assistant librarian Carolyn Dawkins and inter-library loan coordinator Nancy Beasley. *Russ Mackinnon*

some to drawers or flat, wide shelving. When a patron of Bracebridge library borrowed a book, a note was made and the borrower promised to return it within a designated period.

Then came change as the Dewey Decimal System was implemented. Following Melvil Dewey's instructional schedules, Hattie Dickie used the library's Oliver typewriter to make three- by five-inch catalogue cards for each book, one for the title and author, and one or more others for cross-referencing subjects dealt with in the book. The cards were placed in suitable drawers or boxes, then the books to which they referred placed on the shelves according to the 10 logical classes of the world's knowledge as grouped by Melvil Dewey. As the collection increased, a librarian of the day could use further numbering as needed for sub-classification. "Cuttering" organized authors within each sub-classification. Vertical filing cabinets, which New York State librarian Dewey also invented, were used to contain alphabetized subject files on topics of interest, such as the collections on local history and current affairs still in use as an information retrieval system in the Bracebridge library today.

Automation again introduced a new dynamic. From 1984 when a computer first augmented library management in Bracebridge, books and other materials became identified, purchased and catalogued online. "In fact," notes author and librarian Donna Ivey, for some years a resident of Bracebridge, "libraries seemed to be preparing for the world of computerization for centuries as they had always been devising systems for logically sorting the physical books and documents, and the information they contained. The information was all ready to be 'dumped' into the logic-hungry mid-twentieth century electronic machinery called computers."

Chief librarian Ann-Marie Mathieu was frequently in the town newspapers and at community events explaining the nature and benefits of taking up the new technology. Even within days of first arriving on the job she told the *Herald-Gazette* on January 15, 1986, "The next step is to computerize the library. Terminals were put in when the building was renovated." Some people might not think they like the idea, "but it means finding things quicker and getting your books out a lot faster. We're already partly automated for our acquisitions; that's why we get the new best-sellers so fast, and it saves us money." Mathieu heralded the new era: "I'd like to automate circulation and the catalogue: no fiddling with cards, you just type in what you want and it comes up on the screen. And circulation: instead of stamping and writing a number you just wave a wand and you're done."

LONG SERVICE BY YOUNG WOMEN. Mary Denomy and Elisabeth Rainey, two long-time employees of the library, enjoyed a satisfying moment in April 1996 when the town of Bracebridge honoured their years of dedicated service. Gathered outside the Bracebridge town hall at the time are library board chair Paul Follis, Mary Denomy, chief librarian Ann-Marie Mathieu, and Elisabeth Rainey.

In 1990 Bracebridge Public Library joined this march to automation, as briefly noted in chapter 10. Computerized data packages could now handle the ordering of books and periodicals, the cataloguing of books and production of cards, patron records, newsletters and other functions, whether for single libraries like Bracebridge's or large interactive networks of library systems. Acquisition of such library data processing systems and the requisite training of library staff became a necessity. The always-tight budget had to stretch for something no longer a frill. Several months of careful planning and hard work by the library board and staff readied the stage for implementation. The board approved spending $109,000 for this move into the computer age. Ontario's Ministry of Culture and Communication contributed $65,000, and the town of Bracebridge added $44,000 spread over two years.

By April 1990, the 6,800 patrons of Bracebridge public library were advised to register for their new plastic library membership card with its personal barcode, the new passport for the electronic age. The barcode was key to borrowing books or videos, and in a dozen more years, to accessing the digital library of the world online through the portal of the Bracebridge Public Library. The barcode interacted with the checkout system and became the unique identifier for all publications within the system. This new system, developed by Dynix of Waterloo, Ontario, promised faster checkout routines and more accurate record keeping of reserves and loans.

For the July 1 Canada Day weekend, Bracebridge Public Library closed for the holiday and inside the sequestered 13 staff members and a number of board members worked hard several days to apply the "smart" barcode to some 20,000 books on the shelves. With 7,000 other books still circulating, their barcodes were affixed as they returned later. The August 7 target date for automation was met. The staff, three scanners and three terminals accepted the new dynamic of computerization into the Bracebridge Public Library. This was a revolution as much as an evolution. To celebrate the new age, an "official opening" of the automated library system took place at 11 o'clock on the morning of September 8, 1990. The card catalogue was now redundant, an artifact of library history.

Late in 1995, the next stage in this relentless dynamic of automation came when the library offered patrons access to a CD-ROM workstation. The public could now conduct their own searches of four CD-ROM services the library subscribed to: KIOSK (an index of Canadian periodicals), Canadian NewsDisc (the full text of 13 newspapers and wire services), Magill's Survey of Science (full text essays in all scientific fields) and Masterplots (essays in literature). A sign of just how dynamic the new era of librarianship and information retrieval was becoming, all four would be replaced by subscriptions to online versions of the same thing within a decade.

Progress continued. Library staff kept upgrading methods and retraining themselves as inventions of new technologies accelerated. By February 2003, the online collection database and the patron database—in short, the entire library system—"migrated" to Horizon, a web-based program that allows remote access for anyone via the Internet. From outside the library, patrons could now search the catalogue, place items on hold, renew already checked out items (provided they were not overdue!), and ask questions of the reference librarians online—even after closing hours.

Upgrading the skills of those working at the Bracebridge library came in two versions: re-training those already on staff for the new applications of computers to libraries, and hiring individuals with higher qualifications than, even just a few years before, had been possessed by the head librarian. In 1992, for instance, both Ruth Holtz and Nancy Wilson came on staff as reference librarians. Ruth had graduated from University of Western Ontario in 1977 with a Master of Library Science degree, worked in medical libraries in the Sault Ste. Marie hospitals, then raised her children before joining the Bracebridge library part-time, first at the circulation desk, then moving to reference in 1993. During her maternal absence, computers had taken over the libraries so Ruth again became a student of something not part of library training in the 1970s. In addition to reference duties, her talents were extended to writing the weekly newspaper column about library doings, running the "visiting library service," cohosting the "Read to Succeed" program with Cindy Buhne, and creating the library's book displays.

Nancy Wilson had proceeded with a bachelor's degree in French and history from Victoria College to a Bachelor of Library Science degree at University of Toronto and then to her first position in librarianship at the University's Rare Books and Archives library. From there she worked as a cataloguer in the North York Public Library system, then the acquisitions department of University of Calgary library, returning several years later to the North York system in Toronto as the first online database searcher in pre-Internet days, answering questions for the entire 20-branch system. After Nancy joined Bracebridge Public Library in 1992 as a reference librarian and cataloguer, she also earned her Master of Library Science degree.

A third reference librarian is Mary Armstrong, who joined Bracebridge Public Library in 1996, coming with her Master of Library Science degree from the University of Toronto and prior library experience at the Urban Institute and then at the University of Toronto's Robarts reference library.

Nancy has special skills in genealogical research that helped the Bracebridge library become renowned for exceptional service for those seeking genealogical information, and the library continues to expand this resource in important ways for ease of access and even greater comprehensiveness. *Ancestry® Library Edition* is a reference tool from ProQuest that lets someone search their family history by accessing more than 4,000 databases of genealogical data from the United States, the United Kingdom, Canada and beyond. This resource is available in the library on the public-access computers. The valuable Muskoka Collection currently includes registers of births, marriages and burials for the Muskoka Mission (1865–1875) and the Uffington Mission east of town (1884–1923) from the records of the Anglican Diocese of Algoma as well as registers from the Nazareth Lutheran Church at Germania (1873–1994). More information for those seeking their family's roots in the Canadian Shield woods or piecing together early Muskoka history is also provided by this collection's more than 100 years of the Bracebridge newspapers, census returns for Muskoka and Parry Sound for 1861 to 1901, scrapbooks, newspaper clippings, local histories, genealogies and other resources such as online searches and visits by Nancy to the Bracebridge Mormon Church's extensive records of families. In the absence of a public archive in Bracebridge, the librarians have increasingly been filling the void.

Reference librarians add value to the library, making it much more than a place, as Andrew Carnegie envisaged, for librarians to hand out books. They are the inquisitive, intelligent, knowledgeable human connectors between individuals looking for specific information and the infinite body of knowledge out there to which they can refer them.

How specific? At the Bracebridge reference desk, librarians have been asked: the location and information about the vanished Muskoka villages Jerusalem and Candytown; whether Sam Steele really came from Purbrook, Muskoka; any phrase in any aboriginal language meaning "by the water" for a cottage sign; pictures of the interior of the diner on the "Happy Days" set for décor in a local restaurant; the history of carousels for Santa's Village in Bracebridge; a bibliography of novels depicting war and wartime life "suitable for young adults" to read in class during November in conjunction with Remembrance Day; and instructions for building an igloo.

Many questions are received at Bracebridge Public Library by email

VERY GOOD REFERENCES. Ruth Holtz, reference librarian, never knows what the next request will be when someone, such as Rob Cooke, approaches the Bracebridge library's reference desk on the upper level. Although Cooke lives in the town of Gravenhurst to the south of Bracebridge and also uses his Gravenhurst library card there, he finds as a Purolator driver that getting into the Bracebridge public library works better for his hours.

The reference desk is a constantly animated hub of information traffic, both inbound and outgoing, and the reference librarian is the information services equivalent of an air traffic controller at Pearson International Airport. Ruth Holtz and two other seasoned reference librarians, Nancy Wilson and Mary Armstrong, keep up with this increasingly important service at the community's library. All three have master's degrees in library science.

At this desk people also sign in for computer time, controlled access to the locked Muskoka Collection, or to see the library's vertical files on many topics clipped from the local newspapers. There is growing demand for help by those searching their family trees, a particular specialty of Nancy Wilson, whose wide-ranging genealogical tracing activity includes drawing on the Mormons' extensive records of family history at their Bracebridge library. In the process, Wilson keeps records to build up the "early Muskoka families" records at the library, for future reference. *Jan Pitman*

from around the world, the result of posting an invitation on the library's website to "Ask a Librarian." No two days are ever the same. What makes this reference service attractive to users is the freedom it offers, including the fact the reference librarians, as Nancy Wilson emphasizes, "never ask why a person wants a certain piece of information. All questions, answers and names are kept in strict confidence." As she also notes, "Any question that can be asked, has been asked—and answered!"

Ruth Holtz adds that nowadays the skill set of the reference librarians, since they are close to the computer section of the library, is to be computer experts. They assist patrons with a variety of computer problems, send attachments with an email, download programs, and access government forms online for them. Nancy Wilson points out that technology in the smaller public library has put extra demands on the staff to troubleshoot such problems as computer hardware, network connections, software such as Word, Excel, Zoom-Text (computer software to enlarge print for people with diminished vision), or printing to the coin-operated printer.

As Bracebridge Public Library advanced its contemporary full-service operations in an atmosphere of friendly professionalism, the budget has kept pace for this transformation to happen. Long buried in history, now,

LIBRARY TOURISM. June Riley came into Bracebridge Public Library in January 2008 and is seen here speaking with circulation clerk Hasti Jonfeldt. Riley told the author she "loves Carnegie libraries for their beauty and goes into them wherever she travels." When she saw a majestic library in a Saskatchewan city, she went in and told the librarian the same thing, only to be told, "We didn't get a Carnegie grant so we built it ourselves." *Jan Pitman.*

LIBRARY LEADERSHIP AND ADMINISTRATION. Caught by a photographer in a working session, library chairman Robert Dolphin and town clerk Kenneth Veitch consider a matter while chief librarian and CEO Nancy Jones works at her desk. All three held these respective offices through the most significant single event in the history of library service in Bracebridge after the building of the Carnegie structure in 1907–8: its restoration and substantial expansion in 1984–5.

are the days of Bracebridge town council shirking its responsibilities for the town's library.

For fiscal year 2007–8, the library operated with a budget of around $625,000, and the largest portion of this, by far, is from the municipality. Currently, some five percent of the town's budget goes to the library, which is on a par with fire protection. Mayor Don Coates describes the library to townspeople as "your first choice for staying informed, inspired and in touch with current and historical collections in a variety of formats."

A decade earlier, the budget had been $330,000. The increase is significant and reflects the larger role the institution is playing in the growing community. The last three years have, however, seen virtually no increase. In fiscal year 2005, for example, the budget was $626,000. Making up that year's $626,000, to give some idea about the sources of money, since a library on its own is not much of a revenue-generating entity, the town of Bracebridge granted $495,000, the province of Ontario $32,000, and the government of Canada $18,000. Another $51,000 came in from Corrections Canada under the Fenbrook contract, while $30,000 was generated from fees, fines and donations. These numbers are rounded. On the

LIBRARY CARDS, LIKE PASSPORTS, reflect changes over time. Member's tickets of the Bracebridge Mechanics' Institute library, printed at the local Herald shop, were filled in and signed by librarian R.H. Smith. This one sold to Edward Hunt on August 4, 1891, for 80 cents. The library card issued April 1, 1977, to former town librarian Patricia Boyer was printed in the United States where companies specialized in supplying libraries with everything from chairs and shelving to windows and printed items like library cards, beating local suppliers with their large volumes and low prices. The card issued March 14, 1990, to R.J. Boyer had not changed a word, but was again being printed locally at the Herald-Gazette printing office.

Today the "card" is plastic and includes barcode and personal identification number (the last six digits obscured here for security). The patron signs it on the back, forming a contract by which he or she agrees to abide by the library's regulations. The smaller version is the latest thing in library card style (the barcode is on the reverse). It can be worn on a chain around a patron's neck, close to the heart.

expenditure side that year, again rounded, most money went to salaries and benefits for the library staff, some $400,000 out of $626,000. Administration claimed $57,000, building maintenance, $68,000. Another $44,000 was allocated to capital projects, and for acquisition of library resources, there was $55,000.

The "acquisitions" item itself illustrates the dynamic or changing nature of the library and the librarians' role. For a long period of the library's history, any items acquired under a budget for "library resources" would have been words printed on paper—in books, magazines, periodicals and newspapers. Today, a significant part of these payment covers acquisitions for the digital library. The issue that both Bracebridge Public Library and Bracebridge and Muskoka Lakes Secondary School, each town-supported public educational institutions in the same municipality, spend a significant dollar to subscribe to online databases, is explored in chapter 13 where the connection between the library and the schools and costs of duplication are considered.

Just as books are vital to the library, so now too are the programs and resources that patrons can access in the "virtual library." The payments each year for subscriptions to online databases are examples of getting value-for-dollar. The millions of books, articles, newspapers and research scans, maps, photographs, diagrams, films and cultural and scientific artifacts that no library or museum could ever hope to acquire, pay for or house, are now magically available to anyone paying the nominal fee for a Bracebridge Public Library card. If the library was once a passport into the world, the world is virtually delivered into the library now.

A patron need not even physically visit the Bracebridge library to access the world's information and culture. Since 2003 with the launch of the library's website, remote access allows anyone anywhere with a Bracebridge library card to log on and search the library's extensive newspapers, encyclopedias and periodical articles, reached through a dozen different principal website subscriptions. Beyond those sources, the library's reference staff can assist in locating other electronic sources. The powerful search engines like Google and the populist encyclopedia Wikipedia can provide quick help for many purposes, but for more serious or focused research the library offers online resources ranging from *Auto Repair Reference Centre* with information for all makes and models of vehicles from 1954 to 2006 with clear instructions and diagrams designed for the do-it-yourselfer, to *Science Reference Centre* with full text scientific and technical information from 640 science encyclopedias, reference books and thousands of periodicals, including images.

Electric Library provides full text articles from magazines, newspapers and news sources around the world. This database also includes scholarly journals useful in secondary school studies. *Encyclopedia Britannica*, the classic reference work for years, is now only available in electronic format, as the new technology allows constant updating so much more efficiently than for printed editions of the work. Access is provided through the Bracebridge library account with *Encyclopedia Britannica* to elementary, student and adult versions of this authoritative encyclopedia as well as a dictionary, thesaurus, atlas, timeline and year in review. *Knowledge Ontario* is a province-wide collaboration of libraries, archives, museums, heritage organizations, educational institutions, and community groups to create an interactive digital environment for Ontarians. *Canadian Reference Centre* provides full text content and images from magazines, newspapers, newswires and reference books. It is updated daily. *Gale* is an accurate and authoritative reference tool that includes 600 databases with full text magazine and newspaper articles. *ProQuest/Globe & Mail—Canada's Heritage from 1844* is a rich resource where one can search by word, phrase or date through the entire archive of the Toronto *Globe and Mail* and its antecedent newspapers.

E-books (Net Library), a searchable collection of electronic books available to be read or consulted online on a variety of topics, is especially useful for access to literary criticism, the classics, technical books and items beyond the scope of a small public library. This service even includes downloadable audio books. The TumbleBook Library is a collection of TumbleBooks (animated, talking picture books) TumblePuzzles, TumbleQuizzes and TumbleResources for Teachers, and this *Tumblebooks* website account includes French-language editions. Also through the website a patron can access and read ebooks online. Electronic books are available in this format for children, teens and for adults.

Another way the resources of Bracebridge Public Library have increased, which has also altered the work of librarians in the process, has been advent of inter-library loans. For years a library had only the books under its own roof. Inter-library expanded collections considerably, and once such cooperative lending of books between libraries was coupled with computer technology and the Internet, the sky was the limit.

This service in the Bracebridge library advanced dramatically in 1984 with installation of a computer terminal for inter-library loans. It was made even more efficient by introduction of a twice-weekly, then

BRACEBRIDGE HEAD LIBRARIANS

Josiah Pratt	1874–1891	Kay Cave	1968–1972
R.H. Smith	1891–1903	Mary Jorgensen	1972–1977
Moses J. Dickie	1903–1915	Eugenie (Gene) Smith**	1977–1982
Harriet (Hattie) Dickie	1915–1934	Nancy Jones	1982–1985
Patricia M. Johnson	1934–1938	Ann-Marie Darling***	1985–2001
Genevieve Johnson	1938*	Jill Foster	2001–2006
Winifred Richards	1938–1944	Cathryn Rodney	2006–
Hilda Leake	1944–1947		
Emma Fryer	1947–1956	*September to December	
Betty Reid	1956–1963	**surname Graham on marriage 1981	
Agnes Tough	1963–1968	***surname Peachy 1989, then Mathieu	

NEWFOUNDLAND - HISTORY.

971 Mowat, Farley, 1921-
.804 The New Founde Land / Farley Mowat. -- Toronto :
Mow McClelland & Stewart, c1989.
330 p. : map.

5 0 2 6 7

1. Mowat, Farley, 1921- 2. Newfoundland -
Description and travel - 1951-1980. 3. Newfoundland
- Social life and customs. 4. Newfoundland - History.

17347   89SEP15   28/   1-00933035

LIBRARIANS' CODE. Moses Dickie was first introduced to the Dewey Decimal System in 1909. All Bracebridge librarians since have used this code to classify books. Until the library catalogue was computerized in 1990, each book was identified by typed cards, such as the specimen above for a book purchased near the end of the era of the high wooden cabinets with their neat rows of drawers containing the cards. A search could be made through either the card catalogue indexed by the author's last name and by titles, or by subject. The above example, from the subject catalogue, the "971" places the book in Dewey's 900-series of numbers, allocated to "geography, history, biography and travel." The "804" provides further subdivision within this category. Dewey's system had 10 general categories, 0-99 through to 900-999.

thrice-weekly, courier for the loaned and borrowed books. By the final year of the twentieth century, for example, as a counterpoint to the start of the century when the only books available where the ones owned in Bracebridge, the library borrowed 1,805 items and lent 1,223 items in exchanges with other libraries. Such numbers underscore why today a particular library can only fulfill its role by becoming a working part of a larger system. When Joe Ursano went to the Bracebridge library with a friend from Spain to find *Lazarillo de Tormes*, the novella was located at a provincial university and soon in his hands in Bracebridge. "In effect," he said of the inter-library loan system, "it gives us a passport to every library in Ontario." Nancy Beasley is the librarian responsible today for inter-library loans, another service provided upon the mere display of one's Bracebridge library card.

The interface between the library and the community is another important dimension of the dynamic in which librarians operate. For decades one of the most consistent channels for this connection had been the weekly news from the library published in the town's newspapers.

Bracebridge papers regularly reported on library news from the start of library service in the 1870s. Until the mid-1930s these took the form of news items, occasional paid notices, and intermittent editorial comment. Starting in 1934, the presence of the library in the community advanced to a new level of prominence when librarian Patricia M. Johnson began a regular weekly column "Library Corner" in the *Muskoka Herald*. Ever since, weekly offerings from the Bracebridge library have become a staple of the local sheets, its content shifting to reflect the different emphasis and interests of the changing guard of local librarians. The title of this news budget of library happenings has also changed several times, from "Library Corner" to "@ the Library" and later to "What's New at the Bracebridge Public Library." The weekly column, written currently by librarian Ruth Holtz, continues to be a primary voice for the library in the community, now supplemented since 2003 by the library's website channel for reaching and informing the public about library services and developments.

Just as a library's internal operation is a linked system of systems, the library itself is part of a vast external library system. Regional, national and international library relations became part of a new structure within

GRAVENHURST PUBLIC LIBRARY. South of Bracebridge, Gravenhurst townsfolk established a Mechanics' Institute library in 1883. For a while this "part-time library" was housed along with the town clerk's office in a small brick building behind the imposing Opera House Gravenhurst had built for $5,000 on its main street, Muskoka Road, in 1901. On the same day, March 24, 1906, that Andrew Carnegie granted Bracebridge $10,000 for its new library, he offered Gravenhurst, with a smaller population, $7,000 for its.

Gravenhurst's progress was glacially slow, however, making the dragged-out process in Bracebridge seem like speedy assembly of a pre-fab in contrast. In 1922 when Gravenhurst Council finally got serious about the project, the Carnegie Foundation was no longer making library grants, the last one in Ontario having been Ottawa's new West Branch for $15,000 on March 31, 1917. However, because Gravenhurst's application had been in the works, the Carnegie Corporation "grandfathered" its grant and in 1923, contractor Andrew Ferguson completed the building.

Gravenhurst's library then operated in its Carnegie building on the main street beside the Opera House until late in the twentieth century, with a $45,000 expansion in 1975. Then this new building, designed by architect Brian Chamberlain, who had restored Bracebridge's heritage Carnegie library, opened on May 8, 2000. Gravenhurst's public library, back behind the Opera House once again, had left the "Carnegie Family." *Jan Pitman*

the family of libraries as the twentieth century advanced, which certainly made the situation in Bracebridge all the more dynamic. Started as nothing more than a local organization to provide books for its members, Bracebridge's library evolved into a component of these larger systems, from introduction of the Dewey classification system to renovation by computer technology. Because the Bracebridge library also became a "Carnegie library" it shared common paternity with some 2,800 other libraries in Canada, the United States and places around the world from Scotland to Fiji and wherever else the American steel baron's philanthropy extended

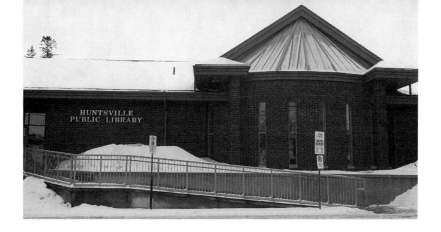

HUNTSVILLE PUBLIC LIBRARY. North of Bracebridge, library service began in the town of Huntsville in 1885, when the town's supporters of the literary life established a Mechanics' Institute. The Huntsville library offered subscribers a "comfortable reading room, a library of over 400 volumes and the leading periodicals of the day," according to the *Toronto Mail* for July 9, 1892. Like its counterpart in Bracebridge, the library of the Huntsville Mechanics' Institute moved from place to place over various stores or offices along the main street. Finally—by this time a public library—the Huntsville library found a permanent home at a building at 7 Minerva Street. It was completely renovated with a spacious addition in 1995. Huntsville's library is an important member of the Muskoka family of libraries, but did not join Bracebridge and Gravenhurst in the Carnegie family, apparently never having asked Andrew Carnegie to pay for one. The Huntsville, Bracebridge and Gravenhurst librarians collaborate in many ways, from friendly competitions to sell library memberships through co-operative efforts on inter-library loans to consortium searching of one another's holdings. *Jan Pitman*

a century ago. As a member of this large but scattered family of institutions, therefore, the Bracebridge library exemplifies not only the universal story of the evolution of all modern libraries, but also typifies a number of attributes common to libraries of the Carnegie class.

The inter-library relationships in which Bracebridge Public Library and its librarians find themselves are also woven together through participation in a number of institutional and professional associations. These, too, have evolved over the past century but at all points have been a formative factor in the nature and development of individual libraries such as the one in Bracebridge. In 1984, for instance, to select a marker prior to the revolution in communication between libraries with the introduction of computers and advent of the Internet, this extensive linkage included: Bracebridge's affiliation with the Algonquin Regional Library System; its membership in the Administrators of Medium-Sized Public Libraries

MUSKOKA LAKES PUBLIC LIBRARY. West of Bracebridge, the citizens of Port Carling established a Mechanics' Institute library in 1887. By 1895 it was converted to a public library, and in 1905 taken over by the municipality and located in a room at the back of the Village Hall. On August 18, 2001, this new library building opened with the library renamed "The Norma and Miller Alloway Muskoka Lakes Public Library." The Alloway family made a large donation to enable the dreams for this library to become reality, he having been a printer and publisher, she an author and editor, and both passionate about education and learning. The Muskoka Lakes library includes branches in Walker's Point since 1990, Milford Bay since 1992, and Bala, where the small 1880s library, frequently relocated, has been in the Community Centre since 1994. *Jan Pitman*

in Ontario; and, its membership in the Association of Library Boards of Ontario. The library itself had an institutional membership in the Ontario Library Association, while librarian Nancy Jones had a professional membership in both the Ontario Library Association and the Canadian Library Association.

Intermittently, re-alignments in the "library family" brought changes for Bracebridge Public Library and its librarians. Along with the other public libraries in Muskoka, for example, it was switched from the Algonquin Regional Library System to the Ontario Library Service (Trent) in the mid-1980s in consequence of Ontario's new Library Act that reduced the number of Ontario library regions from 14 to seven. It was an orientation south, with new partners. The careful participation in this process by Bracebridge chief librarian Nancy Jones, as Muskoka's representative at the amalgamation negotiations from January to September that year, made the realignment as smooth as could be expected.

The inter-library relationship took on its most significant aspects, not surprisingly, with Bracebridge's closest libraries in Gravenhurst, Port Carling and Huntsville. In the 1980s a closer connection between the three libraries in Bracebridge, Huntsville and Gravenhurst developed in several ways. One novel move was the switching of librarians between the three town's libraries for a day. Another was, as chief librarian Ann-Marie Peachy reported to the board in 1987, the "Muskoka Membership Marathon" which was "a friendly competition to see which library could open the most new memberships" during the month of October as a Muskoka means of celebrating Ontario Public Libraries Week. It was a close race with Bracebridge and Huntsville each opening 89 new memberships. A third illustration of greater cooperation came, thanks to the Ontario government's role in advancing library collaboration, with funding through the province's "automation program for small libraries" to study how feasible it would be to automate library procedures at all three libraries. Yet another is that today, Bracebridge Public Library offers consortium searching to the holdings of the three other libraries in Muskoka.

The change of terminology in Bracebridge from "public librarian" to "chief executive officer" hints at some of the much deeper transformations that have taken place at the local library and its growth and evolution as an institution. Still, the human element endures as the most central component making a library reach its potential and fulfill its role in building the community.

"Despite the advancing presence of technology," states Ruth Holtz, "libraries are still people places. Public libraries welcome people, invite people, enjoy people and help people. We are always looking for ways to better serve the people of our communities." Nancy Wilson added, "It all comes down to the people who choose a career in libraries. There will always be the need for staff who have a thirst for knowledge, a curiosity about the world, a love of books and reading, a desire to help patrons find the information they need or match them to a good book to read."

Cathryn Rodney, Bracebridge chief librarian, returning fully energized from a three-day Ontario Library Conference in February 2008, exuded, "I love what we do!"

TWELVE

Shhh! Children in the Library

K ids will be kids, which is why for a long time adults believed a library was no place for them. Serious books like serious drinking were for adults, and kids were not allowed in taverns or bars, either.

This "idea of the library" as a centre for adults expressed a culture more than a century ago that was simply not as child-centric as today's. Most libraries were unwelcoming for children, by design. Adults who patronized these public institutions valued the silence and austere sense of intellectual purpose embraced within, a place and condition which in turn allowed bookish individuals to journey deeper through calm reading and undisrupted research amidst the comity of fellow adults. Noisy children created an unpleasant nuisance. Efforts to placate them or accommodate them only diminished the library and made it more of a nursery hall or playground.

In any number of libraries this line against rambunctious intrusion was maintained by providing a separate children's entrance to the building, if there was even any segregated space allocated for them at all. In this many libraries took their cue from such leading institutions as New York City's public library which was built with a separate entrance and separate stairs for children so patrons engaged in proper library pursuits would not be disturbed by the commotion of children running up and down stairs and the noise of them gleefully calling out.

In Bracebridge, the decision in 1901 to allow children over the age of 12 into the reconstituted Free Library, now that it was changing from a private Mechanics' Institute library into a public institution, was a compromise between the factions. Framed more starkly, this decision by town

IT'S ABOVE ME. The dramatic angle in this picture of the front entrance to Bracebridge public library in the early 1980s recaptures what every little kid experienced for several generations. It was like going up to see god without having to die first.

council meant children under 12 were prohibited from entering the library. Bracebridge Public Library was not alone in trying to take the noise out of children or even better, as a pre-emptive measure, to keep the children out of the library altogether.

Children would no longer kept apart from the library, however, once the town had its new Carnegie building in 1908. If they could climb the steps to the great entranceway, they were in. From these early years after 1908, the rapidly growing collection of books for "juveniles" were an integral part of the operation and signified that it was a place for them, too.

Still, it took some effort to inculcate in the youth the special code of conduct appropriate to the library experience. This problem was thrown into sharp relief by how kids acted in other places nearby.

The town library and Bracebridge movie houses have been closely connected since their inception, the theatres operating in some six or more different locations over the years but always in close proximity to the library. In many ways these paired cultural centres were suitable neighbours because each provided their respective patrons with passports into wider worlds through information and entertainment.

During the first 25 years of the twentieth century, before sound was introduced into films and they became known as "talkies," someone who was present recalled how "noisy audiences watched silent movies." As one of the children in these audiences, Bob Boyer described the Saturday afternoon matinees and after-school special two-hour matinees shown in a street-level room on Manitoba Street just south of the library. Sherman Kirby operated the movie house. There with no theatre seats and only one projector. The children, having parted with their nickels and dimes, sat on planks raised up on boxes above the wooden floor on which they drummed their feet to protest delays in starting the movie or slowness in changing films on the single projector, or to send up loud noise to accompany their wild cheering when the films' silent heroes like Charlie Chaplin or Buster Keaton triumphed over dark villains.

It was exactly this energy and noisiness of children that was anathema to the town's other place of information and entertainment, the library. "Silence Is Golden" proclaimed a sign fastened by the circulation desk. Hattie Dickie was the vigilant enforcer of this rule, standing by herself between order and chaos.

One of the boys in those movie audiences who came into the library was Freddy Hammell. He could still remember, decades later when he'd become chair of the Bracebridge Library Board, the withering looks and stinging admonishments he'd received as a noisy kid from librarian Hattie Dickie. She could swiftly cut down any ill-disciplined child who spoke above a hushed whisper, if at all.

Bracebridge library's holdings by 1915 had grown to some 800 books for juvenile readers, including one on philosophy, four in the field of fine arts, seven of literature, eight classified as "useful arts," 18 on sociology, 27 history, another 27 clumped together under biography and travel, 34 natural science books, and 629 juvenile fiction works. That represented an early and significant effort by the library board and librarian to engage the young and provide for their interests. Hattie Dickie wanted to be sure children knew there were books written for them, especially given the effort and cost of getting them. Yet the two-fold problem she faced in doing so was common to many: not knowing when youngsters were no longer children, and not understanding that by aspiring to something more adult is how we grow up.

Children found this propensity on her part to control their reading frustrating and even humiliating because often she would not let them have books at all. Eva Ecclestone, a Bracebridge high school student, was one of many who came to resent this librarian's censorship. Eva selected a book from a list provided by her upper year continuation school teacher and then went to the library to sign it out. Taking the classic to the check out counter, she was greeted by a stern look over the top of Miss Dickie's eyeglasses and an equally strict admonishment: "Oh, you can't have that to read! That's not a suitable book for a girl your age." Dickie seized the book, went back into the stacks and returned with another book for Eva to take home. It was a child's book, suitable for a seven- or eight-year old-girl at the introductory level of reading, not a young woman in high school.

Such efforts by the devout Baptist spinster to protect children from mature evil were not isolated incidents. In 1925, 12-year old Bobby Boyer turned up at the library keen to borrow Jack London's novel *The Call of the Wild*, only to receive similar treatment. "You may leave the library," scolded librarian Dickie, "but that book does not leave with you!" Young Boyer for months had already been reading London's adventure writing in serialized installments in the *Toronto Daily Star*. Despite the salacious content Miss Dickie apparently surmised would be in a book with so racy a title, it was just a boy's story about a dog. The dog's name was Buck.

Such humiliations at the local library obviously stung deeply because they were still remembered vividly by Ecclestone and Boyer even into their old age, but they were not unique. Similar experiences greeted many other youngsters of Bracebridge during the lengthening years of Hattie Dickie's reign as librarian from 1915 until 1934. For them, in this era, the local library was not the passport either they or Andrew Carnegie had hoped it might be.

Librarian Hattie Dickie encouraged children to read, but exercised her strict Baptist morality and narrow-life judgments about books appropri-

ADULT READING STANDARDS.
In 1925 Bobby Boyer was 12 years
old and a voracious reader. When he
sought to borrow Jack London's *The
Call of the Wild*, librarian Hattie Dickie
exercised censorial discretion and
refused him the book. It was a boy's
story about a dog named Buck.

ate to their tender years. Whether that discouraged reading by youngsters
or served to increase it by investing books with the allure of the forbidden
thereby driving these young people to other places for different books
that would truly shock her, is a moot point. However, in this librarian's
judgmental approach she was an integral part of a larger morality play
being continuously re-enacted on the stage of the town library. She, like
most people working in institutions, take their cues from those in charge.
That was her father Moses Dickie, who was helpful and kindly to young
readers coming in to look for a book but was nevertheless mindful that
reading was a risky business.

One example of many arose in the spring of 1911 when, as reported
in a public notice to townspeople issued on order of the library board,
Moses Dickie as board secretary stated it had been brought to the board's
attention that "some person had discovered immoral books in circulation
from the Public Library." It had also been brought to the board's notice,
he added in the *Bracebridge Gazette* of April 27, "that parents were complaining that their children were reading too many books, to the neglect
of their school work. If such is the case, parents can easily remedy this by
intimating to the Librarian that they wish the supply of books reduced
during the school terms and it will be done." The librarian, though the
visible personification of the library, was but one part of a complex equation as Bracebridge continued to sort out its engaged relationship with
books, including in their role as a suitable escape from boring homework.

Hattie Dickie's successor as librarian in 1934, Patricia Johnson, had a profound yet stoic interest in children of the community and enjoyed seeing them rise to heights of self-surprised discovery. She, too, had Baptist values and could be censorial if she considered a youngster was reading something that was either a waste of their time or a bad influence, but she did not try to mother or scold children so much as lead, teach and inspire them.

This quality was displayed in Patricia's time as Bracebridge librarian and later in other roles as schoolteacher, Sunday school superintendent, producer-director of plays and pageants with children, and as one of the co-founders of the Victoria Street School for children with mental disabilities. But it was her very first initiative in Bracebridge as a 22-year-old university graduate which paved the way for much of her later community involvement, and that initiative was to start up the library's first "Children's Book Hour."

Parents could drop off their youngsters on Saturday morning at the Bracebridge library just before starting time at 10 o'clock, then go shopping for groceries and run other errands around town, confident their offspring were not just being safely supervised but enthusiastically launched with glee or awe into another enchanting enactment of some drama from a children's book. The Book Hour was for children 10 or over. Perhaps this morning they would be acting out the roles of Aladdin, Ali Baba and as many of the Forty Thieves as there were children on hand. Librarian Patricia read and told the story. The children played roles and their love of books grew. They were transported week after week on the magic carpet of a single book to far-away worlds in Arabia, the South Seas, Old England, the American South, or the Canadian wilds. Before these children even understood much about overseas travel in their 1930s small-town world, far more self-contained than ours today, they had discovered at the local library their own gateway into a vast universe.

The grand finale of this Children's Book Hour featured a visit to the children's books. Each child had his or her own library card, itself a proud marker of how they were growing up. They could choose a book for themselves. Patricia would perhaps make a constructive or enticing comment about their choices as she signed out the books for the week. The 30 or 40 children coming to Book Hour on Saturday morning brought last week's book back with them, eager to get another.

One child drawn to this magnetic setting was Ruth Tinkiss, whose father was a steamboat captain on the Muskoka Lakes. "I never wanted to leave," she later recalled. "When the Children's Book Hour ended, I

DOLLS AND BOOKS. The resources of the children's library as they appeared in the early 1980s.

couldn't wait for the next Saturday morning to roll around again." Years later Ruth Tinkiss, by then retired from a highly esteemed career as a teacher of children with special needs in the city, proposed that the new children's library being created in the Bracebridge Public Library as part of the expansion of facilities be named to honour this librarian who in the 1930s gave a generation of Bracebridge and central Muskoka youngsters their passports to the magic world of literature.

This Children's Book Hour has remained a part of the core activities for children in the Bracebridge library ever since, twice temporarily suspended during reconstruction of the library building, but mostly expanded and today called "Storyhour" and aimed at a much younger group of children.

Adventures with books can start early in life and this is why the intelligence and sensitivity of a librarian is so important.

There are, to be sure, many ways for a librarian to figure out what books children could suitably read, but of the 18 librarians who have ministered over Bracebridge readers from 1874 until today, it is unlikely that any was more intuitively intelligent on this score than Emma Fryer. As town librarian from 1947 to 1956, Emma may have been short and stocky but she was also attentive to readers in a possessively observant way.

One youngster coming in to the library daily was Cynthia Thomas, a granddaughter of legendary G.H.O. Thomas, and her father, his son, Douglas C. Thomas, was a lawyer who then became Muskoka District Judge. Not only did Cynthia come in daily, she signed out three books at a time, bringing them back the next day for another selection of three more. Day after day this happened, until Mrs. Fryer finally said to her, "You can't read three books in one night."

"Yes," replied Cynthia, "I can and I do."

Normally a librarian might not be so challenging of a patron, but the fact that Miss Thomas was eight years old probably caused Mrs. Fryer to treat her like a child. "Well then," she said, "read them to me and let me see."

"I can't read them to you now because I'll be late getting home and my mother will be upset." Mrs. Fryer telephoned from the circulation desk to the Thomas residence. "Your daughter wants to sign out three books every day and says she reads them in one night."

"That is correct," confirmed Arla Thomas. "What my daughter has told you is precisely what she does." Emma realized she had a truly gifted child standing impatiently in front of her.

"Well, I just want her to read to me awhile so she might be late getting home." Ringing off, she asked young Cynthia to proceed with a reading. Although the girl felt the librarian was intrusive and judgmental, she did read to her.

"You are very good," she interrupted after a time. "You should be reading books," she continued as she walked Cynthia to the adult section of the stacks, "from over here." That night the book the eight-year-old took home, at the librarian's insistence that she could now read at this more advanced level, was *Gone With the Wind*. For the next several days she read the book and enjoyed it, partly for the story and partly because she was now considered more adult.

"You're letting your daughter read *Gone With the Wind?*" declaimed shocked friends of Cynthia's mother when the saw her curled up with the thick novel. "That's too ... mature for a child!" Mrs. Thomas astutely knew, as librarian Fryer did too, that an eight-year-old would only understand things that were within her personal realm of experience. The seamy passages that were so steamy for adults simply passed over her head as she read through them.

For a century now Bracebridge Public Library has been a place where youngsters become acquainted with reading and discover a place away from home that could be as important in their lives as school, the arena or a church.

The space for children at Bracebridge Public Library has changed to reflect an increasingly child-centric universe. In the 1930s, when the Children's Book Hour began, the Saturday morning session was held in a front corner of the library where youngsters assembled for the event. Children had to be 10 or older, but the librarian adjusted her reading and dramatic presentation to the ages of those who turned up or who were dropped off by parents. In the process, the children were introduced to the atmosphere of the "adult" library as a special and somewhat awesome place.

Building a children's library, in conjunction with other changes to the original Carnegie building, became a town-wide project in 1967. Commemorating a century of Canada's past by looking to the future with library services for children was strong evidence that for sure they now had a place in the library and that this town whose history was interwoven with books would continue that way into future generations. The "Centennial Wing" was not itself the new children's library. That unprepossessing structure only housed a stairway and entrance. The new children's library was housed entirely within the Carnegie building's lower level. When the 1985 restoration and expansion was completed, the children's library remained in this space and was designated the Patricia M. Boyer Children's Library. In 2002 it was relocated to a larger and brighter area in the lower level of the 1985 addition, which between 1985 and 2003 had been the community room. In this shift, made as part of a larger plan to accommodate a new reading room in 2003 where the children's library had been, the community room was sacrificed. So such a space for community meetings and events became an item placed on the list for new accommodation in the next expansion of the library to come.

Wherever located, by designating a distinct space for the collection of books for young readers and children-centred learning activities for the past 40 years, a significant evolution occurred in Bracebridge Carnegie Library. Children had become a major component of the institution. With the 2002 relocation to what had been the programs room, moreover, the Patricia M. Boyer Children's Library evolved further, a place complete unto itself. Instead of the adults keeping the kids out, children had now migrated to a place of their own away from adults and teenagers. Glass doors and a passageway separated this space and muffled any "noise" between it and the rest of the library.

The design of a unique place for little people now included low tables, small chairs and book-related games and learning programs that emphasized animal themes. This degree of reasonable separation according to age groups provided a greater comfort level for all concerned throughout the library. A separate space on the upper level of the library for young adult readers ensured that early teenagers would not have to diminish themselves by being in a place designed for children. Visibility from staff stations allows continuous supervision of all these areas.

After the 2002 move, the children's library in its new larger space was further transformed into a lively area to house the children's collection and programs. Julia Saulnier, children's coordinator at the library, inspired to recreate the walls and ceiling as an African jungle scene, called on the services of a young artist, Sonja Rainey, whose mother, Elisabeth, worked at the library. Sonja took her ideas from a children's pop-up jungle book to create a collage of different animals—lions, zebras, monkeys, hippopotami, a turtle—roaming green forests and immersed in blue waters amidst the floor-to-ceiling jungle mural. The ceiling sky includes overhead ductwork, once bright yellow, that now has become a serene blue expanse with puffy clouds. The room is a happy place. Once the mural was sketched by Sonja she then enlisted fellow art students Meaghan Binstock, Mike Lem, Jasmine Last and Liz Loute from Bracebridge and Muskoka Lakes Secondary School to paint the scenes in cheerful colours during a three-week period in March 2002. "The room has taken on a life of its own," declared chief librarian Jill Foster to *Bracebridge Examiner* reporter Mary-Lyn Tebby on May 8, 2002. "We wanted a room that was child-friendly and welcoming." Julia Saulnier added, "During story hour, the children keep looking around and commenting on all the animals they see. They love it. The lion is their favourite."

One woman, a long-time user and supporter of Bracebridge Public Library, on first looking through the door into the children's library harrumphed, "It looks more like a playroom than a library!" Certainly it combines attributes of both. Yet the books are there, some on traditional shelves, others in an island bookcase that resembles an elephant. It does not take long for anyone open to new images of what a library can be to see the intelligent effort being made here to connect youngsters with books through a sense of adventure and fun.

One of the ways children in this space are connected to books in their early years is through association with other things in their lives, like trees and dogs, with which they are already familiar. The "Forest of Reading" program, for example, involves readings from the Ontario Library Association's selected book list of Canadian authors. The reading levels are

UNIQUE HOME. Children are discovering, in these activities around 1983, that the library is a place they can be nourished in engaging ways.

divided into "Blue Spruce" for kindergarten to Grade 3, "Silver Birch" for grades 4 to 6, and "Red Maple" for Grades 7 and 8. To ramp this up a bit, youngsters are encouraged to vote for their favourite authors, good preparation for CBC Radio's annual "Canada Reads" on-air elimination contest over the works of five Canadian authors.

Another example is the "Paws to Read" program, which involves not just a play on words but also a partnership with certified therapy dogs. The idea here is that canine-reading buddies can increase a young person's enthusiasm for reading, promote confidence, and improve reading skills, especially when it would come to barking scenes in books such as Jack London's *The Call of the Wild*. A third example of connecting to other things kids know is "Readopoly," the library version of the popular board game Monopoly. This is a self-paced game that encourages children to read books on a wide variety of subjects.

The way interests of young citizens at the library are engaged, and their needs met, run along three avenues of activity.

One is to provide a welcoming space for children and younger readers where their introduction to the adventures of discovery can take place. This ranges from the children's library with its wall murals and books creating a pleasing association and transition space, to the simple desk on which a student can work. Students who lack a place to do "homework" at home may find it at the library, where the mood is respectful of those quietly applying themselves to their research, reading and writing. Generations of Bracebridge students have made the library their home in this way. Providing this welcoming environment is essentially passive, which is its own strength. People of all ages may crave time and space to be on their own in a setting that, while public, respects privacy. This provision of space is appreciated by the helicopter generation of parents who hover over their offspring in a constant state of protective apprehension, because the library is considered "safe." As supervised spaces, the educational and entertaining roles of the library have this additional bonus of being a secure environment.

A second way also takes place within the library premises, but is more

CHILDREN HAVE THEIR PLACE. This shows the entranceway to "The Patricia M. Boyer Children's Library" at Bracebridge Public Library following the expansion of the facilities in 1967. In 2003, this space was redesigned as a much-needed reading room for the library and named in honour of Robert J. Boyer, while the Patricia M. Boyer Children's Library was relocated across the foyer to what since 1967 had been the programs room. The children's library is a cheerful and lively place, with animal motifs in both the painted murals and the shape of some shelving, offering a robust series of programs for junior readers of all ages. *Joe Ursano*

engaging. The library's programs for both preschool and school-age children are intended to develop the habit of reading for a lifetime, and there is no barrier of cost because the wide-ranging library service for kids is offered free with valid Bracebridge library card. Through special children's programs youngsters participate in book-centred activities. The connection between books and the joys of learning become actively fused in their formative years. The characters in stories, and the stories themselves, become their make-believe companions. In these programs a librarian tells an audience of children about a book adventure and in some way it is brought to life for them, creating a setting for a child's own explorations along the nebulous frontier between "reality" and fantasy.

A third way Bracebridge Public Library connects with children and young readers is through outreach programs. If the kids don't come to the library, the library will go to them. One part of this outreach is directed to the schools themselves. The "Read to Succeed" program for Grade 4 students in schools of Bracebridge and central Muskoka is a manifestation of this strong culture centred at Bracebridge Public Library to connect youngsters and books. The Grade 4 students get to participate in class visits, have an orientation tour of the library, listen to book talks, and participate in library themed games. They are registered for their own library cards, as well, through this program. A number of incentives are offered for them to read books and these students are encouraged to come in and use the library on their own time. Other outreach initiatives include events in the community, such as the "Books for Brunch" program with participation by the children's librarian in activities hosted by community organizations focused on children and learning.

A Youth Book Club now operates through the Patricia M. Boyer Children's Library. Open to all Grade 7 and Grade 8 students, the club's members read a selected book at their own pace and then meet for "a fun book talk pizza party" under the supervision of children's librarian Cindy Buhne, herself the mother of a young child. Club members email Cindy their book suggestions at cbuhne@vianet.ca.

Face painting became the rage and children seem to enjoy both the process and its effect, so this washable body art is frequently incorporated in such activities. What children enjoy far less, however, to the point of almost universal fear and discomfort, are clowns. Adults nevertheless often include clowns in such activities, not realizing the counterproductive force they are setting up to their other good efforts. A survey of 250 children 4 to 16 reported January 15, 2008, found clowns universally disliked by children including the older ones who find them "quite frighten-

P.M.B. The former Bracebridge librarian Patricia Mary Boyer continued her busy program of supporting cultural life in the community, including many articles and columns in the *Herald-Gazette* and *Muskoka Sun* which she signed, with a slight touch of anonymous if authoritative detachment, simply as "P.M.B." Many of these related to library doings. In this period she also helped found the Muskoka Arts and Crafts Society to mount an annual exhibit by local creators and served as the organization's first president, the Bracebridge Chapter of Amnesty International, and the Victoria Street School for children with mental disabilities. She chaired Toronto Conference of United Church Women, was Sunday school superintendent at Bracebridge United Church, and directed the annual Christmas pageant where talented teenagers like Robin Knowles began her acting career. She was inducted as a Fellow of Huntington University. At the suggestion of teacher Ruth Tinkiss, the library board named the new children's library to honour of Patricia and to emphasize her pioneering work in developing special programs for children at the Bracebridge library in the 1930s. When she died from a brain tumour in 1978 at age 66 she was working on her novel "The Matriarch."

ing and unknowable." Clown images are even found on the website of a Muskoka library. At the Bracebridge library the adults in charge do not make such assumptions about what children like, which is the key to success in attracting them.

Resources for kids at the Bracebridge library today include "chapter books" for readers at all levels, "easy read" books to encourage new young readers, expansive non-fiction books for leisure reading and school research, and comprehensive juvenile reference books. Yet just as the adult library is about more than books, so too children have available many more resources: vertical files on subject interesting to them, electronic resources, online databases, videos, DVDs and music. A public computer in the children's library enables access to the Internet if parental permission has been given.

The pioneering work at the Bracebridge library in the 1930s to establish programs and a presence for youngsters emphasized especially school age children of age 10 or more, which at that time meant kids in Grade 4 and up who would have developed reading skills. Since those early days the drive has been to extend programs and library services down to ever-younger years. Today, Bracebridge Public Library has its comforting arms around preschoolers.

One arm offers many preschool resources, such as "board books" for babies and toddlers, up-to-date parenting books, a great selection of picture books, DVDs and music. The other arm provides preschool programs intended to encourage and develop a love of reading. Three separate such programs, each for a different age group, are available. "One-derful" is offered on Monday mornings at 9:30 a.m. and creates a relaxed, fun and supportive environment. The one-year-olds read simple board books, learn songs, rhymes and bounces. On Wednesday and Thursday mornings in the same 9:30 slot, two-year-olds get their turn, when the "Tales for Twos" program initiates the joy of reading for them with picture books, pop-ups and feltboard stories. These children are also led into interaction with one another through songs, finger rhymes and fun with musical shakers. "Story Hour" comes next up this ladder, offering a one-hour program for active three- to five-year-olds on Wednesday and Thursday at 10:30 a.m. In addition to the main event of reading stories, these youngsters also sing songs, engage in action rhymes and do simple craft work. These preschool sessions are available from September to June, with special programs offered in the summer months. All are free, but because space is limited registration is required.

The program for two-year-olds is highly popular, and about half the accompanying parents are fathers. Grandmothers also attend with their young grandchildren and enjoy the nursery rhymes and finger games, happily recalling them from their own childhood and taking satisfaction both in remembering those years and in witnessing how our culture lives as the story gets passed down through the generations.

This is not free play but directed activity with a librarian in charge.

BOOKS FOR ALL AGES. These two junior patrons, photographed by library board member Russ Mackinnon for a photo essay about the library published in 2005, appear rightly at home in the Patricia M. Boyer Children's Library. Several arts students from Bracebridge and Muskoka Lakes Secondary School painted its walls with animal murals.

The amusements offered a child may appear similar to what happens in a recreational playroom, but they are being used to lead children to books. Many of the games are book-based. The videos shown are based on stories from books, a number being television series that tell the adventures of book characters. Disney is one supplier among many. Scholastic has the series of "doggie detectives" featuring Clifford the Big Red Dog, for ages three and up. Scholastic also has a number of award-winning video adaptations of classic children's picture books. *Harry the Dirty Dog* is one of many where "beloved stories come alive in celebration of friendship, learning and growing up." From Nelvana comes the Franklin Hockey Hero series, in which a turtle, bear, muskrat and coyote engage in hockey and morality plays. Here a hockey hero can be someone who never even scores a goal. Warner, "the strongest name in educational products" offers its "Letter Factory" video for pre-readers aged two to five to help them learn letters and their sounds.

The many resources and programs for youngsters at the Patricia M. Boyer Children's Library and the sustained efforts of librarians in Bracebridge for many decades to raise up youngsters as readers have, cumulatively, created a strong culture that has a life all its own. This makes the library institution all the more indispensable to the social and intellectual life of the community, because it lays the tracks on which young Bracebridgites are going into the future. Librarians, teachers and parents who have read books to babies have seen positive results as these children grow up understanding the importance of books in expanding their lives.

In 1999 many Ontarians were bewildered when Fraser Mustard, Margaret McCain and other top people of that highly educated kind produced their *Early Years Study* focusing on every aspect of children's lives from zero to six without mentioning the role of libraries in this process. *Early Years* had extensive discussion on how critically children's lives are influenced by the stimulation, care, nutrition and parenting received in their first six years, but it all apparently happens in a library-free universe.

When, based on this report, the Ontario government prepared to launch its Early Years Challenge Fund to stimulate community initiatives for improving the lives of children, it certainly heard from pro-library forces. They explained how part of the core service of public libraries has included successful programs for reading aloud to preschool children precisely because it has been long and widely known how this is critical to their brain development and promotes early literacy. As a result, the Fund was opened with criteria for libraries. Most of the projects across Ontario submitted by libraries were not funded, but one of the 15 that did make the cut was a joint submission by the Bracebridge and Gravenhurst public libraries. In 2002 the two created a weekly "new parent and baby group" as a project under this Fund to provide "positive modeling and interaction" through song, rhymes, finger plays and short verse. With the two public libraries only ten miles apart, one part-time program coordinator could serve both and conduct outreach programs as well through community resource centres to serve some 300 parents with their babies. Components from this initiative are now included in on-going programs.

The neglect of libraries in the *Early Years Study* itself served, for some, as one of those "wake-up calls" that prompts new action. For instance in fall 2002 Jennifer Franklin-McInnis, an early years advocate for libraries at the Windsor Public Library, suggested to Ontario librarians in *Access* that libraries may have been overlooked because "the library community has been somewhat unsuccessful at advocating for libraries as an institution serving young children and families. Libraries have to be more than library buildings. They need to take on a social role, not simply exist as a book repository. There is no organization better positioned than the public library to serve the community's needs and yet we are often not thought of as a community resource for early years work." She urged all who work in public libraries "to become advocates—the louder the voice the stronger the message. This may mean that we need to think differently about our libraries. For our future viability, we must be seen as a community centre that serves the needs of young children and families."

The Bracebridge Public Library has in fact been doing this. It has been a leader for years on many fronts extending the library as a democratic institution, demonstrating a sustained instinct for community relevance and library advocacy. Some of this spunk came out in the public support for two major renovations and expansions of the original Carnegie

TRAVELLING IN COMFORT. Jonathan Cho and sister Jessica Cho use their passports to a larger world of their own choosing in the Robert J. Boyer Reading Room. A fireplace is to the right. This welcoming room was furnished in 2003 by a donation from Boyer's daughter, Victoria, who worked closely with chief librarian Jill Foster to ensure that the act of reading would be easy and enjoyable at Bracebridge Public Library. *Jan Pitman*

library building in the 1960s and again in the 1980s, the computerization and new relevance of global interconnectivity for the library from the 1990s on, and inauguration of Canada's first branch library in a prison a decade ago.

Especially as it relates to children and their early development, this same imperative to be a living part of its community also saw the Bracebridge Public Library develop a disproportionately large collection of children's books in the new Carnegie library from early in the twentieth century, initiate a children's book hour in the 1930s, make a centennial project with support from the whole community to create a children's library within the public library in 1967, and expand the children's library and enlarge its programs in bigger child-friendly quarters as the Patricia M. Boyer Children's Library in the early years of this century.

In the long view of Bracebridge's evolution in library service, only the introduction of computers is as significant as the quiet revolution that unfolded over the past century to establish a strong place and presence for children in the library. Each innovation has transformed the character and reach of the institution. Both the children and the computer age are resilient forces now fully twinned for the future into which Bracebridge Public Library is heading.

THIRTEEN

The Library and the Schools

"What action can be taken," asked the Hall-Dennis provincial committee on Aims and Objectives of Education in the Schools of Ontario in 1968, "to develop library services as a single, integrated force for the total community?"

The question was profoundly important in Bracebridge, and not just because Lloyd Dennis, who co-chaired this landmark Ontario committee for far-reaching education reform, was a Muskokan who, as he would later describe in *Treasure Chest of Muskoka Memories*, had "grown up on the wrong side of the tracks in the 1920s and 1930s." This question went to the heart of an unresolved issue in the very constitution and structure of Ontario libraries that had become increasingly costly for dollars spent, efforts duplicated, resources wasted, and opportunities missed. Bracebridge Public Library had struggled for decades with the structural fragmentation of library service.

The Hall-Dennis Report answered its own question with the forthright recommendation: "Integrate the development of school libraries with community library services." That was 40 years ago.

Today Bracebridge is home to one public library but many schooling venues: at the primary level, Bracebridge Public, Monck Public, Macaulay Public and Monsignor Michael O'Leary schools; at the secondary level, Bracebridge and Muskoka Lakes and St. Dominic Catholic schools; at the tertiary level, local campuses of Nipissing University and Georgian College; in the private schooling stream, Montessori School of Bracebridge and several others founded on alternate pedagogical or religious blueprints. The strength of this arrangement lies in its diversity, its weakness in the lack of awareness of the others' library resources and in not maximizing the potential for collaboration and resource sharing in the same community. That is the conundrum.

Recent location of three of the town's four main schools at the outer perimeters of the municipality has left the ghettoized students separated from the community and severed from easy access to Bracebridge Public Library. Neither the location of the schools nor the strong legs of the students, however, is the biggest problem for library service. Formerly, the unity in Bracebridge's schooling system expressed an egalitarian and democratic instinct profoundly present in the community's development well into the twentieth century. It was still strong in the 1960s when public school principal Neil Haight, a Roman Catholic, took a principled stand against certain of his fellow Catholics who wanted to create a separate school system in Bracebridge so children of the community could be segregated by religious differences. In time, however, the ardent minority prevailed. The institutional fragmentation of schools according to religion has since divided the young people of Bracebridge and central Muskoka. The reality of this segregation was underscored by isolating Michael O'Leary School at the westernmost edge of the town and St. Dominic Catholic Secondary School at its easternmost perimeter. Books and other resources now in these schools' libraries are chosen through the filter of a particular organized religion to satisfy denominational imperatives of adults rather than the universal interests of the students showing up for classes. During these same decades, private schools were also being established in and around Bracebridge, some along religious lines, others based on alternate theories of education, all with students, books and some form of school library.

Still, these fragmenting developments at the local level were not the greatest problem to the Bracebridge library interfacing with other educational institutions in the community. One could always celebrate diversity and note that students now had greater freedom of choice among schools to attend. The larger institutional challenge was the provincial framework for libraries and schools within which this fragmentation was taking place in Bracebridge. That was what led Lloyd Dennis and his committee to recommend placing "all libraries under the jurisdiction of a board of education in areas where the board of education and existing library boards mutually agree that this action should take place."[1] That was why the issue was so crucial to the Bracebridge Public Library and libraries wherever else the same structural divisions hobbled development of community library services.

From the province's inception, public education was a prime focus of policy, thanks to the widespread influence of Eggerton Ryerson, a Methodist minister and leading figure in education and politics in the 1800s and a strong-willed advocate of universal and compulsory education. If Andrew Carnegie was the patron saint of libraries, in Ontario Eggerton Ryerson was the patron saint of schools. Grants to libraries started early in the 1800s as government policy in support of education. Meanwhile other government grants early in the 1800s began flowing to libraries, most operated by Mechanics' Institutes, as another expression of support for education.

Schools and libraries had started in the early days of settlement, not from any central directive from a provincial government, but from local initiatives. This was as true in pioneer Bracebridge as elsewhere. As the Department of Education increased its control over libraries and schools, provincial officials just took things as they found them. Ontario policymakers inherited the separate physical existence of schools and libraries and did nothing to try to connect them.

As time passed, these separate tracks for libraries and schools institutionalized a fundamental schism. Under separate Ontario statutes, the Libraries Act and the Education Act, the Bracebridge institutions were governed by two different local entities, the Bracebridge Library Board and the Bracebridge School Board. Policies toward education had matured through administration into formalized structures that were now becoming as entrenched as they were separate. Ontario was left with a basic flaw in its institutions for education: the school system did not embrace the importance of libraries, and libraries were not linked to schools.

A century ago, leaders of the library movement, in Ontario as elsewhere, saw this problem. They sought to formalize links between school libraries and public libraries in the belief "they are all parts of the provincial system of education." In April 1903, the president of the Ontario Educational Association, John Seath, delivered an address urging such convergence. Until public opinion was ripe for integration, he added, school principals should be members of the public library board, as well as the school inspector. "These school functionaries should be members ex officio," he explained, adding that "if they are what I trust our principals and inspectors always are, enlightened and forceful men, our public library statistics and our public morals should tell a different tale before many years go by."[2]

This call for integration, or at least closer collaboration, was taken to heart in Bracebridge. If the province didn't address the matter forthrightly by restructuring schools and libraries in this important respect, self-starting Bracebridgites could at least make the connections on the ground. In 1906, when town council was riven over whether to proceed with the costs of supporting the Carnegie library, councillor Henry Bird on April 9, 1906, stated the library "was an education second only to that of the school" and the money for it "should be continued." He was not the only one seeing it this way. In 1889 Andrew Carnegie had called libraries "an adjunct" to the schools.

A noteworthy shift came, too, in the composition of the public library board as the twentieth century advanced. After the first decade or so when Bracebridge council made a strong effort to include a clergyman in the board's membership, representation on the board shifted from the churches to the schools. In place of a caution to keep "certain books" out of the library came a quest to get the schools in. For most of the twentieth century the presence of incumbent and retired teachers, current or former school principals, spouses of educators, and school inspectors has overwhelmingly dominated the Bracebridge Library Board. In 2008 its membership, consistent with this pattern, includes retired Bracebridge teacher Joe Ursano and retired teacher-librarian Arlie Freer. Local arrangements sought to bring Bracebridge's educational institutions into harmony despite their formal separate structures and in spite of legal and administrative practices of the Ontario government that kept them apart.

A number of schools have operated at different sites around Bracebridge, but construction of the large red brick public school on McMurray Street in 1880, a year prior to the completion of the town hall, consolidated instruction in one place for many decades. Its books were few, mostly readers and arithmetic texts, histories and books of geography for classes. In 1908 another school was opened for 100 pupils in booming Ward IV east of the river above the falls, but it closed during the Depression when factories fell silent and people moved away from Bracebridge. The McMurray

COUNTERPART TO THE LIBRARY. Bracebridge Central School on McMurray Street received additions to this structure to keep pace with expansion of the town's population of school-age children. The continuation classes were in a separate wing until the municipality's first high school was built farther south along McMurray Street in 1925. Both schools had separate rooms for the collection of books that constituted their libraries.

Street school housed both the elementary classes and the upper forms of the "Continuation School" in wings added to the structure as the student population grew, until in 1925 the town's first high school was built to relieve pressure and give students in Grades 9 to 13 their own space.

Books from the Continuation School were moved down McMurray Street into the new high school that year, but library services at the high school remained limited for many decades and students came regularly to the town's public library. The high school's collection of books was housed in a long cloakroom off the north side of the school auditorium on the main floor. This was adjacent to the corner homeroom, for many years, of diminutive and soft-spoken history teacher Dorothy Millar, who was responsible for the books circulation until her retirement in 1960. The library's resources were mostly used by the Student Literary Society. The year Bob Boyer was president, the book that he, Fred Hammell and other members began with was *The Importance of Being Ernest*, which was still in the collection a generation later when their offspring passed through Bracebridge High. It did not matter that the school library remained a backwater because the public library was the real deal and it was handy for students.

Bracebridge Public School in the post-war recovery got an up-to-date library, begun in 1947 with support by the Bracebridge Rotary Club. The school's principal, Bruce Minns, was a Rotarian and each year he supervised the addition of new books to the growing collection. A decade later, when a new school was built on the site of the 1880 structure, it included a dedicated library room in the front of the building. When Minns died the following year, it was named the B.R. Minns Memorial Library and the Rotarians continued their project, adding more books yearly to a collection that included good atlases, an encyclopedia and other reference works. This was not competition for the public library so much as convenience for the students, if the link between the two could be maintained.

In this context, the Bracebridge Library Board seized the initiative to advance the cause of library outreach and stronger connection with the town's schools during the late 1950s and early 1960s. In April 1961, for example, the board used Canadian Library Week to organize an educational evening for parents of public school children and residents of the town. On April 19 several hundred gathered in the auditorium of the public school to see a play performed by pupils, watch colour movies of Banff and Jasper national parks rented by the library from the National Film Board, and study displays and services available at the town library.

With the 1960s school population surging, the Minns Library became a classroom. Baby-boomers so packed the school that all space including the staff room had been turned into classrooms. After four more classrooms were added in 1963, one became the "library" by virtue of having bookshelves around a couple of the walls, but since classes were taught in there it was not very accessible, and the collection had shrunk. "Only with the big 1970 expansion that added several classrooms and a new gym did the library regain a room of its own," recalls Gary Long of those days, "when the books took over the former auditorium. The Bracebridge Public Library was effectively the school library during the Sixties."

In September 1963 a \$1.5 million addition to the high school provided new facilities for technical, vocational and commercial education as well as new gymnasium and library and additional classrooms. For the first time the high school had a real library, and a real librarian. Under the leadership of Diane Clipsham, "the first trained and qualified librarian on staff," as principal Kenneth Black recalls, "she carried out the transition from a room with some books in it to a real library." The set-up was in a block of rooms overlooking the new double gymnasium. Gerry Murphy, an English teacher on staff, became her successor. Though not trained as a librarian, adds Black, he "quickly began providing a new sense of direction in the library."

A student Library Club was formed, and a strong link forged with Bracebridge Public Library. On the morning of Thursday, May 4, 1967, the Library Club visited the town library to examine the new facilities. In what school librarian Murphy described to the *Herald-Gazette* as "a thoroughly professional visit," the 14 club members were given a tour through the rearranged and renovated adult library, then browsed through the new children's library. Public librarian Agnes Tough discussed the differences between a high school and a public library. One student asked what could be done to promote both their own and the public library, to which Tough replied, "Use the library and encourage others to do the same." Murphy said the visit enabled students "to compare libraries which use the same basic cataloguing and processing systems and yet effectively service dissimilar reading needs and interests."

Expansion of Bracebridge High in this period transformed it into the Bracebridge and Muskoka Lakes Secondary School, hitting its historical high for enrolment with 1,200 students, which has receded to 960 today with further decline in numbers ahead. Just three blocks from the public library, BMLSS was still the only secondary school in town.

Ron Jacques followed Murphy as teacher-librarian in 1976, remaining in this position for a two-decade run until 1998. To prepare himself Jacques used his sabbatical and headed to England in 1977 for a year's post-graduate degree in archive and information science at the University of London, while teacher Wayland Drew oversaw the library. The English, he discovered, in contrast to the Ontario approach, simply placed a trained librarian in a school and thought it "quite unnecessary" to also be a teacher. Yet Jacques would find that being a teacher helped him know better how to assist students and also to know from experience and direct daily contact with his peers what teachers needed as resources from the school library. Being integrated into the school, rather than socially and professionally segregated from it as his stand-alone counterparts in their English schools were, seemed to him smarter in the Canadian context. Both, however, represented attempts to cope with the relationship between libraries and schools.

Town librarian Ann-Marie Mathieu and school librarian Jacques met and planned how best to share resources, a further step in addressing this issue, then implemented a division between them for future acquisitions. With a larger budget than the school, the public library would focus on pricier reference works and Muskoka-specific works, leaving the school free to build up other sections of its library. Arrangements were also put in place for sharing and exchange between the two libraries. Both by now had their catalogue of holdings online. This was the zenith of a structured connection between the school and the library. It had been entirely developed by policy worked out at the community level.

By this time there was no longer a school Library Club, but a cadre of students interested in the library was in constant orbit around it, helping out and enjoying it as a special place to be. Agnes Tough, hired by principal Black in 1969 after her retirement as town librarian to be the school's assistant librarian, valued by students and staff alike for her no-nonsense approach yet droll sense of humour, was fully in stride until her retirement in 1979.

During the Jacques' years, Sandra Askin became a mainstay of the school library too. As librarian-secretary she knew the students well and delighted to apply her skills as a planner in preparing for the school's new library. She observed what happened in the library and then translated behaviour into optimum configurations of space.

After three and a half decades it was time to update the library. In April 1997 the Muskoka Board of Education approved a major renovation of the BMLSS library and resource centre. The library was relocated from a single room beside the gymnasium to three reconstructed rooms at the back of the school with a spectacular countryside view. Making the library fully computerized and heavily wired with facilities for audio-visual gear, the project cost close to $700,000.

"We couldn't have a book on everything," explained Jacques in February 2008, "but we wanted to put kids in Bracebridge on an equal footing with city kids." Some 40 computers were added to the library, and a closed-system throughout the school enabled students and teachers anywhere in the sprawling complex to access the catalogue of the school library's holdings, and even reserve a book that way. When head of the English Department, Dennis Denomy, took over from Jacques as head of the library for three years, he was predisposed to good relations with the town's public library. His wife Mary Denomy was one of its librarians. Denomy aligned new acquisitions closer to curriculum, whereas Jacques had been more wide-ranging, but he could build on the solid foundation of the modern school library planned and developed by his predecessor. A presentation area was added to the library for classes, and a blackout area for film presentations in response to suggestions by students unable to see them when screened in lighted classrooms. The high school library and resource centre was no longer a backwater relying on the town library; it had become essentially self-sufficient.

Today the BMLSS librarian is Wendy Nicholson, supported by Ron Stevens and Ruth Jones. With the school relocated in 2007 to a new building north of town, where now fully 98 per cent of the students must be bused to attend, its new library is centrally located just inside the main entrance. The costly library facility on McMurray Street abandoned, its books and computers were moved to their new quarters. Some 18,686 items of "materials" are in the school library which has space for 25,000. These include textbooks and course materials, other books, and a large collection of videos, DVDs, memory sticks, iPods loaded with audiobooks, and a number of graphic novels. The library, with a 40-foot high sloping ceiling and painted concrete block walls has an institutional aspect that will take time to overcome, but with students painting three full-sized murals it will begin to make the place less sterile. "It's not a traditional library setting," comments Nicholson, who is in charge of this multi-media centre where new technology takes pride of place. There are about 35 computers (a mix of 16 desktops and 19 laptops), a smart board, TV screens for DVD research, photocopiers and scanners. There are study carrels and, at the back of the library past the stacks, an open space with large tables for studying and comfortable chairs for reading. It is more self-sufficient than ever, and remote from the town's public library.

Although Bracebridge Public Library provides its resource list to the school library, it is just one of many sources to which students can turn. Nicholson devotes half of her $15,000 materials budget to data base subscriptions, while a contractor funded by the Government of Ontario sets up videoconferencing for students, for example, a bioinfomatics lecture from an expert at Washington's Smithsonian Institution. The Department of Education has a regional coordinator interacting with school libraries to connect them to educational resources, and the administrative side of the education system is very busy coordinating activities. Bracebridge and Muskoka Lakes Secondary School and Bracebridge Public Library operate today as two solitudes.

Collaboration with local public schools has been undertaken by Bracebridge Public Library since 1996 with its "Read to Succeed" program, launched cooperatively with Muskoka Board of Education and Simcoe County Roman Catholic Separate School Board, for students in Grade 4. Librarian Ann-Marie Mathieu on April 2, 1997, explained the program's goal in the *Examiner* as being to introduce the Grade 4s "to the joy of reading and familiarize them with their local library." Activity includes two class visits by a librarian, a tour of the Bracebridge library, and instruction in how books are classified and use of the library's computers to search for materials. Students receive special library card folders, plastic book bags and reading lists for use on future visits to the library. The "Read to Succeed" program has given confidence and familiarity to youngsters in accessing the library's books and research sources, all the more important with reduction of library services in the public schools. The reduction of staff in the schools for library-related activity has meant only the most rudimentary skills for using research tools and getting relevant books and periodicals are being imparted to a rising generation.

By 2007, however, of the five Grade 4 classes in Bracebridge a number were not participating. Even from the same school, one Grade 4 class was engaged in the program, the other not. When the library's coordinator of children's programs Cindy Buhne wrote the teachers asking if the "Read to Succeed" program was missing something, if it needed refreshing, whether the load was too heavy, or the materials inadequate. None of the teachers replied. When the principals of the schools were then asked, their response was the same inelegant silence. "The teachers are just overwhelmed and overworked," was an explanation offered to Cindy Buhne by one teacher in the community. "They're stretched to the limit and cannot deal with that program." Teachers of the other Grade 4 classes who do participate in the program, however, because they see its benefit to their pupils, were not invoking that excuse.

"What action can be taken," asked Muskoka's son Lloyd Dennis four decades ago, "to develop library services as a single, integrated force for the total community?" What the province does not answer, local communities like Bracebridge seek to address, with mixed results.

The most positive developments for Bracebridge Public Library connecting with other institutions for education have been recent, and outside the structured separation of the primary and secondary school system. The first was to create a satellite library operated at Fenbrook institution. This pioneering effort to connect a public library with a prison now has a successful 10-year track record. This operation is based on rehabilitating offenders through education and excellence in library service. It is accomplished by integrating institutional resources in the same community. Fewer dollars go much further.

A second advance came in 2004 with the Bracebridge library's new partnership with Nipissing University of North Bay. It is a stellar example of how those with greater freedom in running their institutions can make sensible arrangements locally to leverage resources and bring the greatest benefit to students with the least cost and effort. The partnership was officially launched at the library on October 20 that year, when CEO Jill Foster spoke at ceremonies to explain the background of the project, talks were given by Professor Robert Hawkins, Nipissing's vice-president academic, and Brian Nettlefold, the university's executive director of library services. Mary Armstrong, reference librarian at the Bracebridge library, gave a service overview of how the partnership would work for students.

The Bracebridge library provides students at Nipissing's Muskoka Campus with a collection of materials corresponding to course requirements, which are housed on the upper floor in their own stacks in the northeast corner. Two nearby computer terminals, dedicated to the use of registered Nipissing students, provide access to the main campus catalogue and its electronic resources. Nipissing material can also be located in the Bracebridge Public Library online catalogue. This material may only be borrowed by Nipissing students, but is available for consultation in the library by all users. Reference staff of the Bracebridge library provides in-depth assistance to Nipissing students.

Instead of attempting to create a freestanding library, Nipissing University has worked with the Bracebridge library to make what once would have seemed a science fiction library a reality of the present day. The remote is now near at hand. Through a partnership, cost-effective and efficient use of resources is being achieved. Nipissing University of North Bay is more closely connected to the Bracebridge Public Library than the town's own high school, a sign of the new configurations of our age.

Third, in 2008, the success of this Nipissing partnership in turn is prompting Georgian College of Barrie, which also has a Muskoka campus in Bracebridge, to explore plans to follow suit.

The sensibility of these models demonstrates the spirit of what president John Seath of the Ontario Educational Association had in mind back in 1903 when he advocated that school libraries and public libraries be more closely connected because "they are all parts of the provincial system of education." They advance the goal aspired to by Lloyd Dennis four decades ago to "integrate community library services." Neither man could have imagined this would work out the way it has, with the Internet, with satellite libraries in a prison and satellite university campuses in small towns.

FOURTEEN

Prisoners of the Library

The year 2008 would mark a double anniversary for Bracebridge Public Library—a full century in its Carnegie building and a full decade for its satellite library at Fenbrook. In both cases, earlier history paved the way to these milestones, from 1874 with creation of the Bracebridge Mechanics' Institute in the case of the town library, while in the case of the Bracebridge library's prisoner patrons, the tale begins in the 1960s.

In 1959 when the Diefenbaker government created several new prisons across Canada, efforts by Parry Sound-Muskoka MP Gordon Aiken to secure one for the electoral district he represented paid off. The Beaver Creek Institution was constructed east of Bracebridge around facilities previously used for training Norwegian fighter pilots during World War II. More than most correctional facilities, Beaver Creek soon began filling up with a high proportion of well-educated inmates. As a minimum-security prison, it housed business executives, lawyers and other white-collar, non-violent criminals. The imprisoned men posed minimal threat and were unlikely to attempt escapes. Soon the 200 spaces for them at Beaver Creek were fully occupied.

Prisoners suffer a loss of most freedoms during their incarceration, but the freedom to read is not one, provided there is a steady supply of interesting books. Their greatest punishment now came in the form of the institution's paltry "library." There were few books at hand.

I asked one employee at the time, "What's the library like?"

"Nothing!" came his immediate, strong reply.

The mish-mash of old magazines and a few tired books depended on discards from the Bracebridge and Gravenhurst libraries. It was, at best, a

collection point for remnants from other penal facilities, with a few donations of worn-out books for which there was no other storage space.

Danny Poland, local hero as a star player on the Bracebridge Bears
hockey team and owner and operator of a local service station, by 1963
had become a guard at Beaver Creek. Every day at work prisoners asked
him for more to read than Ben Weider's weight-lifting and muscle-build-
ing magazines. If prisoners wanted better reading material, Danny Poland,
like anyone from Bracebridge, knew right away what the solution was.
After getting clearance from the superintendent to take a few prisoners
to the Bracebridge Public Library, he then called Agnes Tough, recently
elevated to position of chief librarian. Following a few more calls and a
meeting of the Bracebridge library board to give consent, the prisoners'
great escape through literature was planned.

On the appointed summer evening, Danny drove eight inmates wearing civilian clothes into town in a van. Because no books were in the
prison, the prisoners would come to the books.

Agnes Tough had already been given their names in advance. She
had created new library cards for each and placed them in a separate section of the wide pull-out drawer in the circulation counter housing rows
of alphabetical records of all Bracebridge library members. The town's
librarian had done everything she could think of to prepare for the first
arrivals from Beaver Creek. Then she waited.

The prisoners climbed the front steps and passed between the columns
into the high vaulted freedom of the Bracebridge Public Library. Emerging from behind her tawny hardwood counter that separated the reading
and reference section from the open stacks behind her, librarian Tough
lowered her glasses and smiled in her pleasantly austere way to greet the
new recruitment of dedicated readers. She then conducted a tour, pointing out the sections and shelves of books she believed would be most
interesting, having deliberated on prisoners' probable reading interests.
She guided them to crime and detective novels, adventure stories, the
romance section, and some "current releases," adding that she was sure
the Bracebridge Public Library would have books that appealed to them.

After a silent pause, one inmate cleared his throat and asked softly if
there were any books on electrical circuitry. Another was interested in a
good text on astronomy. A third hoped to find something new on accounting principles and practices. A couple were interested to know, "Is there a
section for philosophy?"

These criminals had not robbed convenience stores at gunpoint at 2
a.m., raped and murdered their fellow citizens, or otherwise exhibited

violent behaviour or anti-social pathologies. They had, instead, used their intelligence to extort money from their compatriots and fleece their own companies. Embezzlement, fraud, tax evasion and calculated tricks to abuse trust and violate fiduciary relationships had been the gambits which brought them into the custody of a minimum security prison the locals referred to as like a resort or "Camp Muskoka" and its inmates as "residents." A simple fence marking the perimeter of the Beaver Creek grounds was as much to keep friends and the curious out as the prisoners in, although in July 1963 the camp's four-year "unblemished record" was spoiled when three inmates did escape.

Most of these men had a good education and reasonably high social standing. Class analysis of how they were being accommodated in a privileged style to which they could quickly adjust with very little trauma, could certainly make one cynical. On the other hand, economic and risk analysis showed the taxpayers did not need to foot the bill for more costly security arrangements needed for escape-prone hardened criminals. The active minds of such men as these at Beaver Creek could not be satisfied with a Harlequin romance or even good crime novels by William Deveral or Howard Engel. Nor were they entirely fulfilled by the projects they undertook to earn goodwill locally, such as making penny banks for the Bracebridge Children's Aid Society. The Bracebridge library was in the opening phase of acquiring yet another of its unique elements, a significant group of avid readers with clever minds and an insatiable quest to know more about particular subjects than anybody else.

In following years, Beaver Creek inmates quietly came into town for other reasons than to return books and sign out new ones at the library. They helped the Bracebridge community by painting the seats and interior of the arena when the new Junior C hockey team was being launched. Arena manager Doug Smith had no money for the needed paint job, so in exchange for their services the inmates got to come into town to watch the hockey games for free. Beaver Creek prisoners helped erect fencing around the riverside grounds at Williams Memorial Park on which paintings would be displayed for the Muskoka Arts & Crafts show. When moving day came for Bracebridge's new hospital, a busload of inmates pulled up to carry beds and other equipment from the old facility under the supervision of nurses. Few townspeople knew about these activities. In time, however, critical comment in the community about inmates mingling with other patrons and handling the same books as law-abiding people spelled an end to their outings to the local library.

On May 7, 1998, a time capsule containing that day's Far Side cartoon, a couple of best-selling books of the day and other memorable artifacts was locked away inside a concrete and stone cairn above ground and observable from all four sides, to mark the official opening of a new prison.

In a few days, other confined spaces at Fenbrook Institution would begin to encapsulate the human artifacts of the criminal justice system. Fenbrook, the first medium-security prison for males built in Ontario in a quarter century, was initially to be constructed near Kingston alongside Millhaven Prison, known as "Gladiator School" by inmates who learn to fight there in order to survive. Then Corrections Canada realized most offenders emanated from the greater Toronto area and that building the new facility closer to them suggested co-locating it with Beaver Creek prison just south of Bracebridge. Both Beaver Creek and Fenbrook share some services and facilities. Prisoners in both are reminded of the outside world by flights of small planes taking off and landing at adjacent Muskoka Airport and by their own flights of imagination and inquiry launched through books.

In March 1998, ahead of the prison opening, Bracebridge Public Library entered into a contract with the Government of Canada's Department of Correctional Services to establish and maintain the institutional library in Fenbrook to serve the reading and information needs of the inmates and staff. Libraries are generally well down the list of prison priorities, but fortunately for inmates of Beaver Creek and Fenbrook, both were in the orbit of Bracebridge, the book town.

While it was to be the prison's "institutional library," it would in effect operate as a branch library or satellite operation of the public library in Bracebridge. The fact that Bracebridge Public Library had completely modernized itself, from its building to the computers and the skills of the staff, provided the essential basis for this agreement. The contract called for the library board to use the Bracebridge Public Library's state-of-the-art automated library management system in establishing and maintaining the Fenbrook branch. It also was agreed that the two libraries would share resources in order to maximize library services. Another feature of the deal was to provide library training and employment opportunities for prisoners in the institutional library. The money to pay for staffing, collection-building and managing the library would be provided by Corrections Canada. It was perfect.

On August 12, 1998, the *Bracebridge Examiner* reported on the signing of this historic agreement to bring books to the inmates, noting that, "This innovative partnership is the first of its kind in Canada." Librarian

Ann-Marie Mathieu had taken an active role, it was noted, and the library board was reported being "extremely excited about this partnership" and "looking forward to a long, mutually beneficial relationship with Fenbrook."

A particular strength of this partnership was its two-way flow of books for the combined reading populations. The patrons of both parts of the library, one in the town and the other in the prison, could place holds and borrow materials from the other. Once the branch operation became fully operational, patrons of the town library could have access to the materials purchased and housed at the Fenbrook Library. This would be facilitated by a shared database of library materials which could be cross-borrowed. "The items will be delivered by library staff to the membership branch," explained Mathieu, "and the process will be simple and timely." She anticipated in August 1998 that "it will be approximately six months before the Fenbrook collection becomes available to Bracebridge patrons."

The books and other materials might pass freely between the two branches and sets of readers, but the existence of a prison wall between the two communities required special measures. The library board committed to safeguard the confidentiality of all patron membership and borrowing information. Correctional Services Canada had its information technology specialists review the system's security, and it was reported that it satisfied their requirements.

Meanwhile, at Beaver Creek the library, such as it was, fell under the responsibility of Acheron College. This was a different model from the new arrangement just created between Corrections Canada and the Bracebridge library, but it was where things ended up after the puritanical sensitivities of some Bracebridgites spelled an end to the visits by Beaver Creek inmates to the town library. Acheron College for Adult Education was a so-called private school operated from Kingston to provide schooling for prisoners. Its "campuses" were Canada's prisons. The word "college" gave the entity a lustre it would not normally warrant, which was among the considerations for the Ontario Ministry of Education terminating its status as a private school in 1994. Because Acheron College was teaching inmates who were obligated to get Grade 10 while in prison if they hadn't already reached that level on the outside, and because many of them had vowed "never again" to return to a school classroom, it perhaps helped to call the room with desks and a contract teacher a "college." Inmates, who are not fools, also realized the better value when applying for a job after their release to be able to show prospective employers their educational qualifications on a document issued by a "college."

The two main things Acheron College did were teaching prisoners and buying books for the prison libraries. The choice of the name Acheron for this organization was remarkable. Translated as "river of woe," Acheron is the name of one of the five rivers flowing through Hades, was presented by Dante in the *Divine Comedy* as the river boundary of the hellish inferno, and is often used as a synecdoche for Hades itself. A "true satanic black/death metal revolution" band uses the name Acheron, too. Acheron College bought books for use by the prisoners in courses it gave them, both at Beaver Creek and Fenbrook, and this constituted a prison library of sorts. Books bought by Acheron College are now among the holdings of the institutional library operated by Bracebridge public library.

At Fenbrook there was plenty of money. Once it was decided the place should carve out its own niche in the Canadian penal system—that it would serve as a special prison for Inuit offenders—considerable expense was incurred to send the prison's designers and contractors to the Arctic to see and study features they would replicate in Muskoka, from inukshuks to a stone carvers' hut. About ten percent of the Fenbrook prison population at any given time may be from the far north, and in addition to the normal costs of $70,000 per inmate a year for housing prisoners in a secure facility, about $400,000 a year goes to flying elders south, subscribing to newspapers in the two Inuit languages, and bringing whale blubber to Fenbrook to supplement the southern diet. Elsewhere on the grounds, First Nations have a teepee, gardens and a sweat lodge. The enclosed area incorporates a reasonably sized forested area and gardens for prisoners, as well as a baseball diamond. The somewhat secluded facilities for personal family visits to prisoners provide accommodation where a man with his wife and children can be for up to 72 hours. There is also, and especially, the library.

Housed in Juniper or "J" Block among the dozen buildings making up Fenbrook Institution, the branch of the Bracebridge Public Library shares clean modern premises with classrooms and athletic facilities, including a good-sized gymnasium where long high-arced shots swish through the basketball hoop without touching the rim. As in the main library in town, shelving next to the circulation checkout counter displays new titles.

Library cards are not issued, but the prisoner's number is used to keep track of books being signed out or inter-library loans. This is more convenient and efficient, since the same number is used for all other purposes, including credits for work and debits at the canteen, as well as general security purposes. In terms of book borrowing, it probably also helps contribute appropriate anonymity.

About 4,000 books are in the Fenbrook branch, and inmates have access to books from the Bracebridge library, with drop-offs and pick-ups twice a week. A substantial collection of videos is available, but their number is no longer growing as new materials for viewing come increasingly in the form of DVDs. There are audio books, ranging from novels by Diana Gabeldon to Johnny Cash, beloved singer of "Fulsome Prison Blues," reading the entire New Testament. Newspapers and magazines are in demand, and for many offenders constitute their main reading in the library.

Vertical files hold such reading materials as brochures on industrial trades and fact sheets on Hepatitis and HIV/AIDS. A collection of phone books is shelved in the library, a handy resource for checking numbers and addresses for friends and relatives outside, learning contact information for churches, half-way houses and AA groups, and scoping out prospective employers serving the community an inmate will be released into.

All the titles are interesting books. The staff librarian and the prisoner assistant librarian run a contest between themselves, selecting from the new books arriving the one each thinks will be first to be borrowed. The prisoner librarian seems to win more often, suggesting the advantage of an insider's sense of his fellow residents instincts and tastes.

A number of government documents, binders of policies and programs, lists of officials with contact information are available in a prominent section of the library, and a number of these are required by law to be available to prisoners, including matters relating to Corrections Canada. If you examine the access to information requests made to Corrections Canada, you will see that many arise from an informed understanding of problems and incidents or investigations inside the prison system. Also available is each current year's *Martin's Criminal Code*, and its counterpart volume on *Criminal Procedure*, along with similar texts and resources which may be helpful to inmates working on their appeal or understanding better the workings of the criminal justice system in its legal framework.

Most books are in English, but one section houses a large number of books in French, German, Dutch, Vietnamese and Spanish, among other languages, while another section has significant holdings of books and booklets and pamphlets in the Inuit languages.

Books are donated to this library from many sources. Sometimes a local clergyman who is retiring or a local lawyer whose small office is overcrowded with old law books are suddenly inspired to share their worthy collections of shop-worn theology and time-trapped laws with those less fortunate than themselves. Other times the donated volumes arrive when an educational trust spends money on books for offenders and sends its acquisitions to Corrections Canada for redistribution through the prison system.

Books on certain topics or themes are censored. Corrections Canada indicates books that should not be available to prisoners, and the librarians at the Fenbrook Branch keep a running list of them posted in their office, a room forming part of the library to which only they have access. Banned books include those that deal with making or using weapons, such as describing the workings of different hand guns or the use of explosive devices. Also prohibited are books discussing or showing types of restraint manoeuvres used by guards, such as Tai Chi and the Dynamic Sphere. Books portraying images a prisoner might desire as a tattoo, such as illustrated books on dragons, are also outlawed, since Corrections Canada seeks to discourage body art. A book discussing the advancing technology of hydroponic gardening was not available when requested by an inmate convicted for masterminding marijuana grow operations. Banned books also include those documenting particular crimes or criminals, such as those that might educate about how a particular armed robbery or kidnapping was pulled off, or about a celebrated or infamous criminal now a fellow inmate in the same institution. Still, it is hard to draw lines. A book that serves an innocent purpose for one may be an instrument for triggering a diabolical plan in the mind of another.

One of the librarians, Sherry Fish, at least sees the problems of censorship she must address at Fenbrook in a comparative context. Previously, when she worked in the library of a girls school in Dubai, the "protection" was based on religious morality rather than criminal morality, so the male censor went through the fashion magazines before the girls saw them, and with a black magic marker covered over body parts too sensationally revealed by current Western clothing designers and their models. With a few flicks of the black felt tip, a low cut dress that exposed excessive cleavage had its neckline raised to a height of fetching modesty.

The Fenbrook Library is open longer than most prison libraries, from 1 to 8 p.m. on Monday and Thursday, 8:30 a.m. to 3:30 p.m. on Tuesday and Wednesday, and 12:30 to 4 p.m. on Friday. These hours accommodate the counting of prisoners that takes place with inmates reporting to designated locations at 8 a.m., 12 noon, 4:15 in the afternoon, as well as other times in the evening. There are mounting requests to open and operate the library during part of the weekend as well.

The library at Fenbrook is rated highly by prisoners who have known similar facilities in other institutions. It is a highly popular centre, usually reaching its busiest just after one o'clock in the afternoon. A row of eight or so computers is constantly in use, just like at the library in town, except that patrons in Fenbrook have no Internet access. Their time at the screen ranges from playing computer games to drafting documents or writing letters.

Inmates are encouraged to work inside Fenbrook prison, so the three positions at the library are coveted as pleasant, interesting and easy jobs. The pay is as moderate as that in any other line of prison employment. Money does not actually change hands. Rather, credits are built up that are then debited elsewhere, buying cigarettes, candy or other items at the canteen, or renting a patch of garden to grow vegetables.

The uniqueness of the Fenbrook Branch of the Bracebridge Public Library was noted at the time of its creation in press releases from Corrections Canada. A year later it was also recognized when Ontario's Minister of Culture designated it the sole winner of the Minister's Award for Innovation in the Small Public Libraries category and the "Bracebridge/ Fenbrook Library Partnership" was celebrated as "the first of its kind in Canada." The culture ministry's website noted how this "represents a shift in philosophy toward rehabilitation and re-integration of offenders into society." The library at Fenbrook is to be applauded, said the minister, "both for the service it provides staff and inmates, as well as for the difference this innovative partnership has made in the lives of the people who live at the Fenbrook facility."

On November 8, 2000, Mary-Lyn Tebby, writing in the *Bracebridge Examiner*, reported that Fenbrook Institution was investigating what warden Michael Provan called an internal breach of security involving the Fenbrook Institution Library. "It was discovered within the last three weeks that someone had given a set of keys to some of the buildings to an inmate," he said. "Our internal investigation revealed that the keys were given to him by a member of the library staff."

Warden Provan was reported having spoken to Peter Jekel, chair of the Bracebridge Public Library Board on Monday and the entire Board on Thursday. "This is a significant breach of security. That individual [library employee] will no longer be able to come into the prison." The incident involved keys to two buildings only, and the inmate did not have access to the keys that would enable him to get out of the institution. Investigation had not yet involved the police and it was "too early to say" if criminal charges would be laid.

The Town of Bracebridge issued a cryptic press release Friday announcing the breach of security. Neither Mayor Northmore nor Board chair Jekel would say more, however, since the investigation was still underway at that time.

Warden Provan said he hoped the incident would not jeopardize the operation of the library in the prison. "We are very satisfied with the service and the population is very happy with it," he stressed. "We are reviewing our key policy and will determine if there is a better way to handle them. We have to be able to rely on people to keep the keys out of the wrong hands."

Reports that did not make the papers suggested that the attractive town librarian had developed a close relationship with a handsome and attentive prisoner in the course of their library work at Fenbrook. His request for keys to their facilities so that he could carry on with the program in her absence failed to provoke a sufficient caution, in the circumstances.

On December 6, 2000, an update from library board chair Peter Jekel was published in the *Examiner* stating that Ann-Marie Mathieu, former CEO and Chief Librarian of the Bracebridge Public Library, had left the employ of the Town.

"So many books, so little time to read them!" is not a complaint of those living at Fenbrook. The operation of Bracebridge library's branch has been a great success. Prisoners headed for a spell in solitary confinement often load up with books, frequently exchanging some of their own for new ones in the "swap" rack in the library. For many, their time in prison has brought a new companionship for the first time: the pleasurable company of books.

In August 2007, the contract between Bracebridge Library Board and Corrections Canada for operation of the library at Fenbrook was renewed for two more years.

FIFTEEN

Always the Book, Never the Book

If it wasn't for books, no library could exist. Yet if it had only books, no library would last for long. The magic of this unique institution is born from how it embraces this paradox.

Libraries today include classrooms and lecture halls, facilities for writers-in-residence, recital halls for music events, archives for historical records, rooms for civic events and community organization gatherings, and displays of art and museum pieces. "It is not unusual for the public to see their library as more than a place to find books and other forms of information," observed Joe Rizzo in *American Libraries*. Some librarians welcome a broader range of these complementary uses more than others, but all libraries accommodate at least some special functions, not just because it is expected but also because it enriches the library experience.

Are there limits? In the 1980s, when Bracebridge councillors, a newspaper editor and seniors' organizations wanted the town library to include a place for dancing and food preparation, the town debated the issue and resolved that not all outside functions can be supported by a library's set-up. Smells of burning grilled cheese sandwiches and calls to "swing your partner" lost out as contenders for a Bracebridge library, just as a gymnasium and public baths failed to make the cut for the town's new Carnegie library in 1906.

While a library is certainly about more than its books, it can never be less than a core library. Some activities are incompatible with the library's need for quiet atmosphere, security, and hours of operation. If good design of a library building enables compatibility of different functions,

BOTH THE BOOK AND THE MOVIE WERE GOOD. Across the street from Bracebridge Carnegie library stood the Lyceum Theatre, the building with the wide archway in this row of stores, one of the town's several early movie theatres. In 1907 Sam Lamb opened The Lyceum once he knew where the new public library was being built, seeing it as a drawing card for people interested in the arts and culture, but he was not the only one to see the affinity between books and film. The same year the library opened its doors so also did the Wonderland Theatre, just around the corner on Thomas Street.

Successive movie theatres have remained in close proximity to the library over the century in Bracebridge, including the Strand, the Princess and the Norwood in both its locations. The association between them is not just geographic but cultural. The various creative art forms are important in Bracebridge culture with the library playing a pivotal role in the dramatization and actualization of ideas.

this can increase a library's use and enhance its importance and support from the community. Yet too many non-library roles risk diluting its higher function as a centre of culture, education and democratic life.

In Bracebridge Public Library a young woman smiles to herself as she writes responses to messages left on The Wall by "friends" who had visited her facebook on the Internet. Andrew Carnegie gazes with placid resolution from his portrait over the scene. The very name face*book* invokes the medium of this place, even though it is not a physical book but exists virtually with pictures and text and even movies in cyberspace and on screens. As a place where individuals write about their interests and responses, their wants and worries, to share them with others, facebook is a phenomenon that is loosely akin to the book in an early twenty-first century electronic form, a mélange of true confession and manifesto, of memoir and diary. Yet because it is not a book as we are conditioned to understand the paper-printed and bound volume, it illustrates a parallel truth about the library itself: format exceeds form.

"The medium is the message," Marshall McLuhan told us, and interpreting what the University of Toronto linguistics professor and communications guru meant when he dispatched that epigrammatic insight into our consciousness has since fuelled uncounted books and conferences. Yet applied to libraries as a medium of communication, his idea is helpful by showing how the place itself is not the essence but rather what goes on at the library is what really counts. The library is the message.

The dynamic life that is possible, intellectually and socially, through the facilities of the community library, is both qualitatively and quantitatively greater than the individual elements that comprise it—the building with its stairs and smells, its lighting and temperature, the books and computers, the librarians and other patrons, the tables and carrels, the newspapers and artifacts, the washrooms and windows. Still, as the caretaker or any member of the library board can remind us, you do need the building to make it all happen, and you do have to be sure ice falling from the roof doesn't kill an approaching patron or that the toilets don't back up or the kid who defecated in a cupboard is dealt with, somehow.

Sitting in the library beside the teen immersed in her facebook, a middle-aged couple huddles in front of another computer screen identifying friends in photos of a ski team. Across from them, a staff member gathers up piles of books and publications that, each day, a woman from the community hauls onto the research tables even though she might just as well read them upside down. The library is a refuge to many. Eccentrics are not odd to others who share their perspective. Who is to say what the norm should be?

This is where the library confronts a great challenge, at the outer boundaries of community values and normative behaviour, where issues about the books often have little to really do with them, where the contentious title becomes proxy and symbol for a cause. While the Bracebridge library generally takes an all-in approach to its collection and the materials or information its staff will help patrons track down on the premises or through Internet searches or bring in through inter-library loans, there are limits. Censorship is contentious because civil libertarians see it as thought control, a restriction on freedom of expression, an imposition of someone else's judgment about what is good or bad, right or wrong. Those who support and practise censorship, meanwhile, have their marshalled arguments about maintaining standards, about providing good examples that uplift rather than bad ideas that corrupt.

It is not only the prurient that can upset. One patron in February 2008 brought the Bracebridge librarian a book he found in the collection that decodes the dense symbolism on the United States paper currency, suggesting it be withdrawn because it revealed too many secrets of the Masonic Order. The library will always be about more than the book because every book in it links in one fashion or another to something beyond the page, outside the experience of that library's time and place.

ROM CERAMICS AT BRACEBRIDGE LIBRARY. Officials connected with the local library meet with Dr. Walter Tovell, director of the Royal Ontario Museum, when a ceramics display arrived at the Bracebridge library in 1973. Mrs. and Dr. Tovell are seated in front. In the second row, from the left, are Paul Hitchcock and Mrs. Hobbs, members of the library board; Ann Malton, chair of the board; and chief librarian Mary Jorgensen. The five across the back row are: Frank Miller of Bracebridge, Muskoka MPP and Ontario cabinet minister; Ray Smith of Parry Sound, representing the Algonquin Regional Library Service; Mayor George Parlett, also a member of the library board; Marion Boothby of the library board; and Dr. William Monk of Bracebridge, a member of the ROM board of trustees and the library board.

HAPPY IN THE KNOW. Six years prior one of the Bracebridge newspapers carried a photograph of activity at the library which featured Thelma Marrin studying the coming community events on this notice board by the circulation desk. On the very afternoon taking photographs of how Bracebridgites currently use the local library, Thelma Marrin was to be found again looking over the cultural fare ahead. The events on the well-referenced board may come and go, but the constant is Thelma Marrin's bright cheerfulness. Her husband Jim and her brother-in-law Michael Marrin are also frequent users of the library's facilities and services, part of Bracebridge's large community of "library regulars." *Jan Pitman.*

The library is always about books, but it is also never about the books. The first accounts of library operations in Bracebridge describe an evening's entertaining lecture by Henry Bird, owner of the local woollen mill and strong supporter of the library as a centre of education. He had the "limelight" as he provided a demonstration of a mechanism of his own invention in the Mechanics Institute Library.

Those lectures at the Mechanics' Institutes were just as integral to their much wider project as the libraries they created. The library was a drawing card and a component for a full-bore program that also included facilities like lecture rooms and reading rooms and meeting halls, and offered courses, meetings, talks and presentations in a general educational thrust to improve workingmen and strengthen citizens. The whole enterprise went far beyond anything confined to borrowing books. That was the foundation of library service in Bracebridge, with creation of the

IS THE BOOK BETTER THAN THE MOVIE? In times past, patrons of Bracebridge Public Library might have read the book, then seen the movie. Since 1908 first-run movie theatres in town have (except for the drive-in) even been in close proximity to the local Carnegie library. Now even closer, movies are available in the library, to be borrowed like books. They may not be Hollywood blockbusters since the Library seeks to provide films with educational as well as entertainment value, but the expression in Harper Harrison's eyes in this 2005 photograph suggest he has just found the treasured flick he'd been searching for. *Russ Mackinnon*

Mechanics' Institute in 1874. It is in the genetic code of the local public library in 2008 still. It is an institution whose cultural, educational and democratic mandate is profoundly about more than books, even while it is all based upon books.

Given its nature from inception, it is understandable why Bracebridge Public Library has remained a primary vehicle to carry culture and education in the community. Throughout the 1960s and 1970s the library was used for art exhibitions regularly, including exhibits from the Royal Ontario Museum. For many decades the bust of William Shakespeare was prominent in the library, fitting for a town with a long-standing love of drama and legitimate theatre. Yet other playwrights get their due, too. In January 1972 a production of T.S. Eliot's play *Murder in the Cathedral* was staged in the library and enjoyed as "an exciting cultural experience." In this period after the Bracebridge theatre disappeared with the town hall burning down, the library became a venue for mounting several plays. At various times there have also been puppet shows, for a change of pace.

Frequently lectures were delivered on a library evening. Garden talks by Al Bonnell helped round out the program for several years in the 1970s. The library offers children's story hours and drama workshops. During the summer of 1975, reported the *Herald-Gazette* on June 19, a summer

RARE PERFORMANCE. This small platform over the original entrance, called a "Juliette balcony" by Judith Brocklehurst in a *Herald-Gazette* article on the library, is seldom used. Sometimes a decorated Christmas tree is placed there in December. Size does not limit the imagination, however. After the library's armaments displays had been removed in 1967, a new object of fascination for some boys became the hidden ladder and "secret passage inside a wall" to reach this balcony.

Perhaps the last time it was used theatrically was in conjunction with the local production of T.S. Eliot's play *Murder in the Cathedral*, beautifully directed by Peter Malton in January 1972, when the whole library became a theatre. The stage settings were minimal, but effective use was made of the well-known library furnishings and special lighting was added, noted Patricia Boyer in her review for the *Herald-Gazette*, which along with the extreme simplicity in costume design, "gave visual pleasure as well as mediaeval effect." The presentation in the library under auspices of the library board, she added, was "an innovation" that could "well be part of an exciting expansion of the cultural and educational influence of the institution."

Anyone wishing to perform from this balcony now, however, or even to dust it, will need a stepladder to get over the railing. The fabulous secret ladder is lost to all but memory: the interior passageway was permanently closed off in 1985.

course on Canadian literature, sponsored by McMaster University of Hamilton, was a highly popular offering at the Bracebridge library. In 2005 Martin Avery, as the library's writer-in-residence, headed up writing workshops and organized poetry readings. Other authors like "susan sa" have conducted writing tutorials, and workshops of Melody Richardson, writer-in-residence in 2008, include memoir writing.

Even though the public library has never had its own concert facilities, that never stopped it fulfilling this "more than just books" mission in Bracebridge. Before the town hall theatre disappeared in 1959 through fire, it was the venue of choice, the best auditorium in town and just a block

THE ART OF A LIBRARY. Over 130 years, library service in Bracebridge has included a range of cultural activities and educational programs that complement its book-centred role in the community. The library intermittently stages dramas, conducts gardening talks, operates puppet shows, hosts lectures, sponsors readings, displays historical artifacts, and presents art shows. Artist May House of West Gravenhurst, a charter member of the Muskoka Arts & Crafts Society, poses here in the mid-1960s with paintbrush and some of her completed canvases at this art show in the Bracebridge Public Library.

from the library. The library booked Canadian poet Pauline Johnson to appear in that hall for several recitals in 1904. Classical guitarist Liona Boyd performed a concert in Bracebridge Public School auditorium sponsored by the library. Jan Rubes sang here. The Canadian Opera Company was here. Saxophonist James Galloway, dancer Norma Edwards, authors from Margaret Lawrence to Robert Munsch, the library brought them all.

Until it was removed in 1967, everyone in town knew about the display at the library of weapons and war gear, a military mini-museum not noticeably connected to the books in the place. While it is not a bookstore, the library regularly gives away or sells at nominal prices books being culled from its collection. Nor is it a print shop or an Internet café, yet the library is a place you can make photocopies and connect to cyberspace.

In 2006 the Bracebridge library participated in co-operation with TVOntario in the "Telling Our Stories" writing contest with entrants submitting no more than 500 words on their relationship with the library. Some 19 entries were garnered by Bracebridge library for the province-wide competition and one of the three top winners was Jennifer Milne of Vankoughnet village east of Bracebridge. A retired librarian 30 years in the Toronto system, her winning entry was entitled "Ronnie's Story," a true tale of an impoverished immigrant boy from Ireland who struggled to find pennies for the movie until discovering the children's story hour and free books as the Beaches Public Library in Toronto. The boy had been her father. Published in an attractive edition by TVO, the collection of these short essays provides an engaging and informative education about the centrality of libraries to a vital life.

On Wednesday November 1, 2006, Bracebridge's chief librarian Cathryn Rodney was "thrilled" to welcome Ontario's Lieutenant-Governor James K. Bartleman to the library where an eager audience crowded the Robert J. Boyer Reading Room to hear him promote the "Telling Our Stories" writing contest. His Honour, member of the Mnjikaning First Nation and author of deeply moving books that tell his story of a close relationship with libraries that started in Port Carling after World War II, was home. The audience included his mother Maureen, still a resident of Port Carling, and his brother Robert, now living in Bracebridge. He presented a signed copy of his first book, *Out of Muskoka*, to longtime library volunteer Diana Eaton.

Mr. Bartleman had the large attendance laughing at anecdotes from his early days but also feeling the sharp edge of his ironic humour. "Reading was my ticket out of my delightful young life as a ditch digger in Port Carling," he said. He had "read virtually every book" in his school library and, as Matt Driscoll reported in the *Weekender*, he "was certain his access to books put him on the road to a good education and a fulfilling career."

James Bartleman's "home coming" to Muskoka that afternoon brought him full circle: from the margins of society into the Port Carling library and on to roles as Canadian ambassador on six continents, top foreign affairs adviser to Canada's prime minister, and creator of libraries for Indian children in isolated northern settlements so that they can discover, as he did as a boy, as Andrew Carnegie did as a boy, their passport to the wider world.

That is why, at the end of the day, the library is still always about the book.

SIXTEEN

A Library of the Future

A book like this on the history of a town library is focused on the past. While looking back is profoundly educational and can even be pleasantly nostalgic, a deeper motivation for our historical interest is that we may pick up clues to guide us into the days of our lives still ahead. What will they be like? What can we do? This desire to see the future more clearly, like driving forward with the benefit of a rearview mirror, is neatly summed up in the aphorism, "The best predictor of future behaviour is past performance." We are interested in history because we are even more interested in what is up the road ahead of us.

From the mid-Sixties to the recent past, Bracebridge Public Library kept pace with rapidly changing times, maintaining "dynamic stability" as it evolved with its community.

The progress came with a renovation in 1967, creation of children's library, a restoration and expansion by 1985, creation of a reading room and relocation of the children's library in 2003, but the loss of a community meeting room at that time. The facilities were transformed with introduction of computers in 1990 and inauguration of the library website in 2001, bringing significant changes for staffing and space allocation while renewing the library as a patron's passport for the computer age.

Over four decades since 1967 nine different head librarians have come and gone. There have been many other changes in staff too as the number of employees grew and their acquisition of contemporary library skills increased.

Services have expanded starting with a satellite library at Fenbrook prison in 1998, books-on-wheels for shut-ins, new collections of large-print books and audio books, addition of videos and DVDs, development of the Muskoka Collection of historical records, expansion of genea-logical research support services, computerization of inter-library loans, programs for preschoolers, new activities to connect children and the adventure of reading books, and augmentation of the library's collection of books.

Library service in Bracebridge, begun in 1874 and institutionalized in 1908 with the Carnegie library building, has clearly passed through many phases of renewal. Only by looking back through the smoothing lens of time do these events now seem to have followed a natural course of evo-lution. At the time each occurred, however, the possibilities were many, the drama unscripted, and the episodes often as surprising as the town's earlier twists and turns between 1903 and 1908 when a straightforward process of getting one of the many Carnegie libraries being handed out was anything but smooth.

The cycles of library life in Bracebridge over 13 decades have come in and gone out like the tides: from having limited space and cramped quarters to expanded facilities with lots of room, then with passage of time becom-ing again fully occupied and overcrowded, leading to another campaign for new facilities. In 2008, the library is ready for this cycle to repeat itself once more with major expansion of space and facilities. The tide has already begun to rise. Bracebridge is looking to its library of the future.

In 2002 the board commissioned a survey of the future library needs of its patrons and staff, which culminated in the *Bracebridge Public Library Needs Assessment Report* from consultant Gwen Wheeler in June 2003. In the surveys, "The library building was frequently mentioned as a valued aspect of library service," noted Wheeler. "Overwhelmingly, people con-sider the library to be a great public space." Library patrons comments made clear that "being in the library space itself is an important aspect of visiting the library." People specifically expressed appreciation about the lighting, atmosphere, comfortable places to sit and read newspapers or magazines, openness, décor, quietness, and being "a cool place to visit in summer."

By 2005, under the steady leadership of library board chairman Robert Taylor and chief executive officer of the library Jill Foster, a committee of board and library staff members developed a vision for the library's

LIBRARY STAFF IN 1908. Hattie Dickie stands alone at the front steps to the Bracebridge Carnegie library shortly after its completion. Miss Dickie remained the sole employee until relinquishing the position of librarian upon marriage in 1934.

future and a strategic plan to achieve it. Central to the plan is "a commitment to focus on community needs, acknowledgment of the library's value to a vibrant downtown core, and the need to expand and update the existing Carnegie building." All three elements are centred on the heritage building that has served Bracebridge for 100 years from its flagship position in the heart of the community.

As good as all the community surveys and comparative library statistics indicate it to be, the Bracebridge library is evolving to meet new demands. These have been coming in waves from at least a half-dozen identifiable groups, in addition to the regular needs of Bracebridge's general population of library users. First are the many young people who have grown up in the town's library culture in recent years as they continue to utilize its electronic services as well as more traditional library resources.

Second are a large number of educated and affluent retirees who have sold their homes in the city and moved in financial comfort to Bracebridge with both free time and high expectations for utilizing the resources of the local library. They may have come to a small town, but do not want small town library service. Fortunately, Bracebridge and its library have been astride the mainstream for a long time now, so this merely involves the extension of an existing pattern.

LIBRARY STAFF IN 2008. Today the 14 members of the library staff work on different rotations at the library in town and the satellite library at Fenbrook so rarely are all in one place at the same time. Even for this historic photograph at the beginning of the library's centennial year, two employees were away, circulation clerk Joyce Hallworth and library assistant Julene Jones of the Fenbrook Branch.

Present in the semi-circle around the railing, from left to right, are: Lynn Stewart, library aide; Sherry Fish, Fenbrook Branch library assistant; Bonnie Parkhill, library aide; Ruth Holtz, reference librarian; Carolyn Dawkins, office manager and library assistant; Cindy Buhne, children and youth services coordinator, and Hasti Jonfeldt, circulation clerk and library aide.

In the inner circle, from the left, are: Mary Armstrong, reference librarian; Mary Denomy, circulation clerk; Cathryn Rodney, chief executive officer and chief librarian; Nancy Wilson, reference librarian, and Nancy Beasley, interlibrary loan coordinator.

Third are the thousands of summer residents and tourists who have long kept Bracebridge from being a backwater municipality. They place a much larger demand on library services in Bracebridge than is indicated by traditional methods of extrapolating a library's space and collection needs based on the town's census population. Fourth is the greater diversity in the multi-cultural make-up of the town's population, which translates into some shifting in the library's resources. Fifth is the continuing impact on the library of research methods and available sources resulting from the Internet and 24-hour a day access to the "virtual library" in cyberspace.

Sixth is the state of library services and facilities in schools that ambiguously shifts a greater role onto the town library in taking up the slack for students who seek an alternative. Far more significant in terms of specific space and staffing requirements, the expanding operations at the library of Nipissing University's Bracebridge campus, and the current emergence of a similar partnership for the local offerings of Georgian College, add a vital component to the Bracebridge library as university students use Nipissing's on-premises computers and read and borrow from its extensive library of books for the university courses now housed in a separate corner of the main library hall. If Bracebridge Public Library can operate a satellite library at Fenbrook, Nipissing University can operate a satellite library in the Carnegie building on the main street of Bracebridge. Each has its holdings of books and use of computers, each is linked with other institutions, and both show the bright prospects for the library of the future.

The planning process is now taking all these factors into account. It is not as if there is a starting date for evolution of a library, because it is continuous, like the tide that has been rising steadily. Already the usual complex interplay of forces in town is engaged in determining Bracebridge's library of the future. No doubt its evolution will include, as well, some unusual twists and turns that are a Bracebridge hallmark. A feasibility study was prepared on different configurations for additional space. The curse of the shortsighted council of 1906 is on the town yet, as this most significant institution in the heart of the community sits atop its small plot of land, surrounded by potential expansion space that it does not own but the town once did. Yet there are possibilities, and necessity will surely produce inventive results.

If the past really does provide helpful clues, so that the future Bracebridge Public Library will unfold along the path the institution and its place in the community have followed up to now, this would mean three things.

First, new technologies will be embraced and incorporated into the library's operations at a reasonably early take-up date, but only once it is understood in practical ways how this new method will really make an improvement. This was the pattern in adopting the Dewey Decimal System for cataloguing books, converting the building's heating system

CUSTODIANS OF THE LIBRARY IN 2008. All members of the Bracebridge Public Library Board, who represent diverse parts of the community, stand proudly on the front steps in January 2008 to inaugurate the centennial of the town's first purpose-built library building. From the left are board chair Robert Taylor, David Goodyear, Arlie Freer, Joe Ursano, chief librarian Cathryn Rodney, council representative Barry Young, Pam Dunlop, Mark Benson, Lynn Taylor and Russ Mackinnon.

The board meets in the early evening on the second Tuesday of each month, in the library's reading room. Like the library itself, its meetings are open to the public.

from coal to oil, developing a system for inter-library loans, installing an elevator to enhance accessibility, converting the heating system from oil to electricity, installing computers to track holdings, and adding portals for patrons to connect to the Internet. The established norm is prudent yet progressive pragmatism.

Second, expansion of the library's facilities and programs will take place, consistent with a pattern since the 1960s, in ways that enable the institution to accomplish two purposes at once: fulfill basic yet evolving library service for a much larger and changing community, and enhance a higher level of intellectual performance by members of the community. This will include a significant enlargement of the present heritage building by a large addition in harmonized style and structure that respects the distinctive architectural character of the present Bracebridge Public Library. Here, too, past performance in the mid-1980s expansion and restoration points to how satisfactorily this can be accomplished. There are many possibilities for this waiting extension, so Bracebridge currently has the pleasurable activity of designing what the optimum arrangement will be. Physical expansion of Bracebridge Public Library now required by the growing town will permit a variety of services, both new programs and extension of existing operations, to meet the community's rising needs. Those needs flow from the seven groups mentioned above—the general population of library patrons, members of the X and Y generations, newly retired people, seasonal residents and tourists, people of minority cultures, the Internet community, and students. As well, current needs in Bracebridge for community meetings rooms, a venue for cultural presentations, and a proper public archive, are on the wish list to be included in expanded facilities connected to the library.

Third, the Bracebridge Public Library will integrate the cultural and human dimension of peoples' interests with immediacy and relevance as an institution providing citizens' primary contact with information and offering a context for intellectual life in the community. That sounds pretty dense, but it means that as one resident said in the 2002 survey, "the library is the place to be." In short it will be central, not marginal, to the lives of people in the community. This, too, will represent continuity with the book-centred tradition in a town that created its library even before it organized its fire department. Many cultural activities of the community that in the past were interwoven with the library, but recently could not be due to space limitations, will be resumed upon re-acquisition of suitable facilities in the library for them.

Those are the clues that history gives.

In whatever forms the Bracebridge library of the future emerges, however, it will entail more than a construction job. The town learned that in 1967. A good library must necessarily evolve with the times, but as it grows and evolves it must still operate as a cohesive organism. Communities that added to or renovated their libraries, as Bracebridge did twice, discover how inflexible these buildings can be when one tries to add space or divide functions. "During the 1950s and 1960s," said Joe Rizzo in *American Libraries*, "reaction to the old Carnegie-style library resulted in a call for modular, open and very flexible planning." This made libraries easier to change physically when later adding a wing or renovating existing space, "but in many cases resulted in losing the sense of place that many people need." The lesson learned in 1967 was applied in 1985, thanks to Robert Dolphin's leadership and Brian Chamberlain's architectural design, to make the library the finest public building in Bracebridge.

A controlled environment serving as a sanctuary to many, the library's space needs to achieve a unique blend of providing privacy, inspiration, and freedom from distraction, even when it is also a busy centre where many people simultaneously pursue quite different interests and display highly dissimilar personality traits. While some patrons crave the privacy of secluded study carrels, others work together in small groups, while still others like the open space at large library tables under high ceilings.

"Traditionally," points out Joe Rizzo, "libraries have provided quiet places to study, but many years of analyzing study habits have expanded our view of what an appropriate study space is. People study in different ways at different times. Because individuals have disparate needs, their preference of work environment varies—from central to remote, from busy to isolated." Achieving variety in the spaces available is desirable because patrons will naturally self-select what suits them best, which has the added benefit of reducing crowding and competition for a place to read and work. "Variety is not simply a matter of layout," he notes, "but of all the aspects that create an environment: the size, shape and height of the space; its degree of enclosure; its lighting, acoustics and furnishings; the colour and texture of its finishes; and the views it provides."[1]

"Dynamic stability" is a principal attribute of a successful library over time, and as evolution of library service in Bracebridge over more than a century shows, this is achieved by the library being more than an isolated repository of books. Its dynamism flows directly in proportion to the institution's active engagement with its community. That is why the current strategic plan of Bracebridge Public Library has a "commitment to focus on community needs" and sees "the library's value to a vibrant downtown core." This relationship is pivotal. The "community" in question is extensive: the people who use the library, those who fund it, the ones who work at or volunteer for it, the reporters who cover it, the officials who supervise it, the network of other libraries with which it interacts, the professional associations and community organizations with which it connects.

The Bracebridge Public Library is the central institution in a town

STABILITY AMIDST CHANGE. A good library achieves dynamic stability as a community institution by upholding civilization's traditions even while embracing changes in values and technologies. Sometimes this concept almost seems to apply literally, as well, to the library building. Winter of 1939 finds an automotive garage to the library's north, a service station to its south, and cars moving by in front. By the 1970s the gas station was replaced by a restaurant, the garage by a post office, but cars remained in front.

The library and the automobile share an ability to change how someone sees the world. Just as over time the Bracebridge library's institutional model would evolve legally, physically, technologically and culturally in the ways described in this book, these 1938 motor cars would likewise modernize over the next 70 years into today's vehicles, but in both cases a primary function of each stayed the same: helping a person reach new places.

where books are part of life. In the settlement's early years, bookshops appeared as additional manifestations of how much Bracebridgites wanted books as well as groceries and hardware. Today some five independent retail bookstores operate in town: Readers' World, Scott's of Muskoka, the Owl Pen, and My Book Store—all within a block of the library—and a bookstore in a shopping mall at the west side of town specializing in remaindered works. At the same time, more than a dozen other retailers in Bracebridge offer books amidst a wider inventory of goods. The town is still the place of the book. This culture is both cause and effect of the town library and its vibrant nature augers well for the Bracebridge library's future.

The more things change, however, the more they remain the same. Today a quiet sense of expectancy still beats in the heart of anyone opening the door to the library, because now as always there is something new to discover. The treasury of books in the library has always rewarded patrons over the years, and the volumes have grown in number from 2,000-plus in 1908 to more than 35,000 today, with new classifications and a constant flow of fresh titles to replenish the collection.

Most important of all, the enduring constant over the years of Bracebridge Carnegie library's evolution is the presence of librarians of quiet intelligence willing to help anyone find the information they are seeking, in turn helping them to find themselves.

Credits

The help of many people who care about libraries and know the history of Bracebridge and Muskoka made it possible for this book to now be in your hands. Chief librarian and CEO of Bracebridge Public Library Jill Foster took the initiative to have it written. Her successor, chief executive officer Cathryn Rodney, has likewise been helpful in many ways, including an extensive tour of the library's satellite operation at Fenbrook Institution together with Assistant Warden Nancy Kinsman.

The staff at Bracebridge Public Library has been enthusiastic in sharing experiences, explaining things and tracking down information. I gratefully acknowledge the cooperation of reference librarians Nancy Wilson, Ruth Holtz and Mary Armstrong, office manager Carolyn Dawkins, inter-library loan coordinator Nancy Beasley, children's services coordinator Cindy Buhne, and circulation clerks Mary Denomy, Joyce Hallworth and Hasti Jonfeldt. Pages Bonnie Parkhill and Lynn Stewart, as well as Sherry Fish and Julene Jones at the Fenbrook branch, have collaborated with friendly professionalism. Librarian Marsha Ann Tate, Ph.D., at Pennsylvania State University, shared her research about "Little Pittsburgh" in Muskoka and the Carnegie connections. Librarian Robena Kirton of Gravenhurst Public Library provided photographs and an account of that town's library history.

Members of the Bracebridge Library Board, while governing the library in the present and guiding it into the future, have also taken time to share their memories, current perspectives and aspirations about the town's library. For their support of this book and their service to building a community through its library, I express deep gratitude to chairman Robert Taylor, council representative Barry Young, and their fellow board members Mark Benson, Pam Dunlop, Arlie Freer, David Goodyear, Russ Mackinnon, Lynn Taylor and Joe Ursano.

At Bracebridge municipal offices, Mayor Scott Northmore and his successor Mayor Donald Coates, as well as members of staff past and present, have been interested in this project. For help with information and access to the town's archival records, I thank treasurer Andrew Nelan, chief administrative officer Murray Clark and his successor John Sisson, former town clerk Kenneth Veitch and his successor Lori McDonald, assistant clerk Matthew Gower and reception administrator Donna Mae Tolton.

Many people "interviewed" for this book were individuals I grew up over the years at Bracebridge public library and other libraries, long before knowing their ideas and insights would cumulatively work themselves into this story. However, since starting on this history, those spoken with in addition to those mentioned above include: Wallace Anderson (née Tough), Kenneth Black, Keitha Boyer, Brian Chamberlain, Brenda and Arthur Cox, Ted and Carolyn Dickie, Jo Anne Dewan (née Dickie), Robert Dolphin, Eva Shields (née Ecclestone), Gene Smith Graham, Martha Jackson, Sybil Jackson, Ron Jacques, Ruth Jones, Gary Long, Audrey McNabb, Grace Melvin, Wendy Nicholson, Danny Poland, Cynthia Smith (née Thomas), Ron Stevens and Cheryl Tough (née Hammell).

Canada's former Governor General Adrienne Clarkson has long been a supporter of libraries and holds particular enthusiasm for Carnegie libraries, so I was delighted when she wrote the preface to this book to explain why. The Carnegie Corporation president, Vartan Gregorian, has likewise added a rich perspective to the opening of this book, drawing not only on the Carnegie legacy for libraries but his own feelings and experience as the former head of the New York City Library. To both, I am grateful that they have enhancing this book by sharing their thoughts about it with you.

I am grateful to William R. Young, Marina Nemat, Diana M. Daniels and Pamela Ryan for their positive appraisals of this book.

Donna Ivey, a librarian and researcher, author and indexer, helped with her good cheer and attentive prospecting through years of earlier newspapers. Current photographs in this book include those taken by board member Russ Mackinnon to accompany a magazine article he wrote about Andrew Carnegie and the library, board member Joe Ursano to illustrate a library calendar that raised awareness and money, and professional photographer Jan Pitman of Orillia. Editor Dominic Farrell assisted with a number of chapters in cutting them down to size. Board members Joe Ursano and Pam Dunlop read chapters.

Gary Long, a Muskoka historian who has authored several titles and edited and published many more, became indispensable in the creation of this book through all stages of editing, working with photographs, indexing, proofreading, designing, completing layout, and production—as well as sharing many stories about experiences at Bracebridge Public Library over the years as he grew up in Bracebridge. This book would not have come to life without Gary's professional focus, technical skills and rich enjoyment of the inspiration and irony that all local history entails.

This book uniquely owes its existence to my parents, for the gift of life they first gave me, for the gift of reading they instilled in me, for the joys of a library they made known to me, and, though both have been dead since this book formally began, for their continuing presence of place and spirit with me in its writing: by their enduring remembrance at Bracebridge Public Library in facilities named in their memory, the Patricia M. Boyer Children's Library and the Robert J. Boyer Reading Room, and by the books they wrote and newspaper articles they left behind to preserve the record and uphold the memories for those of us who carry on.

Sources

PHOTOGRAPHS

Photographs in this book are from Carnegie Archives, Chamberlain Architect Services, Boyer Family Archives, Bracebridge Public Library Collection and other private collections, unless specifically credited otherwise. Recent photographs include those taken by Russ Mackinnon, Bracebridge, Jan Pitman, Orillia, and Joseph Ursano, Bracebridge. Some images have been reproduced by scanning previously printed photographs which accounts for variations in quality.

PRIMARY SOURCES

Carnegie Foundation files
Town of Bracebridge Record Book of By-Laws
Town of Bracebridge Council Minutes
Bracebridge Public Library Board Minutes*

*Note: Loss of many years of Bracebridge Public Library records remains a mystery. When writing about library history in 1962, reporter Lou Specht of the *Herald-Gazette* noted "nowhere could we find documents" about the Library Board in the early years of the century. Later in referring to George Johnson's 30 years as member and chairman of the Bracebridge Library Board, he wrote, "Unfortunately, the records covering these periods are not complete, and so it is possible that we have failed to credit him with a few more years."

A complete search and town-wide inquiry by the author, assisted by many library staff and town office officials, failed to turn up the missing minute books of the Bracebridge library board prior to the 1970s.

Town librarian Gene Smith stated in 2007 that she had read them during her tenure at the library from 1977 to 1982 on the library premises at that time, and that the minute books consisted of some five or six maroon leather-bound volumes. This was prior to the extensive renovations carried out at the library between late 1983 and 1984.

In this period, a summer student found the original 1906 plans for the Bracebridge Carnegie library in a box of items for the garbage and retrieved them.

COLLECTIONS

Bracebridge Public Library "Muskoka Collection"
Lillie M. Johnson (Bracebridge) Scrapbooks 1931–1972
Audrey McNabb/Bracebridge Public Library Scrapbooks 1979–1996
Bracebridge Public Library vertical files, Library History 1996–2008
Records of The Muskoka Herald Company Limited from 1888, Boyer Archive.

LOCAL NEWSPAPERS

The Northern Advocate, Bracebridge
The Free Grant Gazette, Bracebridge
The Muskoka Herald, Bracebridge
The Bracebridge Gazette, Bracebridge
The Herald-Gazette, Bracebridge
The Bracebridge Examiner, Bracebridge
The Weekender, Bracebridge
The Advance, Bracebridge
Muskoka Magazine, Bracebridge
MuskokaTODAY, Gravenhurst

BOOKS AND ARTICLES

Aiken, Gordon H., *Looking Out on the Twentieth Century* (Orillia: R O Publications, 1993).

Barrow, Shirley et al, *Gravenhurst: An Album of Memories and Mysteries* (Gravenhurst: Gravenhurst Book Committee, 1993).

Bartleman, James, *Raisin Wine* (Toronto: McClelland & Stewart, 2007)

Battles, Matthew, *Library: An Unquiet History* (London: Random House, 2004).

Beckman, Margaret, Stephen Langmead and John Black, *The Best Gift: A Record of the Carnegie Libraries in Ontario* (Toronto: Dundurn, 1984).

Bow, Eric C., "The Public Library Movement in Nineteenth-Century Ontario." *Ontario Library Review* March 1982: 1-16.

Boyer, Robert J., *A Good Town Grew Here: The Story of Bracebridge, Ontario, from 1860 to 1914* (second edition) (Bracebridge: Oxbow Press, 2002).

——, *Bracebridge Around 1930* (Bracebridge: Oxbow Press, 2001).

——, *Early Exploration and Surveying of Muskoka District* (Bracebridge: Herald-Gazette Press, 1979).

Brisson, Jeffrey D. *Rockefeller, Carnegie, & Canada: American Philanthropy and the Arts & Letters in Canada* (Kingston and Montreal: McGill Queen's University Press, 2005).

Bruce, Lorne, *Free Books for All: The Public Library Movement in Ontario, 1850-1930* (Toronto: Dundurn, 1994).

Campbell, Harry C., *Canadian Libraries* (Toronto: McClelland & Stewart, 1969).

de la Fosse, Frederick Montague, (Scott D. Shipman, ed.) *English Bloods in the Backwoods of Muskoka, 1878* (Toronto: Natural Heritage Books, 2004).

DuVernet, Sylvia, *Muskoka Assembly of the Canadian Chautauqua Institution: Points of View and Personalities* (Bracebridge: Herald-Gazette Press, 1985).

Fitch, Leslie and Jody Warner, *Dividends: The Value of Public Libraries in Canada* (Toronto: Book and Periodical Council, 1997).

Gravenhurst, Town of, *The Light of Other Days* (Cobourg: Haynes Printing, 1967).

Hamilton, W.E., *Guide Book and Atlas of Muskoka and Parry Sound Districts* (Toronto: Muskoka Publishing Company, 1879).

Hendrick, Burton J., *The Life of Andrew Carnegie* (Garden City, N.Y.: Doubleday, 1932)

Hulse, Elizabeth, *The Morton Years: The Canadian Library Association, 1946–1971* (Toronto: Ex Libris Association, 1995).

Jackes, Lyman B., *Indian Legends of Muskoka and the North Country* (Toronto: The Canadian Historical Press, n.d.)

Krass, Peter, *Carnegie* (Hoboken, N.J.: John Wiley & Sons, 2002).

Manguel, Alberto, *A History of Reading* (Toronto: Albert A. Knopf Canada, 1996).

——, *The Library at Night* (Toronto: Albert A. Knopf Canada, 2006).

Mason, D. H. C., *Muskoka: The First Islanders and After* (Bracebridge: Herald-Gazette Press, 1974).

McMurray, Thomas, *The Free Grant Lands of Canada, from Practical Experience of Bush Farming in the Free Grant Districts of Muskoka & Parry Sound* (Bracebridge: Northern Advocate, 1871).

Moodie, Susanna, (Robert L. McDougall, ed.), *Life in the Clearings* (Toronto: Macmillan, 1959).

Ontario, *Report of the Provincial Committee on Aims and Objectives of Education in the Schools of Ontario* (Toronto: Ontario Department of Education, 1968).

Pryke, Susan, *Huntsville: With Spirit and Resolve* (Huntsville: Fox Meadow, 2000).

Thomas, George H.O., *Bracebridge in 1884* (Bracebridge: Gazette Press, 1934).

Thomas, Redmond, *Reminiscences* (Bracebridge: Herald-Gazette Press, 1969).

Thompson, Nancy R. (editor), *A Good Town Continues: Bracebridge 1915 to 1999* (Bracebridge: Town of Bracebridge 125th Anniversary Committee, 1999).

Van Slyck, Abigail A., *Free to All: Carnegie Libraries & American Culture, 1890–1920* (Chicago: University of Chicago Press, 1995).

Notes

CHAPTER 1

1. James Bartleman, *Raisin Wine*, passim.
2. Matthew Battle, *Library*, 2003, p. 180-1.
3. Ibid., p. 214.
4. Alberto Manguel, *The Library at Night*, p. 117.

CHAPTER 2

1. Lyman B. Jackes, *Indian Legends of Muskoka and the North Country*, p. 2.
2. D.H.C. Mason, *Muskoka: The First Islanders and After*, p. 1.
3. Ibid, p. 2.
4. Robert L. McDougall, introduction to Susanna Moodie, *Life in the Clearings*, p. xiii.
5. *Historical Kingston*, Vol. 5, October 1956, p. 45.

CHAPTER 3

1. *The Canadian Encyclopedia*, 2nd edition, vol. 2 (Edmonton: Hurtig, 1988) p. 1203.
2. Ibid.
3. A close review of atlases—for example, *National Geographic Atlas of the World*, rev. 6th ed. (National Geographic Society: Washington, D.C., 1992)—discloses that around the globe can be found North Bay,

North Beach, North Bend, North Branch, North Buttress, North Cape, North Cay, North Channel, North Creek, North Down, North Fork, North Haven, North Head, North Highlands, North Island, North Lagoon, North Lake, North Land, North Pass, North Peak, North Plains, North Point, North Pole, North Port, North Portal, North Prairie, North Reef, North Ridge, North River, North Rocks, North Sea, North Shore, North Side, North Slope, North Sound, North Star and North Trap—but no other "North Falls" anywhere on the planet.

CHAPTER 4

1. Robert J. Boyer, *A Good Town Grew Here*, p. 22.
2. Ibid., p. 21.
3. Ibid, p. 11.
4. W.E. Hamilton, *Muskoka and Parry Sound Districts*, p. 23.
5. Lorne Bruce, *Free Books for All*. See especially Part Two, pp. 51-119.

CHAPTER 5

1. Remarks at official opening of enlarged and renovated Bracebridge Public Library, May 24, 1985.
2. Robert J. Boyer, *A Good Town Grew Here*, p. 76.

CHAPTER 6

1. Peter Krass, *Carnegie*, p. 44.
2. Speech at Grangemouth, Scotland, September 1887, quoted in Hendrick, *Carnegie*, vol. 1, p. 67, and in Krass, *Carnegie*, p. 44.
3. Krass, *Carnegie*, p. xi.
4. Ibid., p. 419.
5. Ibid., p. 244.
6. *Independent* 60 (31 May 1906) pp. 1277–9.
7. *Collier's* magazine, quoted in Krass, p. 502.
8. Quoted in Krass, p. 436.

CHAPTER 9

1. Harry C. Campbell, *Canadian Libraries*, p. 17.
2. *Herald-Gazette*, Jan. 31, 1957.

CHAPTER 13

1. *Report of the Provincial Committee on Aims and Objectives of Education in the Schools of Ontario* (Toronto: Ontario Department of Education, 1968), recommendation 39.
2. Quoted in Lorne Bruce, *Books for All*, pp. 130-1.

CHAPTER 16

1. Quoted in *Chamberlines*, Issue 7, n.d., Burlington, Ontario, p. 1.

Index

Aboriginal peoples (Ojibwa) in Muskoka, 18
Acheron College, 319, 320
Administrators of Medium-Sized Public Libraries in Ontario, 282
Aiken, Gordon H., 199, 315
Aird, John Black, 233, 234
Algonquin Regional Library, 199, 250, 282, 283
Allison, R.M., 211
Anderson, James, 76, 77
Anderson, T.J., 70
Andrés Wines, Bracebridge Library Edition, 223, 225
Appleby, Henry Oscar, 125
Armstrong, Margo, 201, 264
Armstrong, Mary, 272, 273, 314, 337
Armstrong, Samuel H., 118, 120, 121, 131
Askin, Sandra, 311
Association of Library Boards of Ontario, 283
Aulph, I.B., 69
Avery, Martin, 331

Bachman, Mrs. P.J., 100
Bailey, Alexander, 32, 34
Bain, James, Jr., 28–30, 150, 169, 192
Bala, 183, 283
Ballantyne, J.M., 139, 144

Baptist Church, 148, 149, 184
Barrie Carnegie library, 196
Bartleman, James, 1–3, 333
Bartleman, Robert, 3
Bartram, James, 83, 101, 105–113, 155, 158, 166, 189
Bastedo, David Edgar, 93, 163
Beal, John, 22
Beasley, Nancy, 268, 280, 337
Beaumaris, 88, 90, 176
Beaver Creek Correctional Camp, 206, 216, 261, 315–19
Bell Telephone Company, 61
Benson, Mark, 339
Berlin, B.A., 151
Best, Russell M., 90, 188
The Best Gift, 84, 222
Bible, 23-5
Billingsley, Victoria (Vicki), 247, 249
Binstock, Meaghan, 294
Bird, Henry James, 45–7, 55–7, 62, 69, 114, 118, 119, 121, 139, 307, 329
    free library, 65
    Mechanics' Institute Library, 51–52, 54
Bird, Peter J., 213
Bird Engineering Ltd., 213
Bird Woollen Mill, 35, 39, 47, 60, 124, 154, 161
Black, Kenneth, 206, 309-11

Blacks, excluded from libraries, 4
Bonnell, Al, 330
Booth, Harry, 39
Boothby, Marion, 328
Borden, Robert, 152, 153
Bowron, Albert, 210
Boyer, Alison, 247
Boyer, George W., 41, 93, 145, 150, 163
Boyer, Hannah, 24, 41
Boyer, Harry S., 69, 103, 138, 139
Boyer, J. Patrick, 233, 234, 247
Boyer, James, 27, 40, 41, 43, 44, 52, 60
Boyer, Keitha (Kit), 242, 260, 264
Boyer, Patricia Mary, 233, 249. *See also*
    Johnson, Patricia Mary; Patricia M.
    Boyer Children's Library.
Boyer, Robert James, 66–69, 84, 139, 180,
    182, 198, 199, 202, 233, 234, 248, 288,
    308
    chairman, library fund-raising
        campaign, 226
    Reading Room, 247
Boyer, Sam, 138
Boyer, Ted, 264
Bracebridge, 27, 29
    bookstores in, 39–41, 343
    books in pioneer society, 26
    falls, role in location and development,
        32
    first settlers, 22
    hydroelectric development, 32, 60
    incorporation as town 1889, 60
    incorporation as village 1875, 49
    industries, 32, 33, 60, 124, 173
    name, origin of, 34, 36
    post office, 34, 128
    railway, arrival of, 34
    waterworks system, 60
Bracebridge and Muskoka Lakes
    Secondary School, 5, 211, 261, 294,
    310, 311, 312. *See also* Bracebridge
    High School.
Bracebridge Business and Professional
    Women, 184
Bracebridge Carnegie library building,
    93
    "The gore" site proposed, 115–17

architectural style, 132, 133, 141, 142,
    207
architect for, 123, 126
construction of, 124–138
Manitoba St. site approved, 118–120
Memorial Park site, 103–105
opposition to, 93
Town Hall proposed as site, 103–108
Bracebridge Citizens' Band, 153
Bracebridge Examiner, 210, 220, 231
Bracebridge Falls (North Falls), 22, 32,
    35, 36, 47
    water-power harnessed at, 32
Bracebridge Free Library, 64, 70–73, 285
    attempts to establish, 64–69
    board considers Carnegie funding,
        95–96
    first board of trustees, 70
    municipality assumes responsibility,
        69, 70
    Town Hall location inadequate, 91
Bracebridge Gazette, 94, 138, 158–61, 165,
    248
Bracebridge Granite and Marble Works,
    138, 139
Bracebridge Hall, 33, 36
Bracebridge High School, 125, 308, 310.
    See also Bracebridge and Muskoka
    Lakes Secondary School.
Bracebridge in 1884, 40
Bracebridge Ladies' Literary Society, 73
Bracebridge Literary Society, 145
Bracebridge Memorial Community
    Centre, 208
Bracebridge Public Library. *See also*
    Bracebridge Carnegie library
    building; Bracebridge Free Library;
    Mechanics' Institute Library
    (Bracebridge).
    Centennial Wing, 198, 200, 216, 293
    children's collection and programs,
        286–8, 290, 291, 293, 294, 296–9,
        301
    children's library, 197–204, 249, 293,
        294
    co-ordination with school libraries,
        310–14

Fenbrook branch, 313, 318, 320–4
firearms display, 202, 241, 243
floor plan 2008, 238
genealogical resources, 272, 273
government publication repository, 251
inter-library loan services, 240, 250, 278, 280
librarians, list of head, 279
Muskoka Collection, 235, 335
newspapers microfilmed, 235
number of members, 9, 236
plays staged at, 330, 331
Read to Succeed program, 312, 313
rebuilding/re-location options studied, 206, 208–10
restoration and expansion 1984-5, 217–35, 237–9
Royal Ontario Museum exhibit at, 328
statistics (collection and circulation), 143, 144, 156, 168, 236, 240, 287
"Talking books", 236
website, 256
writers-in-residence, 331
Bracebridge Public Library Needs Assessment Report, 335
Bracebridge Public Library Restoration-Building Fund, 226
Bracebridge Public School (Central School), 307, 308, 309
Bracebridge Rotary Club, 309
Bracebridge Town Hall, 59, 91, 128
fire destroys, 190, 202
Free Library in, 91
Mechanics' Institute Library in, 59
new town hall 1958, 202
post office in, 59
proposed as Carnegie library, 103–8, 112
theatre at, 331
Bridgland, Harry, 183
Bridgland, Samuel, 37, 52–54, 59, 73, 170, 172, 18
Briscoe, Henry, 20
British Lion Hotel, 51, 61
Britton, Edward, 210, 220
Brocklehurst, Judith, 231, 331

Brooks, Dan, 227
Brown, Singleton, 65, 66, 68
Browning, James B., 51, 52, 54
Bruce, Lorne, author of *Free Books for All*, 195, 264
Buck Island, 89, 92, 176
Buffett, Warren, 80
Buhne, Cindy, 271, 297, 313, 337
Buller, Grace, 221
Burden, Mr. and Mrs. W.F., 51
Burlington Public Library, 221
Byers, Dr. J.N., 52

Cabinet Centennial Committee (Ontario), 198
Caisse, Joseph, 61
Caisse, Rene, 61, 252
Cambridge Public Library (Preston Branch), 221
Campbell, Harry C., author of *Canadian Libraries*, 187, 192
Campbell, Henry, 210, 211
Campbell, John, 28, 29, 30, 169
Canadian Chautauqua, 104
Canadian Library Association, 259, 283
Canadian Library Council, 187, 192
Canadian Library Week, 309
Carnegie, Andrew, 76–90, 93, 98, 107–9, 155, 180, 189, 227, 233, 307
Carnegie Hall, 85
Carnegie libraries, 93, 94, 100, 112, 122, 195, 237, 281
criteria for funding of, 80, 101, 102, 167
number built, 84, 85
Cave, Alick, 206
Cave, Kay, 206
Chamberlain, Brian, 127, 134, 220, 222-5, 230, 231, 281, 341
Chamberlain Architect Services, 223, 235
Chancery Lane, 40, 61
Charter of Rights and Freedoms (Canada), 11
Chief's Island, 53
children in libraries, 65, 237, 285
Cho, Jonathan, 10
churches. *See* Knox Presbyterian

Church; Methodist Church; St.
    Joseph's Roman Catholic Church
Citizens' Band, 104
Clipsham, Diane, 206
Coates, Donald, 275
Cole, Rev. J.S., 51
Colville, W.H., 39
computers in library, 240 250–52, 254,
    255, 269–71
    Internet, 252, 254, 256
Cooke, Rob, 273
Courthouse, District of Muskoka, 44, 97,
    97, 98, 128, 204
Cox, Brenda, 188
Crawford, Anna, 264, 265

Dana, John Cotton, author of "How a
    Town Can Get a Library", 83
Darling, Ann-Marie, 192, 240, 250, 251,
    264, 265, 269, 310, 312, 319, 324
Dawkins, Carolyn, 268, 337
Dawson, Harold, 215
Dennis, Lloyd, 304, 313, 314
Denomy, Dennis, 311
Denomy, Mary, 269, 337
Dewey, Melvil, 155, 156, 268
Dewey Decimal System, 155, 156, 268,
    279
Dickie, Cecil W., 183
Dickie, Harriet (Hattie), 72, 99, 150, 154,
    156, 157, 167, 174–8, 248, 258, 259, 268,
    287, 288, 336
Dickie, James Arthur, 72
Dickie, Jeremiah (Jerry), 72, 157, 170,
    172, 173, 178, 181, 182, 184
Dickie, John William, 72, 147
Dickie, Jo Anne, 184
Dickie, Moses Jones, 71, 72, 113, 114, 124,
    136, 138, 139, 142, 144, 146–52, 157,
    164–6, 182, 196, 258, 266, 267, 289
    appointed librarian of Bracebridge
        Free Library, 74
    retires as librarian, 156
    secretary, Bracebridge Free Library
        board, 70
    treasurer, Bracebridge Free Library,
    74

Dickie, Sarah, 72, 143, 147, 150
Dickie, Stanley, 147, 149, 150, 152
Dickie, Ted, 184
Dickie, Violet, 72, 147
Dickie, Wesley, 72
Dickie, William, 149
Dickie Lake, 147
District Exchange, 33
Dollar, James, 149
Dollar, Robert, 55
Dolphin, Evonne, 250
Dolphin, Robert, 215–28, 233–5, 242, 250,
    263, 275, 341
Drew, Wayland, 310
Dundas Public Library, 221
Dunlop, Pam, 339
Dunn's Pavilion, 183
Dunn, Gerald, 183
DuVernet, Sylvia, 170

Early Years Challenge Fund, 301
Early Years Study, 301
Eaton, Diana, 333
Ecclestone, Albert, 92–93, 95, 174, 176
Ecclestone, Eva, 92, 174, 288
Ecclestone, George W., 103, 118, 121
Education, Ontario Department of, 197
Education Act, 306
Ellison's photography gallery, 59
Elmira Carnegie library, 218, 219
Essiac cancer treatment, 61, 252
Etobicoke Public Library (Albion
    Branch), 221
Everett, Harry, 183
Everett, Robert E., 183, 246
Everett's Drug Store, 183

Fenbrook Institution, 318, 320, 322,
    323, 324. *See also* Bracebridge Public
    Library: Fenbrook branch
Fenelon Falls library, 217
First Nations, book programs for, 1–3
Fish, Sherry, 322, 337
Follis, Paul, 269
Foot, W.E., 51
Ford, Henry, 89
Ford, Robert, 65–68

Forth, Barbara, 254

Foster, Jill, 245, 247, 256, 264, 266, 294, 335

Fourth Ward School, 137, 173, 307

Franczyk, Walter, 247

Franklin, Benjamin, 14, 52

Franklin-McInnis, Jennifer, 301

Franks, Robert, 83

Fraser (teacher), 40

Freer, Arlie, 307, 339

Free Grant Gazette, 38, 43, 160. *See also Bracebridge Gazette.*

The Free Grant Lands of Canada: from Practical Experience of Bush Farming in the Free Grant Districts of Muskoka and Parry Sound, 43, 46–48, 51

Free Libraries Act (1882), 58, 63–64

Fryer, Charles, 188

Fryer, Emma, 188, 189, 197, 260, 291, 292

Gates, Bill, 80, 84

Georgian Bay Regional Library System, 221

Georgian College, 314, 338

Glass, Aubrey, 215, 227

Glennie, Mary Dee, 225, 227

Goodyear, David, 339

Graham, Barry, 206, 262

Graham, Eugenie. *See* Smith, Eugenie.

Grand Trunk Railway, 152

Gravenhurst, 32. *See also* Gravenhurst Public Library.

Gravenhurst Banner, 89

Gravenhurst Public Library, 223, 281, 301

Great Depression, 173–5, 179, 182, 307

The Grove, 50

Guelph Carnegie library, 195, 196

Gutenberg, Johannes, 19

Haight, Neil, 305

Hall-Dennis Report, 304, 305

Hallworth, Joyce, 337

Hamilton, W.E., 50, 51, 52, 62

Hamilton Public Library (Terryberry Branch), 221

Hammell, Fred, 157, 186, 197–9, 208, 216, 260, 287, 308

Hampton, Howard, 229

Hardy, E.A., 151

Harkness, Norm, 201

Harrison, Harper, 330

Hawkins, Robert, 314

Hawn, Verna, 265

Henderson, Aubrey, 40

Henderson & Thomson Bookstore, 38, 40

Herald-Gazette, 198, 202, 231, 248

Hess Furniture Factory, 124

Hitchcock, Paul, 328

Holtz, Ruth, 271, 273, 274, 280, 284, 337

House, May, 332

Huber, Isaac, 38

Hunt's Hill bridge, 119

Hunt, Alfred, 60, 61, 112, 13, 139, 144, 149

Huntsville Public Library, 6, 282

Hutchison, Peter, 67, 69

Hutchison Bros. store, 61

Hyunga, Emma. *See* Fryer, Emma.

Independent Order of Foresters, 148

Independent Order of Odd Fellows, 59, 145, 147

Inn at the Falls, 45

Irving, Washington, author of *Bracebridge Hall*, 33, 36, 87

Ivey, Donna M., 252

Jackson, Sybil, 189

Jacques, Ron, 310, 311

Jekel, Peter, 323, 324

Johnson, Alvin A., 189

Johnson, Genevieve (Paddy), 178–82, 184–6, 196, 197

Johnson, George S., 170–73, 180–82, 185, 196, 197

Johnson, Lillian, 179, 182, 186, 236, 237

Johnson, Patricia Mary, 13, 178–181, 182, 260, 280, 290. *See also* Boyer, Patricia Mary.

Johnson, Pauline, 73, 74

Johnson, Stephanie, 179, 182

Jones, Julene, 337

Jones, Nancy, 234, 250, 262–4, 275, 283
Jones, Ruth, 312
Jonfeldt, Hasti, 337
Jorgensen, Mary, 206, 260, 328
Joseph, Lake, 30

Kingston Mechanics' Institute Library, 22
Kingston, Ross (Kingston & Powell Ltd.), 212, 213
King Township Public Library, 221
Kirby, Sherman, 287
Kirk, W. Reginald, 199, 201
Knox Presbyterian Church, 70, 71, 115, 116
Krass, Peter, author of *Carnegie*, 77

"Library Corner" column, 13, 181, 189, 249, 260, 280
Ladies' Literary Society, 258
Lamb, Sam, 326
Lang, James D., 225, 233, 234, 242
large-print books, 237
Last, Jasmine, 294
Leake, Frank, 186
Leake, Hilda, 186, 188
Lee, Chris, 29
Leith, J.M., 70
Lem, Mike, 294
LeSueur, William Dawson, 34–7
librarians, professional training of, 260, 264
Library Associations and Mechanics' Institute Act, 54
Library Club (BMLSS), 310, 311
Lindsay Carnegie library, 217
Liquor Control Board of Ontario, 224
Livesay, Harold, author of *Andrew Carnegie and the Rise of Big Business*, 77
Locke, George H., 151
London Public Library and Art Museum, 221
Louden, James, 29
Lount, C.W., 44
Loute, Liz, 294
Lyceum Theatre, 326

M&T Roofing Contractors, 216
Macaulay Township, 40, 49
MacIntosh, Robert M., 226, 235
Mackinnon, Russell, 84, 339
MacMillan, John M., 69
MacNaughtan, James, 182
Mahaffy, William Cosby, 44, 45, 52, 62, 68–70, 93, 124, 139, 144, 157
    chairman of Bracebridge Free Library board, 74
    efforts to obtain Carnegie library funding, 95, 96, 101–3, 105–10, 113, 117, 121
Malton, Ann, 328
Malton, Peter, 331
maps, role in Muskoka's development, 19–21
Marrin, Jim and Thelma, 329
Marrin, Michael, 329
Marshall, Duncan, 160
Mason, Alex, 14
Mason, Douglas H.C., author of *Muskoka: The First Islanders*, 20, 21
Masonic Order, 128
Mathieu, Ann-Marie. *See* Darling, Ann-Marie.
Matthiasville, 24
Mayes, R., 64, 65
McBride (mayor), 182
McCabe, Mickey, 28
McCabe's Landing (Gravenhurst), 33
McCaffrey, Bruce, 227
McCain, Margaret, 301
McCann, W.H., 39
McEwen Tailor Shop, 61
McFadyen, Heather, 7
McGill, Anthony, 52, 54
McGill University, library school, 260
McGuinty, Dalton, 2
McIntyre, Gordon, 185, 197
McIsaac, Alfred, 160
McLeod, Angus, 69
McLuhan, Marshall, 327
McMurray, Thomas, 27, 43, 50, 51, 235
McNabb, Audrey, 263, 264–6
McPhail, Bruce, 227
Mechanics' Institute Act of Ontario, 67

Mechanics' Institute libraries, 14, 15, 22, 23, 52, 57, 58

Mechanics' Institute Library (Bracebridge), 39, 55–63, 71–3, 276, 329
  collection, 66–67
  establishment of, 52–4
  Free Library, seeks to become, 63–69
  locations, 54, 57–9, 61
  municipality assumes control of, 69

Mellon, Andrew, 89, 90

Memorial Park, 103–5, 118, 153, 186

Menken, H.L., 86

Methodist Church, 150

Millar, Dorothy, 308

Miller, Anne, 233, 234

Miller, Duane, 201

Miller, Frank S., 226, 228, 233, 234, 328

Miller, George M., 121, 123–133, 136

Millionaires' Row, 88, 90, 176

Milne, Jennifer, 333

Minns, B.R., Memorial Library, 309

Minns, Bruce R., 309

Mitchell, Margaret, 201

Monk, William, 197, 198, 328

Morgan, J.P., 77

Monsignor Michael O'Leary School, 305

Morrison, Hew, 86

movie theatres, 287

Mowat, Oliver, 44

Mundy, Alfred E., 74

Murphy, Gerry, 206

Murray, Alexander, 21

Muskoka
  exploration of, 19–21
  judicial district, 97
  settlement of, 22, 23
  tourism, 28, 29, 31

Muskoka, Lake, 21, 28, 29

Muskoka Agricultural Society, 147

Muskoka Arts & Crafts Society, 104, 317, 332

Muskoka Assembly of the Canadian Chautauqua, 169

Muskoka Board of Education, 311, 312

Muskoka Club, 29, 32, 169

Muskoka Computer Centre, 256

Muskoka Herald, 38, 61, 64, 65, 93, 94, 145, 147, 162, 163, 165, 180, 248

Muskoka Lakes Public Library, 283. *See also* Port Carling Library.

Muskoka Navigation Company, 34

Muskoka River, 18, 21, 22, 32, 33

Muskoka Road, 23, 30, 33

Mustard, Fraser, 301

Nemat, Marina, author of *Prisoner of Tehran*, 4, 5

Nettlefold, Brian, 314

newspapers. *See Bracebridge Examiner; Bracebridge Gazette; Gravenhurst Banner; Herald-Gazette; Muskoka Herald; Northern Advocate*

Nicholson, Wendy, 5, 312

Nipissing University, 314, 338

Norma and Miller Alloway Muskoka Lakes Public Library. *See* Muskoka Lakes Public Library.

Northern Advocate, 27, 38, 43, 52, 163, 235

Northern Business Academy, 40

Northmore, Scott, 249, 324

North American Review, 80, 82

North Falls, 29, 33, 34. *See also* Bracebridge.

Norwood Theatre, 326

Nursey, Walter R., 151

Oakville Public Library, 220

Oatley, Joe, 176, 178

Ontario Educational Association, 306, 314

Ontario Library Association, 29, 30, 150, 151, 192, 259, 283

Ontario Library Service, 250

Ontario Library Service (Trent), 283

Ontario Lottery Corporation (Wintario), 209, 211, 218, 220, 228, 230

Orillia Carnegie library, 196

Ottawa Public Library, 224

Packard Bell Electronics, 250

Parkhill, Bonnie, 337

Parlett, George, 199, 204, 328

Patricia M. Boyer Children's Library,

233, 234, 249, 266, 293, 297, 301, 303
Peachy, Ann-Marie. *See* Ann-Marie Darling.
Pedersen, Mary Jo, 255
Perrin, Jim, 226
Pierre, Ashley, 10
Plummer, Geoff, 256
Poland, Danny, 205, 261, 316
Port Carling, 2, 152
Port Carling Library, 2, 3. *See also* Muskoka Lakes Public Library.
Pratt, E. Josiah, 40, 54, 55, 59, 61, 62, 257
Provan, Michael, 323, 324
Provincial Library Service, 221
Public Libraries Act, 151, 306
Public Library Institute, 150, 151
Public Works, Department of (Ontario), 44

Queen's Hill, 142

Raeburn, Sharon, 201
Rainey, Elisabeth, 265, 269, 294
Rainey, Sonja, 294
Raynor, John, 209, 211
Reid, Betty, 189, 191
Reid, Harold, 189
Richards, Archie L., 181
Richards, Winifred, 181, 186
Richardson, Melody, 331
Riley, June, 274
Rizzo, Joe, author of *American Libraries*, 325, 340, 341
Robert J. Boyer Reading Room, 245–7, 249, 266
Robinson, T.M., 151
Rockefeller, John D., 80, 82, 89
Rodney, Cathryn, 264, 267, 284, 337, 339
Royal Canadian Legion, 137, 242
Royal Hotel, 33, 40
Ryan, Richard W., 61
Ryerson, Eggerton, 306

"sa, susan", 331
St. Dominic Catholic Secondary School, 305
St. Joseph's Roman Catholic Church, 242

Salmon, Alexander C., 118
Salter & Allison (architects), 198
Sander, Fred, 118, 120, 121
Saul, John Ralston, 11
Saulnier, Julia, 294
schools (Bracebridge). *See* Bracebridge High School; Bracebridge and Muskoka Lakes Secondary School; Bracebridge Public School; Fourth Ward School; Monsignor Michael O'Leary School; St. Dominic Catholic Secondary School; Victoria Street School.
Schroeder, Glen, 206, 209
Seath, John, 306, 314
SellWithPictures, 256
Shepherd, James, 74
Sherriff, Alexander, 20
Shier, W.C., 70
Sieber, Linda, 201
Simcoe, Maureen Benson, 3
Simcoe County Roman Catholic Separate School Board, 312
Smith, Eugenie, 206, 209, 211, 215, 216, 217, 218, 242, 250, 262, 263
Smith, John, 39
Smith, Peter A., 118, 120, 121, 139, 144
Smith, R.H., 62, 64, 257
Smith, Ray, 199, 328
Smith, W.M., 29
Sons of Scotland, 147
South African-British Empire war (Boer War), 103, 104, 146
South Muskoka Agricultural Society, 42
Specht, Lou, 173
Stephenson, E.F., 160
Stevens, Ron, 312
Stewart, Lynn, 337
Student Literary Society (Bracebridge High School), 308
subscription libraries, 14, 52, 58, 59
Survey of Libraries in Canada, 259, 260
Sweetman, David, 103

Taylor, Bert, 198
Taylor, Lynn, 339
Taylor, Robert, 249, 335, 339

Thomas, Arla, 292
Thomas, Cynthia, 291, 292
Thomas, Douglas C., 292
Thomas, George H.O., 39, 40, 118, 136,
    138, 146, 156, 160, 188, 292
    library funding, campaign to reduce,
        158–65
    opposed to Carnegie library, 93, 114,
        115, 119, 120, 122
    opposes Memorial Park site for library,
        103, 104
    supports "the Gore" site for Carnegie
        library, 115, 116
Thomas, Noah D., 39
Thomas, Redmond, 117, 118, 150, 159
Thomas, Shelagh, 188
Thomas and Booth (store), 39
Thomas Bros. (store), 39
Thompson, David, 20, 21
Thomson, James, 38, 40
Thomson, John, 69, 118, 120
Tinkiss, Ruth, 249, 290
Tough, Agnes, 191, 201, 205, 206, 260,
    261, 264, 310, 311, 316
Tovell, Walter, 328
travelling library, Ontario Department
    of Education, 179, 180
Trimmer, Mrs. E., 151
Twain, Mark, 85, 155
Tytler, William, 29, 30, 169

United Workmen, 148
University of Ottawa, library science,
    260
University of Toronto, library science,
    260
Ursano, Joe, 8, 280, 307, 339

van der Meulen, Hank, 222
Veitch, Kenneth, 226, 275
Victoria Street School, 290

Walker, John, 89, 90, 92, 108, 109,
    174–76
Wall, Joseph, author of *Andrew Carnegie*,
    77
Warne, Francis P., 62, 65, 67, 70, 74, 95,
    139, 144, 151, 164
Watson, Cheryl, 201
Watson, Lori, 201
Webster, Noah, 155
Wenonah, 32
Wheeler, Gwen, 335
White, Aubrey, 51, 53
White, Mary, 24
Whitten, James, 139, 144
Wilson, Nancy, 8, 252, 271–4, 337
Windsor Public Library, 301
Wintario. *See* Ontario Lottery
    Corporation.
Wonderland Theatre, 326
Wood, Elspeth, 250
Woodchester Villa, 47
Woodrow Wilson, 89
World War I, 152, 153, 154
Wright, Richard, 4
Wright, W.J., 199

York (Toronto) Mechanics' Institute
    Library, 22
Young, Barry, 339

J. PATRICK BOYER, born at Bracebridge March 4, 1945, as the second child of a librarian, writer and teacher, and a newspaper editor, author, historian and publisher, seemingly fating him to write a book about the institution that had first brought his parents Patricia M. Johnson and Robert J. Boyer together.

That his family also included a 30-year chairman of the town's library board in grandfather George Johnson, a long-term administrative secretary to the board in aunt Genevieve Johnson, and three generations of Boyers who supported the library through their family newspapers and public offices, respectively for James, George and Robert, as town clerk, mayor and member of the legislature, further help explain that Patrick Boyer's predisposition to write this history of Bracebridge Public Library is a genetic condition beyond his control.

Patrick has worked as a typesetter, pressman, bookbinder, print journalist, television host, lawyer, university professor, member of parliament, and parliamentary secretary for foreign affairs in the Government of Canada. He has chaired parliamentary committees on equality rights, the status of disable persons, and electoral reform. His work for democratic development takes place in Canada and around the world from Cambodia, Thailand and Vietnam to Bulgaria and Ukraine and Iraq.

His university degrees include an honours degree with first-class honours in economics and political science from Carleton University, a master's degree in history from University of Toronto and a doctor of laws degree from the faculty of law at University of Toronto. He has also studied at Université de Montreal and the Academy of the International Court of Justice in The Hague, The Netherlands.

Patrick has chaired a number of public policy organizations, from the Couchiching Institute on Public Affairs to the Pugwash Park Commission in Nova Scotia dealing with nuclear disarmament. Following his wife's death in 1995, he founded the Corinne Boyer Fund for Ovarian Cancer Research and Treatment which today is the National Ovarian Cancer Association operating across Canada.

Local Library, Global Passport: The Evolution of a Carnegie Library is his seventeenth book.

Patrick, who multiplies his time by living at 2583 Lakeshore Boulevard West in Toronto, 59 Kimberley Avenue in Bracebridge and the west side of Browning Island in Lake Muskoka, can be reached at patrickboyer@sympatico.ca.

BRACEBRIDGE is a Canadian town with a strong connection to books. In 1874 as a tiny settlement, it organized its first library even before creating a fire brigade to protect lives and property. In 2008 Bracebridge would celebrate a century of its Carnegie public library. The story of each community's library is unique, as this book recounts with many twists and turns that could only happen in Bracebridge, but this is also a case study whose details reveal universal truths about libraries everywhere.

As the central town in the famous Muskoka lakeland district of Ontario, Bracebridge has long been home to remarkable individuals, from its first tourists and summer residents James Bain and William Tytler in the 1860s who founded the Ontario Library Association in 1901, to Andrew Carnegie's business associates like steel tycoon John Walker and United States Secretary of the Treasury Andrew Mellon who had summer island homes in "Little Pittsburgh" near town and influenced the course of the Bracebridge library.

Sometimes town councillors and newspaper editors seemed intent on jeopardizing the venture in scenes from a comedy, but the town's "book culture" prevailed, and the patience of Andrew Carnegie and his assistant James Bartram in New York helped Bracebridge overcome the danger and join the world family of several thousand Carnegie libraries a hundred years ago.

Efforts to expand and restore the library since then have been battlegrounds of rival architectural designs and competing uses for a community institution, including public baths and square dancing, but the surprising leadership of individuals like Robert Dolphin and Brian Chamberlain turned the tide. Today Bracebridge's Carnegie library is an award-winning "heritage building" and is consistently tops in its class as it keeps re-inventing itself to meet exceptional new demands.

The evolution of this library as a democratic institution, with the sometimes melodramatic adventures of the 18 different librarians since 1874, matched the revolutions in library systems, from Melvil Dewey's book classification system through inter-library loans to fully computerized library service, and now the Internet.

Yet the "virtual library" of today is still a place of humans—the patrons, the board members, the governing officials, the librarians' associations, leaders and members in the library organizations and, especially, the goddesses of librarianship whose friendly professionalism reinforces individual freedom of citizens and builds the community of culture.